REFOCUSING ETHNOGRAPHIC MUSEUMS THROUGH OCEANIC LENSES

REFOCUSING ETHNOGRAPHIC MUSEUMS THROUGH OCEANIC LENSES

Philipp Schorch

with

Noelle M.K.Y. Kahanu
Sean Mallon
Cristián Moreno Pakarati
Mara Mulrooney
Nina Tonga
and
Ty P. Kāwika Tengan

University of Hawai'i Press
Honolulu

Paperback edition 2021

Printed in the United States of America

26 25 24 23 22 21 6 5 4 3 2 1

Library of Congress Control Number: 2020933166

ISBN 978-0-8248-8986-9 (pbk.)

Cover art: *Mahina Poepoe* (the many faces of the full moon) by Hawaiian kapa artist Verna Takashima (Kanaka ʻŌiwi). Made of wauke (paper mulberry) and natural dyes in 2017, this artwork conveys how pō/darkness gives birth to beauty, diversity, and creative complexity.

University of Hawaiʻi Press books are printed on acid-free paper and meet the guidelines for permanence and durability of the Council on Library Resources.

Contents

List of Illustrations

Figures

Plates (*following page* 140)

Acknowledgments

This book is the outcome of collaborative research carried out between 2014 and 2016 and written up between 2017 and 2018. First, I am indebted to Noelle, Cristián, Mara, Sean, Nina, and Ty for engaging over several years to see this book come into fruition. As an experiment in rethinking, or refocusing, and writing, the process was complex and exhausting, but ultimately very rewarding. I also thank the three museums—Bernice Pauahi Bishop Museum, Hawai'i; Museum of New Zealand Te Papa Tongarewa; and Museo Antropológico Padre Sebastián Englert, Rapa Nui—as well as its various staff members (many of whom are named throughout the text) for making the research possible. Those individuals, like many others I have encountered over the last fifteen years of traveling, working, researching, and living across Oceania, have turned this part of the world into my second home, and have made me become a scholar—I shall never forget and always treasure.

Further, I extend my gratitude to my dear mentors Eveline Dürr and Conal McCarthy, who supported and advised me on the project while I was a research fellow at the Institut für Ethnologie at the Ludwig-Maximilians-Universität München, Germany, funded first through a stipend from the Fritz Thyssen Foundation and then a fellowship from the European Union's Horizon 2020 Research and Innovation Programme under the Marie Skłodowska-Curie Grant Agreement No. 659660 as well as European Research Council Starting Grant No. 803302, Indigeneities in the 21st Century. I also appreciate the anonymous reviewers and the acquisitions editor, Masako Ikeda, who assisted with their critical comments and reflections in the development and completion of the manuscript.

Finally, I extend my heartfelt thanks to my family and friends for their continuous support and to my wife Eliza for being Eliza, the backbone of my life.

Philipp Schorch, December 2019

Note on the Text

When using the general category of Indigenous, we use uppercase, on par with other conventional markers such as Western, and observe the use of capitals in reference to specific Indigenous people: Native Hawaiian, Māori, Rapanui, Sāmoan, and so on. To avoid Othering Indigenous languages, we italicize Indigenous words and concepts only on first use.

We follow the conventions of using macrons for Hawaiian, Māori, and Sāmoan words to indicate a double vowel, and of using the glottal stop or *'okina* in Hawaiian, Sāmoan, and Rapanui. However, in the titles of books, organizations, and in historical archival sources and texts these words have been left in their original form. Although the country remains formally New Zealand, we use the double appellation Aotearoa New Zealand where appropriate to reflect the increasing formal use of this term.

Introduction

This book, *Refocusing Ethnographic Museums through Oceanic Lenses,* offers a collaborative ethnographic investigation of Indigenous museum practices in three Pacific museums located at the corners of the so-called Polynesian triangle: the Bernice Pauahi Bishop Museum, Hawai'i; the Museum of New Zealand Te Papa Tongarewa; and the Museo Antropológico Padre Sebastián Englert, Rapa Nui (Easter Island). Since their inception, ethnographic museums have influenced academic and public imaginations of other cultural-geographic regions. The often resulting Euro-Americentric projection of anthropological imaginations has come under intense pressure, as seen in recent debates and conflicts around the Humboldt Forum in Berlin, Germany, which attempts to reconfigure the rebuilt Berliner Schloss (Berlin Palace) as a museum forum for the world.[1] This ambitious project has brought Germany's difficult and long-silenced colonial legacy back to the surface of a changing national commemorative environment and subjected it to international scrutiny, critique, and protest.[2] At the same time, (post)colonial renegotiations in former European and American colonies, such as the cases under scrutiny in this book, have initiated dramatic changes to anthropological approaches through Indigenous museum practices. The book shapes a dialogue between both situations—Euro-Americentric myopia and Oceanic perspectives—by offering historically informed ethnographic insights into Indigenous museum practices grounded in Indigenous epistemologies, ontologies, and cosmologies. In doing so, the book employs Oceanic lenses that help reframe Pacific collections in, and the production of public understandings through, ethnographic museums in Europe and the Americas.

Refocusing Ethnographic Museums through Oceanic Lenses arises from a movement of museum critique and reevaluation that can be traced back to the critical, and by now classical, studies by authors such as Michael Ames and James Clifford as well as Ivan Karp and Stephen Lavine in the late 1980s and early 1990s.[3] These studies epitomize a shift toward the collaborative reconceptualization of museum processes and structures, in line with related arguments for the decolonization of anthropology and research methods, and the foregrounding of Indigenous perspectives. Building on these groundbreaking interventions, more recent scholarship has moved beyond Euro-Americentric views of ethnographic practices by revealing the hidden processes, both collaborative and contested, through which a range of actors, such as European scientist-collectors, Indigenous people and "objects," become involved in the co-constitution of ethnographic collections. Such analytical focus has enabled scholars to zoom in on museum collections as relational and dynamic assemblages rather than static sets of material items.[4] These historically minded studies have alluded to the mutual, albeit often asymmetrical, construction of ethnographic knowledge, but remain largely disconnected from contemporary Indigenous museologies emerging across the Pacific, including the Americas.[5]

Pacific museums have provided a particularly fertile ground for innovative developments in museum theory and practice, especially through the active engagement with Indigenous concepts and paradigms.[6] In Aotearoa New Zealand, for example, changes in the parameters of curatorial roles, which have been inflected by the ongoing Indigenization and decolonization of museologies, have led to the evolution of new models of the curator as facilitator, intermediary, and even activist.[7] It has further been argued that curatorship, if approached as an inherently cross-cultural method, is well placed to decenter the predominant association of science with Western ways of thinking and being by engaging with Indigenous epistemologies and ontologies.[8] Despite these developments, however, only a few examples of historically informed ethnographic insights into Indigenous museum practices exist, and scholarly European involvement is minimal.[9] As a consequence, and despite their close connection to the Pacific through the "ethnographic objects" in their collections, European museums remain often distanced from these experiments in Indigenous scholarship.[10]

This is not to claim that no progress has been made since the critical reassessments, or that no collaborations with Indigenous artists, curators, and scholars are pursued by European museums. Such initiatives indeed have a history.[11] Yet, the debates, or rather conflicts, around ethnographic museums, especially in Germany, evidently go on and even gain in intensity. This is all the more perplexing given that promising terms such as "multiperspectivity," "shared heritage," and "source communities" circulate in nearly each museum-related document, grant application, conference program, professional publication, policy statement, and press release. The question remains, however, whether the critical potential of these concepts is really mobilized toward epistemic, political, and institutional reconfigurations. Or can their articulation instead be unmasked as an insidious act of "strategic reflexivity," as Friedrich von Bose observed of the Humboldt Forum, that is, the co-opting of postcolonial critique for the sake of stabilizing the neocolonial status quo?[12]

Answering these questions, however important they are, is not the ambition of this book. In other words, it is not my intention to analyze the wider European or specific German ethnographic museum landscape, which is a laudable goal that has been pursued by other authors.[13] Instead, I address the evident critique and crisis of the ethnographic museum—a much berated yet, as we shall see, still vital institution—by offering epistemic assistance generated elsewhere. As James Clifford reminds us, "the museum is an inventive, globally and locally *translated* form, no longer anchored to its modern origins in Europe."[14] In a similar vein, Elian Hooper-Greenhill speculated nearly twenty years ago that the intellectual development of what she called the "post-museum" was likely to take place outside the "European centers which witnessed the birth of the modernist museum."[15] Following this line of reasoning, *Refocusing Ethnographic Museums through Oceanic Lenses* sets out to offer insights into Indigenous museologies across Oceania to recalibrate ethnographic museums, collections, and practices through Indigenous Oceanic approaches and perspectives. This, in turn, should assist any museum scholar and professional in rethinking and redoing their respective institutional settings, intellectual frameworks, and museum processes when dealing with Oceanic affairs; and, more broadly, in doing the "epistemic work" needed to confront "coloniality," not only as a political problem or ethical obligation, but "as an epistemology, as a politics of knowledge," as Ciraj Rassool reminds us.[16] At the level of content, this book thus offers an in-depth analysis of Indigenous museum practices grounded in Indigenous epistemologies, ontologies, and cosmologies that are of significance to ethnographic museums in general. In terms of form, the book's distinctive feature is its layered coauthorship and multivocality, drawing on a collaborative approach that has put the widespread philosophical commitment to dialogical inquiry into infrequent practice by systematically co-constituting ethnographic knowledge. Before the unfolding chapters offer substance to these claims, I first explain the Oceanic framework of the study, introduce the collaborative ethnography in the doing, and map out the content and structure of the book.

Reimagining and Reenacting Oceania

"Imagining the Pacific and its peoples," Christopher Balme concludes, "has been an activity that Westerners have followed with almost as much energy as they have invested in its colonization."[17] Moreover, the label Pacific itself is a Euro-American invention.[18] The associated "foreign representations" deriving from and feeding into visionary attempts at imagining the Pacific or Oceania continue to be contested through Indigenous perspectives, concepts, and paradigms.[19] Recent research has paid close attention to concrete life worlds and cultural practices to highlight the moment and processes of reimagining. This, in return, has facilitated the reimagining of Oceania on the analytical plane through empirical insights into insider conceptualizations instead of perpetuating the predominant imposition of outsider cartographies, maps, and other visions and imaginaries.[20]

Polynesia and the Polynesian triangle, as particular categories of history, remain contested to this day and warrant a closer introduction since they represent the regional focus of this study. The outsider remapping of the Pacific through its partition into Melanesia, Micronesia, and Polynesia, usually assumed to be invented by the French navigator Jules Dumont d'Urville in 1832, was "not so much a cartographic progress, a simple addition to universal geography with new maps," as Serge Tcherkézoff has argued, "but . . . the outcome of a racial agenda."[21] At the time, this was no hidden plot but seen to assist in developing scientific knowledge, which becomes apparent when d'Urville refers to "all the Oceanic peoples who have more or less black skin, curly and frizzy hair, and often frail, deformed limbs. We shall give [them] the name of Melanesia."[22] This racial-cum-scientific intervention has been extensively researched and debated.[23] Its subsequent consolidation as a geographic-cum-ethnological division and typification has been intensely critiqued.[24] All three terms linger in the present and have largely entered the consciousness of Oceanic people, often with detrimental effects in terms of hierarchy and superiority.[25] However, only the label Polynesia—first coined not by d'Urville but by Charles de Brosses in 1756, prior to Captain

James Cook's voyages, and initially referring to a different geography of all Pacific Islands—carries empirical weight and conceptual purchase. Patrick Kirch sums it up neatly:

> Although based on a superficial understanding of the Pacific islanders, Dumont d'Urville's tripartite classification stuck. Indeed, these categories—Polynesians, Micronesians, Melanesians—became so deeply entrenched in Western anthropological thought that it is difficult even now to break out of the mould in which they entrap us. . . . Such labels provide handy geographic referents, yet they mislead us greatly if we take them to be meaningful segments of cultural history. Only Polynesia has stood the tests of time and increased knowledge, as a category of historical significance.[26]

Despite the ongoing justifiable academic critiques of the label Polynesia and its regrettable opposition to, and contrast with, other categorizations, it still refers to a geographic region characterized by a common cultural history clearly discernible in languages, stories, genealogies, and cosmologies.[27] Hawaiian scholar Lilikalā Kameʻeleihiwa lends support to this claim by reminiscing about her first visit to Aotearoa New Zealand:

> I learned that the Māori cosmogonic genealogy and gods were incredibly similar to those of my Hawaiian ancestors. The prayers of the dawn blessing echoed the ones we do at home and I found that our languages were incredibly similar. . . . I was stunned by the similarities . . . because for the very first time I realized that we Hawaiians were not alone on the earth, either as a separate people or in our philosophical understanding of the world.[28]

Kameʻeleihiwa proceeds by equating the Polynesian triangle, which is equally contested in the academic literature, with the ancient triangle of Hawaiʻi-nui-akea (Great Hawaiʻi of Atea).[29] "The Hau-atea alliance," she further argues, "was a religious political alliance between all of the cousins in Hawaiʻi-nui-akea, including Hawaiʻi, Rapa Nui (Easter Island), and Aotearoa/New Zealand."[30] The term "Hawaiʻi-nui-akea" thus draws on a common genealogical history.[31] This hibernating ancient alliance is reawakened in the face of geographic-cum-political reconfigurations, such as its remapping onto, what Eveline Dürr and I called elsewhere the Transpacific Americas, through the colonial incorporation of Hawaiʻi into the United States and of Rapa Nui into Chile.[32] A particular historical-ethnographic vignette illustrates well the ongoing process of reconnecting and rebonding in response and resistance to colonial impositions.

On January 26, 1779, the reigning chief of Hawai'i Island, Kalaniʻōpuʻu, encountered Captain James Cook, whose ship landed in Kealakekua Bay. As a demonstration of his peaceful intentions, Kalaniʻōpuʻu gifted the *mahiole* (feathered helmet) and *ʻahu ʻula* (feathered cloak) he was wearing to Cook. According to Lieutenant James King, the chief "got up & threw in a graceful manner over the Captns Shoulders the Cloak he himself wore, & put a feathered Cap upon his head, & a very handsome fly flap in his hand."[33] Both material treasures were subsequently taken to England and in the following years passed through various private and museum collections. They eventually arrived at the Dominion Museum in Wellington, New Zealand, the predecessor of the Museum of New Zealand Te Papa Tongarewa (Te Papa), and were displayed as part of the latter's opening exhibitions in 1998. Over the last decade, an increasing number of Hawaiian artists, activists, researchers, and school groups included Te Papa on their travel itineraries to Aotearoa New Zealand so they could visit Kalaniʻōpuʻu's mahiole and ʻahu ʻula. The display at Te Papa was described by the Wellington-based Hawaiian academic Emalani Case as a *puʻuhonua,* a place of refuge, sanctuary, or peace. But others openly challenged the status quo and demanded their return. For Native Hawaiians, the ʻahu ʻula, mahiole, and all other featherwork were reserved exclusively for the use of their *aliʻi* (royalty), symbolizing their chiefly divinity, rank, and power. From 2013, Te Papa was visited by delegations from the Bishop Museum and the Office of Hawaiian Affairs in Honolulu. Conversations began about the possibility of a long term loan of the ʻahu ʻula and mahiole to Hawaiʻi. In 2015, they were eventually taken off display to be prepared for their return to Hawaiʻi, which took place in March 2016 (see figures I.1–I.2).[34]

Sean Mallon, coauthor of chapter 5 in this book, observes

> As a curator of Pacific cultures, the most significant shift I have witnessed since I joined Te Papa in 1992 has been in how we talk about the ʻahu ʻula—from its value as an ethnological specimen collected on voyages of European exploration, to an artefact with the potential to strengthen the connections of contemporary Hawaiian people to their history and cultural identities; from Cook's cloak to Kalaniʻōpuʻu's cloak, and from feather cloak to ʻahu ʻula.

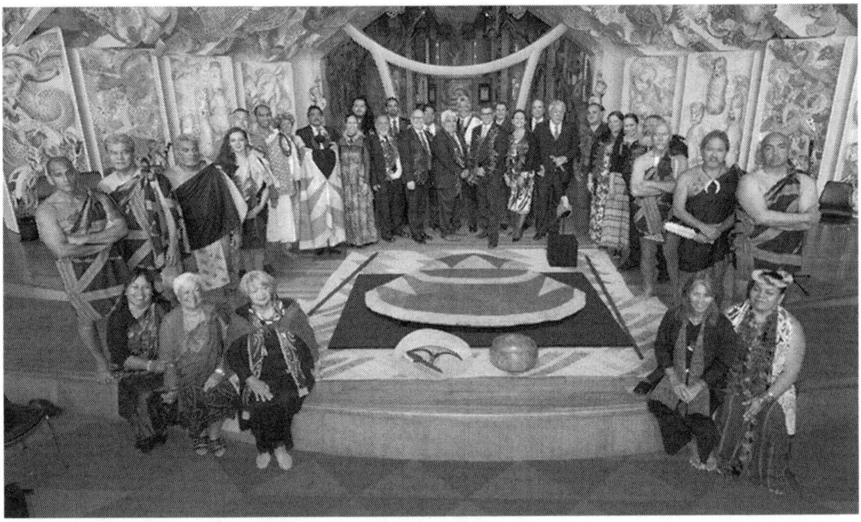

Figure I.1 Participants at the ceremony marking the return of the mahiole and ʻahu ʻula of Kalaniʻōpuʻu, from Te Papa to the Bishop Museum in March 2016. Te Papa, Cable Street, Wellington. Photograph courtesy of Norm Heke.

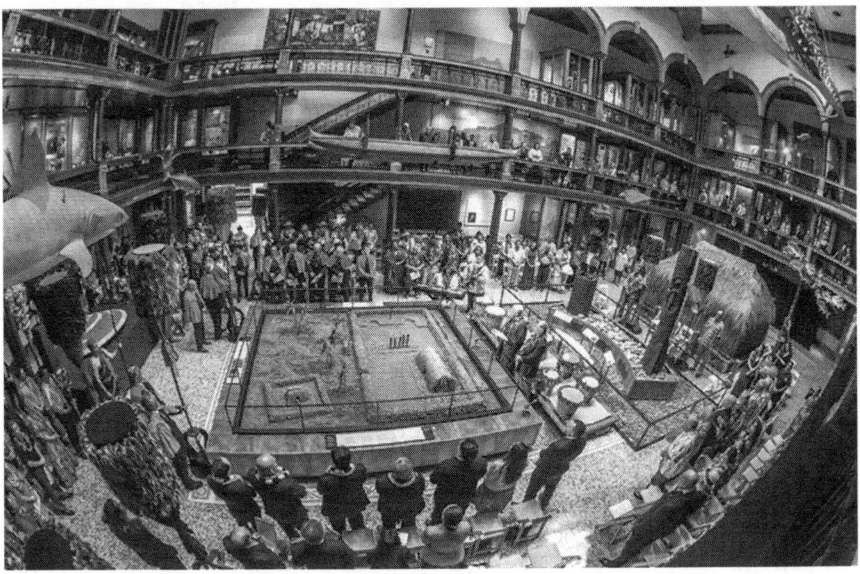

Figure I.2 Private ceremony honoring the arrival of Kalaniʻōpuʻu's mahiole and ʻahu ʻula at the Bernice Pauahi Bishop Museum, March 2016. Photograph courtesy of Kai Markell.

The associated "curatorial reworking of the catalogue," Mallon concludes, "is part of a decolonising of museology that is an ongoing project in various parts of the world."[35]

The return of the ʻahu ʻula and mahiole from Aotearoa New Zealand to Hawaiʻi, which reconnected two corners of the ancient triangle of Hawaiʻi-nui-akea, is remarkable for several reasons. First, it enabled a historic "reconnection of ancestral ties"[36] to take place through the enactment of Indigenous museological practices in the twenty-first century.[37] Second, it was a voluntary return as an act of restitution, underpinned not by (post)colonial redress but instead by pan-Pacific notions of gift and reciprocity shared by many Māori and Hawaiian people, as well as other Pacific Islanders. As Arapata Hakiwai, Kaihautū or Māori co-director of Te Papa, stresses, these *taonga* (treasures) "will be anchors in the revitalisation of the Hawaiian language and identity, and in the ongoing journey for Hawaiian self-determination." The relationships between the three involved organizations (Te Papa, the Bishop Museum, and the Office of Hawaiian Affairs) were woven into the title of the exhibition—*He Nae Ākea: Bound Together,* thus reflecting the ties that bind—the *hulu* (feathers) bound to the *nae* (netting) of the ʻahu ʻula, from the ancient past to the present.[38] Third, as Noelle Kahanu (coauthor of chapter 1 in this book, who initiated the return from the Hawaiian side) emphasizes, it is significant to many in Hawaiʻi that these *mea waiwai aliʻi* (chiefly valuables) were left by an act of Pacific generosity and returned by an act of Pacific generosity. "Both acts were of lasting cultural and political importance," Kahanu concludes, and "one might argue, commitments intended to bind future generations."[39] Such rebonding had historical precedents, the corners of the triangle of Hawaiʻi-nui-akea having remained largely separated for hundreds of years due to halting migration across the Pacific as well as the European arrival and subsequent colonial onslaught. Prevailing transpacific networks have facilitated momentous reconnections between Māori and Hawaiian people and practices (see chapter 1), and other returns radiate from Hawaiʻi to Rapa Nui (see chapter 3).

In terms of the regional framing of the study underpinning this book, defining geographic scope and attributing the associated vocabulary is tremendously tricky. As we have seen, markers such as the Pacific and Polynesia are, of course, Euro-American inventions, which are intensely contested through Indigenous conceptualizations. At the same time, however, the term "Polynesia" has been perpetuated by Indigenous perspectives—in the case of Hawai'i, from the political affiliations of the Hawaiian Kingdom through the scholarship of Te Rangihīroa to the Polynesian Voyaging Society and contemporary museological productions and representations at the Bishop Museum (see chapters 1 and 2). And in the case of Rapa Nui, the term "Polynesia" allowed for the remobilization of ancient ties to resist Chilean colonization, as through the political actions of the Consejo de Ancianos (Council of Elders) (see chapters 3 and 4). The best strategy to face this ambivalent dilemma is to define and justify one's choice, leaving space for lived ambivalence (which can neither be fully explained by any category of history nor completely overridden by its critique). In the context of *Refocusing Ethnographic Museums through Oceanic Lenses,* the approach is straightforward:

First, the book is based on a collaborative investigation of Indigenous museum practices in institutions located in the *so-called* Polynesian triangle. Despite being a European category, this triangle is, as we have seen, built on a common genealogical foundation that manifests itself in shared cosmologies, epistemologies, and ontologies that framed the research design. Second, in the discussion so far the category Polynesia was critically historicized. In the remainder of the book, we (the coauthors and myself) will mainly switch to "Oceania" and use "Pacific" synonymously. However, whenever individuals appearing in the text use Polynesia or Polynesian as a self-identifying label, as in the case of coauthor Christián Moreno Pakarati, this not only is to be respected, but also makes simple and profound sense for the reasons outlined.

In our use of "Oceania," we follow Epeli Hau'ofa, who invokes the "Sea of Islands" in its "topological rather than topographic sense," as Chris Ballard concludes.[40] That is, we perceive of Oceania as a spatial entity that remains intact despite ongoing transformations: being deformed but not ripped apart, maintaining its integrity within flexible boundaries through processes of what Hau'ofa calls "world enlargement."[41] On the one hand, the multisited ethnography[42] conducted in Hawai'i, Aotearoa New Zealand, and Rapa Nui, and employed in this book thus built on common genealogies and histories of ancestral voyaging, as well as shared experiences with Euro-American exploration and colonialism. On the other hand, museum "things," such as the mahiole and 'ahu 'ula, have been thought of as "ships" or canoes—*vaka/wa'a*—as mobile interpretive vessels that embody and navigate the material and discursive relations between different places across Oceania.[43] In other words, museum "things," collections, and exhibitions are always *in the doing:* they move and circulate, they cut across territorial boundaries and resist topographic framing.[44]

Apart from articulating what this book does (offering a museological study of Hawai'i-nui-akea through particular Oceanic lenses), it also has to be highlighted what it does not or cannot do (presenting an exhaustive study of entire Oceania to offer all Oceanic lenses or *the* Oceanic lens), to make it clear that the use of Hawai'i-nui-akea as a specific Oceanic region does not amount to be taken synonymously for entire Oceania; nor does it amount to a distinction with the adverse effects in terms of racial hierarchy and superiority. Furthermore, Oceanic collections can be found in Euro-American institutions where their anthropological and museological separation into Polynesia, Micronesia, and Melanesia is largely maintained. Although this book neither focuses on those collections nor covers all regional foci, it does offer some Oceanic lenses that may spur further collaborative research endeavors, as the one I now introduce in detail, to zoom in on the topological enlargements of Oceanic worlds.

Collaborative Ethnography in the Doing

Beginning in the late eighteenth century, the academic disciplines of anthropology and ethnology emerged in the wake of scientific exploration and colonial expansion beyond Europe and North America, as well as the establishment of ethnographic (or ethnological) collections and museums in Europe and North America. To this day, "anthropology," "ethnology," and the "ethnographic" remain, once again, complicated and contested terms with different histories in different parts of the world.

In Germany, for example, *Ethnologie* is used synonymously for social and cultural anthropology, while *Anthropologie* originally referred to physical anthropology and has recently also been adopted for cultural anthropology, as in *Kulturanthropologie.* Similarly, ethnographic museums tend to be called *ethnologisch* or are still associated with *Völkerkunde* (which has disappeared in the academic context). Spurred by the intensified debates around Germany's long-silenced colonial legacy, semantic shifts are occurring. In October 2017, the Deutsche Gesellschaft für Völkerkunde was renamed to Deutsche Gesellschaft für Sozial- und Kulturanthropologie (German Association for Social and Cultural Anthropology), largely to distance itself from prior racialized notions of *Volk.*[45] At the same time, there is a "pervasive shift" toward renaming museums and replacing the ethnologisch, as in the case of the Humboldt Forum.[46] In this book, I opt for the terms "anthropology" and the "ethnographic" because of their prevalence across Oceania and internationally. Although I critically interrogate (rather than just rename) these categories of history, I also opt for the ethnographic—for lack of a better word—as an omnipresent interpretive field and condition as well as action, movement, and performance through which difference—in whatever form—has been studied, (mis)understood, governed, critiqued, subverted, and so on. My aim, then, is to refocus rather than deny the ethnographic—by decentering, multiplying, and undisciplining—through Oceanic lenses.

The research informing this book took nine months of fieldwork, between September 2014 and July 2016, and met its objectives through a methodological triangulation of archival research, oral histories and narrative interviews, virtual and collection-based research, and photography, as well as "thick participation" throughout the entire research process.[47] That is, the project was conducted with rather than about the participants, thus representing a collaborative ethnography through which knowledge is coproduced, co-interpreted, and co-represented, as I now elaborate in detail.[48]

The struggle over what in German is called *Deutungsmacht* (power of interpretation), over the question of who interprets whom and who speaks on behalf of whom, erupted in the 1980s in vigorous clashes caused by the "crisis of ethnographic authority" and the "writing culture" debate.[49] In response to the ongoing discussions about culture and representation induced by postmodern and postcolonial critiques, proponents of the ontological turn have argued,[50] for example, for "ontological delegation," which turns the anthropologist into an "ontological negotiator or diplomat,"[51] or the "ontological self-determination of the other," which redefines "anthropology's role [as] not that of *explaining the world of the other*, but rather of *multiplying our world*."[52] Yet, despite these laudable suggestions emerging in the debate, one can note a "relative absence to date of certain kinds of other," as Amiria Salmond has concluded, "those who might consider themselves *native thinkers* [and] might want to share a stage with these [nonnative] thinkers, to offer their own accounts of . . . ontological struggle—of *self-determination* and *decolonization*."[53] This virtual absence of Indigenous scholars has prompted Zoe Todd, who identifies as Métis/otipemisiw and Indigenous feminist from

Amiskwaciwâskahikan (Edmonton), Alberta, Canada, to even claim that "'ontology' is just another word for colonialism."[54]

This book responds to this predicament in a methodological way. The ongoing and perpetually incomplete decolonization in former European and American colonies, as across the Pacific, has prompted drastic changes to museum and anthropological practices through Indigenous interventions that draw on Indigenous epistemological and ontological schemes in order to reshape collecting, exhibiting, fieldwork, and research (often collaboratively conducted in partnership with nearby communities). So-called ethnographic objects in European museums, however, remain largely disconnected from the distant cultural milieus of their Indigenous makers and customary sources of anthropological knowledge. The roots of the widely observable conflicts between Euro-American institutions and Indigenous people go deep, below the surface of ethical and political contestation into the realm of different philosophical foundations through which humans, material things, bones, mountains, and other living entities come into being. Unlocking these ways of knowing and being becomes a methodological task.[55] The desperately tight grasp on *Deutungsmacht,* which continues to dominate and stifle anthropological and museological discussions, is thus not only often ethically and politically reprehensible but also methodologically flawed.[56]

To be sure, anthropological knowledge production has never been linear, despite the undeniable power dynamics underpinning such a destructive process as colonialism. Co-creation has been ongoing since the moment of first encounter, from the development of anthropology as a discipline to the formation of ethnographic collections in museums. These Indigenous interventions might not have entered official or public perspectives at the time but they still took place.[57] Anthropological work has never been an exclusive business because it has always relied on, and had to engage with, others as informants, negotiators, interlocutors, and so on (see chapters 1 and 3). At the same time, we should not glorify the present situation in which co-creation seems to become a trend, an almost fashionable must-have, at least in the museum world.[58] Quite often, however, such initiatives can be unmasked as shallow political gestures, which arguably lack methodological rigor and fail to address the key question raised in this book: how can we seriously co-create knowledge across boundaries, which do exist, however porous, malleable, and relational they are?

This is essentially a methodological question; it seems to me that few approaches in current scholarship are able to move beyond the orthodox self-other-dichotomy. This persistent block appears to have caused the ontological turn to lose track, rather than setting course toward the *muliwai*—a Hawaiian concept of the "own space" in-between people, things, places, and knowledge across their global connections—as I argue with Noelle Kahanu elsewhere.[59] "Articulating visions of anthropology's future, at least from an Indigenous Oceanic perspective"—the focus of this book—however, "can be done only through genealogical work—the search for, production, and transformation of connections across time and space."[60] Given the topological reshaping of the globalized "sea of islands," such Oceanic genealogical work is indeed—through the endemic traveling of material entities, ideas, concepts, and so on, and the associated expansion and reconfiguration of connections across time and space—a global affair to be tackled simultaneously from within Oceania and Europe, as pursued in this book. The main concern should therefore not be how anthropology (re)defines the perceived difference of others—such as in cultural or ontological terms—but rather how the anthropological inquiry itself is done with them. In this book, then, the focus is on collaborative ethnography in the doing.

Hawaiian scholar Manulani Meyer, an advocate of the rigor and depth of Indigenous knowledge systems, speaks of the muliwai, a place where fresh water and salt water meet, where the river flows into the sea.[61] It is a critical habitat where marine life congregates as the muliwai ebbs and flows with the tide, changing shape and form daily and seasonally. In metaphorical terms, the muliwai is a location and state of dissonance where (and when) two potentially antagonistic elements meet, but it is not a space in between, rather, it is its own space, a territory unique in each circumstance, depending on the size and strength of the river, the width of the opening, and the strength of a recent hard rain. Rather than being a threat to encountering inhabitants, this living, breathing, and changing muliwai is a source of life and potentiality. Anthropological knowledge production seems most meaningful if it captures and opens the locations and moments of the muliwai as the own space of potentialities arising from in-between worlds. This might, again, be approached in ontological, cultural, or other terms. I opt here for cultural, or rather cross-cultural, but more important than the label is the concrete empirical reality it refers to.

What is much needed, then, is a conscious awareness of and constructive engagement with what might be termed the cross-cultural infrastructure of ethnographic knowledge. What I mean by this is that ethnographic authority can only be dialogically negotiated through a cross-cultural anthropology that is enacted not just through its analytical focus on cross-cultural action, traffic, and appropriation (as research increasingly does), but at the level of method, interpretation, and representation of the anthropological inquiry itself. Such conscious cross-cultural infrastructure of ethnographic knowledge must be put into practice and built up through the translational dialectic of resonances and dissonances. Serious cross-cultural study searches for resonances between different culturally grounded analytical positions and their respective articulation and movement through a "common sphere" while opening spaces for dissonances that are provoked through the "untranslatable."[62] Such dissonances become findings throughout the process of collaborative inquiry rather than an inhibition from the outset caused by Euro-Americentric projections of anthropological imaginations. The muliwai, or the own spaces resonating in between, are insidiously fraught with dissonances.[63]

This methodological ethos was enacted at every stage and in each dimension of the collaborative ethnographic inquiry informing this book: from question and method to interpretation and representation or writing. In terms of both content and form, this book complicates the notion of monograph and its claim of sole authorship. It reveals the underpinning (and often hidden) multiple anthropological relationships by critically revisiting the figure of the informant in the past (chapters 1 and 3), and by methodologically executing anthropology as interlocution in the present (chapters 2, 5, and 6). Although books have been written on how to do collaborative ethnography, one can hardly detect examples that lift the collaborative approach to the level of co-interpretation and co-representation through cowriting.[64] James Clifford's pondering "on ethnographic authority" and his suggestion of an "alternate textual strategy" that "accords to collaborators, not merely the status of independent enunciators, but that of writers" still mostly remains "a utopia of plural authorship."[65] The anthropological potential, indeed necessity, as well as the limits of such polyphonic and utopian work lie at the heart of *Refocusing Ethnographic Museums through Oceanic Lenses.*

Content and Structure of the Book

The deliberate sharing of analytical authority is explicit in the cowritten chapters, which bring forward the distinctive expertise of the coauthors through Indigenous concepts and analyses and render this book a multivocality united in the dual pursuit of historicizing ethnographic knowledge and shifting the register toward Indigenous epistemologies and ontologies.[66] This approach shapes what might be called an ethnographic kaleidoscope (see conclusion). At the same time, however, this book is still a collection process, a curatorial act of selection, inclusion, and elision. This is inevitable in any inherently limited endeavor—intellectual or of any other kind—but the underpinning rationale has to be acknowledged.

This book's intent is to interrogate and question the ethnographic museum, as its focus of analysis, as well as the ethnographic moments of its own inquiry. To do so, it requires a multiplicity of ethnographic relationships and a diversity of analytical languages. With Noelle Kahanu I have a long-held relationship over several years of co-thinking and cowriting; with Christián Moreno Pakarati and Mara Mulrooney I collaborated on the Métraux Photography Project during my fieldwork on Rapa Nui; with Sean Mallon I have engaged for more than a decade (since my time working and researching at Te Papa between 2006 and 2011); and with Nina Tonga I have continued to work on the German-Sāmoan project from Germany. These different relationships necessarily imply different languages—curatorial, artistic, academic, activist, and so on—that build a multifaceted coauthorship and grind the Oceanic lenses of an ethnographic kaleidoscope. Although I initiated the overall project and designed the book, one cowritten chapter per case opens the respective case study: chapter 1 on Hawai'i with Noelle Kahanu; chapter 3 on Rapa Nui with Cristián Moreno Pakarati and Mara Mulrooney; and chapter 5 on German Sāmoa and Aotearoa New Zealand with Sean Mallon and Nina Tonga. These chapters and their research grew out of the fieldwork and emerged throughout our ongoing collaboration.

Chapter 1, written with Noelle Kahanu, considers the founding of the Bernice Pauahi Bishop Museum in Honolulu and its significance as a U.S. institution that is, at the same time, genealogically imbued with the mana of the Hawaiian monarchy. The Bishop Museum appears, in a complex and qualified sense, as an Indigenously constituted institution that was, however, swiftly unsettled by scientific agendas and permeated by the common evolutionary presumptions at the time of its development. Yet, it continuously provided niches for largely unacknowledged or marginalized Hawaiian scholarship and curation, which became the basis for the visible shift toward Indigenous approaches to curation and museology in recent years with broader implications for Hawaiian communities and the endurance of the Hawaiian nation. Chapter 2 fleshes out, in a conceptually driven discussion that draws on my fieldwork reflections and interactions with Indigenous museum professionals, how the Bishop Museum is understood and performed as a dynamic and living genealogical space.

Chapter 3, written with Cristián Moreno Pakarati and Mara Mulrooney, focuses on the Métraux Photography Project as a transpacific exchange between the Museo Antropológico Padre Sebastián Englert in Rapa Nui and the Bishop Museum in Hawai'i. The chapter complicates the notion of informants and discusses the positions and interests of a succession of Rapanui "informants" who engaged in distinct ways and with different motivations over time with visiting ethnologists and archaeologists. Chapter 4, which is again more conceptually minded, delves into the "heritageisation" of Rapa Nui and its discursive reconstruction as "Museum Island." A variety of observable curational interventions—enacted, for example, through the involvement of Rapanui archaeologists and aimed at historical preservation—can be understood as processes of "curing" the scars of the past in an ancestral landscape.

Chapter 5 is written in conjunction with curators Sean Mallon and Nina Tonga, and focuses on Te Papa by exploring the principle of *mana taonga* as a policy that situates Indigenous people at the center of museology. The chapter maps out the collaborative project *Materializing German-Sāmoan Colonial Legacies,* in which I was involved as German community representative, cocurator, and visiting scholar. The chapter also takes a more conversational tone as we talk, always openly and sometimes critically, about our collaborative engagements. In chapter 6, I reflect further on the ambivalent role as one of "anthropology's interlocutors" in the fraught nexus of Germany, Sāmoa, and Aotearoa New Zealand, observing a changing yet perpetuating ethnographic condition that first underpinned German colonial governance and nowadays informs Sāmoan contemporary art practices as Sāmoan-German responses to, and interrogations of, the German-Sāmoan colonial legacy. Throughout the discussion, "objects" are approached as material historical sources (akin to books and archival sources), and artistic expressions and performance are treated as ethnographic interpretations and critiques.

The conclusion, "An Ethnographic Kaleidoscope," proposes a kaleidoscope metaphor as a way of encouraging fluid ethnographic engagements to avoid the impulse to solidify and enclose differences, and remain open to changing ethnographic meanings, positions, performances, and relationships. This leads to an afterword by Ty P. Kāwika Tengan, a poetic reflection on the concept of *maka* as a kind of refocusing lens, and proliferation of the multiplicities of meaning implied by this idea in Oceanic epistemologies and ontologies. Here, the book comes full circle in the coauthors' collaborative effort to mobilize Oceanic eyes, bodies, and sovereignties aimed at refocusing ethnographic museums through Oceanic lenses.

PART I

BERNICE PAUAHI BISHOP MUSEUM, HAWAIʻI

CHAPTER 1

I Kū Mau Mau

Restoring Hawaiian Intent, Presence, and Authority

with Noelle M.K.Y. Kahanu

In Hawaiʻi, as in other places across Oceania, the "canoe making profession of ancient times" was a collaborative endeavor with varying degrees of input from various levels of society.[1] "I Kū Mau Mau" is the first line of a well-known call-and-response chant appearing in David Malo's *Hawaiian Antiquities,* a seminal piece of nineteenth-century Hawaiian scholarship.[2] This chant was customarily sung when large trees were felled for building canoes and carving *heiau* (temple) figures and collectively hauled down the mountainside. Apart from this customary meaning, the chant has also a long history of political significance—being deployed, for example, by the Home Rule Party, a pro-Hawaiian electorate organization, as a call to unity in 1906, a few years after Hawaiʻi was annexed and turned into a U.S. territory, and commonly mobilized today for the same purpose as in protest marches and vigils.[3] The chant line can be translated as "Stand up together," *mau* indicating a sense of multiplicity, collectivity, and unison. But mau also has its temporal sense—as steady, constant, unceasing, continual, perpetual—to continue, preserve, endure, and last. This perspective is supported by the ongoing framing of Hawaiian collective action through mau.

I Kū Mau Mau, then, we want to argue, emerges as a literal manifestation of the longue durée of Hawaiian philosophies, concepts, and practices in general, and the longue durée of a Hawaiian presence in the Bishop Museum in particular, which is crucial for our purposes here. Such Indigenous presence has been and remains vital to the quality and authenticity of the Bishop Museum as an institution. In a 1921 article arguing in support of a federal Hawaiian homesteading program, Native Hawaiian leader John Wise cites Hawaiian canoes as a sign of the excellence (*ka hoailona pookela*) and the fine craftsmanship of the Hawaiian people (*ike hana o kekahi lahui*).[4] I Kū Mau Mau thus conjures forth not just the collaborative nature of canoe-building but also the necessary skill, rigor, and quality of work, resulting in *wa'a* (canoes) that not only endure stormy seas but also ride out centuries within the confines of cultural collections.

The persistent struggle of Hawaiians for sovereignty operates through the discourse of colonialism as well as through an emerging occupation discourse.[5] The latter refers to Hawai'i's status as an independent nation under international law (as the first internationally recognized non-Western nation with an array of international treaties and diplomatic relations in the nineteenth century), and considers U.S. law and a potential nation-to-nation relationship under its umbrella, as in the case of Native Americans, as illegitimate and inapplicable to the Hawaiian Kingdom. In 1993, then President Bill Clinton signed the joint congressional resolution that became Public Law 103-150, which acknowledged and apologized for the role of the United States in the overthrow of the Kingdom of Hawai'i in 1893—a move that has yet to yield any political outcomes.[6] What role, if any, has the Bernice Pauahi Bishop Museum played in this ongoing reconfiguration: as witness, documenter, collaborator, critic?

This chapter discusses the current interpretive shift toward a Native perspective that has emerged over the last decade, arguing that the recapturing of interpretive authority at the Bishop Museum is not a new phenomenon but instead the current manifestation of a continuum of strategies to maintain the institution's Hawaiian intent in the face of the seemingly overwhelming forces of colonization and occupation. This can be observed in the trajectory from the museum's initial purpose as a memorial to Princess Bernice Pauahi Bishop to preserve her (and the wider Hawaiian) legacy for posterity as well as the enduring public presence of Lahilahi Webb, through the scholarship of Te Rangihīroa (Sir Peter Buck) and Mary Kawena Pukui devoted to the perpetuation of Hawaiian customs and language, to the recent restoration of the Hawaiian Hall in 2009 and the landmark exhibition, *E Kū Ana Ka Paia* in 2010.[7]

Throughout our inquiry, we focus on specific cultural and museological actors, who have constituted and have been constituted by larger sociopolitical processes. Such an approach facilitates a "double historicizing" that works through the dialectic between broader historical forces and specific genealogies, thus disclosing how museums and museological figures affect and are affected by wider historical events and transformations.[8] As we shall see, I Kū Mau Mau—understood as restoring the Hawaiian intent, presence, and authority—has not evolved in a linear direction but instead more akin to a temporal *muliwai:* the moment when fresh water and salt water meet, when the river flows into the sea.[9] That is, the Indigenous institutional presence has also been affected by the seasons, swells, and a myriad of other factors, which result in various mixtures of Native and non-Native relations. In this vein, we are interested in exploring how the Bishop Museum's institutional genealogy has been subjected to and is constitutive of Hawaiian rearrangements—involuntary annexation, cultural renaissance, and pursued political sovereignty—through the individual actions and biographies of Hawaiian and other related Pacific people, from Bernice Pauahi Bishop through Lahilahi Webb, Te Rangihīroa and Mary Kawena Pukui, to Noelle Kahanu, coauthor of this chapter. This line of reasoning, we suggest, allows us to refocus the notion of modernity and its institutional manifestation in the museum through Hawaiian lenses.

The Founding of the Bernice Pauahi Bishop Museum

The Bishop Museum's founding in 1889 and subsequent evolution around the turn of the following century coincided with political changes of overwhelming magnitude for the Hawaiian Kingdom that, from the 1840s onward—hardly six decades after its initial contact with Europe on the arrival of Captain James Cook in 1778—was internationally recognized through diplomatic relations with all major world powers, thus evolving into a "hybrid state" that successfully staved off European colonization because of its own political modernization.[10] Then, in 1893, the Hawaiian Kingdom was overthrown by a coup d'état largely executed and supported by U.S. businesses, military, and government; in 1894, it became a republic; and in 1899, Hawai'i was forcibly annexed and turned into a U.S. territory (before becoming the fiftieth U.S. state in 1959). Roger Rose, former curator at the Bishop Museum, thus does not exaggerate in claiming that "no other major museum could cite political change of such magnitude as the context shaping the Bishop Museum's birth and early development."[11]

Dissecting the actual complexity of this highly compact historical account would, of course, exceed the scope of this chapter; further, Rose has already addressed it in *A Museum to Instruct and Delight: William T. Brigham and the Founding of Bernice Pauahi Bishop Museum.*[12] It is enough to say here that, given the enormous instant impact and subsequent influence of the United States, the temptation might be to reduce Hawai'i's destiny to the passively received outcome determined by external forces such as colonialism, Christianity, and modernity, among others.[13] However, if we zoom in on the unfolding drama through a "native agency" or "Ōiwi optics," as done here in regard to the Bishop Museum, "the erasure, or nonrepresentation of the historical native agent" can be partially undone and a more complex picture can be drawn.[14]

The museum as an institution has been widely regarded as being born out of European enlightenment and modernity.[15] In the case of the Bishop Museum, however, this seemingly externally imposed civilizing tool has always had a cross-culturally constituted quality. As museum historian DeSoto Brown has stressed, "Bernice Pauahi Bishop as well as the other *ali'i* (royalty) children of the same generation [were] born and grew up . . . very much in both Western and Hawaiian ways of thinking." Consequently, Brown points out, the "Bishop Museum from the very beginning has always been . . . in both sides of the situation . . . it has always had some level of Indigenous involvement, some level of Indigenous awareness as well as always being within a Western framework of a museum."[16]

This particular museum was initially established by her husband Charles Reed Bishop as a memorial to Princess Bernice Pauahi Bishop, the last lineal descendant of the royal family of Kamehameha I, to preserve her and the broader Hawaiian legacy. If we "accept that the ali'i were able to adapt to foreign systems while maintaining their Hawaiianness," as we certainly do here—how else could one explain any continuing yet evolving Hawaiianness today?—then we can safely claim that the newly arriving idea, tool, and institution of the museum was not externally prescribed but gained, through "native appropriation," a different and uniquely Hawaiian quality.[17] This was evidenced first in the Hawaiian National Museum, which was established by an act of the legislature of the Kingdom of Hawai'i in 1872. Never fully realized for a variety of political reasons, it was dissolved in 1891 and its collections were subsequently transferred to the Bishop Museum.[18] The new museum, which had originally been known as the Kamehameha Museum, was erected on the plains of Kaiwiʻula, within a larger area known as Kapālama (enclosure of lama trees, or *Diospyros*) where, over centuries, chiefly children were educated and trained as future leaders. The site was already home to the Kamehameha School for Boys, which had been established in the 1884 will of Bernice Pauhahi Bishop, and Charles Reed Bishop saw a natural connection between these two entities. According to Bishop Estate Trustee Dr. Charles McEwen Hyde,

> it is Mr. Bishop's desire that these memorials of the past shall furnish suitable instruction and intensify patriotic enthusiasm in the Hawaiian youth of both sexes brought into these buildings, under these influences, for education and training, and, as such, they properly form a part of the equipment of these schools. (figure 1.1)[19]

The Bishop Museum's founding in 1889, both literally and figuratively, underscores how the genealogical significance of its placement contributed, right from the outset, to the evolution of an institution as being both profoundly modern and Hawaiian. Indeed, the *lāhui* (nation) likely looked forward to its opening and considered the Bishop Museum as an extension and embodiment of the will of their aliʻi (chiefs), as exemplified by the dowager Queen Emmalani, widow of Kamehameha IV,

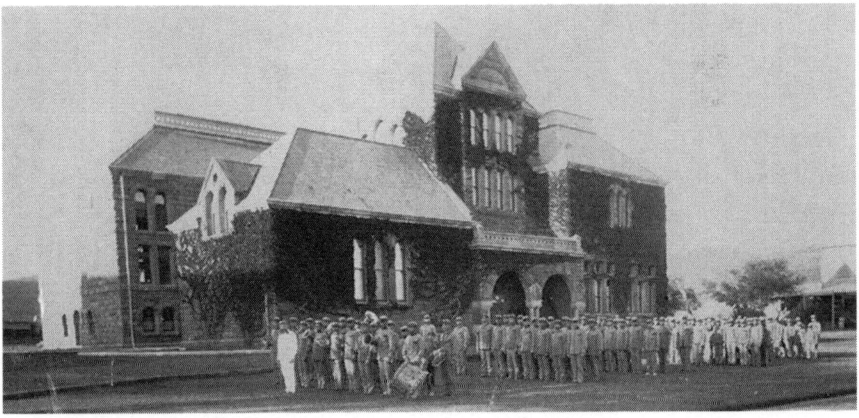

Figure 1.1 Kamehameha Boys' School students in front of Bishop Museum. Honolulu, Hawaiʻi. Taken between late 1894 after completion of Polynesian Hall (back left) and the start of construction of Hawaiian Hall, which would be added at right, circa 1895. Photograph by J. A. Gonsalves, Bishop Museum Archives.

who bequeathed all her "native curiosities" to Charles Reed Bishop so that they might be displayed alongside those of Princess Pauahi.[20] As the museum's collections expanded, so did its facilities, and as Hawaiian Hall was being constructed in 1894, the Hawaiian newspaper *Ka Leo o ka Lahui* observed that "this thing being built is a great treasure [*kekahi mea waiwai nui*]" that "will show our progressive state [*ke kulana holomua*]" and "become a place much visited by visitors and locals."[21] In the face of tremendous upheaval, indeed a mere year after the illegal overthrow of the Hawaiian Kingdom, the *mana* (prestige) of generations of Hawai'i's monarchs as contained within their treasured heirlooms could still be preserved and protected within the basalt structures of Kaiwi'ula.

As the subsequent history of the Bishop Museum shows, however, this point should not be misread as jubilant celebration since the mutual, simultaneous constitution of Western and Hawaiian cultural elements never proceeded in a symmetrical and synchronous manner. Its first curator, William Tufts Brigham, shifted—with the backing of Bishop—the focus from cultural memorial to scientific institution with a global reputation, declaring in 1904 that "this museum is no longer merely an exhibition to amuse an idle hour, but it is, or should be when perfected, a means of collecting, preserving and studying the history of life in the Pacific, a region where," according to him, "the original native life is fast disappearing."[22] This scientific shift in orientation, which refocused on both Hawai'i and the wider Pacific, found its expression in the museum's amended name as the Bernice Pauahi Bishop Museum of Polynesian Ethnology and Natural History. Brigham considered the museum to be a scientifically "living institution," as stated in *A Handbook for Visitors to the Bernice Pauahi Bishop Museum of Polynesian Ethnology and Natural History* published in 1903.[23] His scholarly publications, however, deemed the Hawaiian world a vanishing reality or already dead relict of the past, prophesizing apocalyptically that "the work of a primitive people" and "savage races . . . of a lower order of civilization," such as "kapa-making is fast passing into oblivion" or "already lost."[24] This supposedly scientific stance was thus married with, and informed by, an attitude of racial superiority—an evidently widespread trait at the time that arguably continues to resonate to this day. A prominent example of the often-resulting conflicts was an "open protest," written by Emma Metcalf Beckley Nākuina, curatrix of the Hawaiian National Museum from 1882 to 1887, against Brigham, "that wholesale insulter and villifier [*sic*] of Pauahi

Bishop's race."[25] As a result of the 1897 controversy, Brigham temporarily resigned and Nākuina applied for the position. Although Brigham was reinstated and promoted to director in 1898, the enmity between both persisted until he became director emeritus in 1919.[26]

This complicated narrative is further underscored by Native Hawaiian visitorship of the museum itself, as documented in meticulous attendance statistics kept by race for twenty-five years—from 1899 to 1924. In 1899, annual attendance by Hawaiians was 1,111.[27] By 1924, it had increased nearly fivefold, to 5,204. As a proportion of the overall visitation, Hawaiians averaged 14 percent, the highest—26.7 percent—occurring in 1903, likely due to increased interest following the opening of exhibitions in Hawaiian Hall.[28] Many Hawaiians took advantage of the Sunday afternoon openings, although the director's report of 1924 expressed disappointment that "of all the races the Hawaiians failed to make an advance."[29] Throughout this period, when eugenics studies led to casts of living Native Hawaiian students of Kamehameha Schools and the careful examination and photography of some two thousand Hawaiians and part-Hawaiians (1920–1921), as well as the active solicitation and receipt of Native Hawaiian *iwi kūpuna* (ancestral remains) and burial goods, such as those from the Forbes Cave in 1905, it seems ironic that the museum remained concerned about daily Hawaiian attendance.[30] Although such practices, hailed as scientific inquiry, often happened with the cooperation of Hawaiian entities, such as Kamehameha Schools, they did not appear to impair the trust of the more prominent Hawaiian families of the early twentieth century, as evidenced by numerous donations. In the year 1920 alone, *ki'i* (wooden idols), *kahili* (feathered standards), and other valuable treasures were gifted to the Museum (and subsequently turned into ethnographic material) by Princess Kawananakoa, High Chiefess Elizabeth Kekaaniauokalani Pratt, and the administrator of the Queen Liliuokalani Estate.[31] These seeming contradictions, as evidenced by both visitorship and donor records, indicate that Native Hawaiians had their own relationship to the Bishop Museum, regardless of Brigham's directorial politics.

A Living Hawaiian Presence

Typical of the times, the Bishop Museum was staffed almost exclusively by Western-trained male academics. This changed in 1919 with the presence of Lahilahi Webb (figure 1.2), who "holds a prominent position

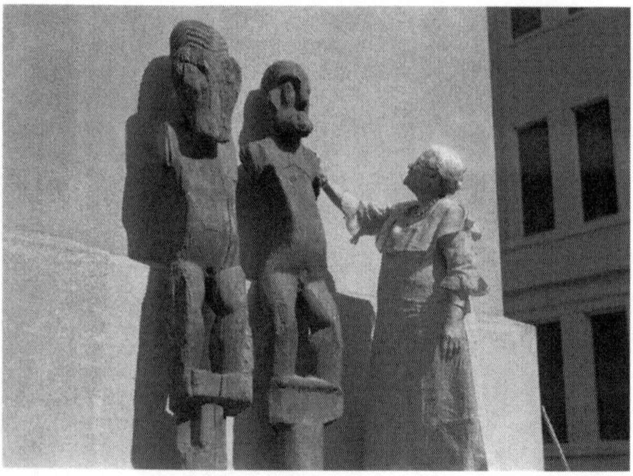

Figure 1.2 Lahilahi Webb with two wooden images at Bishop Museum. Honolulu, Hawai'i, November 1936. The images are from Waipi'o Valley. Photograph by Pan Pacific Press Bureau, Bishop Museum Archives.

among the Hawaiians" and was appointed as guide to exhibits.[32] Webb was fifty-five and had already lived a full and complex life, having served as the last lady-in-waiting to Queen Liliʻuokalani from 1914 until the Queen's death in 1917. She was active in Hawaiian political and social organizations, such as the Woman's Hawaiian Patriotic League, the Kaahumanu Society, and the Hawaiian Historical Society, leading the director to note in 1921 that her influential position in the community "has greatly assisted in bringing the Museum and the Hawaiians into sympathetic relations."[33] As well as her guiding visitors and school children through the exhibits, Webb's intimate knowledge of Hawaiian language, lore, and history contributed substantively to the scholarship of museum staff as she helped edit the Hawaiian dictionary; provided Hawaiian proverbs, stories, and songs; and directed staff to otherwise inaccessible sources, much of which led to published manuscripts.[34] Gradually, Webb's role expanded beyond the museum walls and included presentations at meetings of the Daughters of Hawaiʻi and the opening of the Royal Hawaiian Hotel in 1926, and on the "Technique of kapa making" at the Honolulu Academy of Arts in 1927, an art that Brigham had previously declared as lost, as we have seen. She also penned several articles for the *Paradise of the Pacific* magazine.[35]

Of Webb's remarkable yet mostly hidden career, Rose notes, "For two decades, this one individual, more than anyone or anything else, embodied the Museum's interaction with the local community and general public."[36] She officially retired in 1943 at the age of eighty and continued as a consultant in Hawaiian history and customs for several more years.[37] After her death six years later, the institution she had dedicated herself to for nearly a quarter of a century seemed incapable of recognizing her intellectual contributions, describing her only as "a charming and entertaining hostess," "a colorful link with old Hawaii," and "a valuable informant for members of the Museum staff."[38] Although she had seemingly avoided the designation "informant" for most of her career, in the end, it became one of her most memorable attributes. As we note throughout, I Kū Mau Mau is a persistent but not straightforward journey.

Given the absence of visitor research at the time, we can only speculate about the impact of Webb's "friendly, informal talks."[39] Her lived experiences included witnessing the overthrow of the Hawaiian monarchy and actively protesting the U.S. annexation as a member of the Woman's Hawaiian Patriotic League, but how candid could she be with locals and tourists about her views and perspectives? Perhaps more important, what was it like for her to function as the main Hawaiian face of the museum, both outwardly and inwardly?[40] What we do know is that around 1928, another Native Hawaiian woman would emerge to share this burden, though it would take nearly a decade before Mary Kawena Pukui was formally hired by the Bishop Museum. Their careers formerly overlapped by six years (1937–1943) but due to Pukui's collaborations as a translator and contributor with museum staff E.S. Craighill Handy and others in the mid-1920s, this time frame could easily be expanded to two decades. Their backgrounds were not dissimilar; though separated in age by thirty-three years, both were fluent in the Hawaiian language, exceedingly knowledgeable about Hawaiian *moʻolelo* (stories), *mele* (songs), cultural practices, history, and chiefly genealogies, and both were often called upon to share their Hawaiian expertise. It was probably of comfort to many Native Hawaiians to know that these two women were at the Bishop Museum; and though their titles and tasks were different, a certain complementary relationship seemed to exist. Found in a worn 1938 autograph book belonging to Webb was an intimate handwritten note in Hawaiian from Pukui:

> There are three things: faith, hope and love, and the greatest of these is love. This is a house which we both have aloha for, an endeavor that we both do indeed love. It is you in the front [*alo*] and as for me,

> I am in the back [*kua*]. You beckon the people to enter into this house, and it is I that writes down the history of the royal chiefs and ancestors, whom we have much aloha for.[41]

Both Webb and Pukui's aloha for the Bishop Museum and the ali'i whose heirlooms were contained therein were central to their dedication, purpose, and sense of belonging—a sense of aloha that could seemingly transcend any dismissive, condescending attitudes or conduct they would have been subjected to.

Te Rangihīroa and Mary Kawena Pukui

I—Philipp—still remember the sense of excitement when I discovered a particular photograph in the Bishop Museum Archives (see figure 1.3). A single photo taken in the 1940s seemed to encapsulate what I was trying to understand: the histories and contemporary practices of Indigenous knowledge production and their transpacific dimensions. A notion of caution is again well placed. We do not intend to appropriate this photograph as a sign of postmodern or postcolonial celebration or critique, which in our view, despite being well intentioned, does not mitigate the

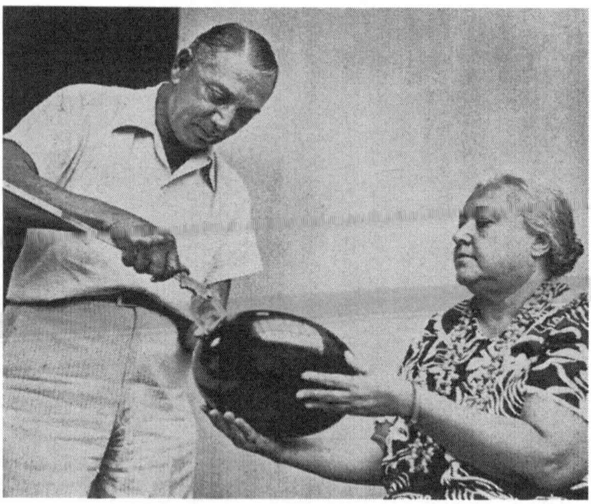

Figure 1.3 Dr. Peter Buck (Te Rangihīroa) and Mary Kawena Pukui study a wooden bowl at Bishop Museum. Honolulu, Hawai'i. From a 1940s edition of "Looking at Honolulu," n.d. Photograph by Martha Homsy, Bishop Museum Archives.

predicament of Euro-Americentric scholarship. Rather, we want to deploy it as a historical trace to complicate such analytical vocabulary by hinting at the ways in which the so-called Western ideas of colonialism, Enlightenment, modernity, and science have been relationally and cross-culturally constituted through the direct involvement and input of Indigenous agency both past and present, most often through the creative and paradoxical dialectic of contestation and collaboration, resistance and accommodation.[42] Given the emerging mutual dependence between scientific travel practices, materialities, and academic disciplines in the eighteenth century, it can be argued that the encounter with Pacific people and their material manifestations yielded a significant influence on the development of new ideas, such as the Enlightenment, thus leading to an interrelation of global encounters and European knowledge practices.[43] In other words, the Enlightenment should not be seen as a singular event originating in some European center and radiating out into the global peripheries, but rather as a "process of global circulation, translation, and transnational co-production."[44] Since the same epoch in the eighteenth century, anthropology (and anthropological curatorship) has emerged through scientific exploration and colonial expansion beyond Europe, as well as the establishment of ethnographic collections and museums in Europe, thus institutionalizing and materializing the global circulation, translation, and coproduction of ideas.[45]

But let us return to the photograph at hand. It appears as an overtly staged intervention for public communication rather than a documentary reflection of everyday practices. Moreover, Te Rangihīroa, or Sir Peter Buck, a prominent Māori scholar who served as the Bishop Museum's director for fifteen years from 1936 to 1951, and Mary Kawena Pukui, a Hawaiian scholar working for decades in various roles at the same institution, seem to be quite uncomfortable with the orchestrated scenario, an interpretation that can be supported by various accounts in which both have been consistently described as exceptionally sharp and hardworking scholars devoted to studying, perpetuating, and sharing Pacific cultural worlds while avoiding the limelight as much as possible.[46] Marie Judd, for example, who worked with both at the museum, emphasized in conversation their inquisitive minds, ability to listen, and "willingness to share." Of course, like any other human being, they had weaknesses. Buck, for example, considered the museum a scientific rather than public institution and insisted, on both ideological and financial grounds, to "devote as much of the Museum's income as possible to research work and the bare necessity to the exhibition halls."[47] This scholarly myopia might partially explain why he seemed to have been a quite incompetent administrator. Rose even saw the Bishop Museum after Buck's reign, due to the latter's "aloofness" and years of depression during the 1930s and World War II, "at its lowest point in history."[48] Although considered an important Hawaiian quality, Pukui's humility and humbleness (*ha'aha'a*) often led to overly terse summaries of her tasks and accomplishments, thus leading many to underappreciate her institutional and academic contributions.[49]

Although such shortcomings might rightly be accepted, critiqued or refuted, most important for the argument presented here, however, is that the bicultural reality of Bernice Pauahi Bishop and other ali'i children described extended, according to Brown, to the generation of Te Rangihīroa and Mary Kawena Pukui, who "had the ability to be in both of those worlds and to appreciate both of those worlds and to know how to act in both worlds." This constant moving between the worlds by Indigenous actors, in this case two scientists each combining European and Pacific heritages, attests to the mutual, albeit often asymmetrical, constitution of global, scientific entanglements underpinning modernity and modern institutions such as museums.[50] Moreover, without perverting the disastrous impact of colonial expansion, it is important to note that Indigenous people consciously and actively occupy the ambiguous and indeterminate spaces that Homi Bhabha calls the "in-between."[51] "We live in those spaces, we live in the cracks, we live below the surface," Maile Andrade, a Hawaiian artist and scholar, explained in conversation. She sees this ontological reality in a rather positive light: "We live really well there and feel really comfortable. It's not a big deal. It's not a negative thing. It's just a different space." Although this "different space" has been commonly described using the postmodern term "hybridity," we argue that a historically grounded ethnographic focus on cultural actors and their actions, as pursued here, reveals that each practice and expression, both past and present, draws on a multiplicity of overlapping and mutually constitutive styles, which make it apparent that "cultures have been hybrid *all along*, hybridization is in effect a tautology."[52]

In this vein, Te Rangihīroa's and Pukui's unwavering thirst for knowledge and commitment to cultural survival in the face of the colonial onslaught required the conscious appropriation of new tools, such as the measuring device in the photo, to carry material expressions, such as the "beautifully made wooden bowl" also in the photo, into the twentieth century, a process that alludes to the centrality of materialities in making connections. Far from being an inanimate thing, the depicted bowl gathers people, in this case two Pacific scholars who self-identified as Polynesian, and provokes their culturally embedded, scientific engagement. In a related research project at Ludwig-Maximilians-Universität Munich, we take materiality and connectivity not as defined properties of "something" but as two interrelated modes in which an entity is or is becoming in a world. With materiality we do not mean the materials as such, but instead the underlying forces and potentialities as material entity. Likewise, connectivity does not denote a single connection, but the underlying mode of being or becoming connected with other entities.[53] In the case under scrutiny, museum things and scientific practices can be considered as "ships"[54]—interpretive vessels that embody and maneuver the material and discursive relations across Pacific localities.[55] More specifically, the depicted wooden bowl allows for Pacific or so-called Polynesian connections to be remade while lending this transpacific Indigenous rebonding a scientific and modern quality, thus effecting not only the "indigenization of modernity"[56] but also the partly Indigenous constitution of modernity itself.

In his speech given at the memorial service in 1952, Kenneth P. Emory, a prominent anthropologist working at the Bishop Museum at the time, lauded Te Rangihīroa's "monumental" contributions to anthropology and his belief in the

> happy blossoming for the museum and a certain renaissance for the Hawaiian People, in that they themselves would be the instrumental ones in keeping alive a knowledge of the achievements of their race and in continuing to explore and understand their own islands and their own history, now aided by all the advantages of modern science.[57]

This laudation with the outlook of a potential Hawaiian emancipation was held at the peak of Americanization, shortly before statehood in 1959 and long before the heralding of the Hawaiian Renaissance in the 1970s. The biographic files of Te Rangihīroa and Mary Kawena Pukui at the Bishop Museum Archives point to the lasting significance of their actions, as seen, for instance, during an exhibition in 1985 commemorating the Museum's former director and facilitating momentous reconnections between Māori and Hawaiian people and *tikanga* (practices).[58] Other historical predecessors of such rebonding through prevailing transpacific networks (as well as their contemporary manifestations witnessed in the introduction) included a Māori women's delegation of the eleventh International Conference of the Pan-Pacific and South-East Asia Women's Association in 1968, visiting the Bishop Museum and paying homage to their distinguished fellow Māori seen in the display (figure 1.4).

At the same time, however, conversations with long-term employees revealed that all three—Webb, Buck, and Pukui—run the risk of being forgotten beyond the museum's walls. Our task, then, is to further historicize and humanize contemporary scholarly notions such as "performing Indigeneity," "Indigenous cosmopolitans," and "Indigenous scholars" through faces and stories, as pursued here, and to not overly

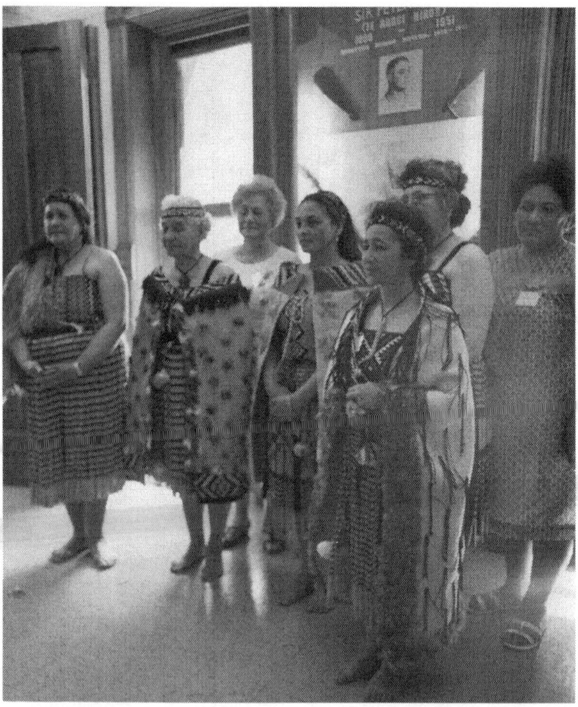

Figure 1.4 The Māori women's delegation of the 11th International Conference of the Pan-Pacific and South-East Asia Women's Association visits Bishop Museum. Honolulu, Hawai'i, August 14, 1968. Photograph by Bruce Erickson, Bishop Museum Archives.

romanticize or glorify their experiences and impact on the Bishop Museum.[59] Buck became a widely published and internationally famous scholar.[60] Pukui represents a museological shift from informant to collaborator. This apparent climbing up the ladder of scientific hierarchy, however, actually meant a downgrading of status given that although much of the original work was hers, when it was subsequently subsumed and published by others, her role was reduced to collaborator rather than acknowledged as author.[61] Yet, despite these obstacles, which Western academia posed (and often continues to pose) to Indigenous knowledge, Pukui still received authorship credit for a significant number of publications.[62] In the same vein is whether Webb also deserves similar treatment for at least some of her contributions. Indeed, the crucial question is not Indigenous presence, but whether such presence rises to the level of Indigenous agency and authority.

Musings of a Former Hawaiian Staff Member

When I—Noelle Kahanu—began my fifteen-year journey at the Bishop Museum in the late 1990s, I was unaware of my genealogical connections to Kaiwiʻula: that my grandfather had lived on the grounds as a boarding student, graduating from Kamehameha School for Boys in 1937, and that my great-grand-aunt, Martha Hohu, had served as a guide to exhibits from 1949 until 1973. I was, however, keenly aware of the tension between the Hawaiian community and Bishop Museum. As one of the oldest institutions in Hawaiʻi, it had much to make up for—a century's-old legacy of purchased burial goods; field work resulting in the disinterment of thousands of Hawaiian ancestral remains, such as the Mōkapu Peninsula disinterment of some nearly one thousand individuals between 1938 and 1940,[63] and denying access to Hawaiian oral family histories and collections. I was struck by the intensity and persistence of resentment that spanned generations; yet with criticism comes both truth and an invitation to dialogue.

The logical pathway forward then was to invite conversation. One of the ways this was achieved was through the creation of a Native Hawaiian advisory committee in 2000, the purpose of which was to dream of a new permanent exhibition in Hawaiian Hall that had not been renovated since its opening to the public in 1903.[64] I did so naively, with no indication that the museum would support such a long-ranging endeavor, and the resulting plan was ultimately set aside—but Hawaiians believe that "*i ka ʻōlelo nō ke ola, i ka ʻōlelo nō ka make*" (in the word there is life, in the word there is death), and that to speak of something, to give it voice, is to animate it. Elements of the plan found thus their way into programmatic efforts, such as the launching of changing exhibitions in the Long Gallery, an area that functions as a vestibule or pass-through gallery leading from the entrance to Hawaiian Hall. The inaugural exhibition in 2003, *E Kū Mau Mau ~ Kū Everlasting,*[65] featured the return following a hiatus for conservation purposes of the Bishop Museum's most celebrated temple image, Kū, god of governance and procreation (among his many divine functions).[66] In the exhibition, the works of nearly a dozen contemporary Native Hawaiian artists and cultural practitioners stood alongside collection items arranged according to Kū's areas of responsibility—a concept directly informed by the prior Hawaiian Hall exhibition plan. Following *E Kū Mau Mau ~ Kū Everlasting,* each year saw three to four Hawaiian exhibitions on a range of

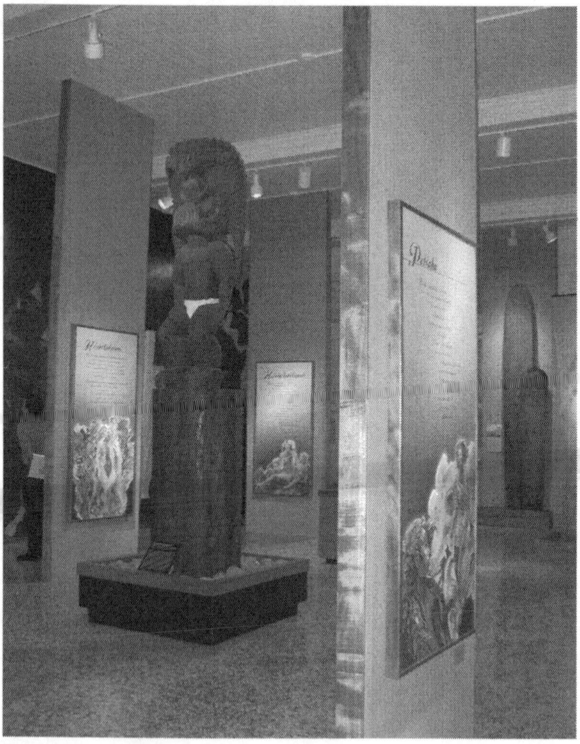

Figure 1.5 *E Kū Mau Mau ~ The Return of Kū,* Bishop Museum, 2004. Photograph courtesy of Bishop Museum.

topics from female gods to the revival of the art of *kapa* (see chapter 2), and, beginning in 2006, an annual exhibition featuring Native Hawaiian master artists (figure 1.5). Exhibitions often resulted from collaborations with Native Hawaiian organizations or guest curators, and ultimately involved more than a hundred Native Hawaiian artists over a ten-year period. Freed from the weighty constraints of a curatorial title, I viewed my role as a coordinator whose job was to facilitate community access—to take what was once a problematic and painful space and make it feel welcoming.[67]

Starting in 2005, when the effort to renovate the three-storied Hawaiian Hall began in earnest, the Bishop Museum had seemingly amassed enough credibility within the Hawaiian community to engage with a host of Hawaiian consultants—scholars, artists, practitioners, community leaders—in all facets of the renovation: from writing label texts on chiefly agency to video vignettes on cultural practices and commissioned contemporary works, to the planning of the grand reopening in 2009. The museum had designated five staff members to the internal content team and the endeavor was truly collaborative: each individual had their respective areas of responsibility and operated at all times by consensus, working closely with exhibition designers Ralph Appelbaum and Associates and the historic restoration expert Glenn Mason. My role was to serve as a community conduit, and to work on the media and contemporary art elements.[68] Perhaps because I did not come from a formal museum background, or maybe due to my own ignorance with regard to accepted practices, I did not know enough to not know.[69] If a conflict arose (and many did), my question was how it measured up against the original intent of the Bishop Museum and the spirit of its namesake, and whether it aligned with Hawaiian cultural practices and values. How did it comport with the Hawaiian community's more recent engagements with the museum? Were we being consistent, honest, and transparent, such as referencing our prior draft renovation plan? It was also helpful to have a holistic approach, for just as physical issues had become problematic, such as peeling paint, outdated wiring, and fluctuations in humidity and temperature, so too had the museum's community reputation suffered the effects of time. Thus, when the Bishop Museum began its Hawaiian Hall project, it was within the context of not just a renovation, but a restoration. And what does one restore? One restores trust, a foundation, a nation (see figure I.2).[70]

Did we succeed? Answering this question is beyond the scope of this chapter, but the Hawaiian Hall of today (see figure I.2) is fundamentally different from the Hawaiian Hall of the past. On November 24, 1903, then Director W. Brigham presided over a public dedication of the new permanent exhibition as the "first distinctively Hawaiian museum in the world." In attendance was the Supreme Court of the Territory, the United States Court, most of the Protestant clergy, faculty from Oʻahu and St. Louis Colleges, the Kamehameha Schools, and by special invitation of the president of the trustees of the Bishop Museum, former Governor Sanford B. Dole, whose treasonous acts against Queen Liliuʻokalani were instrumental in the illegal overthrow of the Kingdom of Hawaiʻi in 1893 and its subsequent annexation by the United States. Brigham's remarks bear repeating:

> This amusement of the people, or even their instruction, is not the chief object of a museum such as this, but we have carefully collected all these things and clustered about them all the facts . . . until at last we may wrest from the unknown the secrets which today puzzle the wisest scientists. . . . It is a waste of time to speculate on most of these questions until we have collected all the witnesses, both living and dead that may be within our reach. That is why a museum like this is never completed, indeed is never finally arranged. If it ceases to grow it dies, and its remains should be scattered to the four winds, that is, to enrich other living museums.[71]

Luckily, the Bishop Museum never met its demise nor did it confine itself to scientific interests. Today's Hawaiian Hall represents a vibrant Hawaiian community whose scholarship is grounded in both our ancestral knowledge and contemporary lived experiences. Each floor now represents a physical and spiritual realm: from the first floor of Kai Ākea, the wide expanse of the sea, to the second floor, Wao Kanaka, the realm of man and daily life, and the third floor, Wao Lani, the heavenly realm. Various cases reflect upon the gods, their different body forms and areas of responsibility, and how the lunar cycle guided how Hawaiians fished, planted, and worshiped. Hawaiian voice infuses each floor, with many of the label texts authored by Hawaiians, past and present. The continuity of the Hawaiian people through time is also shown by including the works of contemporary artists alongside those created by their ancestors.

The third floor addresses the world of our chiefs, not only who they were, but also how they were related, for these are the threads of mana that form the living tapestry upon which Hawai'i was founded.[72] Multiple cases detail the end of the monarchy and the illegal overthrow of Queen Lili'uokalani, as well as annexation, statehood, and the Hawaiian Renaissance movement of the 1970s through today. The opening in August 2009 was a celebratory event with hundreds of participants from throughout the community, including many of our consultants. *Kāhili kū* (tall feathered standards) waived gently in the breeze as *hālau* (groups) performed hula and visitors were welcomed with a mele composed by museum staff: *"Aloha 'ia nā ali'i a mamau loa, lolo aka puna i ka 'ulu kou ka moana, e hele mai i ka hale a, he mai!"* (Enveloped by the eternal warmth that spreads across the lands, our house is ready to receive you).[73]

Subsequent evaluations have reinforced the impact of the exhibition on the visitors, including the fact that 71 percent of visiting guests made it to all three floors, that the median dwell time was seventy-five minutes without a tour, and that on a scale of 1 to 5, 98 percent gave the exhibition a 4 or 5, and 78 percent gave it a 5. Its message seems to carry across the cultural spectrum with comment books excerpts from across the globe: "Very symbolic and touching. So proud to be Hawaiian" (Hawai'i); "May all the gods be pleased with this place" (Texas); "A true revelation!!!!" (Venezuela); "Everyone indigenous could be in this museum. Your story is my story is our story" (Yurok/Pit River).[74] But perhaps most important, the Bishop Museum took major steps toward restoring its relationship with the Hawaiian community. In the words of artist Imaikalani Kalahele, "for the first time, Hawaiian Hall feels Hawaiian."[75]

Holding space within an inherently non-Native space is difficult. To return to the canoe-building metaphor, as Indigenous staff, we must remember the focus, excellence, and drive of our ancestors, and to understand that there is mana in action. Guiding a felled log down a steep cliff is not for the timid; rather, it is a life-or-death task that requires intentionality and a warning to all below. Indigenous presence, whether it be Lahilahi Webb, who was finally relieved of her telephone answering duties so that she could attend more fully to visitors, or Kawena Pukui, whose research and fieldwork were given support and value, or Te Rangihīroa, who even as director was allowed to devote years to the development and publication of invaluable manuscripts, requires institutional commitment. It requires recognition of the validity and importance of Indigenous staff, who not only represent their own personal interests, but also are perceived both internally and externally as the faces of their community. Some staff report their weariness in being tasked with "performing Indigeneity," the requisite opening chant, prayer, or hula for an event. Or being tasked with sharing personal, family, or communal knowledge for programmatic purposes such as cultural demonstrations, yet not being provided equal time for collections research or the presentation of scholarly papers. It is easy to find evidence of pervasive racism at the Bishop Museum more than a century ago, as we have seen; that its strains are more subtle today do not make them any less insidious. Yes, there is Indigenous presence within the Bishop Museum, but is there Indigenous authority? Dare we ask what the weight of decades of cultural knowledge is, relative to academic achievement?

On a U.S. level, museums are increasingly willing to address the difficult subject of structural racism; tackling issues such as diversity and fair and inclusive staffing, collections, interpretation, and equality of access to their resources, and "oppression, privilege and intersectionality."[76] Networks are forming from gatherings such as the three-day *Museums & Race* in Chicago in 2016.[77] Proactive efforts are being made to plant seeds in various geographic areas and museum disciplines to encourage a new philosophical stance on the role of museums that is both morally and culturally responsive and grounded in empathy, respect, and inclusion. Regional conversations are occurring within the Western Museum Association and locally at the Hawai'i Museums Association.[78] At the same time, the Bishop Museum's perceived racial diversity often obscures serious conversations as to the persistence of racism. Given the opportunity years later to reflect on my time at the Bishop Museum, I have come to realize that presence cannot be equated with progress and that progress cannot depend on presence. For example, the Long Gallery continues to host many vibrant and culturally important exhibitions, but the Native Hawaiian artists' and cultural practitioners' participation has been greatly diminished, just as an annual Native Hawaiian arts market was discontinued after a decade due to lack of external funding. Thus, any perceived progress must be institutionalized through the adoption of specific policies and procedures that ensure the continued protection and prioritization of Indigenous programs and practices, regardless of the comings or goings of individual staff. To do otherwise is to leave our fate to the ever-churning muliwai.

In this chapter, we have revisited the current fundamental shift toward a Native perspective at the Bishop Museum, arguing that the Hawaiian recapturing of interpretive authority is not a new phenomenon but the current manifestation of a continuum of strategies contesting the constant crisis of museological representation. The institution of the museum has been widely regarded as being born of European enlightenment and modernity—both being temporal concepts with, once again, Euro-Americentric baggage. In the case of the Bishop Museum, however, this seemingly externally imposed civilizing tool has always had a cross-culturally constituted quality. We therefore want to broadly suggest that Western modernity as such does not exist if misunderstood as a sovereign and autonomous Western achievement. Even laudable perspectives such as Marshall Sahlins' "indigenization of modernity" and Elizabeth Harney and Ruth Phillips' "multiple modernisms" seem to suggest—at least at the level of conceptual semantics—either a chronological precedence of a singular, bounded Western modernity, which is subsequently Indigenized as a response to externally imposed forces, or a multiple co-modernity consisting of separate strands developing in parallel.[79] Instead, we argue that modernity itself has been internally multiple and radically cross-cultural throughout. Rather than juxtaposing different modernities, we should pluralize modernity's history. In the case of the Bishop Museum, the efficacy of Hawaiian and related Pacific actors—from Bernice Pauahi Bishop through Lahilahi Webb, Te Rangihīroa, and Mary Kawena Pukui, to Noelle Kahanu—on a modern institution such as a museum can thus be seen, not as an appropriation or inflection from the outside, but as a partial constitution from within.

Each existed and persisted within the muliwai, the murky confluence of fresh and salt water that is influenced by both external and internal forces resulting in endless changes to Native and non-Native relations. The temporal quality of I Kū Mau Mau resides not in a linear progression of increasing Native intent and presence, but rather within a spectrum that includes both advances and retractions. How best then can the Indigenous perspectives infused within Hawaiian Hall be maintained and allowed to permeate through other facets of the institution?

For Hawaiians and their engagement with the Bishop Museum, illumination can be found within Kū's nature, for as the god of chiefly governance and warfare, protection and procreation, Kū is present and engaged as protector and provider, standing upright, firmly planted, immovable. Despite the fears of the museum's founding aliʻi and the dire predictions of Brigham—that all that could be known of a disappearing culture would reside in the curios of the past—the Hawaiian people have persisted and thrived; the lāhui remains. I Kū Mau Mau, indeed.

CHAPTER 2

Rethinking Temporalities

Curatorial Conversations, Material Languages, and Indigenous Skills

Ethnographic exhibitions have often portrayed Indigenous people as distant in time and place, as "over there" and "back then."[1] Scholarly and public debates since the 1970s—mainly spurred by the so-called crisis of representation and politics of recognition—have accused such externally imposed temporal configurations of denying the museologically produced and represented Other their own sense of history, as the continuously abused misnomer "prehistory" clearly attests, and any contemporaneity or coevalness in the underlying anthropological endeavour.[2] The conference "Museum Temporalities: Time, History and the Ethnographic Museum," which I attended in November 2015 at the Research Center for Material Culture in Leiden, The Netherlands, thus felt compelled to consult several pressing questions: How do ethnographic museums deal with temporal categories such as past, present, and future? What role does history and memory play within these museums? How do they address their now contested histories of representation?

According to the organizers, the conference set out to look critically at this relationship between time and the museum by exploring from multiple perspectives the hitherto underexplored multiple temporalities at play especially in ethnographic museums.[3] The conference's theme appeared to me as immensely topical and its goals as eminently laudable. Most, if not all, papers did not disappoint and offered stimulating food for thought and practice, but it struck me that the most acute questions given the prevailing critiques of Euro-Americentric ethnographic practices were asked last in the conference program: Are ethnographic museums dominated by Western temporalities? What other temporalities can we conceive of for ethnographic curation and display? Reflecting this apparent lack of priority in asking, only two papers of fourteen were devoted to finding answers in the session "Other Times: Indigenous Temporalities in Museum Theory and Practice": one by Genner Llanes-Ortiz, a Maya social researcher, who spoke about curating Indigenous art in Mexico, and the other by myself, attempting to rethink temporalities through Hawaiian lenses.[4]

Should institutions, professional fields, and academic disciplines and conferences as prominently devoted to the Other as their ethnographic variations not devote more attention to "other" times and temporalities? Given the nature of this book, one might correctly assume the rhetorical quality of this question, but I still want to offer a resounding yes. Otherwise we run the risk that even such laudable initiatives and critiques, though importantly alluding to what might be called the temporal colonialism underpinning museological productions and representations of Otherness, remain largely disconnected from Indigenous temporalities and critiques of contemporary museum practices that are reemerging across Oceania, as in Hawai'i. In other words, the critique itself often remains Euro-Americentric, in this instance by reapproaching multiple temporalities through myopic lenses, even if these are repolished as postcolonial or postmodern.[5] Ironically and dangerously, these conceptual demarcations perpetuate, through the supposedly clear-cut distinction between pre- and post-, a linear sense of history and temporality familiar to most in "the West," but not necessarily to "the rest."

This chapter reveals that Hawaiians conceptualize the past as a dynamic ontological source, which is continually recycled to ground the speaker in the present geared toward the future—a temporal ontological reality of a past-becoming-present-becoming-future. As we will see, the Bernice Pauahi Bishop Museum emerges as a living resource rather than a static record, and is actively used by Indigenous actors, such as museum professionals, to self-theorize, self-historicize, and self-interpret, by conversing with ancestors and contemporaries via material languages such as weaving or kapa-making, and to rediscover Indigenous skills in their own right, without necessarily aiming at Indigenizing Western practices, sciences, and institutions. The chapter argues for a conceptual shift from the usual museological focus on exhibitionary productions and representations towards rethinking curatorship as a dialogical practice: facilitating ongoing conversations, which require various common languages and the translational power of Indigenous skills.

Refocusing Museum Temporalities through Hawaiian Lenses

Shortly after I began fieldwork at the Bishop Museum in late 2014, it struck me—and I remember how viscerally it did so—that in Hawaiian and other so-called Polynesian languages no words for "art" and "artifact" exist. Hawaiians do have words such as *waiwai* (goods, valuables), *makamae* (precious), and *waiwai ali'i* (chiefly valuables), but do these equate to an artifact? After posing this question later in a brief presentation given at another European conference, "Positioning Ethnological Museums in the 21st Century,"[6] a colleague called my attention to the apparent banality of my point given the—according to her—inevitability of such equation resulting from any anthropological or curatorial classification. I struggled with her bluntness while appreciating her honesty, and it took me a while to regain my intellectual composure. In retrospect, her statement seemed to be flawed on two grounds, the disciplinary and the methodological.

"The tension between 'art' and 'artifact' is an old one," according to Mark Elliott, "perhaps as old as the discipline of anthropology itself."[7] As we see in chapter 1, the Bishop Museum launched in 2003 the exhibition *E Kū Mau Mau ~ Kū Everlasting*, staging customary wooden *ki'i* (images of Kū)—the Hawaiian deity and male principal most famously and reductively known as the god of war[8]—alongside contemporary interpretations by Hawaiian artists. This exhibitionary conception could be read as an example of the current museological trend to contrast and bring into dialogue the two main intellectual domains through which material and visual cultures of Indigenous people have been studied and exhibited: anthropology and art. That is, many ethnographic museums in Europe and North America have replaced or juxtaposed historical artifacts with contemporary art displays, and hybrid museum spaces blending both disciplinary and curatorial mechanisms are opening up.[9] Yet, both domains and their mixing remain—often despite different intentions—inherently Euro-Americentric. An intriguing example of this seemingly inevitable ambivalence at the heart of current museological reinventions was the acclaimed exhibition *Pasifika Styles* at the Museum of Anthropology and Archaeology at the University of Cambridge in

2008. Successfully opening collections and exhibition spaces to Oceanic material worlds, the initiative was still situated within and between predefined disciplinary parameters aimed at shaping a "new openness between Pacific art and anthropology"[10]—rather than the undisciplining, decentering, and multiplying of the ethnographic itself, as pursued here.[11]

In Hawai'i, one of the cultural environments from which the material expressions under disciplinary scrutiny have evolved, of course, neither the exhibitionary intention nor its analysis can be adequately approached through postmodern or postcolonial recontextualization—from crowded cabinet of curiosities or artifacts to minimalist art displays—and the associated analytical lenses and vocabularies.[12] Much more, as we have seen, was at play in *E Kū Mau Mau ~ Kū Everlasting.*[13] Yet, despite this, virtually all museological interventions (outside Hawai'i and Oceania) produce and represent Hawaiian visual and material culture through the separation and imposition of alien classifications, thus attesting to the fact that so-called ethnographic objects or works of art, especially in European collections, remain largely disconnected from their ecology, that is, the cultural environments of their Indigenous producers and customary sources of disciplinary knowledge.[14]

Engaging with part of this debate, the authors of the influential book *Thinking Through Things: Theorising Artefacts Ethnographically* opted for "things," arguing that this term carries—unlike "objects" and "artefacts"—"minimal theoretical baggage." Further qualifying their line of reasoning, however, Amiria Henare [Salmond], Martin Holbraad, and Sari Wastell insist that the renaming itself does not do the trick and suggest "a shift in the term's status," understood here as a "transformation of 'thing-as-analytic' to 'thing as heuristic.'" The authors explain further:

> Rather than going into the field armed with a set of pre-determined theoretical criteria against which to measure the "things" one already anticipates might be countered, it is proposed that the "things" that present themselves be allowed to serve as heuristic with which a particular field of phenomena can be identified, which *only then* engender theory. So, the difference between an analytical and heuristic use of the term "things" is that while the former implies a classificatory repertoire intended for refinement and expansion, the latter serves to carve out things (as an appropriately empty synonym for

> "objects" and "artefacts") as the field from which such repertoires might emerge.[15]

The broader disciplinary problem thus becomes specifically methodological, alluding to the second flaw of my colleague's statement. Furthermore, there is no denying that any classificatory translation, such as the one from waiwai aliʻi to artifact, is—apart from its heuristic limitations—no innocent linguistic act but instead a philosophically informed and historically grounded move with serious political implications, especially in contexts as ridden with (post)colonial controversy and conflict as ethnographic museums.[16] The question to be addressed then becomes how we can translate differently and avoid classificatory equation or imposition. What is required to address this problem, as I argue throughout, is serious cross-cultural translation maneuvering between different worlds, as undisciplining, decentering, and multiplying analytical performance.[17] Looking back across Oceania to Hawaiʻi illuminates what "ethnographic objects" or "artworks" are or are becoming and doing in contemporary Hawaiian life.

Kamalu du Preez, assistant collection manager at the Bishop Museum and my constant interlocutor throughout the research, suggests that *ʻōlelo Hawaiʻi* (the Hawaiian language) offers with *hana noʻeau kahiko* another term that translates literally as "skillfully created ancient works." Du Preez emphasizes that though these skilled works have been commonly reidentified by anthropological others as "artefacts" and "(ethnographic) material culture," for Hawaiian people, they have remained imbued with *mana* as material "manifestations of . . . kūpuna or ancestors," or as "the kūpuna themselves."[18] This cultural reality is further reflected in the word *mea,* which can refer to *both* people *and* things, thus collapsing the common Euro-Americentric dichotomy between subject and object.[19] At the same time, according to Maile Andrade, a Hawaiian customary practitioner and scholar with whom I also engaged throughout the research, there is "no word in the Hawaiian language for art." Given the widely acknowledged skill in the creation of material culture, one might argue that the Hawaiian material world is imbued with beauty and artistry in every facet of life and not as something aestheticized and separated from function as through the imposition of foreign categories such as, once again, art and artifact. Andrade offers an exit strategy from this anthropological impasse by understanding "art as being a visual conversation or language to express."[20] This, as she insisted in one of our discussions, unfolds as a "mana conversation."[21]

How, then, do these Indigenous conceptualizations embedded in the Hawaiian world drive curatorial practices at the Bishop Museum? This question becomes quite delicate if we consider that the position of the curator was disestablished in the 1990s for its association with scientific colonization and as a reflection of the Bishop Museum's shifting focus from scientific to public institution. However, as a panel discussion, "Indigenous Curatorial Practices: Natives in Non-Native Spaces," that included Māori and Hawaiian cultural practitioners and scholars as well as myself indicated, Hawaiian museum professionals still undertake curatorial tasks if these are understood in the original sense of the word deriving from "curare" and meaning "to care for something."[22] How, then, can Hawaiian material ontologies, concepts, and caring practices travel and speak back to so-called ethnographic museums in Europe?

To address this vital question and conduct serious cross-cultural study between Oceanic and European worlds, it seemed to me that I have to dig deeper into the notion of "conversation" as "mana conversation." I followed this route without attempting to linguistically translate mana, a Pacific or so-called Polynesian concept that has defied foreign categorization and exceeds common translations as "power, prestige and authority," among others.[23] I was instead eager to translate empirically how mana is lived, performed, and gains meaning by the person experiencing it, and what this interpretive-performative *vā* (space between) tells us about the relationship between Hawaiian people and their material manifestations.[24]

In his written "Tauaga" (a Sāmoan dance usually performed as the finale) of the volume *Transpacific Americas: Encounters and Engagements between the Americas and the South Pacific,* Vilsoni Hereniko points out that he

> value[s] museums because they allow [him] to gain valuable insights into our pasts through material culture. . . . such objects were not created for exhibition in glass cases, or auctioned at exorbitant prices to the highest bidder, or displayed in the living rooms of wealthy individuals. This fetishisation of the object serves the interests of capitalism and the market economy, but shifts the focus away from [the fact that] the vast majority of these objects were created for

> reasons that were more to do with making connections, sometimes with other human beings, and sometimes with the supernatural or unseen world."[25]

This making of connections is embodied in, and performed through, the *vā* (*wā* in Māori and Hawaiian).[26] This concept carries purchase across Oceania and is defined by Albert Wendt as

> the space between, the betweenness, not empty space, not the space that separates, but the space that relates, that holds separate entities and things together in the Unity-that-is-All, the space that is context, giving meaning to things.[27]

"The vā," Hereniko concluded, "is abstract and therefore unavailable for sale or display. It is a concept that deserves more attention in scholarly research."[28]

I have listed to Hereniko's call, and the vā has offered a conceptual frame for reapproaching the connections between Hawaiian people and their material manifestations.[29] Not content to remain on the conceptual plane, I have explored empirically how the vā is lived, performed, and gains meaning by those experiencing it. I say "those" because the vā requires at a minimum two "beings" capable of conversing. Even when one of them is a "thing," it too is activated by the conversation. That I delve into the vā through the living human portion of the equation does not preclude the participation and influence on the part of material entities to actively inform and shape the nature of the dialogue, especially when it takes place within their presence. This also brings up the notion of "things" versus ancestral embodiments. When did Kalaniʻōpuʻu's mea waiwai aliʻi, the feathered helmet and cloak seen in the introduction, *become* him incarnate? When does the *makaloa* mat (see figure 2.1) *become* Kalaʻi herself?[30]

The vā, as the "space between," relates and unites people and material treasures or interpretive and material agency and efficacy. This shared space of reciprocal relations needs to be activated, nurtured, and kept alive through curatorial practice, thus requiring curatorial responsibility and care for the physical, historical, and political "weight" of "things" as well as the associated relationships with Indigenous people.[31] Meaning, then, arises out of this interpretive space between people and their material manifestations, and vice versa. At the heart of this simultaneous, mutual constitution of human and material actors lies practice in general and, within the context of the argument proposed here, curatorial practice in particular.[32] This "moment of practice," according to Dipesh Chakrabarty, "is a moment that bypasses—and not just dissolves—the subject-object distinction,"[33] and we shall soon witness its skilled, dialogic, and temporal quality.

I asked Kamalu du Preez and Marques Hanalei Marzan, cultural resources specialists at the Bishop Museum and also constant interlocutor throughout my research, to have a conversation with a museum piece of their choice and allow me to become part of it. Anthropological inquiry conceptualized as such cross-cultural mediation and translation, I argue, channels rather than represents the agency of others, and is not content with generating ethnographic evidence for preconceived ideas, such as "art" or "artifact," but allows different worlds to "dictate the terms of their own analysis" while recursively reframing its points of departure, such as—again—"art" and "artifact."[34] Narrative interviews, which were recorded, allowed for these double conversations to happen.[35] Photography added another methodological layer to document and co-interpret the dynamics of the vā, which gives rise to meanings as feelings beyond words.[36]

Curatorial Conversations at the Bishop Museum

In the previous chapter, we alluded to the longue durée of the Hawaiian world seen through *I Kū Mau Mau*. Here, I suggest that the underlying continuitiy might be best explained through the process of *hoʻala hou* (reawakening) enacted through moments such as, for example, the second coronation of King Kalākaua in 1883, which amounted to a strategic blending of Hawaiian and European symbols and is often regarded as the First Hawaiian Renaissance.[37] Kalākaua was responsible for outward-oriented initiatives, as evidenced in a trip around the world—the first of its kind of any political leader worldwide—and the founding of the Oihana Kea Hoohanohano Alii o ka Hoku o Osiania (Royal Order of the Star of Oceania), which recognized services "in advancing the good name and influence of Hawaiʻi in the Islands of Polynesia, and other groups of the surrounding Ocean."[38] Expansionist policies were aimed at actively and—in the case of the warship HHMS *Kaimiloa's* intervention in Sāmoan affairs—even aggressively, pursuing Hawaiian primacy across Oceania. The king also advocated for the preservation and perpetuation of cultural practices, such as by forming the Hale Nauā society to promote the ancient sciences of Hawai'i and supporting public performances of the hula, thus overturning restrictions and bans issued by Protestant missionaries on their "civilizing" crusade against such "immoral" behavior.[39]

Given this track record of reviving (and expanding) Hawaiian cultural practices and ambitions, it should not surprise that cultural treasures were valued highly during Kalākaua's reign. A particular intriguing example is a makaloa mat, woven by an eighty-year-old woman by the name of Kala'i-o-kamalino from the island of Ni'ihau (see figure 2.1). Kala'i originally made it for King Lunalilo, Hawai'i's first elected monarch and predecessor of Kalākaua. The mat is thus the physical manifestation of the relationship between a particular *ali'i* (leader) and one of his subjects. The makaloa mat then became Kalākaua's by an act of fate, given that he had assumed office following the death of Lunalilo by the time it arrived. Kala'i's intentionality, however, should not be dismissed as a historical footnote. A crucial aspect is the intentionality of the maker to create something for a particular purpose. The creator and

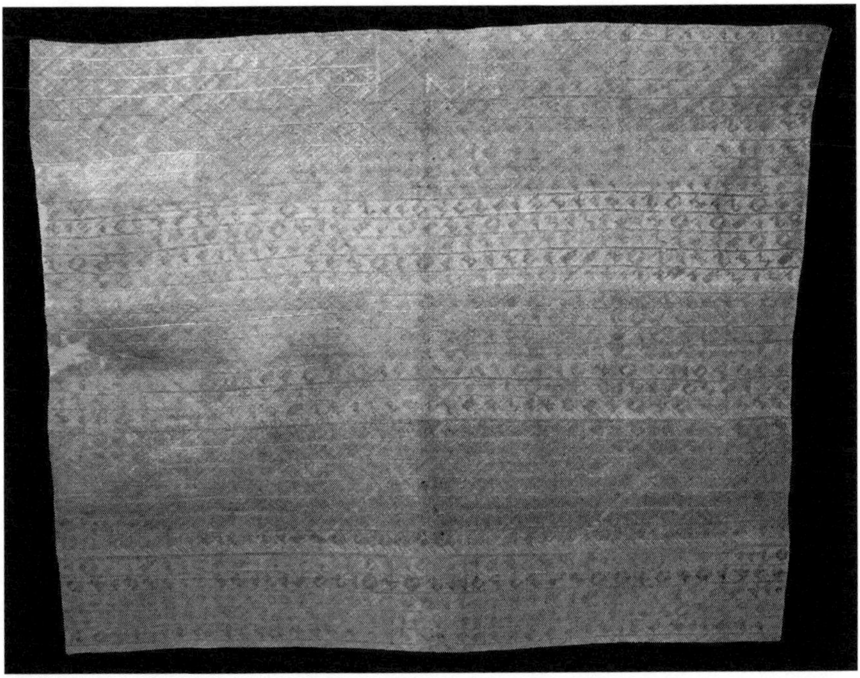

Figure 2.1 Makaloa mat, woven by Kala'i-o-kamalino from the island of Ni'ihau, 1874. Photograph courtesy of Marques Hanalei Marzan, Bishop Museum.

the creation are one and the same; the messenger and the message are one. One may take meaning from it and find contemporary relevance, but must pay due attention to its original context and the intent of its producer, however difficult it is to be reestablished in retrospect (see chapter 1).[40]

According to the "official record," the mat was presented to Kalākaua in 1874 with an inscribed petition asking the "Heavenly One" to lift the "burden" of the newly introduced animal tax at a time of dramatic change for the Hawaiian people. The full petition was printed by two Hawaiian newspapers, the version in *Kuokoa* (1874) corresponding more faithfully (yet not precisely) to the mat. Here we read how Kalai'i refers to King Kamehameha I, who unified the Hawaiian Islands in 1810, and "peace" as the "symbol of his kingdom" and its "constitution," which did not allow for "ruthless seizing . . . because of his love of the people." She calls the reader to "study the great cause for the decrease of the Hawaiian people . . . and to ask the king to change the taxes on animals. . . . O heavenly One," Kala'i concludes by demanding, "release [us] from the burden of the law that keeps us slaves under masters from the sky."[41]

This remarkable woven protest has been preserved in the Bishop Museum since 1891 but was virtually forgotten until recently. Former curator Roger Rose further explains its significance:

> Hawaiians from Ni'ihau specialized in plaiting makaloa sedge mats valued throughout the archipelago for their flexibility and intricate geometric patterns worked in a technique called pāwehe. Such mats were luxury items acquired through taxation and tribute by chiefly class, who used them as bed covers until makaloa mats were abandoned toward the end of the 19th century. One of the last examples created was presented to King Kalākaua in 1874 and incorporates a lengthy petition in the Hawaiian language, interwoven in the traditional pāwehe technique. It requests relief from burdensome taxes on animals and other oppressive conditions, dramatizing the plight of the Hawaiian commoner in a rapidly changing society.[42]

Prior to Rose's detailed scholarly work, the mat had never been discussed in the ethnographic literature. Brigham listed it only in the *Preliminary Catalogue of the Bernice Pauahi Bishop Museum* (1892).[43] He described it minimalistically in *Mat and Basket Weaving of the Ancient Hawaiians*

(1906): "2570. 7ft x 6 ft. Lettered all over, but the rude letters almost faded out."[44] Te Rangihīroa ignored it altogether in *Arts and Crafts of Hawaii* while, in the same work, considering makaloa mats "the finest sleeping mats in Polynesia" (1957).[45] In the first comprehensive study, Rose argues that "incorporating the written language into a makaloa mat is one more example of the creativity of the Hawaiian artisan, and a remarkable adaptation of a traditional decorative technique to an innovative purpose."[46]

This ethnographic-historical interpretation derived from subtle scholarly analysis sounds reasonable and convincing, but what is even more important for our purposes here is that the mat lives on and "speaks to" Marques, who currently looks after it in the Bishop Museum's collection, as he describes:

> This particular mat is unique in that it has text written over the entire surface. . . . The letters as well as the lines are all overlaid onto the surface of the mat, which means it can't be seen on the backside. . . . I think the special way that this particular weaver chose to express herself was in a very Hawaiian type of way. . . . She made this mat to make sure that the king understood his responsibility to his people, just as all of the other kings of Hawai'i did during their reigns, to never forget that your predecessors laid the foundation for your work, and to always walk in the footsteps of your predecessors. If not to do exactly the same thing but to remember the intent, the reasons why they chose to do those things for the kingdom.[47]

Marques goes on to elaborate how Kala'i-o-kamalino's chosen and distinctively Hawaiian manner to express herself and address an issue inspired him to weave the piece, *Nā'ū nā kala,* shown in the other photograph (figure 2.2). He incorporated the petition's final words, "na'u na kala," which he interprets as "let forgiveness resound,"

> to always be a symbol or a reminder that there are things that we all must do, for the betterment of ourselves or our family or our situations, that might not always be easy. And if we look to that and just remember what it is intended for, there's a greater purpose for it rather than just the immediate gratification, but the betterment for future generations, future decision making. Those ideas need to be

remembered and that's how I interpret this wonderful mat that we see here in front of us . . . in the art work that I created that speaks to the mat very closely because I used the same lettering style.

It becomes apparent that both material expressions neither are artifacts nor represent external realities. Instead, both function as vessels through which Marques and Kala'i-o-kamalino converse through the language of weaving and the enactment of cultural skills, thereby mobilizing underlying Hawaiian purposes and values for moral and political ends. It becomes equally apparent that the term "art" has certainly entered Hawaiian vocabulary but is either reframed, for example, as

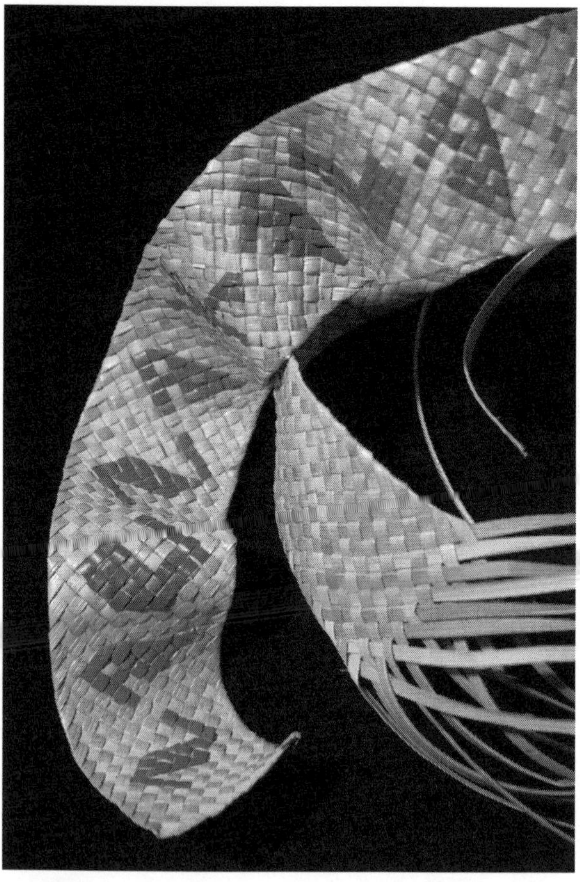

Figure 2.2 Artwork, *Nā'ū nā kala,* by Marques Hanalei Marzan in conversation with Kala'i, 2014. Photograph courtesy of Marques Hanalei Marzan.

"creative expression" in a conscious effort to resist conceptual colonization,[48] or understood differently. In the case under scrutiny, "art" corresponds to a materialized dialogue that "speaks," in Marques' words, "to the evolutionary continuity of culture"[49] and a sense of "the past" as "*ka wā mamua*" or "the time in front or before," which firmly grounds a Hawaiian person in the present with the eyes fixed upon the knowledge of the past and the back facing the unknown future.[50]

Although "no two pieces of . . . any form of creative expression . . . are the same," as Marques asserts, and "will never have the same mana because every person is different," it is, according to him, still of vital importance to "understand the intention and the reasons why those things are being made" so "you can create new things with the same ideology and concept which will look completely different but will be telling the same story." Throughout this dialogical process, the conversation between cultural practitioners, both past and present, through material languages and the translational power of skills informs curatorial conversations of care, as Marques further explains:

> I look to these beautiful pieces in the museum as my inspiration to reconnect with a time period when the culture and the practices and ideas were still very much part of society. I can see how those things visually manifested themselves into these beautiful works in front of us. I take that perspective away from these treasures we care for in the museum and I transform that into my own art of today. I try and understand the practices of our ancestors and the reasons why they did certain things. If we can keep that strong, that will be the foundation for future generations. . . . That's how I look at my artwork. . . . I try to maintain the understanding. The understanding can take completely different forms today and that's why my artwork kind of speaks to that, in different regards.

This conceptual conversation between Marques and Kalaʻi-o-kamalino appears to offer a glimpse into the Hawaiian heart, which continues to beat despite the overwhelming impact of U.S. occupation and colonization.[51] Deidre Brown argues in a similar vein that "while European influence has changed Pasifika art aesthetically, it has not changed it conceptually. Indeed, western media, art practices and technologies have often been employed by Pacific artists to perpetuate Pacific concepts."[52]

The Bishop Museum thus emerges as a living cultural resource, rather than as a static ethnographic record, and is used by Hawaiian practitioners and scholars to self-theorize, -historicize, and -interpret for the purpose of redeveloping Indigenous skills per se, without necessarily aiming at Indigenizing Western practices, sciences, and institutions, as related research has shown in different yet related (post)colonial contexts.[53] Being a cultural practitioner, Marques has an "understanding of the processes and the materials," which "grounds [him] in [his] work." He approaches and looks at the makaloa mat "with a different eye," as Maile put it, and remains in the "special human condition of being *engaged* . . . in a continual dialogue with materials,"[54] both physically and imaginatively. In addition, being a Hawaiian cultural practitioner, the act of caring for or curating the makaloa mat becomes an "act of mana," which is, according to Ty P. Kāwika Tengan, a Hawaiian anthropologist (and author of the afterword) who took part in the panel discussion *Indigenous Curatorial Practices,* "about making those connections" between people and their material manifestations both past and present, "and [about] activating them."

Marques's chosen piece appeared organically in our conversation when he showed me around the collection store. To Kamalu, it amounted to a difficult decision to settle on one piece. As she explained,

> they all speak to me. There's something inside of me, my ancestors, my own being, that really responds to all of the pieces of kapa whether they're from the time of Captain Cook until the time of now. People making things in response to, the same reason why I make it, to continue on what our ancestors have done. Making sure that everything is alive, is alive within us. We just need to enact it. It's kind of inside [and] there are so many that were just speaking to me. I really feel like I have a connection to all of those.[55]

At the beginning of our interview (more accurately, our conversation), Kamalu seemed to offer a glimpse into how and where a conceptual conversation and temporal connection with ancestral characters becomes experienced, enacted, and meaningful: the "inside," or *nāʻau.* As Hereniko argues, the place nāʻau, which literally translates as "inside of the body" especially "of the abdomen," corresponds to a "kind of knowing [that] cannot be explained logically or rationally."[56] Nāʻau is the guts or intestines, but not in their purely biological sense but rather as the seat of one's ability to feel when things are right, or when they are not right. It is not the belly or the heart per se, but the embodied location from where one's grounding comes from.[57] Nainoa Thompson, a Native Hawaiian and expert navigator, even considers na'au to be "the heart of wayfinding" and as something that "from a scientific point of view [is] just unexplainable. It's something very deep that has nothing to do with intellect and everything to do with feelings. It's na'au, the knowledge of the heart."[58] Thompson—also president of the remarkable Polynesian Voyaging Society that helped reconnect Hawai'i with its Polynesian roots and was one of the driving forces behind what came to be called the Hawaiian Renaissance in the 1970s—has spoken about navigating the Hōkūle'a canoe with his nā'au. According to him, when everything else fails, when the moon and the stars have disappeared, or the sky is dark or a storm is raging, he has no other means to steer the canoe but to resort to listening to his nā'au.[59]

In the case of Kamalu, we can observe that this embodied concept or conceptual embodiment has a temporal quality in which "the truth of the ages resides,"[60] and through which the future is shaped. The continuous remaking of *kapa* (bark cloth), a fabric made from the paper bark mulberry tree, emerges as a cultural practice with communicative quality and genealogical efficacy. Kamalu explains:

> Once you start to understand kapa and the designs that are associated with it . . . , it's a way to communicate to people identification, where you come from, without having to say that. Because for any Hawaiian, and I think for any Pacific Islander, they always ask "Nohea mai 'oe?"—Where are you from? But sometimes when you see certain designs . . . and if you are connected, if you know that language sometimes you don't ask that question. . . . It's always talking. Whether we understand it or acknowledge it is another thing. . . . Today it's still talking to me, because it's so relevant not just because I'm a practitioner of kapa but as a Hawaiian. These things from our ancestors. . . . I got emotional and I feel like I can respond to that. I don't know the words but I know the behaviours of how I respond to something like that. I make kapa, I learned how to make kapa. . . . I learned how to do these things so that I can also have a dialogue with my ancestors as well. So it's not just a one-sided conversation. . . .

> And then my children someday can have the same conversation with whether it's with me or maybe they'll find something else from the past that really speaks to them that they need to continue on, or continue on a legacy.

In her creative work "Looking Forward into the Past," which is installed in the Bishop Museum's restored Hawaiian Hall and depicts ancestral layers through superimposed faces made from glass and *wauke* (paper mulberry), Maile Andrade states that "through ourselves we see our ancestors and in our ancestors we see ourselves" (figure 2.3). Prior to the current display, Andrade staged an exhibition at the Bishop Museum titled *Ili Iho: The Surface Within* (2008—2009), which dug deeper into the temporal layers within the "thin veil between the past and present; customary practices and contemporary median." The exhibition consisted of contemporary works created through the relationships that were built with ancestral treasures, thus requiring dialogical engagements between creative practitioner, such as the participating Marques, and ancestors, as well as between the new piece and the ancestral treasure.[61]

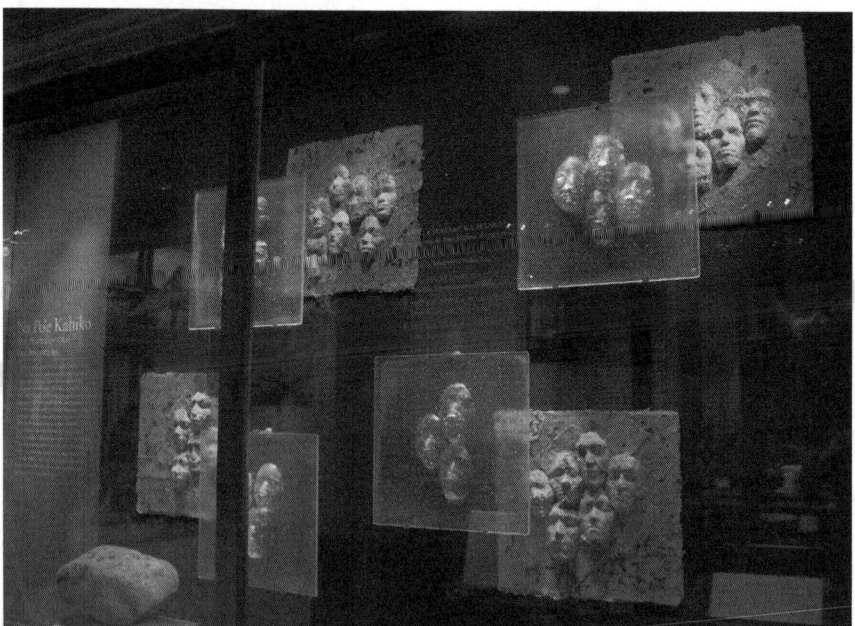

Figure 2.3 Artwork, *Looking Forward into the Past,* by Maile Andrade at Bishop Museum, 2013. Photograph by Philipp Schorch, 2014.

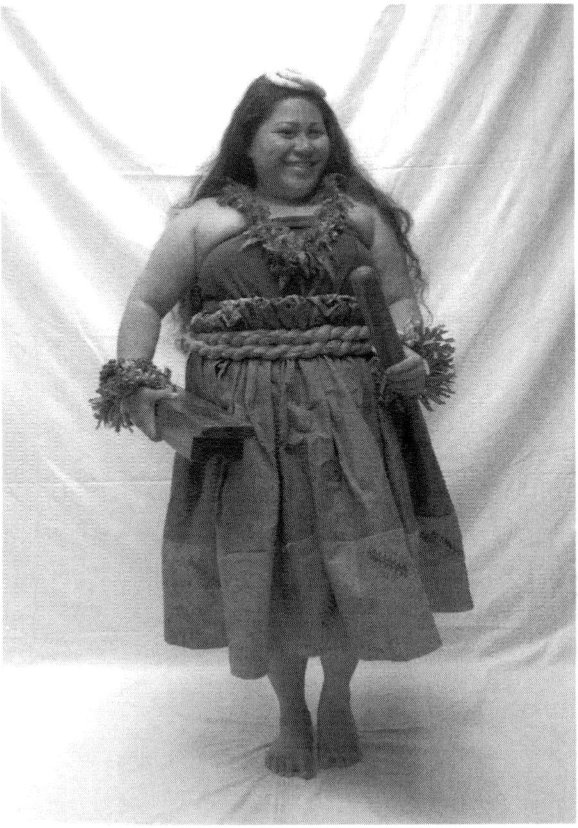

Figure 2.4 Jasmine Kupihea, a dancer from Hālau o Kekuhi, wearing a kapa skirt made by Kamalu du Preez, 2016. Photograph courtesy of Kamalu du Preez.

Such interaction with past and future should not be misunderstood as a flamboyant tactic typical and reserved for the "arts" but, as seen in the case of Kamalu, feeds into her museological work with "artifacts" by merging skilled practices with creative expressions and notions of care. She describes how her conversations with ancestors simultaneously informs her conversations with contemporaries, for example via a kapa skirt that she produced and was worn at a hula festival by a girl seen in the photograph (figure 2.4):

> [The] feeling . . . when I saw this skirt and this person was wearing it and was dancing in it—it totally blew my mind! The feeling I got was all is right in this world. This is how it's supposed to be. I'm getting

> all emotional again, my eyes are glistening. It's like living, like "Oh my god it's 2014!" And this young woman of 2014 is wearing a piece of kapa that I made, doing a traditional dance, speaking the stories of our ancestors, speaking the stories of where she came from through her dance, through the way she's dressed. And I was a part of that and I helped. . . . When she was dancing she was there. It wasn't just "Oh I have a skirt on, I'm doing a performance." She was being it. She was manifesting it. I could feel that when I saw her and I'm like "I'm a part of that."

This chapter began by pointing out that so-called ethnographic exhibitions have often portrayed Native and tribal people as frozen in time (and confined to place). Hawaiians' temporal conception, as reflected in Kamalu's materialized conversation with both ancestors and contemporaries, however, anchors a Hawaiian person in the present confronting the past and mobilizing toward the future, thus shaping an ontological reality lived through the continuum and simultaneousness of a past-becoming-present-becoming-future.[62] Dipesh Chakrabarty—in his efforts to provincialize Eurocentric "histories" through "subaltern pasts"—lends support to such an assertion by arguing

> Pasts *are* there in taste, in practices of embodiment, in the cultural training the senses have received over generations. . . . This is how the archaic comes into the modern, not as a remnant of another time but as something constitutive of the present. Whatever the nature of these pasts that already "are," they are always oriented to futures that also already "are."

Although Chakrabarty alludes to the partly unconscious temporalities underpinning cultural practices, which one "sometimes do[es] not even know [one] engages in,"[63] Kamalu highlights the conscious dimension of a past-becoming-present-becoming-future because, according to her, "you are constantly negotiating past identities with present identities. It's always that in order for us to move forward as Hawaiians, we need to refer to the things in the past." The key question to be addressed by Kamalu while looking after the material manifestation of this dialogue at the Bishop Museum then becomes "How can I show this thing respect that it's not just a thing?" She describes the delicate intricacies of such an endeavour by contrasting it with the handling of a ubiquitous postmodern thing:

> This is an iPad, and this was made in so and so, made by Apple, and this is the maker blablabla . . . But you know, what more can I add to that? It just becomes a thing. But for me because I know that it comes from a system of things, you know, it's related to people, it's related to my own people. Now how do I take care of something like that? How do I treat it in such a way, knowing that it's not just a thing that sits on a table. . . . I do have a relationship to those things. . . . And so because I have a relationship with those things I want to show that I care, that I understand what the context is that they come from. Not just it's a thing and I'm going to just put it away, but it's a thing that is attached to a person, that was used during this time and that it may have been kapu (taboo) and so it's not just history, it's a reality. The history . . . actually dictates to me how I should treat it. . . . Its history is the reality of what it is.

"The times we live in," Kamalu further asserts, "releases us from [certain] practices but it doesn't release [us] from acknowledging that history." For her, this longue durée of cultural significance is "immutable" and "plays into [her] care of those" things, which are clearly more than things, and their history, which is not a stage of the past but a temporal "reality" that permeates the present and reverberates in the future.

What, then, are the wider museological implications of such curatorial conversations enacted through skilled practices via material languages like weaving and kapa-making? And how can we rethink museum temporalities to reframe and "open" up their underlying disciplinary orientations, such as "Ethnology's deep commitment to collecting pasts, rather than pasts-becoming-futures"?[64] According to Marques, the key difference at the Bishop Museum is that although

> anthropologists . . . were just more concerned about the research and preservation but not really interested in the continual perpetuation of those cultures through the interactions with the living people and the community . . . we're looking at it from a different lens. We're looking at how those things of the past are . . . still connected to the people of the present and how those things can help us continue into

> the future . . . in Europe a lot of the collections or the researchers are separated from the collections, they don't interact with the collections in the same way. I think that's, for me, the magic for me being here at the museum is because I am a practitioner of different art forms and understand the different cultural perspectives that were imbued in all of these things that we hold here at the museum. It only allows the museum to access that through me and people like me, so that information can be disseminated in a very positive and proactive way.

This distinctively Hawaiian perspective should, as I argue throughout, not be confined to Hawai'i but travel back to Pacific collections held in Europe. Such a globalized Oceanic lens would assist us in rethinking Pacific collections and their associated temporalities, and ethnographic museums more broadly. If we are accustomed to French and German social theory being exported into Anglophone museum studies, and to using Pierre Bourdieu, Michel Foucault, and Jürgen Habermas to explain virtually any museum in the world, then we should not be surprised that Hawaiian or other Oceanic styles of museology should have something to offer in return.[65] This is, of course, especially the case when "ethnographic objects" or "works of art" housed elsewhere are still related to Hawai'i's living ecology, that is, the originating cultural environment of material expressions and their underpinning sources of knowledge, both customary and contemporary. Marques has personally reached out and embarked on such difficult yet rewarding cross-cultural journeys of reconnection. According to him,

> a number of the institutions that I've travelled to said that they rarely get that kind of in-depth information on parts of their collections because it's so hard to really research, especially if your collections are vast. So to have those people, who have that knowledge come to you; and they really wanted to understand more. I think at those points I'm able to help them get a better understanding and perspective.

Getting a "better understanding and perspective" cannot be confined to the "historical" past or "ethnographic" present but needs to be geared toward Hawaiian and other Indigenous futures. At the Bishop Museum, as we have seen throughout this and the preceding chapter, a gradual, if incomplete and conflict-ridden, institutional transformation has taken place: from a static record devoted to salvaging a dying past to a living resource aimed at revitalizing the present and future. At the same time, current discussions around the evolving Humboldt Forum in Berlin, on the other side of the world, point to the intensity of (post)colonial demands for moral redress, political concessions, and legal reparations. Although legitimate issues may exist in regard to the initial collection of material treasures and whether ethical limits were reached or exceeded, another, at least as important, conversation is whether the journey of these ancestral figures is indeed over.[66] Backward-oriented provenance research—currently the main strategy of Euro-American institutions to pacify Indigenous claims—alone does not suffice. Rather, these museum institutions should be "looking at it from a different lens," as Marques reminds us, that is, "looking at how those things of the past are . . . still connected to the people of the present and how those things can help us continue into the future." Museums across the world, then, can learn from the Hawaiian experience and strive to become active agents in shaping Indigenous revivals and future potentialities on a global scale.[67]

Discussion

This chapter set out to refocus museum temporalities through Hawaiian lenses. It did so by first releasing Hawaiian material expressions of the theoretical baggage and political confinement imposed through externally defined classifications such as "art" and "artifact"—a sort of analytical emptying to allow a "thing" to "speak in its own terms"[68] and reveal what it *can become* and *do*. The chapter proceeded methodologically by exploring how the vā, or space between Hawaiian people and their material manifestations, is lived, performed, and gains meaning by those experiencing it—a kind of empirical recharging of the "things" through their dialogical exchange with Marques and Kamalu throughout the processes of making, conversing, and curating. The historically informed ethnographic insights presented have significant implications for museums in Europe given that they indicate that Hawaiian material ontologies cannot be reduced to, or equated with, Euro-Americentric categories. More specifically, the findings call for a conceptual reframing of museological productions and representations by approaching curatorship as ongoing conversations enacted via common languages and through the translational and traveling efficacy of Indigenous skills.

This ethnographically grounded conceptual vocabulary and its temporal implications, I would argue, serve well to contribute to various academic debates. Curation understood as conversation implies co-presence and therefore contemporaneity with ancestors, contemporaries, and future characters, thus shaping a curatorial response to, and engagement with, the temporal continuum, or past-becoming-present-becoming-future, underpinning Hawaiian life and cultural practices. Understanding curatorship as conversations resonates in a dialogical sense with related scholarly notions such as "conversations with landscapes" as a "more-than-human materiality"[69] as well as, within the human realm, the consideration of art as interpretation or as ethnography.[70] Probing deeper conceptually, a materially grounded conversation resonates with Tim Ingold's thesis that the process of "making is a correspondence between maker and material," "not the imposition of preconceived form on raw material substance, but the drawing out or bringing forth of potentials immanent in a world of becoming." "Making is a journey," Ingold further asserts, and "the maker a journeyman" who takes part in the "becoming of materials."[71]

This point, however, should not be overstretched to the claim that, throughout the voyaging nature of making, the maker embarks on a voyage of discovery *rather than* of creation.[72] As we have seen, the makaloa mat and its material functioned as the means by which a message was conveyed. It conveyed excellence, the best that the island of Ni‘ihau had to offer and the best skill that Kala‘i could present. Yet the message was complicated—remember your *kuleana* (responsibility) to your people, and do not overtax us. It was a difficult message that came beautifully wrapped, as a gift of the highest order. A one-sided overemphasis on material discovery would deny the intentionality of the creator and her ultimately addressed audience of the ali‘i (ruler) and *akua* (gods). The purpose is the point, just as the fish trap is beautiful so that the fish will be enchanted, delighted, and ensnared.[73]

As we have seen, for Marques and Kamalu, this material journey has both temporal and spatial ramifications. Temporally, the processes of weaving and kapa-making links them genealogically to ancestral figures and has, as in the case of the woven protest mat, a political dimension. While studying related Māori weaving practices, Amiria Salmond learned that "the base of a woven *kete* or kitbag is called the *whakapapa*—the same term used to translate 'genealogy'—which literally means 'to make layers.'" Weaving thus throws into relief some of the ways in which relations between Māori people come into being.[74] In fact, whakapapa exceeds the idea of genealogy and should, as Salmond argues elsewhere, be understood as the "relational fabric coexistences with the cosmos," or "woven universe."[75] Translating the underlying reasoning back into the Hawaiian world, we can discern how the Māori word *taonga,* which is often awarded to a material treasure such as a woven kete, is a cognate of the Hawaiian word *kaona,* referring to the layers of teaching and meaning.[76] The layers of material weaving, then, are enmeshed with the conversational layers of meaning and the temporal layers of genealogical connections. This chapter engaged with such relationality and dialogism, rather than with temporalities per se, and working out how relationality and dialogue are temporally mobilized is a significant challenge. There is something to the concept of layering of genealogies that deserves closer consideration, theoretically and materially.[77]

Spatially, these material and temporal conversations are not confined to the Hawaiian context but have a transpacific quality reaching out across Oceania. The exhibition *Binding and Looping: Transfer of Presence in Contemporary Pacific Art* staged at the University of Hawai'i in 2014 is a case in point.[78] During the opening, which I attended, one of the participant artists, Lisa Reihana, expressed her view on "exhibitions as conversations" communicating and embodying "how we relate to each other." Another example is the research project and symposium "Weaving as a Common Pacific Language," conducted by the Bishop Museum in partnership with the University of the South Pacific in the Marshall Islands in 2013. The title indicates that weaving functions not only as a cultural practice but also as a common language that facilitates conversations across the Pacific, which is particularly significant if we consider the linguistic ruptures caused by colonial reconfigurations such as by damaging and drawing so-called Polynesian languages such as Hawaiian and Rapanui into the Americas and the respectively overwhelming colonial languages of English and Spanish.[79] As a consequence, Pacific people today might not be able to communicate linguistically but through material languages such as weaving, which bring us to the conceptual proposition of material languages.

As I argue in chapter 4, curation as an expressive and communicative act involves languages. A language here is not understood as discursive but as a material practice of exchange.[80] Approaching curatorial conversations as enacted through material languages resonates, for example, with the focus on the "expressive qualities of art"[81] and the view that "objects of art are expressive, they are a language. Rather they are many languages."[82] Such a perspective expands the depth and breadth of language by including material languages—such as weaving and kapa-making, which are, as we have seen, not just "thing languages"[83]—and by seeing language evocatively rather than through a structural or representational lens,[84] thus opening the limiting equation of "culture" or "action" with "text"[85] to the performative effect and embodied affect of human expressions and their material dimensions. Language requires communicating or telling, again understood in sense beyond the linguistic realm, as in "telling by the hand," which is a "modality of performance" and "practice of correspondence."[86] "Telling by the hand" through weaving and kapa-making requires particular skills.

As we have seen throughout this chapter, Hawaiian museum practices are primarily aimed at and informed by renurturing Indigenous skills from within (rather than the Indigenizing response to external Western influences). These skills, such as the ones underpinning weaving and kapa-making, are culturally embedded, politically enacted, and genealogically connected—and they become meaningful through the personal investment of meaning. Cultural differences thus appear as variations in skill,[87] which continuously evolve through changing materials and appearances but remain remarkably intact conceptually. Thinking through variations in skill, then, facilitates an ethnographically grounded conflation of abstract dichotomies such as art versus craft, tradition versus modernity, and individual versus culture, which continue to paralyze Western thought.

The notion of skill resonates with recent calls to shift the analytical focus from material "things" as finished products to the creative processes through which they are produced.[88] My conceptualization suggested here, however, moves beyond an understanding of skill as an epistemological compass toward approaching it as cultural performance, political action, and historical force through which material languages become configured and temporal conversations become facilitated. Indigenous skills thus operate as a mode of communing and cosmovisioning, and underpin curatorial practices aimed not at their explanation but at their catalyzation. Throughout these processes of redeveloping Indigenous skills, material expressions and curatorial practices operate as ships, or mobile interpretive vessels that embody and navigate the material and discursive relations across Oceania.[89] Indigeneity, then, is not a spatial and temporal retreat to an isolated place and nostalgic past, but appears as an articulation and performance that retransforms the (post)colonial "double vision"[90] into a cosmovision or *Cosm(o)ceania* on Indigenous terms.

These empirically grounded conceptual propositions also serve to contribute to and reframe broader academic debates. "Oceanic historicities," as "modes of temporal being and awareness specific to particular communities at particular moments in time," are profoundly performative and resist conventional Euro-Americentric conceptions of history as linear, progressive, or teleological.[91] The temporal continuum and simultaneity of a past-becoming-present-being-future proposed here resonates with Epeli Hau'ofa's "notion of the spiral, which connotes both cyclical and lineal movements."[92] Such a temporal awareness might also help explain the longue durée of Hawaiian philosophies, concepts, and practices. Apocalyptical prophecies, as promulgated by William Brigham, first director of the Bishop Museum, predicting in the early twentieth century that "the work of a primitive people" such as "kapa-making is fast passing into oblivion" or "already lost" have been proven wrong by Kamalu and others.[93] Research projects such as The Color of Kapa and Weaving as a Common Pacific Language conducted at the Bishop Museum, as well as student projects such as Revisiting Buck run by Maile Andrade at the University of Hawai'i attest to the vitality of Hawaiian practices and scholarship. These initiatives continue the work of such remarkable figures as Te Rangihīroa and Mary Kawena Pukui, who were introduced in the previous chapter, and call our attention to ho'ala hou (reawaking) rather than renaissance or rebirth.

Being attuned to this historical dimension of cultural life enables scholarship to move beyond the "invention of tradition" debate, which reduced the richness of enduring cultural worlds to the discursive domain of instantaneous political bartering and has thus been rightly branded a "debacle."[94] As Marshall Sahlins sums it up, "When Europeans invent their traditions . . . it is a genuine cultural rebirth, the beginnings of a progressive future. When other people do it, it is a sign of cultural decadence, a factitious recuperation, which can only bring forth the simulacra of a dead past."[95] Somewhat ironically but not surprisingly, the European term and concept of the Renaissance has traveled and been applied to Indigenous populations and their cultural "rebirth"—one of the most remarkable phenomena appearing in late (post)modernity against the certain odds of the fatal impact prophecy—as seen in the case of the Hawaiian Renaissance since the 1970s.[96] The longue durée of the Hawaiian world, however, might be better explained through the process of hoʻala hou enacted through moments such as, for example, the second coronation of King Kalākaua in 1883. The current era, then, simply witnesses new dimensions of a historically grounded process. It is more nuanced to speak of ruptural transformations than of epochal ruptures—without denying the significant (and at times disastrous) impact of critical events, such as the arrival of Christianity and colonialism[97]—and of the reawakening of temporarily dormant cultural facets rather than their alleged renaissance or rebirth which, by definition, implies their former death that, in many instances, evidently did not occur.

In chapter 1, we complicated historically the epochal hubris underpinning claims of death and rebirth through our discussion of *I Kū Mau Mau* as the literal manifestation of the longue durée of the Hawaiian intent and presence at the Bishop Museum. Here I allude conceptually to the embodied anchoring of cultural continuity.[98] Various scholars have insisted that place-bound Indigeneity and contemporary diaspora, especially in the Pacific, cannot be regarded as oppositions but need to be considered in dialectic, productive tension, which builds on a long history of transoceanic voyaging and settling.[99] I suggest another layer through which Indigeneity becomes performed—through the dialectics between concept and body as through nāʻau.[100] As we have seen, many Hawaiians believe that the nāʻau—located in the belly—is where the truth resides. This truth is not the result of intellectual knowledge or rational thought; instead, it is an assurance founded on intuitive knowledge.[101] Nāʻau, I conclude, is the embodied concept or conceptual embodiment through which cultural practices are born, might hibernate, and can be reawakened. It is the very core of Indigenous continuity that has weathered, and continues to weather, the storms of change.

PART II

MUSEO ANTROPOLÓGICO PADRE SEBASTIÁN ENGLERT, RAPA NUI

CHAPTER 3

Cross-Cultural Journeys

Informants, Collections, and Communities

with Cristián Moreno Pakarati and Mara Mulrooney

During a visit to the Bishop Museum in 2014, Paula Valenzuela Contreras (director, Museo Antropológico Padre Sebastián Englert) accessed the photographic collection of Alfred Métraux that is housed in the Bishop Museum's archives. She was working on putting together an exhibition about historic political developments on Rapa Nui and was in search of photographs to include in the display. As she looked through the collection, she noted many photographs she had never seen before as well as others of mostly unnamed individuals who could, according to her, surely be identified by members of the Rapanui community, if given the opportunity.[1] At the time, the Bishop Museum was thinking about ways to improve access to the collections and also increase knowledge about them. Valenzuela's comment led staff members and interns in the library and archives and anthropology departments to devote time to digitizing and inventorying the entire Rapa Nui photo collections, including Métraux's, which contains more than 350 photographs and was generated during the Franco-Belgian Expedition to Rapa Nui in 1934 and 1935.[2]

The evolving Métraux photography project is being undertaken as part of the Bishop Museum's Hoʻomaka Hou Research Initiative.[3] The Hawaiian term *hoʻomaka hou* means "to begin again," and the goal of the initiative is to reexamine and reactivate the Bishop Museum's existing anthropological and archival collections. The photography project was officially launched in early 2016 as a way to reconnect the Rapanui community with collections housed at the Bishop Museum, thus reactivating these collections through community engagement and the addition of new information.[4] In February 2016, one of the authors (Mara Mulrooney) traveled to Rapa Nui and deposited scans of all Rapa Nui photographic collections, as well as accompanying inventories, at the Biblioteca William Mulloy (William Mulloy Library) at the Museo Antropológico Padre Sebastián Englert in Haŋa Roa, Rapa Nui. The primary goal of transferring these files was to provide public access to these important historical collections for the entire community of Rapa Nui. Mulrooney and Cristián Moreno Pakarati (also coauthor of this chapter) decided to focus specifically on the Métraux collection for the project, which aims to add new information to these existing collections and make them more accessible, because only twenty-one of more than 350 photographs were published in Métraux's 1940 monograph, *Ethnology of Easter Island,* and just twenty-four were included in his 1941 publication titled *L'ile de Pâques* (the English version of which, *Easter Island,* was published in 1957).[5]

Such photographs as the ones under scrutiny have "double lives" and record "parallel realities."[6] On the one hand, they have *become* anthropological-ethnological evidence,[7] specimen, or object throughout their journey through scientific knowledge regimes marked by the anthropological interventions of collecting, categorizing, and cataloging aimed at illustrating and supporting anthropological concepts such as race, ethnicity, and evolution.[8] Interest is growing among ethnographic museums in revisiting and exhibiting this side by treating photographs as ethnographic and historical documents in their own right rather than relegating them to the mere role of visual contextualization and graphic illustration, as was often the case.[9] On the other hand, for the depicted people and their descendants, the same photographs have remained embodiments of memories, biographies, and genealogical relations.[10] Little is known about this side, however, and the depicted individuals are often reduced to anthropological types devoid of personal names. In this chapter, we address this lacuna and set out to better understand these "double lives" and bring their "parallel realities" together. This requires a "double vision"[11]—that is, a way photographic (and other) collections can be reapproached by focusing simultaneously on the historicization of anthropological knowledge and the consideration of contemporary Indigenous realities and their underpinning epistemologies and ontologies.[12]

In this chapter, we do so by revisiting the figure of the informant, both past and present. We begin by retracing the journey of the collection of photographs and their acquisition by the Bishop Museum in 1936, and place the ongoing Métraux photography project within the context of the Hoʻomaka Hou Research Initiative. We then proceed by historicizing the ambiguous figure of the informant to show that throughout his innovative ethnological endeavor, Métraux had to rely on genealogically and spatially embedded and partially confined information provided by Rapanui people, such as Juan Tepano, who consciously adopted the foreign scientific enterprise to actively adapt to and creatively shape newly emerging cross-cultural realities. We conclude with the contemporary situation and the return of the digital copies of the original photographs to the Museo Antropológico Padre Sebastián Englert on Rapa Nui, which has enabled members of the Rapanui community and descendants of the initial "informant" to reconnect with their depicted ancestors. The chapter sets out to both "unpack" and "reassemble"[13] this particular collection by retracing the cross-cultural journeys documented and enacted through the photographs, and by writing the next chapter of their histories and contemporary legacies through the lens of collaborative scholarship.

Hoʻomaka Hou—to Begin Again

Following his fieldwork on Rapa Nui that ended in early 1935, Métraux visited the Bishop Museum, which was then directed by Herbert Gregory. During the previous decade, beginning in 1920, Gregory had established a partnership with Yale University, which provided yearlong fellowships to scholars working in fields such as anthropology, botany, zoology, geology, and geography to enable them to write up and publish their research results.[14] The following year, Métraux was awarded a Yale-Bishop Museum Fellowship to write his monograph, *Ethnology of Easter Island,* which was published by the Bishop Museum Press in 1940. While he was in residence at the museum, Te Rangihīroa (Sir Peter Buck) replaced Gregory as director.[15]

By that time, the Bishop Museum had conducted anthropological expeditions, published reports, and completed regional surveys of all so-called Polynesian island groups, except Ellis Islands and Rapa Nui, or Easter Island, as it was predominantly called at the time.[16] In the case of Rapa Nui, the Bishop Museum relied on the Franco-Belgian Expedition, as emerges in one of Buck's letters written in 1935, prior to his directorship, to Āpirana Ngata, his companion on the Board of Maori Ethnological Research and fellow advocate of an "empirical" or "practical" anthropology that geared research toward Native survival and development:[17]

> The ethnologist who was with the French-Belgian expedition to Easter Island wants to come over here and work up his material as he recognizes that this is the centre of Polynesian research. The museum thinks highly of him. . . . He is a Swiss who was educated in France and his name is Metraux.[18]

In his book *Easter Island,* originally published in French in 1941 and in English in 1957, Métraux returns the respect by acknowledging Buck in his foreword:

> In the interpretation of this collection of disconnected and second-rate evidences I was assisted by two eminent specialists on Polynesia—Dr Peter Buck (Te Rangi Hiroa) and Dr Kenneth Emory. During my stay at the Bishop Museum, Honolulu, both these ethnologists were devoting themselves to the resurrection of the civilization of Mangareva (the Gambier Islands), whose traditions and history are much better known to us than those of Easter Island.[19]

While Métraux was in residence, the Bishop Museum operated as a hub in the Pacific, a place where objects, images, and data from the field were reassembled, reordered, and redeployed in the reconstruction of Pacific histories and customary practices on a local and global scale, but under newly appointed Indigenous supervision.[20] As we have seen in earlier chapters, strong similarities are evident between Buck's interest in and reshaping of museums, collections, and ethnological research, and today's museum professionals who are indigenizing and decolonizing professional practices by drawing on customary concepts and knowledge.

The Bishop Museum's Ho'omaka Hou Research Initiative was established in 2013. The goal of the initiative is to foster new collections-based research in the vast anthropological and archival collections housed in the museum. In the first instance, the initiative brings scholars with various interests together to study the collections and apply new techniques to learn more about the past. For example, working with the anthropological collections, researchers have applied new techniques such as AMS radiocarbon dating and nondestructive pXRF (portable X-ray fluorescence) to provide new insights into the ancient Hawaiian past of southern Hawai'i Island.[21] In addition, the initiative seeks to bring collections out from behind closed doors through digitization and dissemination through the building of online, open-access repositories and other methods.

The Ho'omaka Hou Research Initiative continues to attempt to reverse upsetting trends in the historical practice of anthropological and archaeological research in Hawai'i and elsewhere in Oceania. Throughout the last two centuries, a large body of information has been collected through field research endeavors, resulting in vast collections such as those housed at the Bishop Museum. Following fieldwork, field notes, photographs, and other materials were incorporated into archival collections housed at museums, universities, and, indeed, the private collections of researchers. On Rapa Nui, for example, many archaeologists carried away artifacts and samples in addition to their notes, photographs, and other information they had gathered during field research projects. These materials, now far away from Rapa Nui, have been disconnected from the community and are largely inaccessible. Although systems have now been put in place to ensure that cultural materials and associated information stay on the island, the overall historical trend remains problematic. In general, access to information is prohibitive, especially for communities. A key component of the initiative is the improvement of access to museum collections through digitization, which opens the door to reversing the restriction of access, as was the case in the past. New technology has enabled the museum to connect in new ways digitally.

Considerable attention has been paid to the digitization of cultural objects in museology. Such efforts have major implications for descendent communities, researchers, and museum visitors, and these considerations continue to be explored.[22] In light of this, digitization projects carried out under the Ho'omaka Hou Research Initiative are done with community engagement as a core component to every project. For example, the Bishop Museum recently launched an online database containing digital images of more than four thousand fishhooks, which were excavated during archaeological projects on Hawai'i Island in the 1950s. Before the website was launched, museum staff and the descendant community had many conversations about what was appropriate to include in the online forum before it went live. This process was essential to collectively address concerns that had previously been voiced in regard to digitization projects at other institutions and Hawaiian cultural sensitivities in general.

The Métraux photography project contributes to the long-term goal of the Ho'omaka Hou Research Initiative, which is to realize the informative and interpretive potential of collections housed at the Bishop Museum through optimal collections management practices, collections-based research endeavors, and proper dissemination. Once the entire collection was digitized and carried back to Rapa Nui, a community meeting was held, the goal of which was to disseminate the information and begin a project that seeks to reactivate the photographs, as we describe in more detail. Most of the people who appear in the photographs have now been identified. Work is continuing with various community members and Indigenous scholars to compile more information about the people and places documented by Métraux and his "informants," to whom we now turn.

Alfred Métraux and the Ambiguous Figure of the Informant

> You will learn everything about the island and its past. The ones that came before didn't hear all the words, but you will know them all. *I know.* The words of the elders have been twisted but you will get them straight.
>
> Juan Tepano to Alfred Métraux, 1934[23]

The first so-called Rapanui informant was a man named Metoro Tau'a Ure. He was "used" by the bishop of Tahiti, Tepano Jaussen, in 1873 to help in deciphering the *kōhau roŋoroŋo,* wooden boards with the only known script of the Pacific Islands.[24] Many other Rapanui were consulted almost exclusively about roŋoroŋo in the following decades by expeditions from different parts of the world. However, for any other matter, the information was obtained from Western residents on the island. In retrospect, it is unfortunate that the only direct interaction between foreign researchers and Rapanui inhabitants during those early years was focused on roŋoroŋo. It was too late for it to be deciphered and the script remains a mystery, whereas the chance to learn more about the ancient culture of the island was wasted. It was not until the 1910s that "salvage" ethnographic work began on Easter Island (as Rapa Nui was called at the time and often continues to be called to this day), which focused on interviewing the few elderly Rapanui who were born in the pre-Christian era. These elders witnessed the functioning of the old culture and the attempted Christianization of Rapa Nui by French missionaries (from Sacré-Cœur with the assistance of Mangarevan catechists) between 1866 and 1871.

To the present-day researcher, the current canon of oral tradition is based on information collected in this epoch up to the 1950s, which were by then secondhand accounts. The primary sources of our knowledge about ancient society, customs, foundational myths, legends, sociopolitical divisions, and subsistence practices can be traced to two branches of Rapanui "informants."[25] The two branches diverged during the period between the Mohican Expedition of 1886 and the studies carried out by German-Chilean Walter Knoche in 1911.[26] In this quarter century, the types of knowledge manifested by both became distinctive and the areas where they overlapped developed slight differences.

The first branch was formed by most elders who still lived in Haŋa Roa, the main settlement, in the 1910s. All of them were born before 1840 and preserved in their memories the conditions of life on the island before the arrival of the Catholic missionaries. Some of these elders were consulted by Knoche, and practically all of them provided the bulk of ethnographic evidence that Katherine Routledge collected in 1914 and 1915 during her stay on Rapa Nui. Their last appearances were in the Land Commission of 1917, in which they provided topographic and toponymic information for the Chilean government, and during priest Bienvenido de Estella's research into ancient customs in 1917 and 1918.[27] Many of those wise elders died in 1918 during a tuberculosis epidemic and most of the rest during the late 1920s.[28] The main link between foreign researchers and the information held by these elders was a man named Juan Tepano, to whom we turn in more detail later.

The second branch was mostly ignored by foreign scholars and laymen until the late 1930s. It formed around the obscure knowledge obtained from the memories of mostly elderly men interned in the leper colony in the Pare district, several kilometers north of Haŋa Roa.[29] These traditions were kept (and later spread) in a new and unorthodox way for the Rapanui people. After Knoche's ethnographic visit in 1911, some islanders started recording ancient lore in writing by using the Rapanui language transliterated to Latin letters, which resulted in several handwritten manuscripts. Twenty-five years later, the German priest Sebastián Englert caught a glimpse of this second branch by frequently visiting the leper colony and establishing a good working relationship with Arturo Teao Tori, a relatively young man who transmitted to the clergyman what he had learned from the wise elders. However, the manuscripts were elsewhere kept hidden by a few Rapanui families, away from the eyes of foreigners, until the 1955–1956 Norwegian archaeological expedition led by Thor Heyerdahl.[30]

Interaction with these outsiders dramatically changed the importance of people with large stores of information about earlier eras. The now extremely valuable knowledge held by the elders at the leprosarium was preserved for the future through the work of a new type of specialist, transcribers of ancient lore. Among these literates, Simeón Riroroko, Juan Araki, and Gabriel Veriveri (aka Hereveri) were the most important at faithfully recording it, just like the old *maori roŋoroŋo,* the experts of the script, although in an adopted written language. Others preserved the lepers' knowledge through memory, without the aid of printed letters. On an island where only a minuscule percentage of the people knew how to read, this was both practical and sufficient. The prime example here is Arturo Teao Tori, distinguished "informant" or rather collaborator of Englert.[31] Others included a few younger "enlightened" Rapanui such as Mateo Veriveri.[32]

These two branches of knowledge overlapped, but there were key differences between them. The first tended to be much more holistic, covering most aspects of the material and immaterial pre-Christian culture because it derived from long sessions of questions and answers with early anthropologists, as well as from field trips and excavations with archaeologists in different parts of the island. The second branch was much more obscure: Routledge and Métraux, to whom we will turn in more detail, visited the leper colony but did not consider it a primary source for their ethnographic work, unlike Father Englert much later. The recipients of the knowledge from the second branch were therefore younger Rapanui who began their own ethnographic work on their own culture.[33] This explains why the manuscripts that originated from these encounters preserved knowledge mostly through Rapanui codes: narratives, legends, myths, songs, and *pata'uta'u* (recitations), in a nonsystematic way and devoid of interpretations and explanations. It is one of the interesting examples of appropriating a Western method (writing) to support and enhance a Rapanui idea. In other words, the use of Latin script is in line with, arguably, the most pronounced tradition of Rapa Nui of the last three hundred years (and more): adopt to adapt—taking, accepting, incorporating something from the outside, but transforming, resignifying, and developing it to safeguard and advance what is perceived as the Rapanui reality.[34]

The clear differences aside, the two branches overlapped in that both were concerned with the link between past, present, and future. Both covered the same ground when it came to the settlement period and the era of the *moai* (see chapter 4). Both understood this past, or the way to tell its story, as something at risk that could disappear and therefore needed to be preserved for the future. Those of the first branch viewed foreigners as instrumental to this preservation; those of the second thought that using foreign methods was enough to achieve it. Both were right in their own way. They were devoted to a common cause.

Because the manuscripts were kept hidden as sacred family encyclopedias of Rapa Nui's legendary history even from the likes of Father Englert until 1955, and because almost all elders from the first branch were already dead in 1934, the question becomes who Métraux had as an Indigenous source? Working with some of the few first-branch elders still alive proved unsuccessful from the start. The centenarian Veriamo, mother of Juan Tepano, could no longer speak. Eva Hei was not considered, neither were Renga Hopu-Hopu and Catalina Tori, who were almost a generation younger. The old lepers in the leprosarium were also dead and in their place was a much younger and less talkative generation. After his experience on Rapa Nui, Métraux himself points to the sexagenarian Juan Tepano as the living knowledge of the island, as the proud heir of what we today call the first branch, but it is not certain whether Métraux was aware of the differences between the branches. As rigorous as he was, he certainly used what he thought brought him closer to the factual reality of Rapa Nui's past.

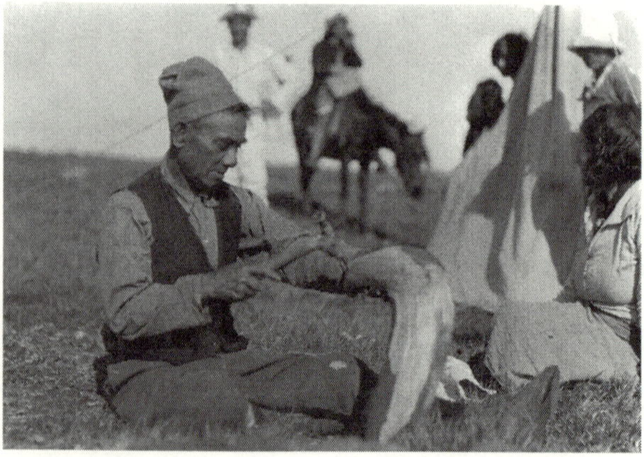

Figure 3.1 "Easter Island. Tepano making a statue." Juan Tepano. Rapa Nui, Chile, 1934–1935. Photograph by Alfred Métraux, Bishop Museum Archives.

Juan Tepano was the son of Rano a Vavara a Rue, a Tupahotu man from the Ko te Kanapu region, the flatland between Rano Raraku and Ahu Tongariki, and Veriamo a Huki, a Hiti 'Uira woman born in the west-southwest of Rano Raraku (figure 3.1). Both parents were from the eastern district called Hotu 'Iti. Tepano was born around 1872, although the conflicting accounts about his age stemmed from his willingness to appear much older than he really was.[35] His last name is derived from the Latin *Stephanus,* given as a baptismal name to his father in the decade of the 1860s during the Christianization of the island. His father most likely died in the 1890s; his mother would live until 1936. Young Tepano traveled to Chile in 1898 as part of a delegation that included the elected and nontraditional king Timeone Riro Kāinga and fellow young ministers Juan Araki and José Pirivato.[36] After King Riro was poisoned in Valparaíso by colonial agents, Tepano and the others were not allowed to return to Rapa Nui by the Williamson Balfour Company, which largely controlled the island.[37] The remaining Rapanui decided to enter the army at the Maipo regiment, where all of them would learn Spanish and to read and write in Latin letters. This would prove invaluable for later ethnologists in an era when almost no one on the island spoke more than a few words in Spanish. Tepano returned to Rapa Nui in 1900 and started to work closely with both colonial powers, the company, and the state. In 1902, he was named the representative of the islanders by the Chilean Navy that held de jure authority. Later in the same decade, he began working as one of the most trusted and reliable islanders for the company that held de facto power. This, together with the need of maintaining good relationships with his fellow Rapanui under the *umaŋa* (reciprocity) social system, forged Tepano into a peculiarly hybrid and controversial figure.[38] He became the ultimate mediator on Rapa Nui, or, as Steven Roger Fischer points out, "he mediated between the Rapanui and the Company, but appreciated the realities of survival: he knew which way the wind blew on Rapa Nui" and, as a master statesman, he was "forever tempering integrity with *Realpolitik*."[39]

Little by little, the naval personnel, and the few archaeologists and anthropologists that ventured all the way across the ocean to Rapa Nui, transitioned from asking questions to Western residents associated with the colonial powers, such as Bornier, Roussel, or Edmunds, and began asking a more direct source, a slightly Westernized but fully fledged Rapanui. Juan Tepano was knowledgeable enough for the occasional visitor. He had the answers for the Chilean sailors of the training ship (the infamous *Baquedano*), who annually appeared asking pretty much the same questions every time. Other islanders were likely more versed in ancient traditions but could not communicate with foreigners. However, that sort of deep knowledge was beyond what most visitors were seeking, at least until Knoche's short visit in 1911. Tepano was indeed one of his "informants," but he also worked closely with another man of the same expedition, priest Zósimo Valenzuela.[40] Knoche wanted to dig deeper, however. He wrote an ethnography in German but published it in Chile much later, in 1925.[41] After these events, Tepano's name became well known in Valparaíso, Santiago, and generally to all those who visited Rapa Nui.

The Mana Expedition of 1914–1915 was the one that profiled Tepano's transformation into the core of what we call here the first branch. Led by Katherine Routledge, the expedition spent almost seventeen months on the island.[42] Routledge was convinced that all knowledge held by elders born in the pre-Christian era, who spoke only Rapanui, was doomed to disappear. Hence, she tried to translate, transcribe, and collect as much as possible in a way that was understandable for a Western audience. Here, Tepano played the role of the intermediary between the elders and Routledge. He made the direct translations to her, and most likely learned even more given that he knew the Rapanui codes far better than she. She processed the information systematically, from the raw translations into Spanish. Meanwhile, Tepano received the information straight in Rapanui, and translated and paraphrased Routledge's questions in a way that made sense for the elders. Because the literal answers would be unintelligible to Routledge, Tepano invested some time translating and commenting in a way that would be comprehensible to the British anthropologist. This is how Juan Tepano learned—through trial and error—amassing knowledge, slowly perfecting his discourse, outlining his image as a source, and making sense of the wisdom of the elders narrated so spontaneously. He knew how knowledge about Rapa Nui's past was of interest to foreigners and decided to forge himself into the custodian of that knowledge, as can be inferred from his attitude to later scholars. Unfortunately, Routledge never published a monograph, but her professional relationship with Tepano would end up having an indirect impact on subsequent scholarly engagements with Rapa Nui.[43]

The end of the 1910s saw the death of half of the elders Routledge and Tepano had consulted. The knowledge was kept in Routledge's secret field notes, and some small bits were published in a few articles and the travel book *The Mystery of Easter Island*.[44] The field notes were inaccessible for decades; the only other place where the cumulative ethnographic knowledge (the first branch) was kept was in Tepano's memory. Priest Bienvenido de Estella was able to gather some of it, but he also published simply a slender book devoid of scientific rigor.[45] In the early 1920s, John MacMillan Brown failed to make sense of Tepano's knowledge, publishing a book filled with naive and absurd hypotheses.[46] It is reasonable to claim that Tepano had not yet refined his act, though his reputation was growing. By the end of the 1920s, the rest of the elders Routledge had interviewed—with the exception of Tepano's mother, Veriamo—had died. This affected only the younger Rapanui generations, who now had only Tepano to ask. Outsiders had no other opportunity given the impossibility of speaking with elders who had no grasp of Spanish.

The Franco-Belgian Expedition arrived in Haŋa Roa, the only village on the island, in July 1934. The expedition was led by the Swiss ethnologist Alfred Métraux and his colleague, the Belgian archaeologist Henri Lavachery, who were accompanied by the Chilean doctor Israel Drapkin. A significant difference between Routledge and Métraux is that the Swiss researcher tried to stay as far away from the island's foreign residents as possible. He wanted to plunge into and fathom the native cultural depths. That is why he quickly refused to become close to the carpenter Vincent Pont, the French resident married to a Rapanui woman, or Nicolás Cardinali, the Italian sailor and survivor of a shipwreck who was also married to a Rapanui. After a quick interview with Murdoch Smith, the English manager of the company, he decided to stay away from him as well.

Métraux would later feel he was fulfilling his duty in the countryside, examining the remains of the ancient culture, away from Haŋa Roa and the Western influence that the younger locals were showing. He did not see a link between the glorious ancient Rapanui and what he considered to be the Westernized inhabitants of the island in the 1930s, thus creating an *"episteme de la discontinuidad"* (episteme of discontinuity) between a monumental past and a dead present in his writing.[47] Paradoxically, Métraux called Veriamo "like Easter Island itself—a body without a soul."[48] At the same time, he relied on her son, Tepano—clearly a body *with* a soul as well as a *living* descendant of the ancient stone carvers—to form the bulk of his ethnographic work. Quickly grasping the foreign scholars' agenda for his own purposes, Tepano delayed his appearance. He baited them, letting the younger people mention him as the expert in the folklore, a hard-earned title he wore with pride. Both Métraux and Lavachery were willing to bite.[49]

Métraux mentioned that, before departing from Valparaíso, they had heard about Tepano as the best informant Rapa Nui had to offer. The Swiss ethnologist and the Belgian archaeologist therefore worked closely with him during the six months of their stay. Métraux acknowledged him as the chief informant of the expedition, though occasionally, the ethnologist would stray away from him and try to verify certain information he did not fully believe. Tepano would usually provide the scholars with closely transcribed narratives of customary history. He would camp with them in different parts of the island, outlining the history of each district and sharing lists of kings, genealogies, names of ceremonial platforms, stars, winds, tides, fishes, birds, as well as the location of statues, petroglyphs, and other megalithic monuments. Métraux pointed out that Tepano's reputation as the most knowledgeable man of Rapa Nui was shared by the islanders themselves: "When other natives are asked about their ancestors they always refer to Juan Tepano. The information I received from others was generally attributed to him."[50]

The Franco-Belgian expedition also benefited from the collaboration of Victoria Rapahango, the last living descendant of the U'i Tau'a line of the royal Miru clan. A proud Rapanui woman in her mid-thirties, she had four children of the departed English manager of the company, Mr. Edmunds. She left an undeniable impression on both scholars, but even more so on Lavachery, who wanted to adopt her youngest daughter Antonia ("Ana").[51] Métraux highlighted that Victoria checked all his notes and helped in the "reconstruction of ancient techniques."[52] Jo Anne Van Tilburg erroneously points to Isabel Chavez (Isabel Haoa Araki, married to Daniel Chavez Manuheuroroa), as a key informant of Métraux.[53] However, no evidence indicates her participation other than her being part of the inner circle of Métraux and Lavachery in 1934 and 1935. She was indeed essential to integrate the expedition members into the social life in Haŋa Roa, but nothing in Métraux's field notes points to her participation in any other way. She is also not acknowledged in the book *Ethnology of Easter Island.* Twenty years later, when Thomas Barthel was going to the island to conduct additional ethnographic work, Métraux asked him to send greetings to Mata Haoa (her sister), even though Isabel was alive and well.[54]

Among the few other people who were consulted to double-check and corroborate Tepano's work, the most noteworthy are Charly Teao, who is mentioned several times, and a few others, such as Nicolás Pakomio and Santiago Pakarati, who appear in specific instances. These three figures would later evolve to become "informants" of foreign archaeologists in the following decades. Teao's knowledge came mostly from a second-branch elder, Tori Harakura, and is likely the reason he is mentioned more than the others. His information departed a bit more from Tepano's versions and thus complemented them well. His brother Arturo Teao in the leper colony would become Englert's chief collaborator given his added knowledge of the rest of the second branch. Teao was somewhat Tepano's equivalent within the leper colony. Pakomio's knowledge had more to do with the customary practices and techniques than ancient lore, which is why he was a trusted assistant. Pakarati, on the other hand, was Juan Tepano's son-in-law, and was preparing to inherit most of Tepano's knowledge for the future.

Can we thus understand Tepano's role as that of a simple informant or an intermediary? From the Rapanui perspective, the intermediary was Métraux (like Routledge, Vives Solar, Estella, MacMillan Brown, and later Heyerdahl, Barthel, and so on). He was part of that—still mysterious—bigger world, commanded the languages of the *taŋata hiva* (foreigners), and had access to resources to publish and distribute his writings. Tepano knew very well, after his previous experiences, that Métraux's notes would become a book that contained the entire sum of his knowledge. It was the culmination of a long process for Tepano to establish himself as the voice of Rapa Nui's past. Métraux and Lavachery were his vehicles to spread his word, which, he understood, was seen as the word of his ancestors. By the time Englert arrived, old Tepano was less lively, and members of a new generation that looked up to him were trying to establish themselves as the living memory of Rapa Nui, but faced much fiercer competition.

In sum, the first branch was developed further by Tepano, whose legacy was inherited by a new generation of "informants," collaborators, narrators, and interpreters. They helped shape the works of several authors, spearheaded by Métraux's monumental work. The second branch remains somewhat of a mystery: Arturo Teao, through Englert, and the manuscripts collected at the time of the Heyerdahl and Barthel-Vargas expeditions between 1955 and 1957 were the shining moments. They appeared just in time, when foreign research on the island had hopes of finding anything that could refute or add to the theories advanced by Métraux. Thomas Barthel was finally the only author that thoroughly worked with second-branch sources in his book *The Eighth Land* and in several articles published in German between the late 1950s and 1970s. In the 1980s, the two branches started to intermingle with the "informants" of the Universidad de Chile's archaeological survey.[55] In the belief that not much more useful knowledge could be amassed by living sources, the focus for research into the past of Rapa Nui in the following years became straight archaeological fieldwork that included consulting extensive archival documentation for context. The only ones that continued relying on living sources were social anthropologists who studied twentieth-century events or Rapa Nui in its present state, as we do in the following section.[56]

The Figure of the Informant Speaks Back, Renames, and Reclaims

> The power to name, rename, or change one's name is crucial to illuminating the ways in which social relationships work between name-givers and name-takers.[57]

> . . . indigenous identities are not necessarily locked into the periodization of past, present and future; rather all three exist, like photography, in the here and now.[58]

This rehistoricizing of Alfred Métraux's main source of information, Juan Tepano, has made it clear that Tepano did not have total access to customary knowledge that could be used to draw a complete ethnographic picture of Rapa Nui (as Métraux had assumed and subsequently often claimed in the literature).[59] Instead, the history of anthropological interventions on the island produced two branches of customary-turned-ethnographic knowledge, which were genealogically and spatially informed and partially confined. This inevitably turned Tepano, belonging to the first branch, into an ambiguous rather than a definite figure. So far we have thus refocused the first lens of our "double vision" by critically historicizing how the photographic collection under scrutiny came into being and, throughout this process, *became* anthropological. We now turn to our second lens, the contemporary Rapanui community and living descendants of the two branches, who reconnect with their depicted ancestors and speak back to, reclaim, and reverse the ethnographic gaze they had been subjected to.

As outlined, the Métraux photography project is part of the Bishop Museum's Hoʻomaka Hou Research Initiative. It was launched in early 2016, when one of the authors (Mulrooney) traveled to Rapa Nui and handed scans of several Rapa Nui photographic collections over to the Biblioteca William Mulloy at the Museo Antropológico Padre Sebastián Englert. The primary goal of the initiative was to reconnect the photographs with the people on Rapa Nui, thus reactivating the collections through community engagement, while increasing knowledge about them. Specifically, the initiative set out to identify those depicted in these unique historical documents in order to preserve the information for the future. The other authors (Moreno Pakarati, the great-great-grandson of Juan Tepano, and Philipp Schorch) found a keen interest in supporting the project and collaborating on it. Here, we lay out how community engagement, which often remains a laudable goal that lacks substantiation,[60] has been put into practice—not as a moral or political gesture, but as a methodological intervention aimed at further reconfiguring the figure of the informant and thus ethnographic knowledge itself.

After the copies of the photographs had been transferred to the Museo Antropológico Padre Sebastián Englert, a public presentation was held at the Biblioteca William Mulloy. The goal was to invite the wider public to attend and participate in the process of reconnecting with the collections. To prepare and then conduct the event, we introduced the collections held at the Bishop Museum, contextualized their coming into being through the Franco-Belgian expedition, and traced the ongoing journey of the same photographs through European collections, exhibitions, and publications. The presentation proved hugely popular and filled the library with a crowd of local people rarely seen in the museum's galleries. Lilian López, who managed the library at the time, printed copies of the photographs to be used in the talk so that we could record the names of the individuals depicted who could be identified (figure 3.2).

Following this event, we discussed how to proceed and get in touch, especially with elderly members of the Rapanui community who could still identify the photographed persons firsthand. Carlos Paoa Huke, a local historian who collaborated on the project and appears in figure 3.2, facilitated contact with Alberto Hotus, who in the 1980s—during the *junta* (military dictatorship) of General Augusto Pinochet—founded and has long led the Consejo de Ancianos (Council of Elders), at the time the only accepted and still influential if contested political body of Indigenous representation.[61] In 1988, one hundred years after the

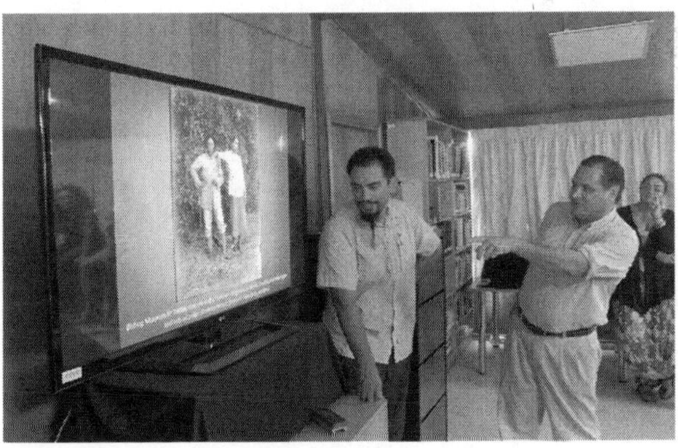

Figure 3.2 Cristián Moreno Pakarati and Carlos Paoa Huke identify individuals in Métraux's photographs, February 2016. Photograph by Philipp Schorch.

acuerdo de voluntades (concurrence of wills), which sealed the political cession of the island to the Republic of Chile, the consejo published a groundbreaking book mapping out the genealogical relationships between Rapanui people and land, and arguing for the unalienable right to and sovereignty over the territory of the island.[62] This part of the deed had never been fulfilled and remains the main source of sometimes severe conflict to this day.[63] The consejo sees itself also as the Comité Defensor del Patrimonio e intereses de Rapa Nui (The Committee defending the heritage and interests of Rapa Nui).[64] It thus follows a cultural agenda and purpose that became apparent in Hotus's unhesitating support for the initiative, despite having been critical of the museum (and other state institutions) in the past (as many other Rapanui are). One afternoon in March 2016, we brought him to the library where he assisted in renaming unnamed individuals in the entire collection.

What has been gained from the photography project? First, the initiative has allowed present-day descendants to speak back to the collection by renaming the unnamed and thus reclaiming the identity of the depicted as well as the genealogical relationship between them, from past to present. Figure 3.3, for example, shows how Métraux's "Natives in Sunday attire" have been identified as Daniel Chavez Manuheuroroa (aka Poroni) and Isabel Haoa Araki (also known as Rita). Figure 3.4

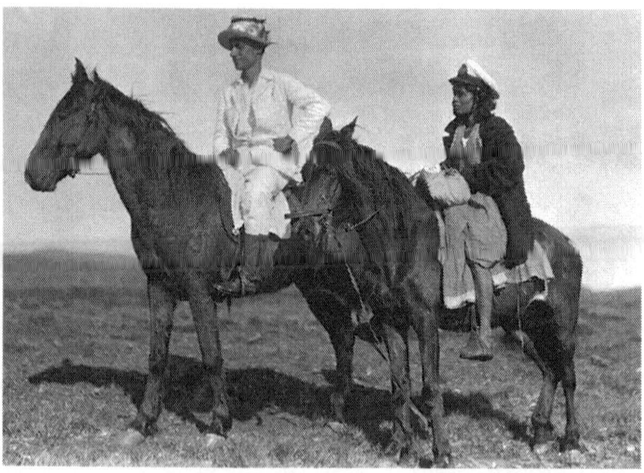

Figure 3.3 "Easter Island. Natives in Sunday attire." People identified as Daniel Chavez Manuheuroroa ("Poroni") and Isabel Haoa Araki ("Rita"). Rapa Nui, Chile, 1934–1935. Photograph by Alfred Métraux, Bishop Museum Archives.

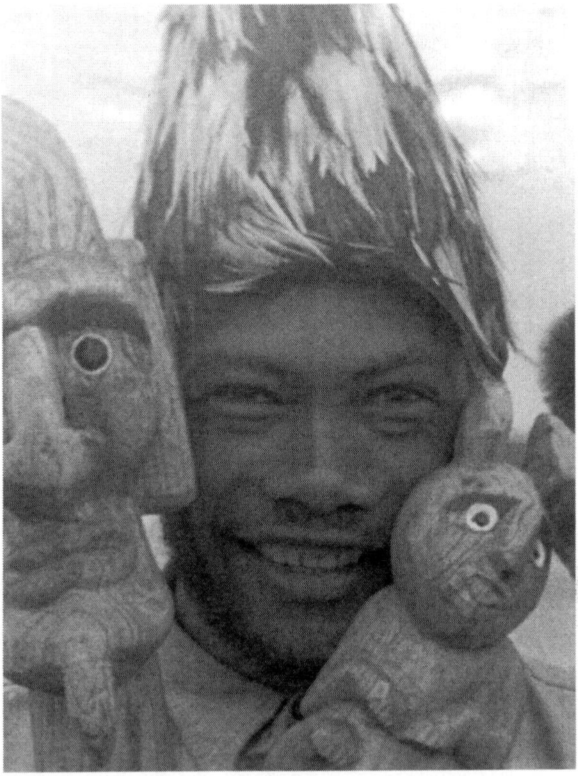

Figure 3.4 "Easter Island. Native boy with statues." Boy identifed as Santiago Pakarati Rangitaki. Rapa Nui, Chile, 1934–1935. Photograph by Alfred Métraux, Bishop Museum Archives.

displays how Métraux's "Native Boy with Statues," has been renamed "Santiago Pakarati Rangitaki." The latter is of particular interest for our discussion here. As pointed out, Santiago Pakarati belonged to the first branch of ethnographic "informants," being the son-in-law of Juan Tepano and great-grandfather of coauthor Moreno Pakarati, and supporting Metraux's work. In this photograph, however, he was not given a name, but instead reduced to a representative of an ethnological type—Native boy—rather than acknowledged and treated for who he really was, an ethnographic collaborator.

Significantly, on the other side of the world, in Europe, the same photographs have been recently published for the first time in books such as *Ile de Pâques 1934–1935: Expédition Métraux-Lavachery* (1995), based on a prior exhibition held at the Musées royaux d'Art e d'Histoire in Brussels, Belgium, and *L'Odyssée pascuane: Mission Métraux-Lavachery, Île de Pâques 1934–1935* (2014).[65] In the second case, we can see how Pakarati, eighty years after the photograph was taken, continues to be portrayed under a generic description: "Jeune Pascuan tenant deux sculptures contemporaines" (Young Pascuan holding two contemporary sculptures).[66] The photography project succeeded in bringing people and their undeniable individuality back into the foreground. In those European publications, however, they are often still relegated to the ethnological background by "branding human beings as types," which "denies them their full humanity."[67] In other words, the photography initiative humanized abstract categories of the past, such as Native boy, by "the mobilization of memories"[68] and "recovering names,"[69] biographical stories, and genealogical connections with the present.[70]

This focus on, and enactment of, cultural continuity between past and present—as opposed to the "episteme of discontinuity" underpinning Métraux's separation between Rapa Nui's monumental past and soulless present—has also been pursued more widely in recent years by the Museo Antropológico Padre Sebastián Englert and the Biblioteca William Mulloy. In 2010, the museum, which stands on contested land, became directly embroiled in the ongoing conflict over territorial ownership between the Chilean state and Rapanui families and interest groups. After five months of occupation, which shut down all operations, the museum first reopened and then reached out to reposition itself within the Rapanui community. To that end, it decided to stage an exhibition on Father Sebastián Englert, the controversial figure after whom the museum was named when it was founded in 1973,[71] and who largely affected the recent history of the island, including the evolving figure of the informant, as we saw in the previous section.[72] An analysis of the museum's situation and plan for its development compiled in 2007 by today's director, Paula Valenzuela Contreras, concluded that people on Rapa Nui were mainly interested in the recent rather than the archaeological history of the island and had a preference for historical photographs.[73] According to Lilian López, who was involved in the conceptual design, it was the first exhibition designed for local people (rather than tourists), and featured numerous and large photographs.[74] Photographs held in the archive have also enabled the library to evolve into a "fuerte nexo con la comunidad" (strong nexus with the community), as López argued in conversation. One of the authors (Schorch) also personally witnessed when local people entered the library—doing something they hardly do in the archeological exhibitions devoted mainly to international tourists, which was to engage with the "historia cotidiana de la isla" (everyday history of the island) and their own place within it.[75]

It is anticipated that the ongoing project Biblioteca Rapanui Digital (Rapanui Digital Library) will further increase and expand such public access and engagement, both on the island and beyond its shores. According to Francisco Torres Hochstetter, former director and now curator, it will assist the museum to become "un agente en la construcción de la memoria" (an agent in the construction of the memory) of the island and its people.[76] In conversation with one of the authors, Torres Hochstetter elaborated that in becoming an "agente dentro de la communidad" (agent within the community), the museum still faces much resistance, and overcoming prejudices is attempted, for example, by bringing Rapanui staff members on board. Photographic exhibitions have also helped to connect more intimately and emotively with local people and their memories. "Memoria," Hochstetter continues, "es más viva. . . . Es lo que la gente recuerda, lo que siente" [is more alive. . . . It's what people remember, what they feel], whereas "todo el tema patrimonial . . . es muy academico . . . y eso genera conflict" [the topic of heritage . . . is very academic . . . and this generates conflict].[77] Chapter 4 reveals some of the conflicts arising out of the reconfiguration of Rapa Nui as "Museum Island" and its governance through what will be termed the heritage complex.[78] In the context of this discussion, memories sparked by and mobilized through photographs allow for "a way of 'doing' heritage from below" and offer a "route to counter authorized accounts or particular sites and practices." Memory thus operates as an "affective tool for the co-constitution of embodied, political narratives" for "feeling the past"[79] from the present and toward the future.

Apart from identifying previously unidentified people in the Métraux collection, the project has also incorporated a comparison between Métraux's photographs and current ones to explore how the landscape of Rapa Nui has changed over the past eighty-plus years. In May 2016, Mulrooney and a small team that included Martín Tuki, Omar Monares, and Aku Ika followed in the footsteps of Métraux and took 212 photographs from the same vantage points from which Métraux took his photographs in 1934 and 1935. The team also shared a selection of these then-and-now glimpses of the cultural landscape with interested community members and Rapa Nui National Park rangers at the end of the four-week field season, the goal being to disseminate information about these collections and raise awareness about cumulative impacts on the landscape during the more recent past. During those presentations, community members shared personal stories and observations about particular places; they also talked about how best to care for their heritage in the future. Such acts of "re-photography" and the responses they generate among viewers "demonstrate a powerful conceptual overlap between the inscription of memory in photography and the inscription of memory in land."[80] Moreover, in regard to the empowering strategies of renaming and reclaiming, this intervention can be seen within the wider context of countering the still lingering "colonialismo toponīmico" (toponymical colonialism), the conquering of places, names, and cartographies.[81] The powerful initiative Terevaka Archaeological Outreach, organized by Britton Shepardson at Northern Arizona University and supported by the museum and other institutions and individuals on Rapa Nui, has recently responded by systematically combining historical archival research with GPS and photographic survey for a publicly accessible and editable digital database of often forgotten or hidden Rapanui place names on the island.[82] Once again, the figure of the informant speaks back, renames, and reclaims.

The photographs of this collection add complexity to the issues pertaining to Indigenous informants, intermediaries, and collaborators. Here, the figure of the informant (or collaborator, to use Englert's more appropriate term) appears in a different light than the Indigenous poster-boy or poster-girl. Most pictures in Métraux's *Ethnology of Easter Island* do not depict Juan Tepano, Charly Teao, or Victoria Rapahango, but instead people who were not really part of the intellectual work of the expedition. Tepano and Rapahango are the only ones who have a personal name attributed; the rest are described as native couple, young Pascuan boy, and so on. Did Métraux choose these photographs deliberately? Or was it the editorial board's wish to satisfy the gaze of the Western reader? The pictures reflect the Zeitgeist of that time, and the poetic and mysterious dreamworld that South Sea islands evoked and continue to evoke, even though Métraux tried emphatically to be associated with serious scientific work. These photos of people without names embody and underscore a conflicting nature in that they contradict the efforts of foreign researchers to transcribe legends even as they name their informants, collaborators, and narrators to lend credibility to the information gathered in the field and offered in the text. The book reduces most Indigenous people to ethnological types, but a few are skyrocketed to complex, magnetic personalities who wield a vast sum of ancient knowledge that adds authenticity to the foreigner's work.

In the contemporary context, the Métraux photography project has shown that "virtual repatriation is, in many ways, about finding a present for historical photographs."[83] What the project has done, then, is to bring the "double lives" and "parallel realities" of the photographs together by "re-implacing" them in the genealogical web connecting Rapanui people and land through inscribed and mobilized memories linking past and present, and gearing both to the future.[84] Thus, the photos have operated as a medium through which the temporal continuum of a past-becoming-present-becoming-future is performed (see chapter 2), and the permanent connection between Rapanui life and land is reclaimed (see chapter 4). In this process, the photographs have played an active role in cultural, political, and environmental initiatives. Métraux's ambivalent figure of the informant continues to speak back, rename, and reclaim, thus exposing the "episteme of discontinuity" as a mythical projection through myopic lenses, and forcing us to refocus our "double vision."

CHAPTER 4

Curating an Island, Curing Rapa Nui

The volcanic island Rapa Nui, or Te Pito o Te Henua, variously translated as end of the earth, end of the land, or navel of the world—as it has been called by its Indigenous inhabitants, Pacific people who migrated there across Oceania more than a millennium ago—is geologically ancient. Fairly recently in comparison, Rapa Nui has been branded an open-air museum or "Museum Island."[1] In the latest chapter of its tumultuous history, the island as a whole has been declared a Chilean national monument, and nearly half of its surface area proclaimed a national park by the Chilean state (1935) and a world heritage site by UNESCO (1995). This ongoing process of "heritageisation"[2] has been embedded in a (post)colonial context of uncertain political sovereignty,[3] enforced through an institutional heritage complex (my term) of overlapping and competing authorities, and subjected to a seemingly stalling pluralism of legal frameworks and normative conventions.[4] But what happens when such a "Museum Island" is not only produced by political decrees, represented through academic analyses and commercial interests, and visited by tourists, but also actually inhabited by real people? In other words, how do the Rapanui people engage with, and respond to, Te Pito o Te Henua's transformation into the arguably biggest open-air museum of the world?

This chapter argues that the answer to this question is to be equally found in seemingly museological terms. Although the monolithic statues called *moai* or *ariŋa ora o te tupuna*—the living face of the ancestor—have *become* samples of archaeological heritage through archaeological definitions, and though ancestral landscapes have *become* sites of natural heritage through scientific discourses, the Rapanui people, somewhat paradoxically, have accommodated and resisted such interventions through similar frameworks. Examples of this—what I call the museological condition—emerge in repatriation initiatives of moai and other material manifestations of ancestors directed at reawakening dormant *mana* (ancestral energy), the rehabilitation of traumatic landscapes such as the former leprosarium, and the performative displays of Tapati, a cultural festival aimed at showcasing and revitalizing cultural practices. The chapter thus points to the different ways in which the Rapanui people have partially reclaimed "Museum Island" by deploying similar gestures, interventions, and tactics, that is, by curating environments and curing or healing their imprinted memories. On the one hand, this curation is—in the conventional museological sense—entangled with, and constitutive of, the national and global heritage-making of "Museum Island." On the other hand, and amid the institutional machinery of the underpinning heritage complex, there is much to cure on Rapa Nui. This calls for another form of curation—in the adopted Rapanui sense—which comes closer to the original meaning of the word *curare* (to heal): the wounds of history, memories of the leprosarium, and the moai, who are not dead but can be seen as patients who are alive and in need of care rather than heritage to be frozen and safeguarded. Curation, in this sense, is then the ontologically grounded answer to and modification of curation governed through the heritage complex; an Indigenous response, appropriating the UNESCO-style discourse for something deeper, as we shall see, something much deeper. After allowing the research material to do the talking, I conclude by liberating curation from its usual museological confines, reconceptualizing it as a lens through which to zoom in on the human condition of attending to, or taking care of, the relationship between environments and memories. In the case under scrutiny, curating an island becomes curing Rapa Nui.

Becoming "Museum Island"

Covering the "turbulent history" of Rapa Nui in depth is beyond the scope of this book, which attempts to refocus ethnographic museums through Oceanic lenses. Such a formidable objective has been achieved elsewhere, as in Steven Roger Fischer's *Island at the End of the World* (2005). In this study, Fischer introduces "Museum Island" as the latest episode in Rapa Nui's history and one of its various "convoluted identities," which followed another episode, "company island"[5]—when it operated as a sheep farm under the split colonial rule shared by British-commercial and Chilean-political interests[6]—and which frames Rapa Nui to this day. Fischer argues:

> Symbolically, Museum Island first emerged perhaps in 1955, when the Norwegian expedition [of Thor Heyerdahl] re-erected the single toppled *mo'ai* of *ahu* Ature Hiki [*sic*] at 'Anakena. . . . After this, particularly under the guidance and/or inspiration of the American archaeologist William T. Mulloy, not only were individual statues re-erected but entire *ahu* and their terrains restored. Eventually this involved many projects over several decades—the last, from 1992 to 2002, being the reconstruction, re-erection and full restoration of the island's largest ritual complex, majestic Tongariki.[7]

I delve into the symbolic dimension in more detail throughout the chapter, but for now it might be argued that politically and legally, "Museum Island" was born even earlier, in 1935, when the island was declared a national monument and national park.[8] As Fischer points out, this legal reconstitution "was a direct result of the Chilean public's consternation at hearing that the Franco-Belgian expedition" (discussed in chapter 3) "had taken away so many artefacts, including a huge *mo'ai*."[9] At that time, however, Rapa Nui was still run as a "company island," Fischer continues, so this apparent legal shift should rather be seen as a discursive "gesture," a "public relation manoeuvre, without result," given that, he concludes, "the National Park would remain a 'paper park' until 1968."[10] Nevertheless, even during that time, the legal frame of "Museum Island" began to be filled with scientific substance. Padre Sebastián Englert (introduced in chapter 3) conducted the first archaeological inventory of all *ahu* (ceremonial platforms) in 1947 and the first restoration of the ceremonial village of *'Oroŋo*—considering Rapa Nui an "archaeological jewel of the Pacific" and "potentially the most significant museum of art and architecture of the Pacific."[11] In 1966, William Mulloy, who collaborated with Englert, set out with his colleague Gonzalo Figueroa to gear the means and methods of archaeological conservation and restoration toward transforming Rapa Nui into an "island-wide museum."[12]

Today, this ongoing "heritageisation" is enforced through a wide array of institutional actors.[13] These often represent ambivalent authorities and competing interests, fueled through the jamming dialectics between an "uncertain sovereignty"[14] of Chile over the island and the associated "*pluralismo jurídico*"[15] of diverse legal frameworks operating at different levels in the same territorial space. In 1995, as mentioned, one of the heritage players and makers, UNESCO, declared the Rapa Nui National Park a world heritage site[16]—a designation that further accelerated Rapa Nui's evolution into a global attraction and travel destination. This happened, however, largely without consulting the Rapanui people, as had been mostly the case throughout the history of the island in general, and "Museum Island" in particular.[17] Although these institutional levels, both political and legal, certainly require closer attention, here I move the analytical focus toward the cultural or rather curational practices—and their underpinning ontologies and temporalities—through which "Museum Island" becomes reconstituted, contested and subverted, experienced and performed. In this context, I prefer "curational" over "curatorial."[18] The latter is more commonly associated with museum practices whereas the former enacts the underlying museological condition which, as we shall see, has traveled beyond institutional walls to reshape an entire island.

Curating "Museum Island"

While elaborating on the symbolic emergence of "Museum Island," Fischer argues that the U.S. archaeologist William Mulloy, who was first a member of the globally famous Heyerdahl expedition that inspired a new generation of foreign scholars to study Rapa Nui, made later the biggest immediate (and lasting) impact of them on the island. This claim is supported, for example, by the fact that the library of the museum is named after him, and that the nearby Tahai Ceremonial Complex, which he restored with Gonzalo Figueroa and countless yet mostly nameless and invisible Rapanui individuals between 1966 and 1968, honors his life's work with a memorial: "Grande fue—como sus obras—su amor y entrega a Rapa Nui. Hai Hapi—Hai Haku Tutu'u I Te Aringa Ora To'Ona Here Rahi Mo Rapa Nui I Haka Tikea Mai Ai. By restoring the past of his beloved island he also changed its future."[19] "Perhaps most importantly," Fischer further notes, "Mulloy regarded his restoration of the monuments as a social campaign to reaffirm the identity and dignity of the Rapanui people."[20] What we can discern in Mulloy's work then, is—broadly speaking—an ideological shift of archaeological interventions from scientific exploitation to cultural restoration, a shift that nowadays continues to evolve into educational dissemination and participation, as seen in the Tereveka Archaeological Outreach program (see chapter 3).

This ongoing archaeological evolution has proceeded through the direct involvement of the Rapanui people—not as informants but as scholars and professionals. Mulloy trained the next generation of Rapanui archaeologists, the first from the island. One of them, Sergio Rapu, first studied under Mulloy at the University of Wyoming in the early 1970s and later became the first director of the Museo Antropológico Padre Sebastián Englert (1975–1990) and, in 1984, the island's first Rapanui governor, appointed by General Augusto Pinochet.[21] In conversation with me, Rapu stressed that his work continued the legacy of Mulloy by being concerned with the "open-air museum," "this huge heritage" that, according to him, continues to be "one of our most important resources of identity and economy."[22] The restoration of Ahu Naunau at 'Anakena in 1978, which he conducted with Sonia Haoa (another Indigenous archaeologist with whom I engaged during my time on the island) and which included the reerection of its seven moai, can thus be seen as a scientific intervention aimed not only at archaeological reconstruction but at cultural revitalization and economic development.[23]

At various points in previous chapters, Te Rangihīroa's Indigenized inflection and reinvention of academic disciplines has been noted as "empirical" or "applied" anthropology geared toward cultural renewal, economic revival, and Native governance.[24] In a similar vein, it can be argued that Rapanui archaeologists, such as Rapu and Haoa, have fostered a particular Rapanui archaeology not limited to the accumulation of scientific knowledge per se, but deployed also as a tool to "empower the community," as Rapu put it. This community-oriented scientific ideal and practice, however, is a contested terrain, as is anything else associated with Rapa Nui's heritage complex. In 2015, the year before I conducted my fieldwork, the national park was occupied by the Parlamento Rapa Nui, a political faction that split from the Consejo de Ancianos to pursue complete independence for the island from Chile. Although its more radical measures are controversial and often rejected from within the Rapanui community, this particular tactic has led, as one element among other initiatives such as those launched by the Comisión de Desarrollo de la Isla de Pascua (Development Commission of Easter Island), to a recent move by the Chilean government to hand over control of the national park and its revenues to the Comunidad Indígena Ma'u Henua after a one-year co-administration—which started in September 2016—with the Corporación Nacional Forestal (National Forrest Corporation), the previous administrators.[25]

Dissecting these political and legal processes accompanying the island's metamorphosis into a heritage site in more detail would, of course, be a laudable task. Here, however, I am more concerned with particular practices that can be understood as attempts to curate "Museum Island." Further, I set out to dig deeper into the underpinning Rapanui ontologies and temporalities, to analyze and speculate what material remnants and landscapes, which have become sites of archaeological or natural heritage, might have become instead or will potentially become again.

Re-membering Ariŋa Ora o te Tupuna, the Living Face of the Ancestor

"This most recent manifestation"—"Museum Island" and "its emblem—the *mo'ai*— . . . an international icon"—"may well . . . derive from the Rapanui's own past," Fischer argues, "but it is no less a foreign obligation, too, once again the product of outsiders imposing on the Rapanui people Western science, values, and goals."[26] In other words, the political and legal discourses, mechanisms, and regimes have mainly come from outside the island, traveled there, and continue to reframe it. As we saw in chapter 3, this external imposition has not been a linear affair but instead a "simultaneous and paradoxical process of resistance and accommodation, contestation and collaboration between Indigenous leadership and settler state," as can be observed throughout other (post) colonial histories across the Pacific.[27] Yet "Museum Island" largely remains, politically and legally, a "foreign obligation" that scarcely reflects the philosophies and concepts, epistemologies, and ontologies derived from the Rapanui's past.

The crucial question and ultimate problem to be addressed, then, is how to Indigenize the principles and conditions underpinning the legal and political frameworks that constitute "Museum Island." This is, of course, an exceptionally difficult task, but recent initiatives from within the Rapanui heritage complex, by institutions such as the Museo Antropológico Padre Sebastián Englert as well as the Secretaría Técnica del Patrimonio Rapa Nui (Technical Secretariat of Rapa Nui Heritage) and the Consejo Asesor de Monumentos Nacionales (Advisory Council of National Monuments), indicate that the "heritageisation" process is increasingly pulled out of the abstract terrains of political and legal discourses into the concrete life-worlds of Rapanui people. For example, the Plan Maestro Patrimonial (Heritage Master Plan) and the education program Manu Iri: Guardianes Por El Patrimonio (Manu Iri: Guardians of Heritage) are developed and executed through continuous community consultation and participation, as I witnessed, and are based on and operate through Rapanui concepts.[28] In the broader scheme, however, *patrimonio* (heritage) continues to be either defined as natural or cultural, which presupposes an ontological separation of people and land (or subject and object), or as archaeological or historical, which, if understood in temporal terms, takes for granted a linear progression of time. Yet these ontological and temporal assumptions do not hold true for the very Rapanui realities they are supposed to protect and govern, as a brief excurse into language and words, as prime sources and carriers of concepts, reveal.

As we saw in chapter 3, the Consejo de Ancianos published in 1988, one hundred years after the *acuerdo de voluntades,* which set the seal on the island's cession to Chile, a book that mapped the genealogical connections between the Rapanui people and the land, and insisted on the unquestionable sovereignty of the former over the latter. Among other things, the authors state,

> Para el rapanui, la tierra pascuense tiene un importante significado y un valor diferente al que tiene para otros pueblos y cultura, pero sí similar al de otras culturas polinésicas. Para el pascuense, existe un profundo lazo emocional con esta tierra que los vió nacer y se refleja en el hecho que la tierra se llama "KAINGA". En nuestro idioma que significa a su vez, matriz o útero y los territorios pertenecientes a cada tribu, llamado "HENUA POREKO" or tierra natal, en donde nacieron los ancestros.
>
> (For the Rapanui, the land of Easter Island has an important meaning and value different to other peoples and cultures, but similar to other Polynesian cultures. For the Easter Islander exists a profound emotional bond with this land where they were born, which is reflected in the land being called "Kainga." In our language this means, in turn, womb or uterus, and the territories belonging to each tribe are called "Henua Poreko" or native land where the ancestors were born.)[29]

For our purposes here, both words—*kaiŋa* and *henua*—refer to both land and parts of the female body associated with giving birth.[30] This ontological unison of people and land is shared across "Polynesia" and unsettles externally imposed ontological separations as natural versus cultural heritage. In regard to Rapanui temporalities, then, Englert notes in the *Diccionario Rapa Nui-Español* (Dictionary Rapanui-Spanish): "las diversas maneras para expresar el término castellano de 'tiempo'" [the diverse ways of expressing the Spanish word "time"].[31] There is no literal translation of "time" in its epochal or linear sense and the closest I could find was *nohoŋa,* which translates, among other meanings, as *permanencia* (permanence) or *vida* (life) as in "*Te nohoŋa ta'e oti.* La vida interminable, eterna" (The interminable, eternal life).[32] Closely related to other Oceanic temporal conceptions, which we encountered in chapter 2, Rapanui time unfolds as an endlessly evolving "spiral, which connotes both cyclical and lineal movements,"[33] through the interweaving of the circular cosmological and the natural seasonal passing of time as well as the linear consciousness of time defined by markers such as birth and death. Present time is merging past and future into a past-becoming-present-becoming-future, which exceeds and cannot be reduced to a purely linear progress broken down into stages, such as archaeological (understood in its temporal sense) or prehistorical and historical, which structure foreign conceptions of heritage.

Given these ongoing temporal and ontological dimensions of Rapanui life, it is worth and indeed needed to ask what the moai might mean, not as "international icon," but in their original yet contemporary sense as ariŋa ora o te tupuna (the living face of the ancestor). In his groundbreaking book *La Tierra de Hotu Matu'a,* which grew—in contrast to most prior and subsequent studies—out of years of permanent living (rather than temporary fieldwork) among Rapanui people, Englert states that "hay nativos que creen ingenuamente, y afirman, que en aquellos tiempos existía el 'mana' o poder mágico de hacer andar a los moai hasta la misma plataforma de los ahu" (there are natives who naively believe, and affirm, that in those days "mana" or magic power existed that made the moai walk to the platform of the ahu).[34] Englert's use of the past—apart from his patronizing gaze as representative of both god and science—insinuates that neither mana nor its capacity to move the moai exist anymore, thus offering further discursive evidence of the "episteme of discontinuity" referred to in chapter 3. Thor Heyerdahl, whose work Englert strongly supported, pushed this even further by "alleging that the Rapanui people had not been the creators, but the destroyers, of the island's archaeological heritage."[35] Other famous explorers before him also claimed a disjuncture between Rapa Nui's monumental past and lifeless present. Katherine Routledge, for example, asserted that "In Easter Island the past is the present, it is impossible to escape from it; the inhabitants of to-day are less real than the men who have gone; the shadows of the departed builders still possess the land."[36] On a similar note, Alfred Métraux referred to Veriamo a Huki as "the poor woman," who "was now like Easter Island itself—a body without a soul" (see chapter 3).[37] Yet the Rapanui people and language are still here, and the pan-Pacific concept of mana, which threads its way through this book, seems to be everywhere, including the Manu Iri heritage education program mentioned earlier. In fact, Fischer argues that "for most Rapanui, ideology always has been secondary to personal *mana* in civil politics."[38] If mana is still alive, then what might have become of the moai instead of a sample of archaeological heritage, or a "frozen picture of the past," as a Chilean living on the island and working in the music industry put it while we spoke in his studio in Haŋa Roa? Or what will the moai potentially become (again), as ariŋa ora o te tupuna, the living face of the ancestor?

Peter Mason has traced "moai on the move" through their global travels and different forms of presentation.[39] He has also laid out "seven ways of being moai," among them the surrealist and exhibitionary modes, which have fueled "perceptions of these exotic colossi. These perceptions," Mason concludes, "are conditioned by an emphasis on either the natural or the cultural aspect of the moai."[40] This outward orientation of inquiry is certainly a laudable undertaking to allude to the process of moai *becoming*—as work of art, museological artifact, or "international icon." What seems even more important, however, is to understand and facilitate the moai *returning*. By refocusing the moai through Rapanui perceptions, that is, through lenses that "derive from the Rapanui's own past," cultural and natural aspects once again merge into one ontological unity in the original or Indigenous process of becoming ariŋa ora o te tupuna, the living face of the ancestor, "through which the deceased and [their] mana would continue to live."[41]

It would be simple, of course, to relegate this way of being moai, or rather becoming ariŋa ora o te tupuna, to an ancient past disconnected from the present. However, such perpetuation of an "episteme of discontinuity" does not do justice to a Rapanui sense of an ancestral present and future. For many Rapanui people, *ivi tupuna* (ancestral remains) are alive, in fact, they *are* the ancestors to whom they are genealogically related,[42] which is a common ontological status across the "Polynesian triangle," as in Aotearoa New Zealand and Hawai'i (discussed in the conclusion).[43] Whether this ontological conviction is shared by all Rapanui people is irrelevant, both philosophically and analytically. It is relevant, however, to detect that these ontological realities—which cannot and need not reach the level of representative totality—enter the Rapanui heritage complex.

The evolving Programa de Repatriación (Repatriation Program) Rapa Nui—Ka Haka Hoki Mai Te Mana Tupuna, which Jacinta Arthur assisted in creating and managing, attempts to establish an inventory of ancestral remains held in Chilean and overseas museums, and, if feasible, repatriate these to the island and their descendants. The initiative reveals the ambiguous structural relationships forming the Rapanui heritage complex. On the one hand, the program faces strong resistance, both legally and politically, on the national level, as Arthur pointed out in conversation and writing.[44] As we have seen, the entire island is categorized as a national monument and thus anything on it, including ancestral remains, is defined as national heritage and property. At the same time, institutions of the same state, such as the Secretaría Técnica del Consejo de Monumentos Nacionales and the Museo Antropológico Padre Sebastián Englert (MAPSE), actively support the initiative and its community outreach, which transforms the museum's role into one of *hoa kona,* or guardian.[45] As Pelayo Tuki, the former group's representative and collections manager at MAPSE (replaced by Mario Villanueva Tuki) stressed in conversation with me, the program has been developed and conducted through *un concepto propio de Rapa Nui* (a Rapanui concept), ivi tupuna, which cannot, according to him, be considered *patrimonio del estado* (heritage of the state).[46] Given these constraints within the national context, Ka Haka Hoki Mai Te Mana Tupuna has reached across the "sea of islands" to their Pacific relatives to seek advice by the repatriation program Karanga Aotearoa at the Museum of New Zealand Te Papa Tongarewa (Te Papa) to dilute or bypass state restrictions as much as possible.[47] What we can see then, I argue, is how the heritage complex becomes—despite the legal and political restrictions—internally, through Rapanui concepts, and externally, through pan-Pacific coalitions, partially Indigenized. Let us return to the moai as ariŋa ora o te tupuna.

For the Rapanui people—again not all, but certainly a significant portion—not only the ivi tupuna, which were placed under the moai, but also the stones, of which the moai are made, are alive and materialize genealogical relations.[48] This vitality of stones is expressed in the name Toki, a word shared across many "Polynesian" languages for a tool used for sculpting stones, which was chosen for the new music school that opened in April 2016 in a stunning building made of recycled materials and is devoted to *un patrimonio vivo* (living heritage).[49] What happens, then, if new moai are made today? One of the most prominent Rapanui artists, Benedicto Tuki, has carved moai for various purposes and locations around the globe.[50] When I visited him in his gallery in Haŋa Roa, he stressed that these endeavors were mostly marred by political controversy on the island, and the resulting moai were always positioned globally to face it. He described the process of carving as a dialogical practice in which *la piedra habla* (the stone speaks) and one needs to listen and respond, which is reminiscent of the discussion on curatorial conversations and material languages in Hawai'i in chapter 2. This is, according to him, the process through which mana emerges, on a deeply personal level. Tuki also features in the film *Te Kuhane o te Tupuna: El Espírito de los Ancestros,* produced by Leo Pakarati and Paula Rossetti, in which he and his granddaughter Mikaela travel to the British Museum, among other European museums, to visit the iconic Moai Hoa Haka Nana'ia (The Stolen Friend), "in search of the sacred power of their ancestors, the *Mana.*" "One way to recover the *Mana,*" according to the primary message of the film, and "to bring back wellbeing to the island, is to bring the spirit of the Moai Hoa Haka Nana'ia back to its shores"[51] (figure 4.1).

Although Moai Hoa Haka Nana'ia might most likely not return to the island in its physical form, despite efforts to this end being undertaken at the time of writing,[52] it might be argued that this cinematic intervention, which has traveled to Aotearoa New Zealand and Hawai'i and continues to be screened at venues around the world (such as the European Society for Oceanists conference in Germany in 2017), has been successful in sparking dialogues among Oceanic people who connect their experiences to those featured in the film.[53] The moai's spirit, then, has been returned, at least partially, to Rapa Nui and spread across

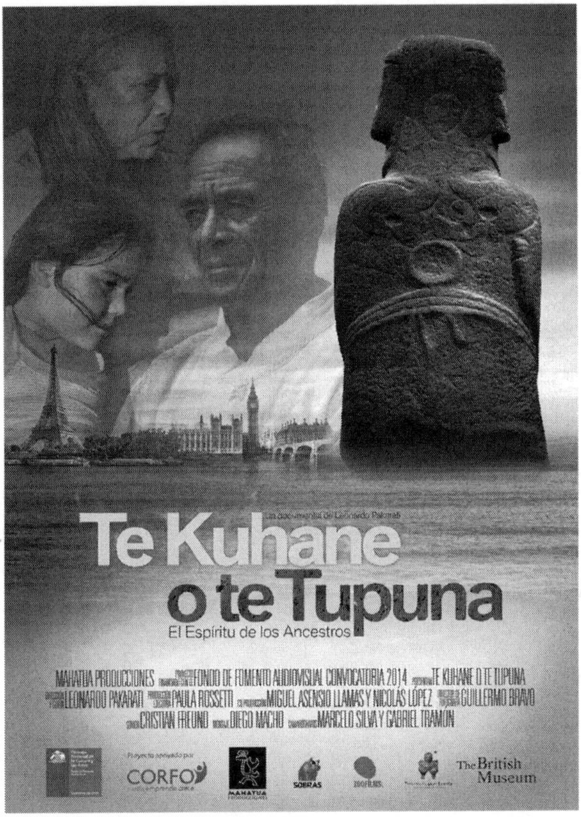

Figure 4.1 Poster of film *Te Kuhane O Te Tupuna—El Espírito de los Ancestros,* directed by Leo Pakarati and produced by Paula Rossetti, 2015.

Oceania and the world. For our purposes here, it is important to ask what this fractured yet preserved ancestral energy or mana perceived through a Rapanui lens may tell us about restored and reerected moai on the island, as seen in the photographs showing Ahu Tongariki, which was restored under both foreign and Indigenous direction (figures 4.2a and 4.2b).[54] What I suggest, speculatively but still through a concept deriving "from the Rapanui's own past" and persisting to this day, is to consider the underpinning archaeological intervention as a form of curation. In the depicted ahu, archaeological curation allows for dis-membered moai to be re-membered,[55] to be made whole again, while reactivating underpinning dormant mana and caring for genealogical relations, thus even producing "new mana."[56] This is not to claim that ahu and moai that have not been restored cannot be activated with regard to

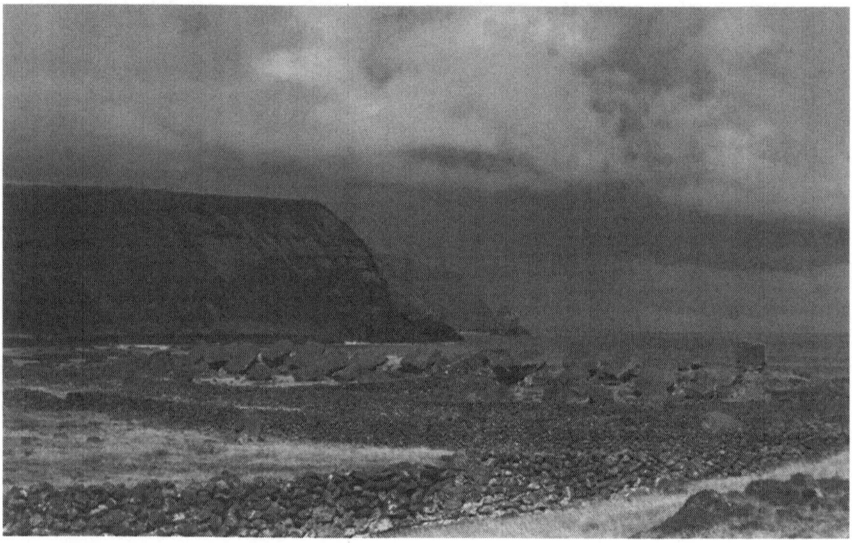

Figure 4.2a "Ahu of Tongariki." Rapa Nui, Chile, 1946. Photograph by Robert Gerstmann, Bishop Museum Archives.

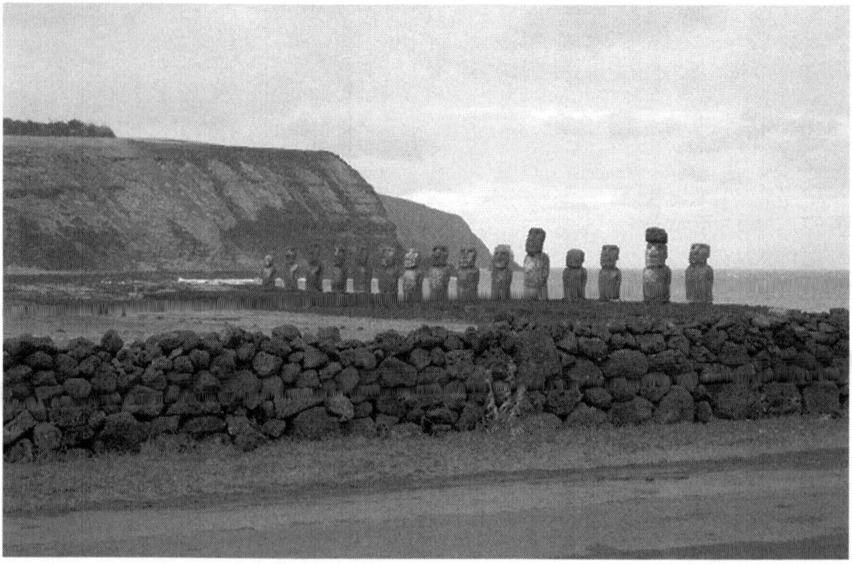

Figure 4.2b Ahu Tongariki. Rapa Nui, Chile, 2016. Photo by Aku Ika, Bishop Museum Archives.

mana, or to deny that archaeological restorations have been—and still are—divisive among the Rapanui community. My argument becomes more concrete in the next example of curating a particular landscape and curing its imprinted memories.

Curing the Leprosarium

Figure 4.3 shows the entrance to the former leprosarium. According to Fischer, leprosy was

> brought from Tahiti by a returnee who had accompanied Nicolás and Elizabeth Pakarati back to the island for the annexation in 1888: 'Tepano' (later Estebán) Ruti Rangi, who had lived for many years on Tahiti. Once he had infected other Rapanui, the Hanga Roa community isolated all lepers at Tara Heu, close to Tahai. (A few years later, they were relocated even further away—to two small shacks 3 kilometers north of Hanga Roa.)[57]

In the years that followed, the disease prompted the Chilean government to declare a "state of emergency," as Rolf Foerster and Sonia Montesino argue, under which the civil rights of Rapanui people were annulled. Leprosy thus enabled the Chilean state to transform the island into a "prison," the leprosarium being "a prison within the prison."[58] In other words, people infected with the disease were not allowed to leave the leprosarium, and the Rapanui people in general were not able to leave the island until 1956.[59] This restriction was purportedly to prevent infections on the Chilean mainland and led to various and most deadly attempts to escape between 1940 and 1958 (two years after Chile had opened the door to the continent).[60] The revolution that began in

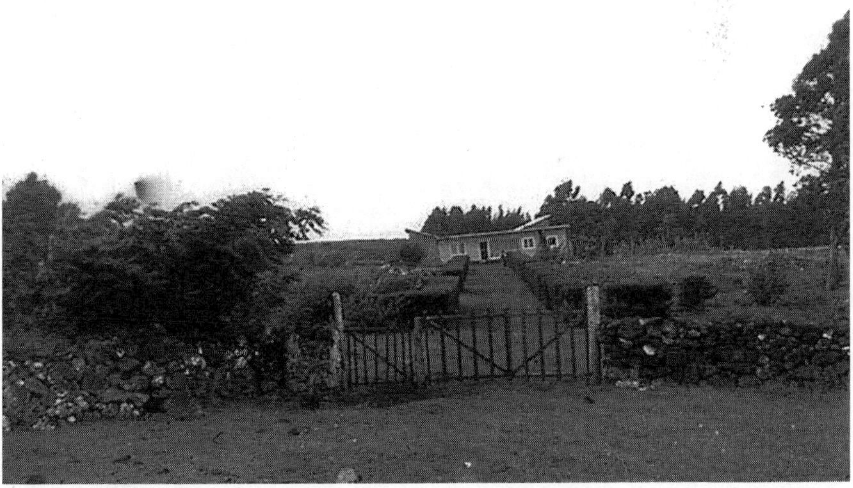

Figure 4.3 Entrance to the former leprosarium. Photograph taken by Doctor Clemente Meneses, courtesy of Tania Basterrica Brockman.

1964 and was led by schoolteacher Alfonso Rapu (brother of the archaeologist Sergio Rapu) brought back or rather expanded civil rights and enabled the Rapanui people for the first time "to be Chileans." This novel status was legally enshrined in 1966 through the Ley Pascua.[61] Rapu became the first democratically elected Rapanui mayor, a position that yielded little political yet sufficient symbolic power to address and eradicate the remains of the "state of emergency" caused through leprosy. Rapu reminisces:

> Apenas asumí como alcalde, hice desarmar la casa donde vivía Gabriel Hereveri en el sanatorio (*leprosario*) y también ordené destruir la mayoría de los pabellones. Fue un impulso, un error, pero tenía mucha rabia por todo el sufrimiento que nos había significado la lepra.
>
> (As soon as I had assumed the role as mayor, I decided to disassemble the house in which Gabriel Hereveri lived in the sanatorium (*leprosarium*) and I also ordered to destroy the majority of the pavilions. It was an impulse, an error, but I was furious about all the suffering which the leprosy had caused us.)[62]

This conscious evasion of the past and particularly traumatic memory continues to this day with both words—leprosy and leprosarium—considered to be *tapu* (taboo) and mainly left unspoken and unheard. Yet heritage professionals such as Betty Haoa Rapahango and Tania Basterrica Brockman have taken up the task of assessing the state in which the few remaining architectural structures are preserved, as *testimonio material de la lepra* (material testimony of leprosy), the ultimate goal being to create a *museo de sitio del leprosario* (on-site museum of the leprosarium) devoted to its conservation and education through musealization.[63] I visited Betty at the Museo Francisco Fonck in Viña del Mar, Chile, before continuing my journey to Rapa Nui, and later joined Tania on one of her field visits of the former leprosarium. Figure 4.4 shows the current entrance of the same site (see figure 4.3), which has, after the demolition ordered by Rapu, in the meantime been turned into Hoŋa'a o te Mana—Aldea Educativa Rapa Nui, an educational village and, as the Rapanui name indicates, a

> lugar donde habita la sabiduría . . . donde se reúnen tradición, cultura, conocimiento e innovación . . . con la finalidad de fortalecer la cosmovisión de la etnia Rapa Nui, en un mundo globalizado.

(place inhabited by wisdom . . . where tradition, culture, knowledge and innovation unite . . . for the purpose of strengthening the cosmovision of Rapa Nui in a globalized world.)[64]

Figure 4.5, then, depicts one of the few historical buildings, which was not completely dismantled because, according to Tania, it was

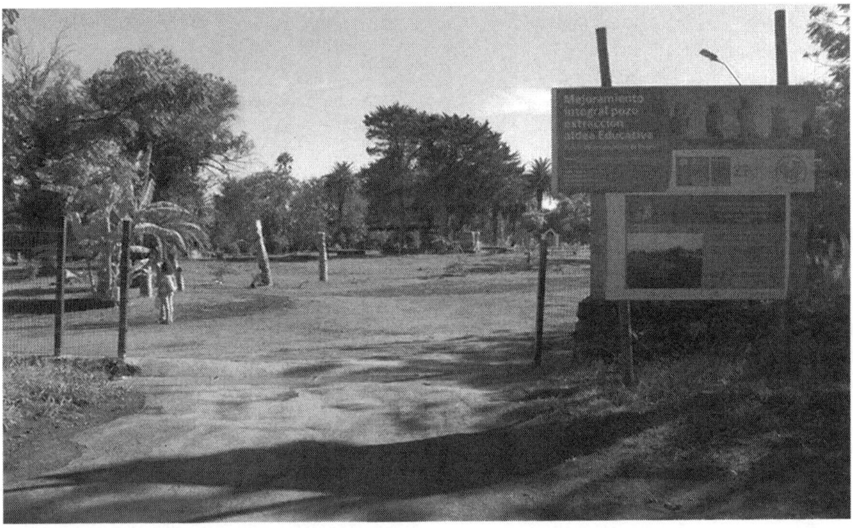

Figure 4.4 Entrance to *Hoŋa'a o te Mana—Aldea Educativa Rapa Nui* (educational village), 2016. Photograph by Philipp Schorch.

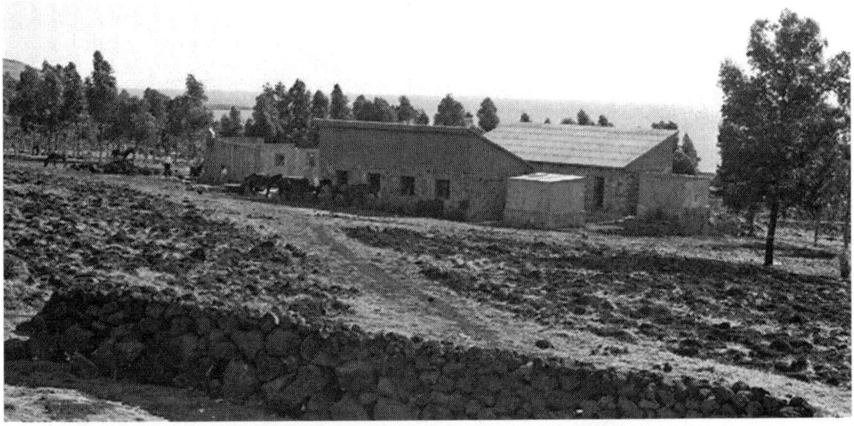

Figure 4.5 *Conjunto central* (central facilities) of the former leprosarium. Photograph by Fritz Felbermayer, courtesy of Tania Basterrica Brockman.

originally used as a kitchen and thus seen to be not directly related to leprosy, disease, and death. Within the repurposed Aldea Educativa, this building's foundation walls were intentionally reused as the basis for a *casa del arte* (house of art) as a conscious expression of life (figure 4.6). As Ana María Arredondo, director of the high school Lorenzo Baeza Vega, put it,

> only walls remained, white walls greenish with moss, the cobbled floor covered with leafs of avocado and rubber tree, all witnesses of a painful past which we wanted to forget but which is present in the air that blows and envelops. . . . The music, the beating of the chisel, the strokes of thousands of colors on the walls, and the words of children remembering a glorious past, began to inhabit this quiet place, which also invites silence, which fosters creation, which makes the spirits smile that have been silent for so long, which makes the wind blow again and whisper us its joy to see this space transformed.[65]

This recovery of history and memory through the *resurrección*[66] of a material space or environment can, I argue, once again be understood through a curational lens. Here, an architectural (rather than archaeological) intervention—which also incorporates a *sala museo* (exhibition hall) destined to exhibit available information about the leprosarium and the history of the place—can be seen as an attempt to restore a physical building and the surrounding landscape, while rehabilitating the imprinted histories and memories. In other words, this particular

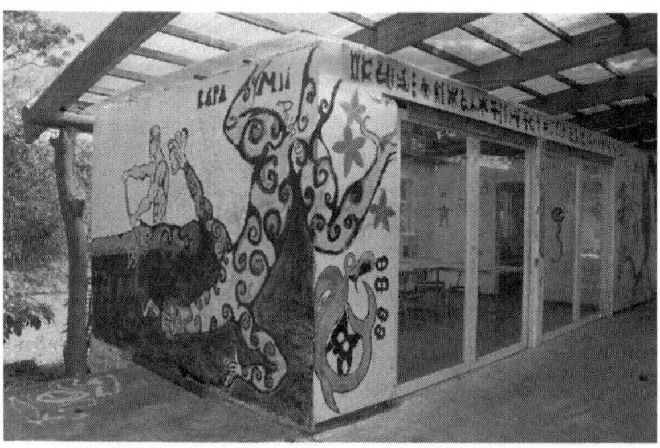

Figure 4.6 *Casa del arte* (house of art), 2016. Photograph by Philipp Schorch.

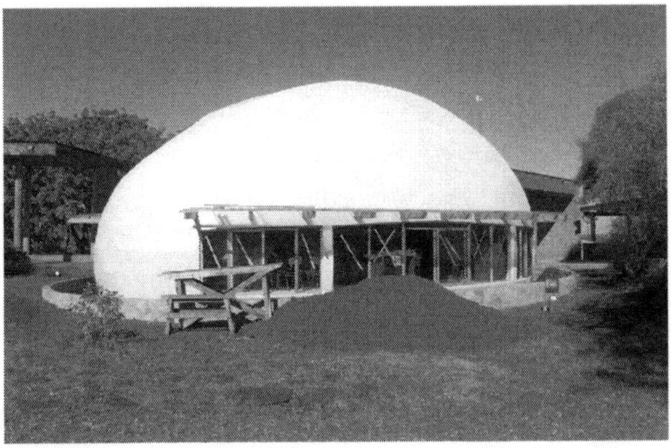

Figure 4.7 The computer lab in the form of an egg, 2016. Photograph by Philipp Schorch.

architectural gesture can be understood as a curative treatment, one that transforms a space of death into a breeding ground of life.

As Walter Benjamin asserted, "the past has not budged; despite aging, decaying, fragmenting or dissolving, it actually piles up in front of our eyes." Further, as Pora Petursdottier and Bjornar Olsen argue, "This material duration of the past moreover represents a form of memory" and is "inevitably contemporaneous, always folding into the present and future."[67] Walter Benjamin's other famous notion—"Allegory is in the realm of thought what ruins are in the realm of things"[68]—thus needs to be temporarily reframed, especially in the case of the Rapanui temporalities. That is, the ruins of the leprosarium repurposed as school allegorically stand for past and present and future, or nohoŋa (permanence). These ideas began to crudely take shape in my mind as I walked around the site, and then gained a sort of enlightened (and jubilant) clarity when we turned around a corner and all of a sudden faced the building housing the computer lab in the form of an egg (figure 4.7). In the most obvious form, this egg symbolizes birth, or rather rebirth, in a place formerly associated with death, and a contemporary reference to the ancient *taŋata manu* (birdman ceremony), which succeeded the religious significance of the moai, and lives on in the present.[69]

Displaying Permanence

> [The] first 'Semana de Rapa Nui' or summer festival—later to be called 'Tāpati' (Tahitian for 'Sunday', from the English 'sabbath')—was held in 1969 after Florencia Atamu, one of Hanga Roa's new

> Rapa Nui councilors, had witnessed the 'Tiura'i Festival' at Pape'ete and had suggested something similar for Hanga Roa. The 'Semana' began small, but enthusiastically. Over the years [the] 'Tāpati Festival' was to become one of the Pacific's most fascinating annual cultural events, attracting tourists from around the world.[70]

Tapati, which began in earnest in 1972 based on the Chilean Fiesta de la Primavera (Spring Festival) with Chilean traditions and games, was later transformed into a reimagined cultural festival that reconstructed ancestral competitions.[71] This evolution indicates that contemporary Indigeneity—in this case, Rapanui—in its various expressions and manifestations—here, a festival—is a multidimensional concept and experience.[72] In other words, we can see how a cultural initiative was born of a changing political landscape—only a few years after Rapanui people acquired full Chilean citizenship—and through the transpacific engagement with their Tahitian neighbors and cousins. Since then, Tapati has evolved into a global tourist attraction, major economic driver, and source of income. To put it differently once again, Indigeneity is at once genealogically (historically), politically, culturally, and economically articulated and performed.[73]

This multidimensionality of Indigenous affairs is also one of the reasons Tapati is, like most other initiatives associated with the heritage complex described, a contested terrain. On the more positive or celebratory side, scholars have considered it as "one of the very few public contexts in which ancient Rapanui traditions are re-enacted for a contemporary audience,"[74] and argued that it contributes to a "cultural revival"[75] so successful that it seems that "culture" is "bursting out all over on Rapanui."[76] A note of caution, which I also overheard many times during the festival in 2016, comes from one of the young dancers with whom Maxi Haase spoke throughout her research: "There are people who do it for the maintenance of culture, for the preservation of our traditions. And there are other people who do it in order to sell, to sell and to attract tourists."[77]

Although I certainly share this concern, I suggest, based on my observations, that this tension between authentic cultural practice and staged tourist performance is more often than not a dialectical variation of degree and not a categorical distinction of kind. A concrete example should help illustrate and support this claim. In 2016, Uri Pate, one of the participants in the Haka Pei competition, which is justifiably called an extreme sport given that the competing athletes rush down the 45-degrees slope of Mauŋa Pu'i on a banana tree trunk sled without any protective gear, was seriously injured and had to be flown to Santiago de Chile, where he remained in hospital for several months. Shortly after the accident, a community fundraiser was organized in which several dance ensembles performed in one of the main venues—not for international tourist audiences (although some were present) but for the Rapanui people themselves. What this suggests, then—not representatively but still empirically—is how the same dance, or cultural practice, can be performed as a personal tribute or can *become* a commercial activity, tourist product, and institutionalized brand. Both cultural practices behind the scenes and tourist performances on stage arise from and are enacted through the same Rapanui bodies and biographies; they differ only in the audience being addressed. The associated dialectics of Indigeneity (my term) thus become articulated and performed from particular yet shifting positions.[78]

In a similar vein, Tapati's main venue—Haŋa Vare Vare—offers (for two weeks) the stage for a tourist spectacle and multimedia extravaganza. Yet, on the first Sunday, the same stage is repurposed for the *misa oficial* (official mass), which brings us into the realm of religion and allows me to wrap up my point. The taŋata manu, or birdman ceremony, was the main manifestation of the birdman cult, a spiritual practice that slowly took over the declining moai cult. The two overlapped considerably, which is materialized in Moai Hoa Haka Nana'ia, who incorporates the *manu piri* figure of two taŋata manu on its back (see figure 4.1). The toppling of the moai statues happened after European contact and during the height of the taŋata manu cult.[79] This co-presence and its persistence reflects, once again, Rapanui temporalities and ontologies I have been alluding to throughout this chapter. In 'Oroŋo, the ceremonial village associated with the taŋata manu ceremony, the manu piri figure is displayed in a conventional museum setting that narrates mainly through the detached third person confined to the past tense. During the Tapati farándula or parade, however, the taŋata manu becomes resurrected by being performatively displayed in the carriage of one of the competing candidates—through the first person (body and biography), and in the present (figure 4.8). Although this rebirth could be easily discredited as a commercially driven and inauthentic

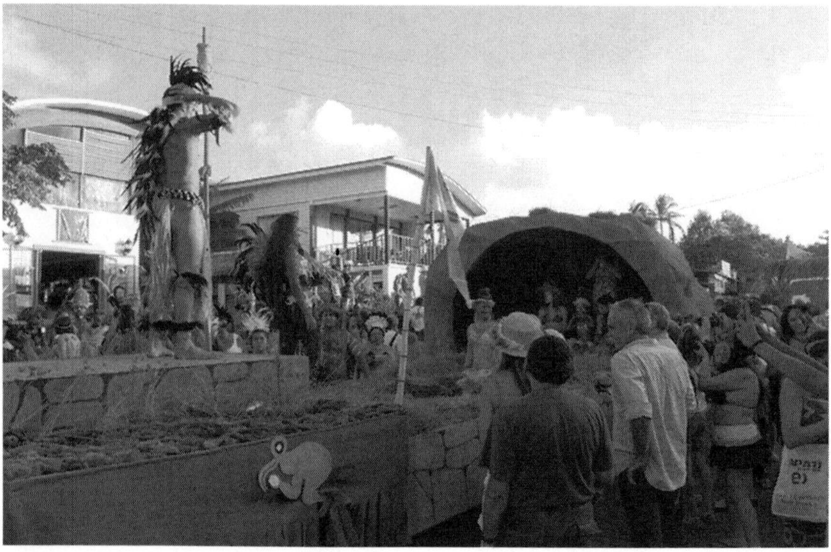

Figure 4.8 *Taŋata manu* (birdman) being performed and displayed at Tapati farándula (parade), 2016. Photograph by Philipp Schorch.

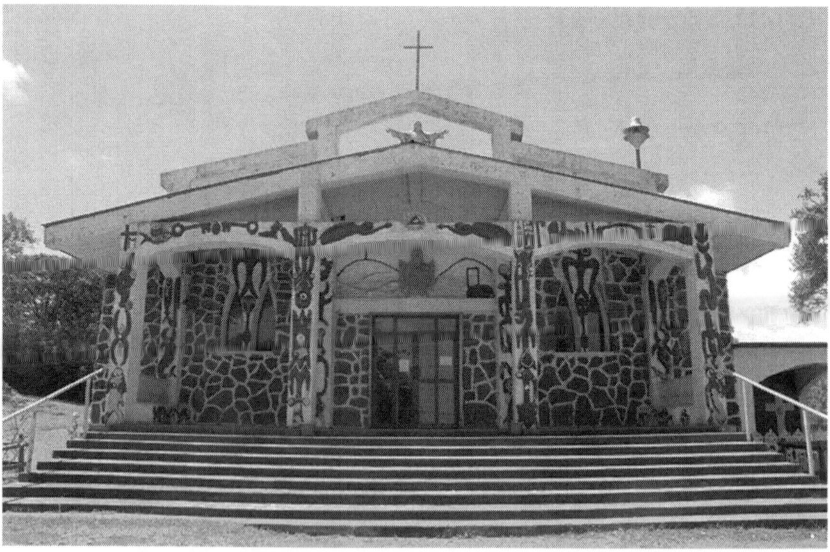

Figure 4.9 *Manu piri* (joined birds) being resurrected outside and inside of Haŋa Roa church, 2016. Photograph by Philipp Schorch.

reinvention of tradition,[80] such an accusation is more difficult to launch in the context of religion (serious) than of festival (frivolous). As shown in the final figure (4.9), the manu piri has entered and lives on in Christianity by being displayed inside and outside the Haŋa Roa Catholic church. What I argue is that distinctions between "ancestral ritual" and "postmodern performance" should not be seen as different stages in a chronological progress of history, but as different manifestations of the same permanent spiral of Rapanui time.[81] Fischer argues—rightly in my view—that "the 'cultural continuity' binding all Rapanui is the transformation itself."[82] As suggested in chapter 3, tradition on Rapa Nui means adopting for the sake of adapting. I add and conclude that this continuing yet transforming bond requires curational efforts, as through acts of re-membering, curing, and displaying. Curating henua (the union of people and land), then, means curing nohoŋa (the permanence of life).

This chapter has been devoted to a particular historical and ongoing episode, in which Rapa Nui was turned into "Museum Island." I have explained the different ways in which the Rapanui people have adopted foreign or external impositions through similar frameworks, and partially reconfigured "Museum Island" by deploying complementary mechanisms, regimes, and strategies. We have seen how practices of re-membering, curing, and displaying have left their usual museological confines and shaped what I term a museological condition underpinning life in a museum. I consider these practices as efforts devoted to the ambition of curating "Museum Island," that is, the curation of ancestral landscapes and curing or healing of their imprinted memories and genealogies.[83]

In the course of my discussion on moai becoming and returning as ariŋa ora o te tupuna, it became clear that "things" can be understood as vessels that become de- or remobilized, de- or reactivated, and reenacted through particular material practices, leaving traces in time (through genealogical relations) and space (though global travel).[84] This process of material becoming is thus characterized by a tripartite relationship through the trajectory from vessel through reenactment to trace. To discern how the process of de- and remobilization and activation might be instantiated, we need to zoom in on the underlying forces, modes, and potentialities. At this point, the notion of curation emerges as an enlightening lens—not as the expertise of individual curators, but closer to its original meaning of curare—to heal—although in a broadened yet specific sense of attending to, or taking care of material environments. Curation facilitates the reenactment of vessels and their traces, thus underpinning the tripartite relation of material becoming. Curation, then, functions as a method, again in a broadened yet specific sense, which is ideologically driven (such as through different archaeological and architectural regimes) and de- or reactivates, dis- or reengages, and de- or remobilizes materials for experiences in relation to, and in dialogue with, environments.

What are the promising potentials of such a line of thinking? This notion of curation allows us to think about ideology and experience in new ways. Curational interventions and the associated processes of selection, configuration, and orchestration render ideology—usually understood as a discursive intervention—palpable in three-dimensional environments. Second, using curation to think through the relations between human beings, "things," and environments enables us to move away from objects, their meanings, and idiosyncratic biographies toward a world where "things" do not simply exist or connect to each other, but where they are instead disposed, ordered, and archived in particular ways. Curation, as a communicative and expressive action, operates through languages. As we saw in chapter 2, language is here not only understood as a discursive but also as a material practice of exchange, and as a way of facilitating the impulse, gesture, and intervention of collecting, ordering, and archiving. Curational impulses, gestures, and interventions, then, mirror layers of the human condition, which are, at the same time, pervasively relational and become dialogically co-constituted given that it is the potency of "things," such as the moai, that affords a particular (ancestral) landscape and shapes (genealogical) experiences.

Curational interventions are full of contestation and compromise, as is clear on Rapa Nui. They have to deal with the traces of other curational efforts—those of the Rapanui activists, the archaeologists, the architects, the tourism entrepreneurs, the environmentalists—and the fact that it takes effort to keep "things," such as the moai, in the doing. In a similar way, the Rapa Nui National Park and the ceremonial village 'Oroŋo with its visitor center and well-manicured surroundings, can be understood as outcomes of layered curational gestures and interventions that, together with the forces of material growth and decay, and the unpredictable ways curated environments end up being used, bring about social realities that give material expression to particular ideological foci: religious, ecological, economical, and so on. The notion of curation understood in this way easily jumps scales; there is never just one curation at work. No curational impulse, gesture, or intervention can be total, because it is always caught up in the course of events and environments already there, never quite stable, and always struggling with the "stubborn persistence of material presences."[85] Moreover, curation is clearly only one of several forces at work. For example, the industrial complex of Vaitea, the former lifeblood of the "company island," is considered a "monumento histórico de Rapa Nui,"[86] even as the site itself deteriorates due to insufficient curational support and is subjected to other interventions, such as a Catholic altar and a barrier erected in 2015 by the Parliamento Rapa Nui to block off the national park. At the same time, reforestation efforts are made across the island, such as by reintroducing native species, such as the extinct Toromiro tree, which are often seen as living and genealogically related relics of a remote past that—just like the ivi tupuna—often exist beyond the island and are called upon to return.[87]

The notion of curation is therefore not to be misunderstood as a comprehensive and exclusive conceptual focus. What it can do is help us understand certain environments as a result of partial and imperfect curational gestures, and of partly failed and fragmented efforts of curational interventions, which are punctuated by ruptures and disjunctures and often layered onto the traces, the material residues and ruins, of older and equally incomplete ones. A moai can thus become re-membered as ariŋa ora o te tupuna, a leprosarium become cured, and permanence become displayed. Curating an island, then, becomes curing Rapa Nui.

PART III

MUSEUM OF NEW ZEALAND TE PAPA TONGAREWA, AOTEAROA NEW ZEALAND

CHAPTER 5

Materializing German-Sāmoan Colonial Legacies

with Sean Mallon and Nina Tonga

The *mana taonga* principle and policy at the Museum of New Zealand Te Papa Tongarewa (Te Papa) was originally a declaration of Māori authority over *taonga* (treasures), and consequently a new way of thinking about the relationship between museums and Indigenous people by putting them at the center of museology. The concept has been extended to other non-Māori collections in Te Papa, to other museums, and even globally. What happens, then, if a collection represents people of dual ancestry such as the Sāmoan-German descendants of colonial German Sāmoa? And what happens if a German representative is drawn into the orbit of a Sāmoan curator in their joint effort to materialize this common legacy? This chapter discusses the project Materializing German-Sāmoan Colonial Legacies, which attempts to retell this larger story through a dual historical and contemporary focus as well as through a double German-Sāmoan/Sāmoan-German lens. Historical objects in the collection and their associated stories allow for the re-historicizing of the past and are brought into dialogue with contemporary objects, such as art works, thus materializing the changing nature of the German-Sāmoan legacy in the present. To retell a story that spans the globe, the chosen objects are inherently mobile—for example flags, stamps, coins, and postcards—and thus function as traveling media symbolizing and enacting the various connections. These objects build the material basis for an online narrative as a virtual and mobile expression of, and intervention in, the reshaping of the shared legacy.[1] The chapter offers a description of, and reflection on the initiative's process and outcome, revealing the resonances and dissonances and convergences and divergences that emerge through and impact the venture of co-collecting and co-curating.[2]

Mana Taonga at Te Papa

Mana taonga can be understood as a contemporary fusion of the ancient concepts of mana and taonga.[3] It thus embodies a contemporary, historically grounded "Indigenous articulation," a creative recoupling, or rearticulation, of constituent elements in response to global forces, rather than an inauthentic product of the "invention of tradition."[4] Te Papa's mana taonga policy was initially framed by influential Ngati Porou leader Apirana Mahuika during the development of the new museum's conceptual design in the late 1980s and 1990s.[5] It states that "Te Papa recognizes the role of communities in enhancing the care and understanding of collections and taonga."[6] In this context, mana taonga means the power and authority (mana) that resides in and derives from cultural treasures (taonga). The policy is therefore a declaration of Māori and other communities' authority over Māori taonga and other cultural treasures, and consequently a new way of managing the relationship between museums and communities. As a reversal of the common assumption that museums owned their collections, it puts Indigenous concepts and all communities at the heart of the museological enterprise. In doing so, the principle of mana taonga acknowledges and affirms the spiritual and cultural connections of the people to whom the treasures belong. This recognition accords rights and responsibilities, such as being actively involved in the care, interpretation, and display of taonga.[7]

The mana taonga policy at Te Papa is a contested terrain, however. Some criticism, for example, asserts that mana taonga in a government institution overrides the *mana whenua* (people of the land) or property rights of the local *iwi* (tribes) in Wellington because of the pantribal inclusion of many iwi within a national body, arguably amounting to an appropriation of Māori values that turns "tribal space" into "our place."[8] Other museums have developed different mechanisms. For example, the Auckland War Memorial Museum's Māori Committee, known as the Taumata-ā-Iwi, recognizes the sovereignty of the local tribe in decision making.[9] Mana taonga is also seen as the product of the biculturalism of the 1980s and 1990s, a government ideology that ameliorated Māori demands for independent development but that has in many cases been superseded by more autonomous arrangements, such as co-governance of cultural institutions or co-management of natural resources.[10]

Despite these debates and the diversity of museum practice around Aotearoa New Zealand, the concept of mana taonga as developed at Te Papa remains an important and potent fusion of customary and contemporary as well as Indigenous and non-Indigenous practices. Although framed in Māori conceptual terms, as a policy it actually empowers and facilitates collaboration with potentially any community in the management and use of its cultural heritage, such as Te Papa's Pacific Cultures collection, which we discuss in this chapter, but also its New Zealand History collections.[11] Mana taonga has also been extended to other museums, and even globally.[12] The challenges and tensions of translating mana taonga from theory through policy into practice, however, have—despite being inevitably experienced by museum professionals—gained comparatively less attention in the literature.[13] We see it as our task here to reveal some of the ambiguities and limits that arise and have to be personally, strategically, and productively negotiated as part of collaborative collecting and curatorial practice.

Mana Taonga and Pacific Cultures at Te Papa

Nina Tonga

As curators of the Pacific Cultures collection at Te Papa and being of Pacific Island descent, we have some specialist knowledge of the Pacific and its peoples, but it is not encyclopedic. We constantly draw on the knowledge and expertise of our Pacific communities to shape our collections, research, and exhibitions. Collaboration with Pacific communities is wide-ranging and covers a spectrum of museum activities from governance to exhibition and events programming and collecting. Conversely, Pacific communities have also sought collaboration, using the museum collections and resources for their own purposes.[14] A recent example of this form of community agency was a commission of a *ngatu fuatanga* (a type of decorated Tongan bark cloth) by the Otaota Fahina, a *koka'anga* (ngatu-making collective) based in Mount Roskill, Auckland. In 2015, we were contacted by the koka'anga, who offered to produce the first ngatu made from paper mulberry plants grown in Aotearoa New Zealand. Te Papa commissioned the koka'anga and in doing so, helped them realize this project and their aspirations to contribute a unique object to the Pacific collection and representation of Tongan material culture. This is one example of many, in which Pacific people are helping us create collections that better represent themselves and their communities.

In 2016, we explored the potential for Pacific people to be more directly involved in our collection development through co-collecting.[15] Our approach was inspired by some of the collaborative work of our colleagues and the groundbreaking fieldworker program started in the mid-1970s at the Vanuatu Cultural Centre.[16] We arranged our inaugural co-collecting project with Monaeka Flores, former coordinator of marketing and programs, and Kimberlee Kihleng, director of Humanities Guåhan (Guam), focusing specifically on the culture of Guam's Chamorro people, including works by master carvers, weavers, and blacksmiths. Our collaborators took the curatorial lead and set the scope and selection criteria for collecting. This allowed us to put the principle of mana taonga at the core of our collecting by creating an opportunity for the Chamorro people to define their representation at Te Papa. Our partners selected the art forms and artists to be represented in this co-collecting project. Throughout this process, the reversal of roles took some effort. On our part as institutional curators, this meant resisting the urge to influence the decisions our collaborators made, particularly when our curatorial advice was sought. The power of our influence was made obvious during one particular studio visit when our excitement about an object influenced the artists and staff of Humanities Guåhan to reconsider including it in their selection. In that moment, we became aware of the difficulties of co-collecting and the practical application of mana taonga. Our presence and involvement inevitably added another set of pressures for our collaborators, who in addition to building a representative collection were also trying to meet our expectations.

Our role was also apparent in our second co-collection project, Materializing German-Sāmoan Colonial Legacies. For this project, we engaged Philipp, a German academic, to develop a collection that materializes the legacy of German colonization of Sāmoa from 1900 to 1914. His approach to this project attempted to use a double lens that refocused the historic colonial framing of German Sāmoa toward a revisionist view that emphasizes an Indigenous present. This becomes clear in his reasoning and the selection of art works by contemporary

Sāmoan artists, who offer critical voices and alternative representations of these histories. First, however, we turn to a detailed run-through of the project's scene setting.

Setting the Scene for Materializing German-Sāmoan Colonial Legacies

Sean Mallon

In April 2016, Philipp approached and asked whether I could suggest a project he could work on relating to his research informing this book. His timing was good because the question of how we develop museum collections collaboratively with the communities we represent in the museum was driving our acquisition work. In late 2015, I gave a presentation on the politics of co-collecting Pacific cultures in Aotearoa New Zealand at the Research Center for Material Culture in Leiden, The Netherlands, and Nina and I were in the process of developing a co-collecting project with people in Guåhan, which took place in May 2016.

Over several years, I had grown frustrated with a growing number of researchers coming to Te Papa and theorizing about our curatorial work without having any real understanding of it from a hands-on or practical perspective. I devised a project called Materializing German-Sāmoan Colonial Legacies, which would involve Philipp's assembling a collection of objects representing the history of the German colonial period in Sāmoa and its legacy. My aim was to position him at once as collaborator, curator, and German community representative so that he would experience the challenges of curatorial collecting and documentation and gain firsthand insight into our practice. My role was to guide the project through the museum's processes. Given other work commitments and the overall intention of the project, I tried to keep my distance wherever possible and let the project unfold. Much of the actual work was progressed by Philipp on his own. We met occasionally to discuss and troubleshoot any issues that arose.

The project involved five core tasks. First was researching the current holdings of Te Papa related to the German Sāmoa colonial period and their associated historical background. As a research baseline for the project, I asked Philipp to look at the representation of German Sāmoa colonial history in Te Papa's collections and think about how to further develop it. I thought that an analysis of the objects in the collection would be a useful way for him to immerse himself in this complex history. The second task was to improve the current catalogue records. I asked Philipp to select a number of objects and to prepare web summary content (catalogue entry data) that would appear on "Collections Online"—Te Papa's publicly accessible web-based catalog. The purpose of web summaries is to summarize the history, significance, and provenance of objects in Te Papa's collections, all of which are often in a diffuse form in the full nonpublic catalogue record. They are like expanded captions, a few paragraphs, and can stand alone or be grouped under a theme or topic, constituting an online narrative for the Collections Online website. The goal was to provide experience of preparing collection-related research for presentation to online audiences. I sent several examples of types of web summaries from across the catalog as guidance because writing for audiences that use Collections Online entails various considerations and challenges that need to be taken into account. These include structuring and organizing ideas, ensuring economy of text, and providing basic museological data that describes the object and puts it in historical context. This procedure would activate skills in the research, analysis, and synthesis of data, but also present tough decisions (with the audience in mind) about word count, readability, and what information to put in and what to leave out.

The third task was identifying suitable objects to acquire for the collections at Te Papa. It was up to Philipp to research, select, and source objects to expand the holdings related to the German Sāmoa colonial legacy at Te Papa. My hope was that this work would be informed by his research into the existing collection and the historical context of their production. The key objective was a process of materializing history (see chapter 6) and creating a small archive or collection. The curatorial challenge was to work with limited resources, such as knowledge, research time, and availability of items, and—in a context of limited vendors and markets—to make choices and curate a selection of objects. The fourth task was to present a preliminary collection proposal to Te Papa's New Zealand History and Pacific Cultures Acquisitions Committee, which took place on July 19, 2016. Philipp discussed his selection of objects with the curators and offered justifications for their inclusion in the national collection. The selection was approved to proceed to a full proposal according to the procedures of the time. The fifth task was to acquire the objects and prepare catalog records for them so they could be submitted as part of a full proposal for accessioning into Te Papa's collection. This part of the process is in progress at the time of writing.

Materializing German-Sāmoan Colonial Legacies

Philipp Schorch

As laid out in the introduction, this book draws on a collaborative ethnographic investigation of museum practices conducted through "thick participation," which implies "apprenticeship and practice, natural conversation and observation, lived experience and sensuous research."[17] The underpinning research design lent further methodological weight to the collaborative approach by advancing a cross-cultural anthropology, which is enacted at any stage and level of the anthropological inquiry: from question and method to interpretation and representation or writing.[18] Within the context of the project Materializing German-Sāmoan Colonial Legacies, this "deliberate and explicit" sharing of analytical authority across cultural boundaries,[19] which transforms the "informant" into a co-anthropologist (see chapter 3), further complicated the anthropological relationship and gave it another twist. As Sean points out, the project put me in the position, or rather positions, of collaborator, curator, and German representative, thus enabling me to slip into the roles of several of "anthropology's interlocutors" (see chapter 6). Furthermore, our subject of curatorial focus was not a common cultural group such as Māori, Tongan, or Sāmoan—which, despite their internal heterogeneous complexities and external fluid overlaps, largely frame and order museum collections and anthropological inquiries—but instead a group characterized by an inherent blend produced through a specific intertwined history and its ongoing yet evolving legacy: colonial German Sāmoa. How could I materialize this legacy from both sides?

When Sean suggested and framed the project, I was immediately reminded of a research initiative at LMU Munich. The aim of that collective exercise has been to think through materiality and connectivity as two ways of existence relating and folding into each other through things that move and thereby connect or, the other way round, connections made through things.[20] As I attempted to materialize German-Sāmoan colonial legacies, which span the globe, it seemed to me that this framework of connecting materialities and material connectivities (mat~con) was useful to think through and work with. Especially the contemporary chapter of the German-Sāmoan story is comparatively little studied and understood but increasingly gaining attention through (post)colonial debates and renegotiations on both sides of the common sphere (see chapter 6). I often asked, and keep on asking myself a single simple question: if the joint legacy has hardly entered cultural memory discourses in school education, public debate, and academic research, what is left apart from the material traces, as "performative utterances of memory," that might be detected?[21]

To address this question methodologically, I followed a threefold approach. First, I picked five objects from a limited number of items in Te Papa's collection related to the German Sāmoa colonial period (1900–1914): three photographs depicting the hoisting of the German flag, the capturing of German flags, and the hoisting of the Union Jack, a hand-held German colonial government stamp, and a Malifa schoolbook created by Sāmoan schoolchildren under the subsequent New Zealand occupation of Western Sāmoa. My main criterion was the overall narrative these objects could assist in rewriting: the beginning and end of German Sāmoa and its transition into New Zealand Sāmoa. In chapter 6, I provide details of the rehistoricizing that these material references allowed; here it suffices to present them as the historical basis from which I developed the next stage of my inquiry aiming to shape a dual historical and contemporary focus through a double German-Sāmoan/Sāmoan-German lens.

Second, I set out to trace the contemporary connections from both sides, amounting to a sort of "virtual ethnography" of "global connections," which, of course, has its shortcomings but served well within the mat~con framework.[22] On the German side, I searched for potential sites of encounter and engagements with Sāmoa: student exchange programs, development aid schemes, religious organizations, tattoo fairs and studios, rugby and other sports events, travel agencies and museums. Remarkably, in the digitized collections accessible via the websites of ethnographic museums in Germany, I found only one contemporary item: a comb of Michel Tuffery's *Siamani Samoa* series (discussed in detail in chapter 6), at the Museum Fünf Kontinente in Munich.[23] On the one hand, this paucity further highlighted the significance of our initiative. On the other, it brought me in touch with Sāmoan artists and their art works as contemporary material traces, which at the same time dissected the very legacy I attempted to understand and materialize. This discovery spurred me to research and contact three Sāmoan artists—Yuki Kihara, Rosanna Raymond, and Leafa Wilson—to engage with their efforts to do the same as I did, just through different methods of analysis and modes of expression. I felt like crossing paths with other interlocutors of anthropology. This discovery also had implications for the curatorial scope of the project given that its initial anthropological-historical focus shifted into the realm of contemporary art, and thus brought Nina on board.

At the third level, I switched from tracing to making, enacting and forging connections. Within the broader scheme of things, this change of methodological register reflected my understanding of anthropological inquiry—(outlined in the introduction)—not merely as a form of detached representation of, but also as an active intervention in the field under scrutiny, that is, as being conceptualized and performed not as "an ethnography *of* global connections"[24] (emphasis added) but as one *as* and *through* global connections. In the context of this project and collecting contemporary items, this means that the chosen objects are inherently mobile and thus function as traveling media both symbolizing and enacting the various connections between Germany and Sāmoa.

The first object is a set of stamps purchased on the online auction site Ebay in 2016 (plate 1). The stamps commemorate the sixth anniversary of Sāmoa's independence, gained in 1962, and depict German and English characters associated with the prior colonial period: two major German figures who shaped the commercial and colonial beginning of the German-Sāmoan legacy, impresario Fritz Marquardt and governor Dr. Wilhelm Solf (see chapter 6), as well as John C. Williams, first missionary to visit Sāmoa for the London Missionary Society, and Thomas Trood, entrepreneur and acting British vice consul in Sāmoa when it was annexed by Germany in 1900.

Apart from their obvious material mobility, the stamps are remarkable for various reasons. Although clearly Sāmoan material expressions devoted to the celebration of Sāmoan independence, they still portray key personalities reminiscent of the colonial era yet to be overcome. Formerly condemned colonial pasts, here personified by emblematic individuals, thus become incorporated into the celebratory process of nation-building and heritage-making in the present. This ambivalence of enduring (post)colonial legacies is further complicated by Sāmoa's multiple colonizing forces and their respective afterlives (see chapter 6). In the case of these stamps, figures of both German and British Sāmoan pasts are displayed and reappropriated. Further, the term "Samoa I Sisifo" (Western Sāmoa), until 1997 the official name of the country, alludes to another ambivalent reality: the continuing separation of the two Sāmoas.

The second object, also a set of stamps, was identified on the online auction site Silvia De Carlo of Milano, Italy, and purchased on Philipp's behalf by Te Papa in 2016 (plate 2). The stamp on the left depicts Prince Otto von Bismarck, the first chancellor of the German Empire, between 1871 and 1890; the one on the right shows the warship SMS *Adler*, which engaged in gunboat diplomacy during the Sāmoan crisis and was destroyed in 1899 by a cyclone at anchor in Apia, Sāmoa. Both stamps are devoted to the Treaty of Berlin in 1899, which was to resolve what was termed the Sāmoan problem between the imperial powers of Germany, the United Kingdom, and the United States, but ultimately led to the Tripartite Convention of 1899, through which Sāmoa became partitioned into a German colony and a U.S. American territory (see chapter 6). Spanning both stamps is one picture of the Brandenburg Gate, the iconic site and architectural feature that has become the key symbol of both German separation (after World War II and during the Cold War) und the fall of the Berlin Wall and inner-German border in 1989, leading to reunification in 1990.

These two stamps, far from being tiny and insignificant items, materialize and reenact complex histories, relationships, and imaginations. On the one hand, they are dedicated—again from within postcolonial Sāmoa—to one hundred years of (post)colonial relations between Sāmoa and Germany. On the other hand, the stamps also refer to the shared destiny of division and potential reunification.[25] Although this has been achieved on the German side, the Sāmoan side remains divided as Sāmoa and American Sāmoa. When the stamps are taken apart for individual use, the Brandenburg Gate is torn apart, thereby not reseparating Germany but instead reenacting the ongoing separation of the two Sāmoas.

The third object is a coin, identified on the online auction site Ebay and purchased from Continental Coin and Jewellery Co. in California, again on Philipp's behalf by Te Papa in 2016 (plate 3). On the front side, the coin portrays Dr. Wilhelm Solf, the governor of Western Sāmoa between 1900 and 1910, dressed in a Prussian uniform of the Wilhelminian era and standing in front of a Sāmoan backdrop, scenery dotted with fale (living and meeting houses) and palm trees. On the back side is an imprint of the coat of arms of "Samoa I Sisifo," or Western Sāmoa, still the official name of the country in 1980 when the coin was issued, including the motto "Faavae I Le Atua Samoa" (Sāmoa is founded on God).

Like the stamps, the coin is an official dedication to the German-Sāmoan legacy, once again launched from the Sāmoan side, by rehonouring the former colonial governor, Dr. Wilhelm Solf (see chapter 6). Initially, this seemingly neocolonial celebration of a colonial past in the purportedly postcolonial present appears odd, even inauthentic. Yet, a close look at the coat of arms on the back of the coin reveals that Sāmoanness—whatever this might entail at the level of lived practice and performed life—can neither be separated into neatly terminated historical stages nor hermetically sealed from other cultural influences. The Christian Atua (God), symbolized by the cross above the coat of arms, is just as integral to contemporary Sāmoa as is the former colonial governor of German Sāmoa. Both embody histories of change, caused through Christianization and colonization, which continue to inform Sāmoan lives. A simple coin, then, materializes the inherent blend and external malleability of Sāmoanness.

The fourth object is a second commemorative coin, acquired from the Münzenhandlung Brom in Berlin, Germany, in 2016 (figure 5.1). On its front is a rendition of the technological evolution of 175 years of German railways illustrated through the contrast between historical and modern trains and train stations. On the back, "Samoa" has replaced "Samoa I Sisifo," which became the country's official name in 1997, before this coin was issued in 2010. The coat of arms and the motto "Faavae I Le Atua Samoa" are the same as on the coin in plate 3.

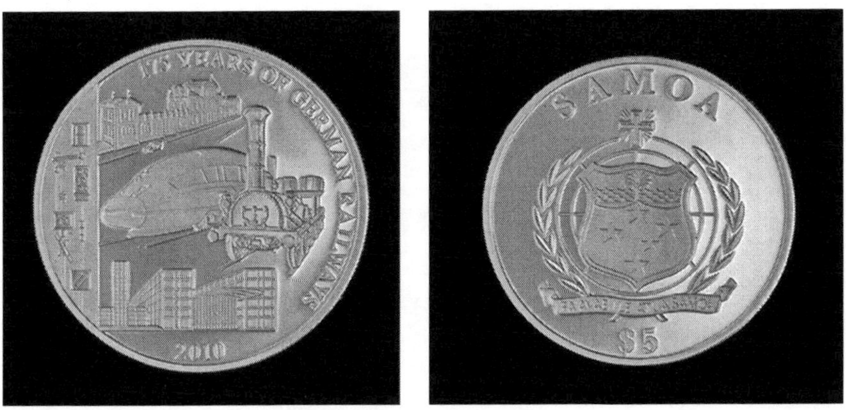

Figure 5.1 Commemorative Coin, 5 Tala (Samoa, 2010): "175 Years of German Railways." Te Papa Reg. No: TMP031576

Although contemporary Sāmoa has no railways, the coin speaks to its former German industrialization:

> In the late 19th and early 20th centuries a number of plantations were established by German settlers. Several of these had their own narrow gauge railway systems. These continued to operate after the occupation by New Zealand forces in 1914, but following the liquidation of the remaining German companies in 1916 the plantations languished and the railways fell into disuse.[26]

As is true of the first coin, a particular aspect of the German-Sāmoan legacy—industrialization, which preceded and developed alongside colonization—is reappropriated from the Sāmoan side and incorporated into the self-fashioning of the nation. German railways, like the Brandenburg Gate, stand for something broader: here it is the pursuit of the ethos of economic development, progress, and modernization rather than a longing for Sāmoan reunification.

The fifth object is a beer bottle label, purchased on the online auction site Hood.de in 2016 (plate 4). The label promotes the lager beer brand Vailima at a time when it was produced by Western Samoa Breweries in Western Sāmoa, before 1997, and "brewed and bottled under German Management." That Germany's industrial influence on Sāmoa should include its beer heritage is no surprise. What is interesting, though, is that the expertise and skill associated with German beer brewing is here used to bolster a Sāmoan brand.

The global entanglements and the reach of Vailima, as a Sāmoan beer and commodity, become even more intriguing in light of recent news, from March 7, 2018, when Samoa Breweries (the corporate successor of Western Samoa Breweries, which celebrated its fortieth anniversary in 2018) "announced a major breakthrough in as far as exporting the taste of Samoa—Vailima—to the world. Vailima Beer will soon be available in the United States." The "taste of Samoa" will be available in Hawaiʻi and along the U.S. Pacific coast in California and Washington State, which are home to diasporic Sāmoan communities. The national sales manager, Aumua George Avia, explained to the *Samoa Observer*: "We know certainly that there's a lot of Samoans who used to leave [*sic*] here in Samoa and in American Samoa that have moved to the U.S, this is about taking a bit of home with you and keeping it there to the U.S.

with yourself." A bottle of beer thus transforms from a commercial commodity into a marker of identity, "a bit of home," that can be taken along to reconnect the knots in the global net of Sāmoan relations.[27]

The sixth object, a pennant and pin, were given to Philipp by the Hamburg-Samoanischer Club in 2016 (plate 5). The pennant functions like an identity card for the club. The pin materializes and symbolizes the broader environment in which this cultural organization operates and the purpose to which it is committed: Deutsch-Samoanische Freundschaft (German-Sāmoan Friendship) embodied in the crossed national flags of Germany and Sāmoa.

The club's main activities, such as the South Pacific Fashion Show, the Polynesian Festival Islands Night, and the attendance of the Rugby World Cup qualifier between both countries in 2018,[28] might be easily discarded as staged and "inauthentic" cultural performances culpable of the perpetuation of stereotypical representations and imagery. Yet a closer look reveals that the club's chairwoman is Maria Pein, of Sāmoan descent, and its activities in the name of German-Sāmoan friendship are officially supported and recognized by the Honorary Consulate of the Independent State of Samoa. The Hamburg-Samoanischer Club thus allows for a Sāmoan presence from within Germany to be reenacted for the wider purpose of cross-cultural diplomacy. The dance ensemble Teuila, far from being reduced to a clichéd misappropriation of "authentic" Sāmoan cultural practices, is instead uplifted to a state affair through which the German-Sāmoan colonial legacy becomes partially re-performed as friendship. The pennant and the pin, then, can be seen as mobile material markers of this transforming relationship.

The seventh object, a postcard, was identified on the online auction site Ebay and purchased on Philipp's behalf by Te Papa in 2016 (plate 6). It promotes a Völkerschau ("ethnic show" or "human zoo"), a widespread form of entertainment, organized by entrepreneurial figures such as Fritz Marquardt (featured on the set of stamps presented in object 1), in which colonized (or otherwise "exotic") people and places were museologized and displayed in European and U.S. metropolitan settings for the colonizing and "civilizing" citizenry. In this case, however, "Unsere neuen Landsleute" (Our new compatriots) rather than "noble savages" are introduced following the incorporation of Sāmoa into imperial Germany (see chapter 6).[29] Given the postcard's iconic status, Philipp was immediately attracted by the opportunity to include it in our collecting effort aimed at materializing German-Sāmoan colonial legacies. It turned out to be a reproduction rather than a genuine article. The trade in genuine and fake postcards is testament to the interest among collectors in Germany's colonial past that continues to loom large in the contemporary imagination as part of the colonial legacy. This past is recognized, commodified, and appropriated by business people.

The eighth object—a patch labeled Bungaswehr—is a contemporary artwork by Sāmoan-German artist Leafa Wilson (aka Olga Krause) and part of her ongoing project, *Ich Heisse Olga Hedwig Krause—Deutsche Kuenstlerin* (My name is Olga Hedwig Krause—German artist), addressing the German-Sāmoan colonial legacy through a Sāmoan-German lens (plate 7). "Bunga" is a racist expression for a person of color, especially a Pacific Islander, in Aotearoa New Zealand, which is here reworked into "Bundeswehr," the German armed forces, further symbolized through the Bundesadler, or German eagle.[30] The item was acquired by Te Papa after Philipp established contact with Leafa aka Olga in the context of the collecting project.

The last object, *Them and Us,* a German-Sāmoan coproduction between German choreographer and performance artist Jochen Roller (Berlin) and Sāmoan interdisciplinary artist Yuki Kihara (Apia), is a mixture of hybrid choreography and film (plate 8). It explores the history of German colonization of Sāmoa and its ramifications in contemporary German society, staging a "folkoloniales Spektakel" to rewrite the German anthropological viewpoint of its former colony.[31] This digital poster promoting the performance was acquired by Te Papa after Philipp contacted Yuki Kihara about the German-Sāmoan project.

What these collected items did was, first, to bring contemporary objects into dialogue with the historical (and rehistoricized) objects already held at Te Papa, thus materializing the evolving nature of the German-Sāmoan legacy in the present. Second, they enabled a double perspective, a simultaneous German-Sāmoan/Sāmoan-German lens. Although I did not have an external Sāmoan collaborator to help shape this lens on more levels, I argue that we nevertheless made headway at the level of the object itself. All collected items, apart from the postcard (object 7), were either material expressions launched in Sāmoa, or even by Sāmoan people from within Germany, such as through the Hamburg-Samoanischer Club (item 6). The artwork in particular not only turns—at least partially—the overwhelming German-Sāmoan colonial past into a Sāmoan-German utopian present and future, they also function as interventions by artists, as interlocutors of anthropology, to reframe and add new layers to historical understandings and their reverberations in the present. Further, the Sāmoan artists and their traveling artistic expressions contribute to the global circulation of imagery, which was for a long time very much dominated by the other side of the colonial equation. Consequently, these "art works need not be taken as objects of analysis, as sources to be interpreted. Rather, they can be seen as interpretations *in their own right*," as Nicholas Thomas and Diane Losche argue. These artists, then, should not be seen as "informants but as co-interpreters of the issues that preoccupy anthropologists and historians."[32] Third, that some items were purchased in Germany and Europe via online auction sites, and that others were acquired on my behalf through online dealerships in Aotearoa New Zealand, Australia, and the United States, attests to the global ramification of the German-Sāmoan legacy and its material manifestation. The online narrative, in which the collected objects will eventually feature, lifts this empirical reality to the level of conceptual design by operating as a virtual and mobile expression of, and intervention in, the reshaping of the intertwined history into a shared one.

The Double Lens—A Shared History?

Nina Tonga

As we have seen, the double lens attempted to represent the perspectives of people from two countries that were and remain connected by colonialism and its ongoing legacy. But as the sole external collaborator who identifies as German—however complex this marker is, and whatever it actually entails—Philipp represents, at the level of identity, only half of this double lens. This raises a major question: who is providing a Sāmoan perspective? The absence of an external Sāmoan collaborator has been problematic throughout the project because collections are ultimately a reflection of the curator or collector. Philipp's selection of objects is fundamentally a reflection of his personal and professional view, and ultimately presents a single perspective. This poses several important questions: would a Sāmoan collaborator select the same objects? Would this person have a different set of criteria and principles guiding their collecting? How would they navigate the multivocal nature of this history? How would their ethnicity and cultural experiences influence their selection?

These questions are important because they highlight the partiality of this curatorial project, and acknowledge that the German-Sāmoan colonial legacy consists of contested voices, perspectives, and positions that are intertwined but not necessarily connected by a singular shared history. Christine Winter states the importance of seeing the German-Sāmoan colonial legacy in its plurality, as polyvocal and fluid legacies: "The histories of German-Pacific Islanders and Germans, including me, are intertwined, but they are not automatically 'shared' histories. 'Shared' histories have to be forged, made and renegotiated continuously."[33] In regard to this project, then, the negotiation of histories must grow from both sides, the Sāmoan and German communities, rather than be imposed by one on the other.[34] The absence of a collector-curator from the Sāmoan community has thus affected and limited the full potential of mana taonga and co-collecting. A Sāmoan collaborator would have afforded a sense of authority and allowed a Sāmoan to be the author of their own memories and stories. Although Sāmoan artists contributed individual works, they did not have the same broad agency to negotiate and decide how to represent the German-Sāmoan legacies within the overall project.

German-Sāmoan Legacies in Contemporary Pacific Art

Nina Tonga

The collection of art and ephemera from contemporary Sāmoan artists in this project attempted to create a dialogue with historical objects to address the evolving nature of the German-Sāmoan legacies. However, this dialogue exists in many different forms and for many Sāmoans because the history is inextricably entwined with the family *gafa* (genealogy). The past is in the present (and future), as described by Sāmoan politician and writer Misa Telefoni Retzlaff in a speech to a German audience in 2011: "the German legacy in Samoa is an enduring legacy. It is both historical and contemporary because it is a story that continues and still has no end in sight."[35] Retzlaff's comment points to the contemporary context of German-Sāmoan legacies as part of everyday life. For example, the daily performance of the Royal Samoa Police Band, marching to Government House in Apia for the ceremonial raising of the flag while playing Viennese brass-band music, continues a tradition that harks back to the German Sāmoa colonial era.[36] Within Sāmoan cuisine, the *pani siamani* (German bun) was heavily influenced by German pastries. Although disparate examples, they demonstrate the many manifestations of German-Sāmoan legacies and provide a wider context for the work of contemporary Sāmoan artists, who are just one component of contemporary culture that Philipp privileged above other forms. This decision was most likely influenced by existent collection items and the overall time and resource limitations of our collection plan.

Within the project, Philipp's selection of art works materializes contemporary German-Sāmoan narratives. Three artists were chosen in this co-collection initiative: Rosanna Raymond, Yuki Kihara, and Leafa Wilson. All of them have addressed the history of German Sāmoa as subject matter and have used different artistic strategies to reclaim, rewrite, and re-present these histories (see chapter 6). During the selection process, it became evident that the collection of work of contemporary artists adds another set of considerations that relate directly to their representation as artists independent of the project. In the broader scheme of museum activities, such thematic collecting inevitably cuts across curatorial and disciplinary territories.[37] The selection criteria for the artists was largely thematic. However, the potential future use of these objects outside of this context was not given much thought. Determining future use is always difficult, but it encourages the collector to ensure that the artist is represented in the best way possible. Some of the curatorial considerations include the number of art works selected to represent a project, their display potential, and where this work fits in the artists' oeuvre. Although Philipp considered the display potential of the artworks, in the spirit of mana taonga, I refrained from enforcing this full set of curatorial concerns to respect the ethos of the project. This has resulted in a partial representation of the selected artists' initiatives that can be resolved with future collecting, but this is not guaranteed.

In terms of existing collection relationships, the chosen works contribute to Te Papa's current holdings of contemporary Pacific art by addressing a relatively underexplored area in Pacific art history. Issues of identity have been central to explorations of Pacific art since the early 1990s, especially among a generation of New Zealand–born Pacific artists. It is within this context that Sāmoan artists explored the colonial histories of Sāmoa, including the legacies of German Sāmoa.[38] As we have seen, however, this art history informed neither the selection of artists in this project nor the inclusion of contemporary art within the collection plan. One of the first artists to explore this in a gallery context was the Sāmoan-German artist Nick Netzler in the exhibition *Unsere Neuen Landsleute* (Our New Countrymen) in 2002.[39] The exhibition involved photographs taken of historical images of Germans in Sāmoa held at the Linden-Museum in Stuttgart, Germany. Speaking of these photographs, Netzler commented, "I've always seen these types of images in our family." Netzler's familiarity repositioned these photographs not as colonial products, but rather as part of his Sāmoan-German genealogy and cultural experience. Netzler's pioneering exhibition reclaimed colonial photographs and demonstrated the possibilities to see and imagine alternative histories. Louis Owens describes this in relation to colonial photographs:

> This is perhaps the greatest paradox of colonial photography. The hand on the shutter and the eye behind the aperture may belong to the colonial acquisitor, and the purpose may well be to document a vanishing culture and in doing so participate deeply in that project of cultural erasure, but the artifact has the power ultimately to help ensure a cultural coherence, to play a crucial role in giving a people a picture of themselves. Admittedly, the picture Native people inherit in such instances is filtered through the dominant, invasive culture, and the frame that defines can obfuscate greatly, but nonetheless what adheres is the living air of a people and a culture, an air visible to those looking from within rather than without. My Yurok friend sees her Yurok family, not vanishing Americans.[40]

Artists, like historians, are able to create new frames for history and to position themselves within or outside this. As Owens explained, they are also charged with the power to counter existing narratives and representations. The artists informing this project—Rosanna Raymond, Yuki Kihara, and Leafa Wilson—are connected by a common subject matter, but they also represent three distinctive generational perspectives that are shaped by ethnicity, location, and point in time, among other factors. Each offers a new understanding of what constitutes German-Sāmoan legacies. To illustrate this point, I discuss the work by Leafa Wilson aka Olga Krause (see object 8 and chapter 6).

Leafa Wilson materializes her German-Sāmoan legacies by using her German birth name, Olga Krause. This honors her late father Charles (Sale) Krause and readdresses a specific history of German-Sāmoan people in Sāmoa during the German colonial rule. She explains:

> Here I claim my 5.125% Germanness and do so without hesitation, for it is this part where Germany has extended her boundaries to encompass me. Notions of the fixity of race are destabilised within this [my] work. Not for the purposes of attack or critique of colonial presence. Instead, the *Germanness* that was not afforded my Grandfather, Augustine Krause and my father, Charles Augustine Krause, is therefore being claimed in this work.[41]

Wilson asserts and claims her Germanness as a revisionist strategy to counter the circumstances her forefathers had been subjected to. During German colonial rule, individuals of German-Sāmoan descent were not afforded dual heritage, but instead had to apply to be granted European status. Those thus categorized fulfilled certain criteria that included having the "correct" blood quota and literacy in European languages, and were expected to maintain "high" standards of behavior.[42] Those who were not considered European, were categorized as Sāmoan and subjugated to different regulations. As a consequence, they most likely had different cultural experiences. However, as Sāmoan academic Malama Meleiseia notes, it is likely that those categorized as Sāmoan saw this as an assertion of their own Indigenous and cultural superiority—and as proof of the inability of Europeans to acquire it.[43]

Wilson's ambivalence regarding her German genealogy and family history is reflected in her practice as an artist and curator, through the multiple names and identities she employs. By mining her ancestry, she asserts the right to claim her fluid identities to speak back, specifically to her German-Sāmoan heritage. In her project, *Ich heisse Olga Hedwig Krause—Deutsche Kuenstlerin*, she has produced a series of prints using her New Zealand birth certificate that names her parents and their place of residence, Tokoroa. These prints and her subsequent works, including the Bungaswehr patch that Philipp selected for this project (see plate 7), reveal that German-Sāmoan legacies operate in personal and public spaces that change between generations. Furthermore, the inclusions and exclusions of the past continue to have implications that are felt and negotiated in the present.

Reflections on Materializing German-Sāmoan Colonial Legacies

Sean Mallon

The survey of the current holdings of Te Papa related to the German Sāmoa colonial period was wide, but the final selection of objects that Philipp chose can be scrutinized. Why did he choose to work with three photographs and only two three-dimensional objects? Why the stamp and not the briefcase? Why the photograph of the flag and not one of the several physical flags in the collection (see chapter 6)? Throughout the development of the project, I did not want to compromise the process in which we were supposed to be privileging mana taonga and allowing Philipp to lead the way. In the process of developing this chapter, I noticed that he left these questions about selection largely unanswered, apart from pointing to the main criterion, which was the overall narrative these objects assisted in retelling: the beginning and end of German Sāmoa, and its transition into New Zealand Sāmoa.

What does the selection reveal or obscure about Philipp's process of choosing? How can we discuss these curatorial choices? What do they tell us about the limits and politics of co-curating history? On reflection, a key influence in the selection was the time frames involved. Time is a finite resource in institutions and sets limits on mana taonga and projects of collaboration. It inevitably influences the development and management of all kinds of museum projects, including this one. As curators, we should not be surprised: time often influences curatorial choices. As one of my colleagues has said, "we don't have the luxury of doing our best work." This is not to say that we do not do our best to work to high standards, but rather that every task has a limited time frame attached to it. The search for a fact or snippet of information that might clarify a point cannot be allowed to run on and on. As an academic, Philipp had a defined period in which he needed to complete this project as well as other competing facets of his fieldwork. We could devote only a limited amount of curatorial time to supervising this project, but any deadline we set was arbitrary.

This project—which I conceived and Philipp developed—did not exist in a vacuum. The Materializing German-Sāmoan Colonial Legacies

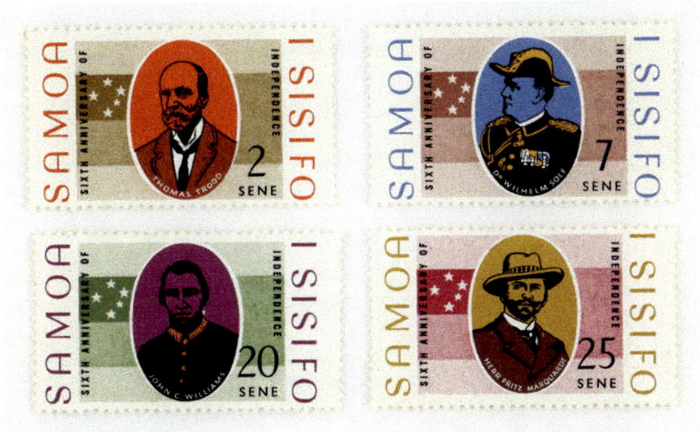

Plate 1 Postage Stamps (Samoa, 1968), "Samoa I Sisifo: Sixth Anniversary of Independence." Set of four stamps, Te Papa Registration Number (Te Papa Reg. No): TMP031573.

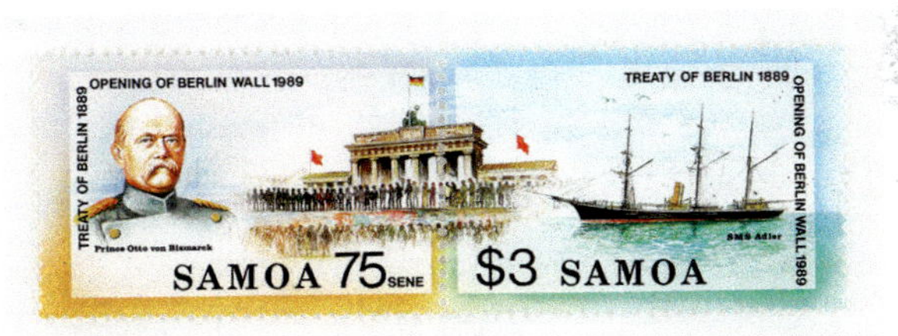

Plate 2 Postage Stamps (Samoa, 1989), "Opening of Berlin Wall, 1989" and "Treaty of Berlin, 1889." Set of two stamps, Te Papa Reg. No: TMP031574.

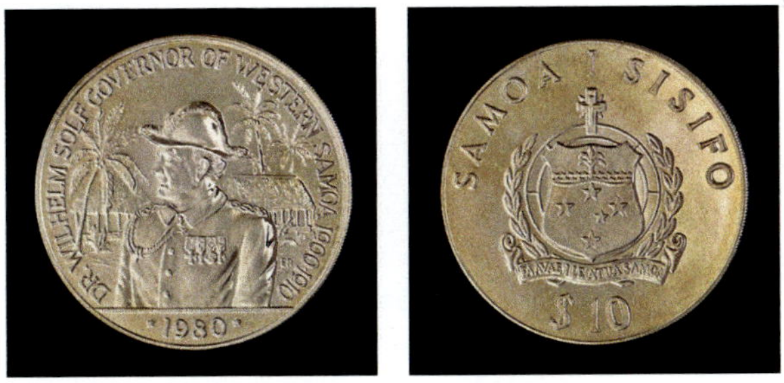

Plate 3 Commemorative Coin, 10 Tala (Samoa, 1980): "Dr. Wilhelm Solf Governor of Western Samoa 1900–1910." Te Papa Reg. No: TMP031575.

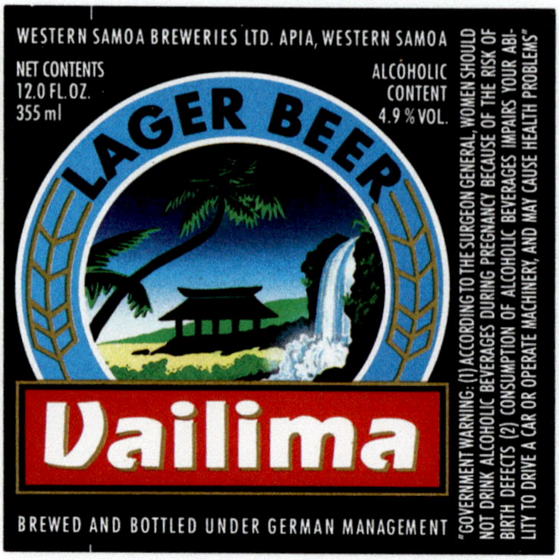

Plate 4 Beer bottle label (Apia, Western Samoa, late twentieth century): "Vailima," Western Samoa Breweries, Te Papa Reg. No: TMP031577.

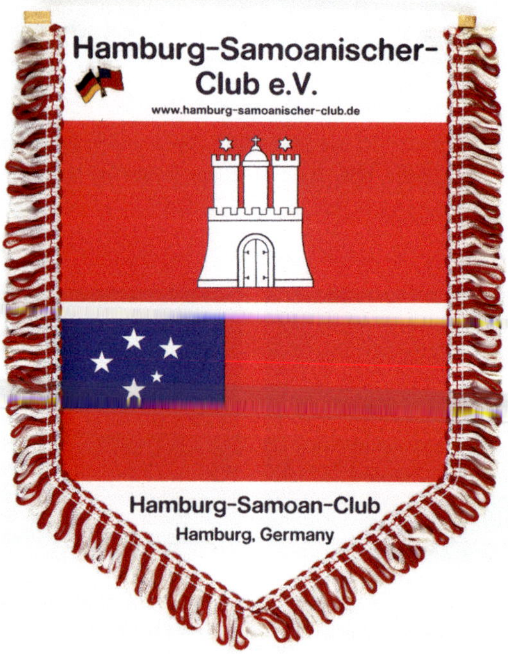

Plate 5 Pennant and pin (Hamburg, 2016): "Hamburg-Samoanischer Club e.V.," Te Papa Reg. No: TMP031578.

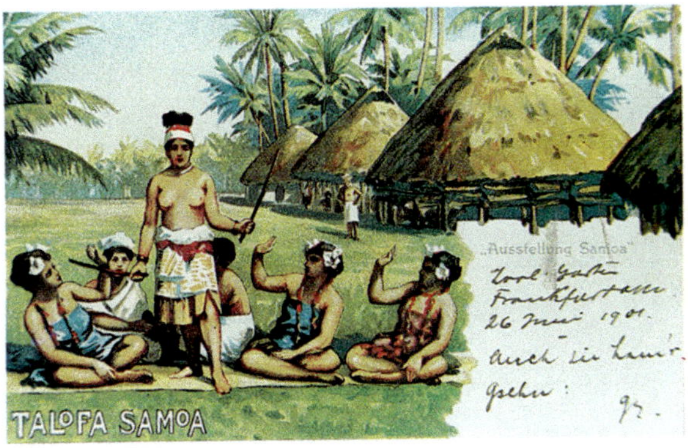

Plate 6 Reproduction of postcard (Germany, 1903): "Talofa Samoa (Ausstellung: Unsere Neuen Landsleute)." Te Papa Reg. No: TMP031579.

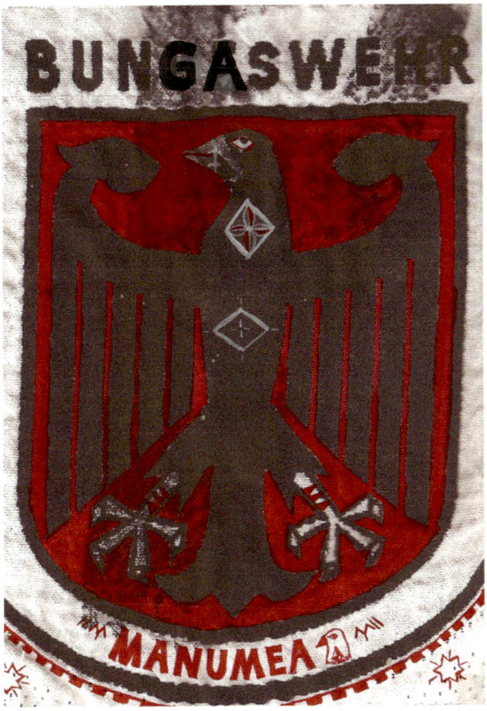

Plate 7 Patch (Aotearoa New Zealand, 2005): "Bungaswehr," Te Papa Reg. No: TMP031580.

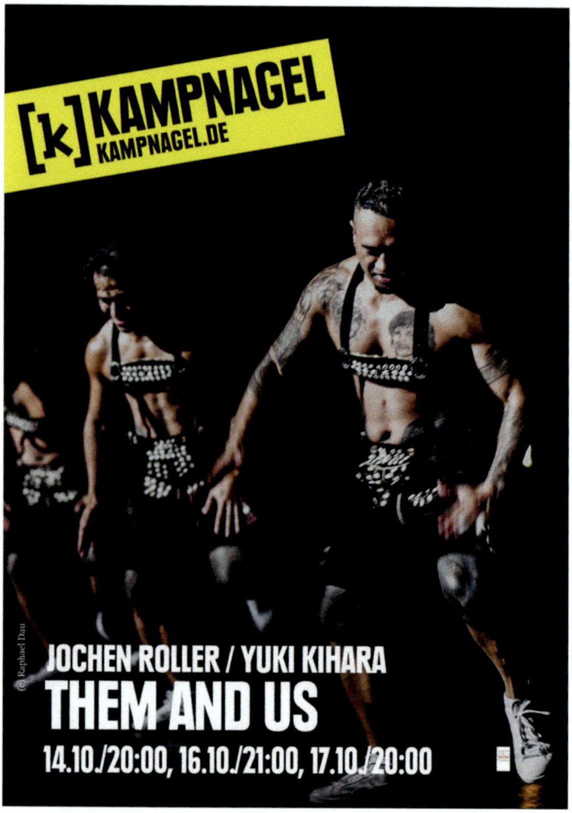

Plate 8 Digital poster (Germany, 2015): "Them and Us," Te Papa Reg. No: TMP031581.

initiative had a starting point but may not have an identifiable end point. As it was progressing, it was feeding into, and articulating with, other projects and centers of knowledge production in other parts of the world. The project has been part of institutional and individual concerns. It has enhanced an existing resource for Te Papa (its online collections database), created a resource for Te Papa (new collection items), and advanced our individual curatorial interests in German-Sāmoan history and the museology of co-collecting, both of which bring tangible benefits to the museum and potentially increase our curatorial credentials in our field. However, from the start, the project was also entangled with Philipp's career trajectory in the European-German academy, and was a resource in his desire and need to establish himself in his chosen fields of anthropology and museology. Throughout the project's development, pressure on Philipp (and us as curators) has been considerable to advance the work to various stages of completion so that Philipp could present our ideas at European academic conferences and then develop the text for this book. His presence at these conferences in turn supported the research agendas of other individuals and institutions, and so on. These circumstances shape the nature of the collaboration and its many outcomes. We may set limits on the collaborative process but we cannot always control them.

Even with the in-house museological processes we tried to stay within the spirit of mana taonga, resisting the urge to control or direct them. Proceedings took their own course. A key example involved the development of the web summaries for the online catalogue records. Overall, they were well researched and highlighted important historical details and were written in a reflexive style (see chapter 6). However, Philipp chose to work outside the well-established structures of the web summary examples I provided him. I would have preferred that they had a basic structure and subheadings for each major paragraph, and I am not comfortable with their length and lack of basic catalogue detail. Guidelines are well established for writing content for the web and for specific audiences, whether a blog format, academic article, or catalogue record. However, Te Papa's website team made no comment on this point when presented with Philipp's work. His determination to work beyond the scope of my curatorial preferences is not unusual in our work with communities, and in the spirit of mana taonga why should not communities work within the structures they are most comfortable with? This type of misalignment highlights how collaboration can and will cause variations in the products museums produce, be they exhibitions, labels, catalogue records, or publications. In this case, the information is well researched and accurate, but the inconsistency relates rather to Philipp's disregarding of the web summary structure, and how audiences and online readerships interact with online content and information. In other forms of museum productions, such as exhibitions, education programs, tours, books, and digital media, variations in content, accuracy, and approach are variables that need to be negotiated with content co-creators. Are curators ready to let go of this aspect of their work in collaborative curating? It turns out I was not. In the interest of readability, especially on handheld devices such as mobile phones, I edited Philipp's text, inserting subheadings, paragraphing, and breaking up long passages.

One of the aims of our co-collecting and co-curating has been to decenter the power of the curator. So far, however, and in practice, I have come to acknowledge that the curatorial role brings with it a crucial skill set that is informed by and underpins a range of key museological practices. It is also a role connected to other museum specialists, each of whom has their own skill sets. Together we know, for example, what is held in collections, the possibilities and limits of display, effective interpretative methods, language and text lengths, and what types of content and in which formats audiences will engage with, and learn from in exhibitions, both physical and online. But in bringing these skills and specialist knowledge to bear in collaborative projects, to what extent do we underline or undermine the "co" in co-collecting and co-curating? And then the matter of the budget and who holds the purse strings. It is one thing to develop and build collections collaboratively, but how do we finance and ensure their broad utility beyond the point of acquisition in the sphere of public display and access?

The objects Philipp selected to expand the collection are also worth examining. Overall, I was comfortable with the form the selection took, as was the acquisitions committee. The selection draws our attention to some surprising aspects of the German-Sāmoan colonial legacy and how it is materialized in the contemporary world, spanning a date range that reaches into 2019, the year of writing. The selection featured commemorative coins, postage stamps, postcards, contemporary artworks, and even a beer bottle label. Philipp's earlier point about the objects being inherently mobile is a pertinent one in that they are all forms of well-established collectibles that circulate around the world on specific markets. We can look cynically on the characteristics of the commemorative coins and the trade they are part of, and in which history, people, and events are reified as part of a profit-making enterprise dictated by overseas collectors—an enterprise that offers hardly any local circulation and possibly limited understanding of the events depicted on the coin. On the other hand, the postage stamps and beer bottle label do offer insight into aspects of German-Sāmoan heritage that passes from hand to hand in Sāmoa and the Sāmoan diaspora every day. Contemporary artworks come with their own set of circumstances of production and have implications for other collections in the museum and future projects. The postcard is a fake, a discovery we only made on its delivery (see plate 6). It is a poor photographic reproduction of a genuine historic postcard, which the vendor or the person the vendor collected it from has signed in blue ballpoint pen with the note "xxxxx". The image reproduces an important historical artwork, but the postcard is just as interesting on its own for the way it finds its way into the marketplace and preys on the interest of the unwary collector of German Sāmoa, duping them (us) into making a purchase hardly worth seeking a refund for. Despite its dubious quality and originality, it is nonetheless a legitimate part of the legacy, the materialization and commodification of German Sāmoa.

To be fair to ourselves, time was again a factor in the assembling of this group of objects. Philipp's time frame meant that his search for new items was restricted to online vendors or dealers he could physically visit during his fieldwork in Aotearoa New Zealand and at home in Germany. A longer time frame might have allowed for the development of other collecting strategies and outreach activities that could have productively involved German-Sāmoan families, as the recent work of German-Sāmoan photo researcher Tony Brunt has demonstrated.[44] One wonders what Philipp would have identified if the project had the time and resources to establish collecting activities in the Sāmoa Islands. I had a glimpse of the possibilities when a friend showed me photographs of wrought iron gate fittings he had salvaged from the rubbish when a German colonial-era building was demolished in Sāmoa. This is a tangible trace of the colonial presence. Future projects could shed light on many intangible and "hidden in plain view" traces of German Sāmoa. On reflection, this focus on the possibilities of the non-Indigenous materialization of the German Sāmoa colonial legacy, such as wrought iron gate fittings, highlights again the creeping of the project from one where Philipp was representing a German point of view and legacy, to one where he was attempting to "materialize this legacy from both sides." He assumed a role as observer and anthropologist gathering or curating Indigenous materials and people (Kihara, Raymond, Wilson), and their artwork and analysis into his purview. Had we designed the project to work with artists in a creative and new exploratory process from the outset, the outcome might have been more collaborative and had different results.

Last but not least, our initial disagreement over the title of the project is worth unpacking as well. I titled it Materializing German-Sāmoan Colonial Legacies. Philipp disagreed and preferred Materializing Sāmoan-German Colonial Legacies. If mana taonga drives our work, who determines what the project is called, even if I named it to begin with? This debate played out throughout the course of the initiative and in some ways was a rather academic discussion. Still, how has the title influenced this project, and in what ways? Has it actually had an impact on what we have collected? The naming in this case could be seen as just a case of semantics, but it is still a mechanism of museological practice that can obscure as much about a topic as it might reveal.

This is Philipp again. I refrained for quite a while from calling the project German-Sāmoan because I wanted to involve, study, and understand the Sāmoan side of the equation. I was also reluctant to limit the focus to the colonial legacy, because I felt that the intertwined and potentially shared history should not be reduced to the colonial dimension, however overwhelmingly powerful and devastating that was. It took some back and forth, but ultimately I was convinced when Sean pointed out that colonialism founded the relationship and that the word "legacy" implies all events and persons that came after. What we really did, then, was materializing German-Sāmoan colonial legacies.

Co-Collecting as Community Engagement and Method of Collaboration

Nina Tonga and Philipp Schorch

Nina: Co-collecting, as a strategy of collection development, can help strengthen old and create new relationships with Pacific communities, which are crucial to ensure that we are developing meaningful collections that respond to the changing needs of Pacific peoples. Within co-collecting projects, relationships such as those established by Philipp with the three artists—Yuki Kihara, Rosanna Raymond, and Leafa Wilson—are activated for the duration of the project. At the completion of a project, it is plausible that we as curators will continue to maintain and reactivate these relationships for different reasons. The reasons can be administrative and curatorial, given that the collecting of works, particularly from contemporary artists, establishes a responsibility to continue representing their oeuvre. This ongoing responsibility reveals the ways in which co-collecting and collaboration can shape our existing plans and in some instances introduce new collecting priorities. In this case, we are faced with the dilemma of whether we continue collecting the work of these artists within the thematic collection areas identified by Philipp. Do we address the gaps in the art history created by his selective collection of artists engaging with these German-Sāmoan legacies? Clearly, co-collecting has parameters of time and resource that will dictate how we are able to manage the myriad relationships moving forward. One of our ongoing challenges of co-collecting will be to create a sustainable model that allows collecting to move beyond a temporary project toward long-term collection development.

Philipp: The museum, James Clifford reminds us, "is an inventive, globally and locally *translated* form, no longer anchored to its modern origins in Europe."[45] Curating and collecting may similarly be recalled and remade through collaborative relationships with communities and "experiments in culture," as we have seen.[46] What can ethnographic museums in the Americas and Europe learn from these distinctive forms of Indigenous museology that are emerging across the Pacific and reshaping museological conventions?[47] If we understand "coloniality as an epistemology, as a politics of knowledge,"[48] and the museum as a "highly contested field of epistemological systems,"[49] then co-collecting (and co-interpreting and cowriting) offers us a concrete way to produce "postcolonial knowledge" of "colonial objects."[50] Co-collecting, in other words, enables us to create, or co-create, knowledge across epistemological (and ontological) boundaries, which do remain, however porous, fluid and shifting.

In the context of ethnographically studying Indigenous knowledge practices, the co-collecting project informing this chapter has contributed to the rearticulation of an "indigenous anthropology in/of

Oceania" through "the search for, production, and transformation of connections across time and space"[51]—here between Aotearoa New Zealand, Sāmoa, and Germany, both past and present. The relationship between anthropology and Indigeneity remains complicated and contested across Oceania.[52] Further, insider-outsider dichotomies are theoretically and politically upheld despite their practical impossibilities in an inescapably entangled world.[53] As soon as we assume a material rather than an ideological perspective, we detect that the German-Sāmoan colonial legacy is articulated from various positions and localities and is global in scope. And once we dig deeper into the intellectual frameworks underpinning these material expressions, as in the next chapter, we see how colonialism, anthropology, art, and Indigeneity become intertwined and potentially shared through the ethnographic condition.

CHAPTER 6

"Anthropology's Interlocutors" and the Ethnographic Condition

The previous chapter discussed the project Materializing German-Sāmoan Colonial Legacies as an expression of, and intervention in, the reshaping of the common legacy. This chapter sets out to historicize and theorize the legacy's underlying processes of anthropological interlocution, and the yet deeper underlying interpretive mode that I call "ethnographic condition." As the title indicates, the work of Edward W. Said has been instructive in this regard. Said's seminal *Orientalism* and his notion of "anthropology's interlocutors" provide useful points of departure.[1] They can and need, however, to be reframed when revisiting German-Sāmoan legacies.

Anthropology has often been seen as the handmaiden of colonialism, as a scientific enterprise developing in the shadow and service of colonial expansion. In *The Devil's Handwriting*, Georg Steinmetz takes issue with this view and convincingly argues that Said's succinct scheme—"from travelers' tales . . . colonies were created"—marked a significant break with the so-called handmaiden thesis introduced in another seminal work, *Anthropology and the Colonial Encounter*.[2] Steinmetz builds on the argument of the effects of precolonial representations—as in travel literature—on colonialism, naming it the "devil's handwriting thesis," but at the same time launches another critique of the reductionist tendencies often held against Said. "What he failed to acknowledge," Steinmetz concludes, "was that many if not most formations of ethnographic discourse are multivocal or multi-accentual." The resulting relationship between ethnographic representations and colonial policy is thus characterized, among other aspects, by "patterns of resistance and collaboration by the colonized" and "symbolic competition among colonizers."[3] Despite defining his sense of ethnographic discourse, however, Steinmetz inevitably remains within the discursive terrain of representation, both textual and visual. He neglects the "material dimension which is all too often absent from works of cultural history"— but still offers rich material examples within his discursive framework.[4] This chapter, without attempting to offer such an impressively rich historical study, changes the order of explication by putting the material first. By revisiting German-Sāmoan colonial legacies at Te Papa through the lens of material history,[5] I zoom in on a range of things as the material nexus that mediates and enacts rather than simply represents the relationship between ethnographic condition and colonial governance, and the latter's ultimate critique and subversion through contemporary art.

This brings me back to the other idea of Said, the notion of anthropology's interlocutors, which requires a brief introduction and revision with the context of the argument presented here. Said wrote in 1989 that

> there is by now a sizable literature in the Third World addressing an impassioned theoretical and practical argument to Western specialists in area studies, as well as to anthropologists and historians. The address is a part of the revisionist postcolonial effort to reclaim traditions, histories, and cultures from imperialism, and it is also a way of entering the various world discourses on an equal footing. . . . For the most part, little of this material reaches the inner chambers of and has no effect on general disciplinary or discursive discussion in metropolitan centers. Instead, the Western Africanists read African writers as source material for their research, Western Middle East specialists treat Arab or Iranian texts as primary evidence for their research, while the direct, even importunate solicitations of debate and intellectual engagement from the formerly colonized are left largely unattended.[6]

Within the context of the Pacific, this statement needs to be qualified. Much has happened since the time of Said's writing, examples being Rainer Buschmann's detection of "indigenous counterethnographies" in German New Guinea,[7] Conal McCarthy's historical study of the Board of Maori Ethnological Research and its influences on both anthropology's evolution and colonial governance radiating across Oceania,[8] and Amiria

Salmond's work on and with contemporary forms of Māori anthropology aimed at disciplinary renewal.[9] Yet Said's view on anthropology's interlocutors, which implies a mutual dialogical engagement but still reduces the colonized to be represented by the colonizer, lingers in the present, and often puts Indigeneity across Oceania at loggerheads with anthropology and its alleged scientific intrusions.[10] It might be argued that anthropology has always been enacted through interlocutions in practice, but a clear distinction between author and informant (or any other designation awarded to the studied) has been mostly upheld in writing.[11]

As we saw in chapter 5, the Materializing German-Sāmoan Colonial Legacies project has put me in the curator's and the community's shoes simultaneously, and framed me methodologically as one of anthropology's interlocutors within the overall picture. In this chapter, I continue with this positioning to analytically aim at unsettling the described dichotomous anthropological oppositions through the German-Sāmoan legacy. I show how the (pre)colonial encounter caused cross-cultural realities that had to be experienced, studied, and understood—thus shaping an ethnographic condition established through interlocutions, navigated for mutual manipulations, and permeated with a dialectics oscillating between salvage and vanishing, cooperation and resistance, stabilization and subversion. On the German colonial side, the ambivalent tension between governmentality and anthropology was personified in governors-cum-scholars, or scholarly informed governors, such as Dr. Wilhelm Solf and Dr. Erich Schultz. In the (post)colonial Sāmoan response, the same ambivalent ethnographic condition is found in contemporary art through which Sāmoan artists-cum-scholars, or scholarly informed artists, such as Yuki Kihara, Rosanna Raymond, and Leafa Wilson aka Olga Krause, speak back to and subvert racial hierarchies and other anthropological frameworks while selectively using ethnographic resources to revitalize cultural practices.

Here, "in the convergence of ethnography and art, it is the Indigenous, rather than the postmodern Western artist who has—pace Hal Foster—become the ethnographer."[12] It is in this moment and location in which and from which the overwhelming German-Sāmoan colonial past is turned—through a reverse anthropological mimicry enacted through bodies, biographies, and artistic-ethnographic interventions—into a Sāmoan-German present and future, however utopian it might be or may remain. As we shall see, returning the ethnographic gaze and rewriting the anthropological perspective paradoxically perpetuates the ethnographic condition and lends it an inescapable quality.

German-Sāmoan Colonial Material Histories at Te Papa

We now approach German-Sāmoan colonial material histories at Te Papa from a somewhat different perspective. Seemingly small material items—three photographs, a handheld stamp, and a schoolbook and banner—thus reappear as significant actors involved in large stories of global reach.

Raising the German Flag

The photograph in figure 6.1 records the raising of the imperial German flag at Mulinu'u Peninsula on the Island of Upolu in Sāmoa on March 1, 1900.[13] This was the act and moment that made imperial Germany the internationally recognized ruler of Sāmoa after years of internal strife among Sāmoan chiefly figures in response to, and association with, the colonial bickering—both diplomatically and violently—among Germany, Great Britain, and the United States aimed at carving out a share of this territorially small yet geopolitically significant piece of land in the Pacific.[14] At first sight and thought, then, the flag raising could be seen as

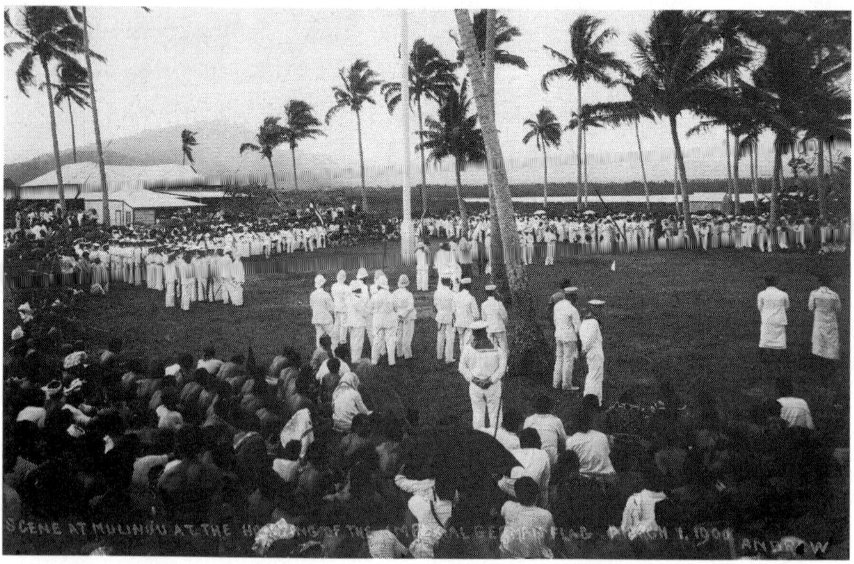

Figure 6.1 Scene at Mulinu'u Peninsula, Upolu, raising the German imperial flag, March 1, 1900, Samoa. Photograph by Thomas Andrew. Te Papa (C.001571)

reflecting these large and overwhelming forces of empire and colonialism. Sāmoa's destiny would be sealed and the whole story told. However, if we take the flag as a specific "material maker(s) of relationships," then we can zoom in on concrete "transactions and transformations" between the people and places involved.[15] What can such a view illuminate?

For example, we discover that the photograph was taken by Thomas Andrew, a New Zealand photographer who lived and worked in Sāmoa, and whose images made their way to the collection of Te Papa.[16] To a certain extent, his photos present a New Zealand perspective on the unfolding event, thus hinting at New Zealand's role in the "Samoan tangle" as another player with its own colonial ambitions. We can also discover more about the photographs' locality, Mulinu'u Peninsula. This is where the German side suffered, during the Sāmoan crisis in 1888, the "first serious defeat of an advanced white power in the Pacific" in its support of Sāmoan chief Tamasese—also proclaimed *tafa'ifa* (king)—against his opponent chief Mata'afa, who was supported by the opposing imperial powers of Great Britain and the United States.[17] Mulinu'u thus gained "sentimental" value to the German navy. It was, however, also where the same Mata'afa—following diplomatic efforts culminating in the partition of Sāmoa—morphed from German enemy to ally by being named *ali'i sili*, or paramount chief (rather than king), the governmental link between the German administration and Sāmoan people. The associated ceremony on June 8, 1901, involved—according to Sāmoan customary practices—the distribution of *'ie toga* (fine mats), thus giving a colonial procedure a distinctive flair, the aim being "to retain and defend as many elements of Samoan customs as possible without endangering German domination or the rule of difference."[18]

This brief excursion to related events taking place at the Mulinu'u Peninsula prior and after the raising of the German imperial flag hinted at the complexity of cross-cultural relations and negotiations underpinning and enacting empire and colonialism, which often failed, at least partially, in their ambition to regulate such events. The photograph shows a carefully orchestrated ceremony in which German officials, sailors, and policemen assume center stage, standing in the first row and relegating seated Sāmoans to the second row. At first sight and thought, once again, the colonial power structure seems clear cut. However, newspaper articles around the time of the event hint at "serious native dissension" and "bitter feelings of native parties,"[19] both among the

Sāmoan chiefly factions and in their relation to the German regime, which could erupt into open resistance and violent conflict at any moment when the acceptable scope of cooperation seemed overstretched. "Each ceremony," Christopher Balme observes, "for all its outward festive appearance and harmony, concealed an underlying dramatic tension and potential for disaster."[20]

Such intense friction and impending catastrophe existed even on the German side. These internal conflicts were mostly not externally communicated by, for example, a newspaper article mapping the spatial design of the ceremony and giving official voice to its protagonists. Here, the main German characters, governor Dr. Wilhelm Solf and naval Captain Hugo Emsmann, appear as holding glorifying speeches seemingly committed to a common cause.[21] Internal documents, however, reveal a major and at times vicious conflict between the actors and their interpretations of colonial governance.[22] Emsmann, being "shocked" that a civilian bureaucrat rather than a military figure would be named governor, continued to protest by even temporarily switching sides and conspiring with Mata'afa (who reappears in yet another context). Meanwhile, Solf—thanks to diplomatic skill and political connections—achieved a "victory in these skirmishes" and "successfully insisted that *he* personally raise the black-white-red flag of the empire."[23] These traces of cross-cultural transactions and mutual transformations—captured in the photograph—indicate that a German-Sāmoan flag was hoisted, not a German one. In fact, given the plurality of claims and interventions on both sides as well as the spaces between them, not just one but many flags were.

Capturing German-Sāmoan Flags

This postcard in figure 6.2, "German War Flag captured at Samoa by New Zealand Expeditionary Force," is one of a small group of items at Te Papa that reference the New Zealanders' landing and occupation. According to newspaper reports at the time, the flag was captured by members of the Fiji defense force who joined New Zealand troops at Apia, Sāmoa, on August 29, 1914. The *Evening Post* reported that the flag was captured by Private Herbert F. Bailey, a member of the Legion of Frontiersmen in Fiji. He enlisted in the New Zealand Samoan Expeditionary Force when it passed through Fiji en route to Sāmoa. When the troops landed, Bailey spotted the German flag, rushed forward, and lowered it. New Zealand troopers who witnessed the event remarked

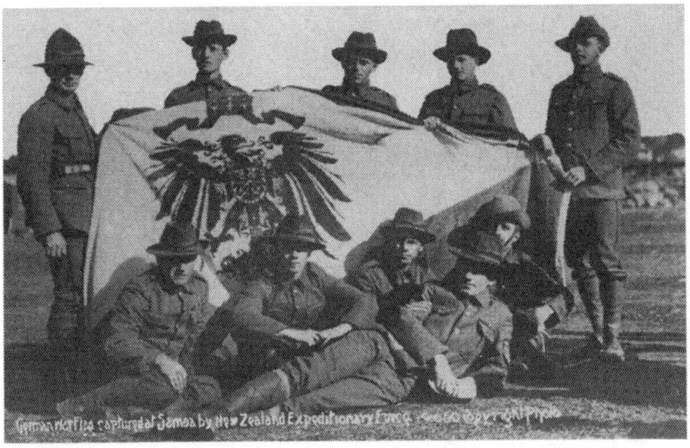

Figure 6.2 Postcard, "German War Flag captured at Samoa by New Zealand Expeditionary Force," 1914–1916, New Zealand, by William Wilson. Purchased 2011. Te Papa (GH023107).

that the scene as the flag was hauled down was dramatic because German government officials were standing in the vicinity. As "they [the German officials] saw it lowered they one and all reverently saluted." Bailey was given permission by military authorities to keep the flag. Later on, however, he and other members of the Fiji contingent decided to present the flag to the New Zealand government. In front of the camp headquarters, the flag was handed over to the commanding officer of the troops from the Auckland district of New Zealand. The Fiji contingent expressed hope "that the Government would see fit to retain the flag in Auckland."[24]

More than a decade later, on August 2, 1930, the same "story of capture" resurfaces again in the *Evening Post*. The article quotes Bailey as writing to the newspaper,

> It was only by accident that I saw a picture of the official German flag hauled down at Samoa on 29th August, 1914, by myself, cut from one of your papers, a week or so ago, and as I understand there is a controversy between the Parliamentary Library of Wellington and the Auckland Public Library as to the ownership.

Bailey goes on to tell "the story of the flag," as described, "to clear the matter up," reiterating that he "presented the flag . . . to the New Zealand Government, and . . . especially asked . . . to have the flag kept in Auckland and hung either in the Auckland Museum or the cathedral." He concluded, "I have stated all the facts. The flag was my property, and,

I think, in fairness to me should be kept in Auckland. Only the citizens of Auckland have a claim to it."[25] The *Auckland Star* then reports a few weeks later, on October 8, 1930, that the library committee of Auckland City Council recommended that a German flag captured at Apia, Sāmoa, which for years had been on view at the Auckland Public Library, should be sent to the Auckland War Memorial Museum.[26] The article does not specify whether it refers to the flag captured by Bailey; nor does his name appear in the current online collection records at Auckland War Memorial Museum where several flags are held and one is on display.[27] The newspaper records tell us that in the decades after the war, several flags captured in Sāmoa appeared. For example, a third flag for the Auckland Museum appears in the *New Zealand Herald* on January 14, 1938.[28] Two weeks later, on January 29, the same newspaper states that "a claim of the capture of two more German flags at Samoa has been made," this time in Christchurch, "bringing the total to eight."[29]

The most intriguing aspect about these claims is not their factual accuracy or provenance, but rather their efficacy in pulling the flags as material traces of the German-Sāmoan colonial legacy into regional rivalries and civic competitions played out in New Zealand, as seen in the example of the controversy between the Parliamentary Library of Wellington and the Auckland Public Library addressed and contested by Bailey. These flags, then, do not just represent material remains of a past gone but are also entangled with, and constitutive of, ongoing processes in the present—in this case, the institutionalization of war heritage for the making of cities, regions, and the nation, and even for the remaking of international relations. The *New Zealand Herald* reports on February 13, 1934, that a flag taken from a German planter's house when the New Zealand Expeditionary Force (including Bailey) landed at Sāmoa, was presented by the Auckland Harbour Board to the crew of the German barque *Magdalene Vinnen*. "The officers of the vessel regard the presentation as a most-friendly gesture,"[30] the article reads. It thus seems as if the flag was turned from war loot into gift, thus transforming former enemies into maritime comrades and assisting in mending fences of global diplomatic affairs, at least for a while, until the next major conflict.

Raising the Union Jack

Figure 6.3 is an example of a commercial postcard depicting incidents during New Zealand's annexation of the German colony of Sāmoa in August 1914. In a British World War I poster also held in Te Papa's

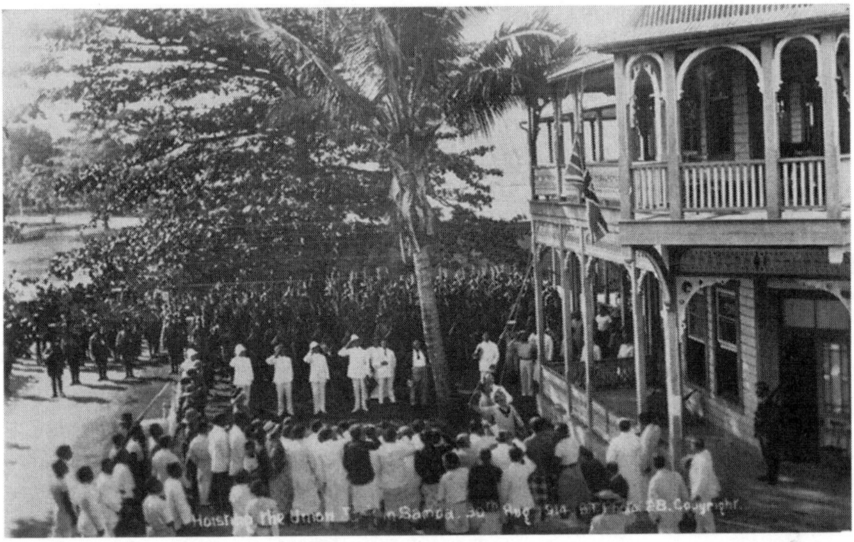

Figure 6.3 Postcard, 'Hoisting the Union Jack in Samoa. 30th Aug 1914.' 1914, Samoa, by Alfred James Tattersall. Purchased 2011. Te Papa (GH023108).

collection, New Zealand is mentioned in relation to the German colonial possessions of the Samoa Islands, which were "captured by the Expeditionary Force furnished by the Dominion of New Zealand."[31] The British government had requested that New Zealand send an expeditionary force to seize the wireless station near Apia. An advance guard of almost 1,400 men was quickly dispatched, ten days after New Zealand entered the war in Europe, and achieved its goal on August 29, 1914, meeting no resistance from the Germans stationed there. The day after the New Zealand force arrived, the British occupation was formally proclaimed, with a British Union Jack raised on the Apia Court House flag pole. The New Zealand military administered former German Sāmoa for the duration of the war though the number of men garrisoned there was reduced to 250 in April 1915. At the end of the war, New Zealand was mandated by the League of Nations to govern Western Sāmoa, and continued its administration when it became a United Nations Trust Territory in 1946. This situation lasted until 1962, when Western Sāmoa gained its independence and signed the Treaty of Friendship with New Zealand.[32]

So far, so good. But what happened to the German and—even more important—the Sāmoan thread of this tangled history? Once again there is more to the story than meets the eye from a glance at a photograph or postcard. Such visual records do not speak for themselves and should not be taken at face value but instead be seen as a window into larger processes. New Zealand's annexation finally fulfilled its long-held colonial ambitions as the "better Britain of the South Pacific,"[33] vividly captured in the reference by former Prime Minister Richard Seddon (1895–1912) to Sāmoa as "New Zealand's Alsace."[34] This historical reality often remains a blind spot in contemporary debates around (post) colonial situations.[35] It comes as little surprise, then, that newspaper articles at the time sold the landing of New Zealand's troops as a "great surprise" or even "complete surprise to the Germans," thus trumpeting military achievements worthy of a colonial force and discrediting the opponent.[36] According to a statement made by Dr. Erich Schultz, the last German governor of Sāmoa, after he landed in Auckland as a prisoner of war, however, the taking of Sāmoa had in fact been expected for days. In the course of an interview, Dr. Schultz remarked on other exaggerations in the New Zealand media, such as the inflating of the number of "white people in Samoa," aimed at making the victory appear even more glorious. Asked whether the visit of the expeditionary force was expected, Schultz replied in the affirmative, highlighting that Sāmoa possessed a powerful wireless station—the strategic target of New Zealand's intervention—and was thus able to intercept messages from troopships. Furthermore, Schultz continued, "we realized from the very outset that surrender was inevitable, because of the primitive defences of the place."[37]

The surrender was even ridiculed, as seen in a postcard titled "Samoa Yielded without a Struggle," which refers to the perception that German colonial ambitions were mainly economically focused, and that these business interests did not mind such takeover as long as trade links were not affected.[38] Imperial Germany's colonial agenda was, of course, more multifaceted than such satirical portrayal can convey, and the surrender itself gained a more respectful acknowledgment in the following years. The *New Zealand Herald* reported on June 26, 1935, after Schultz's death, that he was "said to have used great wisdom and tact when the New Zealand forces landed" and "urged his nationals to offer no resistance, thus avoiding bloodshed." Furthermore, during his term as governor he "was noted for the sympathetic manner in which he treated the natives."[39] This sympathetic treatment, however, turned into hostile policies of political exile once "the natives" resisted to being incorporated into the colonial scheme. After New Zealand's annexation, exiled

Sāmoans were repatriated, and conferences were held with, and promises made to, Sāmoan chiefs to give the "blessings of the British flag" to the recolonized.[40] Once again, even the formerly ostracized "natives" reemerged from the margin to the center of the colonial power play so the next chapter of the "Samoan tangle" could be cowritten. As the *Samoanische Zeitung* remarked aptly at the time, "The Samoan question . . . appears to be eternal. More changes of Government, more diplomatic questions, and more diverse relations have arisen over these islands during the last decade than over any other part of the earth of the size."[41]

The Ethnographic Stamp of Colonial Governance

Having traced German-Sāmoan material histories through the raising, capturing, and again raising of colonial flags, I now return to German-Sāmoan colonial governance and dig deeper into its underlying ethnographic condition. To this end, I continue to follow the material line and turn to a handheld stamp with a wooden handle (figure 6.4). The actual stamp is a rubber plaque in circular relief bearing the words "MALO KAI-SALIKA, APIA SAMOA 100 MARK." In the middle is the German imperial coat of arms. This tiny object—measuring 90 millimeters high,

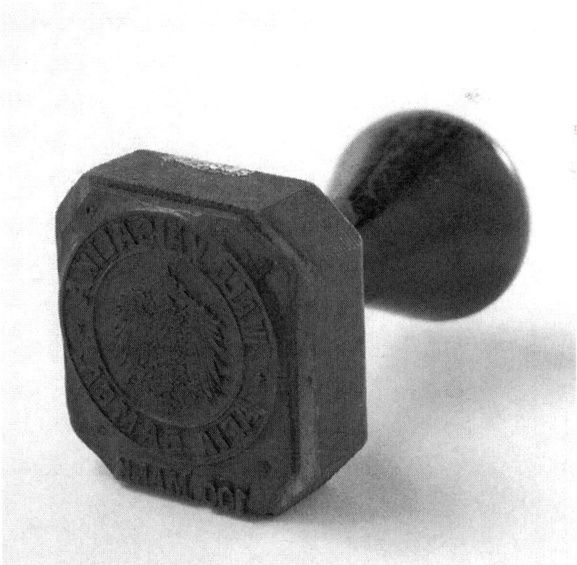

Figure 6.4 German handheld stamp, circa 1900, maker unknown. Purchased 2010. CC BY-NC-ND 4.0. Te Papa (FE012581).

55 wide, and 52 deep—of wood and rubber turns out to be a remarkable witness of and actor in thrilling dramas on worldly stages.

In 1905, five years after Germany became the ruler of Sāmoa, Governor Solf's nominated advisory board of Sāmoans came to be called Malo Kaisalika (imperial government), building on the Sāmoan word *malo,* which initially meant dominant party or faction victorious in war, but in the later nineteenth century signified the Sāmoan governing council of chiefs.[42] Facing the persistent influence of these chiefly structures, Solf announced this on August 14, 1905:

> There is only one government in Samoa, and that is the Government of His Majesty Wilhelm II, which is styled the 'Malo Kaisailika' . . . there is no room in that Government for *tumua* and *pule* [confederations of districts]. The old *fa'alupega* or formal traditional salutation of Samoa which was made use of by the former Council to arrogate power to themselves is no longer in existence, and I shall make a law forbidding use of that salutation in any meeting.[43]

Solf's declaration is absolutist in tone, seemingly prescribing a doctrine that leaves no room for customary and alternative Sāmoan forms of governance. The term "Malo Kaisalika" indicates, however, that the colonial government used Sāmoan terms and coined Sāmoan neologisms, or new terms, to name new institutions, thus inevitably lending the colonial doctrine a distinctively Sāmoan note. What role did the stamp thereby play?

Woven mats occupied, and continue to occupy, a central position in Sāmoan life. 'Ie toga (fine mats) were distributed within the context of weddings, formal apologies, and fines, and were used as currency to pay, for example, for houses or canoes. The Germans struggled to distinguish, on the one hand, between 'ie toga or *'ie o le malo*—fine or heirloom mats—and *lagaga* (common mats), and, on the other, between the monetary values assigned to them. As a result, the colonial government set up an office staffed by Germans and Sāmoans to determine the precise value of each mat and mark it with the stamp. This intervention aimed at turning ambiguous Sāmoan customs into manageable procedures defined according to the value system of capitalist commerce and trade, in the process preventing Sāmoans from mixing monetary and sacred systems of value in ways that were incomprehensible to Germans.

This form of colonial rule geared toward preserving and regulating customary practices—rather than prohibiting them as under New Zealand occupation[44]—is also evident during the installing of Mata'afa as ali'i sili (paramount chief). This ceremony involved, according to Sāmoan custom, the distribution of 'ie toga—in this case more than two thousand—overseen by Solf to "smooth over difficulties"[45] among the competing Sāmoan chiefly districts, and symbolically overshadowed by the most paramount chief of all, the German emperor.[46]

The stamp thus served as a governmental tool but it could function properly only if it was handled with a particular expertise, or "ethnographic acuity," to first make sense of and then manage cultural differences.[47] Not surprisingly, then, we can observe how Sāmoan 'ie toga did not only feature in political events and economic transactions but also in the evolving science of ethnography. A particular fascinating example begins with a detailed article published by Julius Henniger on April 13, 1912, in the *Samoanische Zeitung* (*SZ*) "im Interesse der ethnographischen Wissenschaft . . . feiner Matten" (in the interest of the ethnographic science of . . . fine mats).[48] Following this article, which is still considered by some as one of the most detailed treatments of Sāmoan 'ie toga ever written, a debate on whether fine mats should be encouraged or banned evolved between Henniger, Lieutenant Werner Albert von Bülow, and "Spectator," thus turning the newspaper into a "forum for ethnographic exchange and debate."[49] This debate, however, was not confined to the academic realm. It also became entangled with, and constitutive of, approaches to colonial governance. That is, ethnographic visions and their increasingly scientific framing shaped colonial governmentality. Von Bülow, for example, was praised for his unique acquaintance with Sāmoan customs (apart from Schultz, Solf's successor as governor), even as he was critiqued for his claim that "mat celebration, and the belief in the supernatural, hinder the civilization of the natives."[50] He thus embodied the ambivalent "salvage colonialism" typical of German Sāmoa.[51] On the one hand, he was an enthusiastic ethnographer with a wide range of interests and publications. On the other, he was a staunch advocate of the colonial project, even savagely criticizing the German administration for its allegedly inclusive approach to social and political affairs. There was, he wrote to governor Solf, "an absolute necessity to make the character of this colony more German than has been the case up till now."[52]

One of the other ethnographic authors involved in the ‘ie toga debate in the *Samoanische Zeitung*, Henniger, was also directly involved in the governmental valuation of mats, which brings us back to the stamp. It is not far-fetched to claim that Henniger—if not physically then at least metaphorically—used this stamp (maybe even this very stamp) personally, thus drawing on, and performing his “ethnographic acuity” for the sake of a functioning colonial bureaucracy. This brings us back to the larger relationship between Sāmoan customs, colonial governance, and ethnographic science that the stamp not only symbolizes but also assisted in enacting. Both governors, Solf and Schultz, referred to, and applied ethnographic knowledge, citing, for example, the still-eminent work of Augustin Krämer, who “transported precolonial ethnographic representation to the nascent colonial state.”[53] Their ethnographic curiosity, sensitivity, and expertise might explain the comparatively “enlightened” approach to colonial domination that largely refrained from violent intervention, often in opposition to more militant colonial interests and forces, as we have seen personified in naval captain Emsmann and lieutenant-cum-ethnographer von Bülow. “All radical measures are evil,” Solf advised the Colonial Department in 1901, “time and goodness and justice are the best means to govern Samoa.”[54] This pacifist attitude, however, should not gloss over its clearly racist and social Darwinist foundation, as becomes clear in the debate around the *Mischehenverbot* (prohibition of mixed marriage) in 1912, during which the same cosmopolitan Solf asked the not-so-cosmopolitan and rhetorical question: “Sollen anständige, reinrassige Weisse die Herren in Samoa sein oder heruntergekommene, verkanakerte Menschen mit Halbblut-Nachkommenschaft?” (Should decent and full-blooded whites be the masters in Samoa or degenerated kanakanized people with half-blooded descendants?).[55]

Given these layers of the ambivalent thread weaving through German-Sāmoan relations, my argument supports neither preservationist celebration nor ethnocidal condemnation—the two main strands of the historical literature dealing with German colonialism in Sāmoa[56]—but distinguishes instead, following Steinmetz, “between the colonizer’s treatment of specific indigenous *practices* and their approach to the . . . *institutions* within which these practices were located.”[57] This colonial ambivalence of salvaging and preserving practices while controlling and dominating their institutional framing was permeated with an ethnographic condition, which could assume racist or cosmopolitan qualities (among others) and was enacted (for example) through the ethnographic stamp of colonial governance, and embedded in an ethnographic field exemplified in the next story.

Schultz and Henniger, who worked together for the German colonial administration, were members of the Polynesian Society, a nowadays-professional anthropological organization, which was founded by amateur ethnologists in 1892 in Wellington, New Zealand, and has consistently had a small Indigenous membership throughout its history.[58] Schultz published his *Proverbial Expressions of the Samoans* in 1948 via the society.[59] Henniger attempted to use his ethnographic credentials to regain liberty and the permission to return to Sāmoa while being a prisoner of war in New Zealand after the takeover. He appealed to intercede for his repatriation to the president at the time, S. Percy Smith, who, despite being interested in Henniger's publication plans, dismissed the request by pointing to the political neutrality of the society (which of course never existed in practice). A letter exchange held at New Zealand Archives provides fascinating insight into the ways in which ethnographic expertise gained political weight by being mobilized as a scientific trait with universal value transcending the partisan interests inherent in military conflict (Henniger) while being seen as a potential threat undermining colonial reconfigurations (New Zealand government).[60]

The ethnographic field in which colonial governance operated emerges most clearly in the case of the Sāmoan "problem" with the Mau nationalist resistance movement developing in the 1920s.[61] Suddenly, the struggling New Zealand government gained an appreciation of the "ethnographic acuity" needed to regain colonial control. A memorandum initially written by Solf to the Imperial Colonial Office in Berlin in 1907, in which he spoke of "the fundamental rule . . . that the Samoans can be guided but not forced" as well as the interracial threat of *Verkanakern*, thus reemerged in 1928 and was passed on by the New Zealand government to Colonel Logan, who was in charge of administrating the mandated territory of Western Sāmoa and concluded in his response that the "remarks of Dr. Solf should never be lost sight of" and are of "the very highest value."[62] The Sāmoan "problem" erupted in violence, however, prompting Māori scholars-cum-politicians Āpirana Ngata and Te Rangihīroa (Peter Buck), who shaped an "anthropological governance" in New Zealand at the time, to argue in parliament that "Maori methods" should be applied carefully to Sāmoans (Ngata) and insist in private that "ethnological research" could have prevented the disaster (Buck).[63] Both were involved in the Maori Ethnological Research Board, which became entangled in the "Samoan tangle" by attempting to get Augustine Krämer's seminal *Die Samoa-Inseln* translated from German into English on behalf of the New Zealand government "owing to the misunderstandings . . . existing in Samoa."[64] These misunderstandings were exemplified in and intensified through the prohibition of ‘ie toga. How meaningless this colonial attempt to suppress (rather than govern) customary practices was, becomes clear in its substitution through the giving of *siapo* (bark cloth) pieces on occasions such as feasts, wedding, and funerals.[65] Colonial interventions, then, might have changed material appearances but failed to unsettle the underlying conceptual foundations.[66]

The "Samoan Tangle" Materialized: The "Malifa Handbook" and Banner

Before turning to responses by anthropology's interlocutors through contemporary art interventions, let me complete the historical discussion. The front cover of the "Malifa Handbook" indicates that it was presented to Mr. and Mrs. D.A.J. Rutherford in 1936. The Rutherfords had arrived in Sāmoa in 1919 when Mr. Rutherford was appointed superintendent of schools. Previously, he had been headmaster of Highcliff School near Dunedin, New Zealand, before taking up his position as headmaster of Leififi School, the first government school in Sāmoa established for local European children and children of expatriates. The handbook has hand-drawn images on the front cover and seven pages of handwritten text inside. It was presented to the Rutherfords when they left Sāmoa in 1936.[67] What other stories—beyond such biographical facts—can this handbook tell us?

Written by a student, this object is an example of how New Zealand policies in the early 1900s influenced Sāmoa's educational system. During his eighteen-year tenure, Rutherford left his mark, as attested to in an article in the *Evening Post* on December 3, 1936. Referring to Mr. Rutherford's departure, a "native teacher" is quoted as saying, "The news of Mr. Rutherford's retirement is sad to Samoa. Latafoti, as he is known in Samoa, has been with us in good times and bad times."[68] New Zealand's education policy personified through Rutherford seems to have been awarded with a Sāmoan name, Latafoti, in return. Once we travel further back in time, we can detect more of such personal interactions and cross-cultural alterations throughout the school's institutional evolution.

In 1908, Malifa became the second government school established during the German period in Sāmoa. It was intended for Sāmoan children. In 1909, a boarding school for the sons of *matai* (chiefs) was added to the compound. Only boys were allowed, in respect for the Sāmoan chiefly elite and its underpinning hierarchical and gender divisions.[69] The influence of Sāmoan ways of thinking and being can also be witnessed in the school's founding. Faletoese, a pastor for many years at Fagamalo, Savaii, was asked by Governor Solf to come to Apia to establish the government school at Malifa.[70] A matai thus became the headmaster, demonstrating how "the Germans agreed to move within a world that was draped with Samoan webs of meaning." Even in secret correspondence, officials referred to the school's matai rather than a German equivalent designating the position, thus indicating the level to which "Samoan concepts had permeated the colonial administration."[71] In a similar vein, the Sāmoan language remained the main language at the school, prompting Solf—who spoke Sāmoan fluently—to declare that children of the German school would be allowed to attend Sāmoan language education here.[72] Germany's "salvage colonialism," designed and enacted primarily by Solf and his successor Schultz to preserve Sāmoan customary practices while subjecting them to colonial institutions was—despite the undeniably uneven power dynamics—still a two-way affair, leaving a Sāmoan imprint on the German population. Moreover, this avenue branched out into multiple side tracks, as seen in the *Kulturkampf* (culture war) erupting between Solf and the Catholic Mission over the school's secular orientation.[73]

What broader conclusion can be drawn from such interwoven narrative threads? A banner given as a farewell gift to Rutherford and housed in Te Papa's collection serves well to use a particular object, not as an end in itself but as a brush to paint a bigger picture (figure 6.5). Aesthetically, the banner appears designed in a Sāmoan pattern and made from local material, and is personalized to a New Zealand teacher with his Sāmoan identity—Latafoti—written in German script. Is this banner then Sāmoan, New Zealand, or German? Does it represent one or all of these broad categories, or is something else materialized here? The Sāmoan-German poet and scholar Albert Wendt, in his pondering

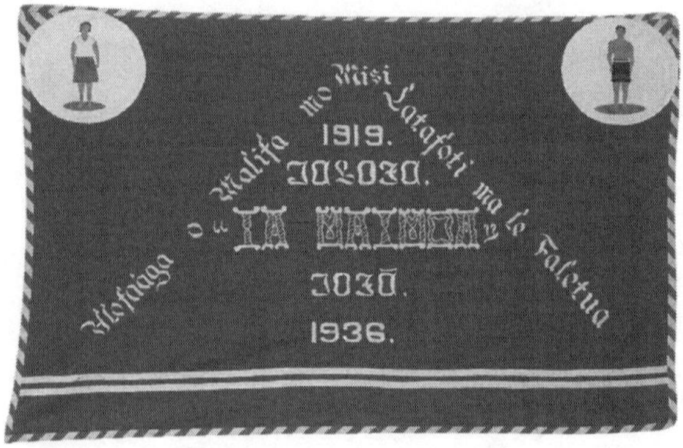

Figure 6.5 Banner (Alofa'aga o Malifa mo misi Latafoti ma le Faletua 1919. Talofa. "IA MANUIA" Tofa. 1936.) Gift of Dr. Alex M. Rutherford, 1954. Te Papa (FE002797).

on the "post-colonial body" as "a body becoming" through the inscription of a Sāmoan *tatau* (tattoo), helps us thinking through the banner:

> it is a body coming out of the Pacific, not a body being imposed on the Pacific. It is a blend, a new development, which I consider to be in heart, spirit and muscle, Pacific: a blend in which influences from outside (even the English Language) have been indigenized, absorbed in the image of the local and national, and in turn have altered the national and local.[74]

The banner, having traveled to Te Papa's collection and now reappearing in this text, continues to perform as a specific "material maker(s) of relationships" through which we can zoom in on concrete "transactions and transformations" between its makers, givers, receivers, viewers, and so on.[75] Throughout its ongoing journey, it continues to blend and newly develop, living on as a multitude of banners.

"Anthropology's Interlocutors" Speaking Back: Reverse Anthropological Mimicry

This chapter set out to revisit the German-Sāmoan colonial legacy by zooming in on its material dimension. It put a few material actors—three photographs, a handheld stamp, and a schoolbook and banner—center stage from which to explore the dramas written by the colonial script. I argued that the German-Sāmoan colonial government was entangled with, constituted by, and enacted through what I term an ethnographic condition. It grew out of the (pre)colonial encounter, which generated cross-cultural realities that had to be studied, understood, and governed, and increasingly gained a scientific quality personified in colonial administrators-cum-scholars such as Dr. Wilhelm Solf, Dr. Erich Schultz, and Julius Henniger. The ethnographic condition (and its scientific upgrading) was permeated with an ambivalent dialectics oscillating between salvage and subjection, curiosity and prestige, cooperation and resistance, stabilization and subversion. In the Sāmoan response, the same ambivalent ethnographic condition gains different qualities and emerges in other variations. It can be detected in contemporary art through which Sāmoan artists-cum-scholars such as Yuki Kihara, Rosanna Raymond, and Leafa Wilson aka Olga Krause speak back to the common legacy by expressing (and once again materializing) Sāmoan-German responses, perspectives, and positions. Before I introduce these interlocutors of anthropology in detail, I first draw the historical discussion into the contemporary situation and the realm of art.

On January 28, 2014, one hundred years after the German colonization ended with the raising of the Union Jack, His Highness Tui Atua Tupua Tamasese Efi visited Bundespräsident (federal president) Joachim Gauck at Schloss Bellevue in Berlin to mark the occasion. In his speech, Gauck stressed the historical proportions of the meeting by stating that this was the first official visit to Germany by a Sāmoan head of state.[76] Yet, in 1910, the latter's grandfather, Tupua Tamasese Lealofi, also visited Berlin when a Sāmoan *Völkerschau* (ethnic show) organized by the German side (through the impresarios and traders of ethnographica, Fritz and Carl Marquardt) reached the officially diplomatic status that the Sāmoan side had always in mind.[77] Governor Solf at the time was directly involved by first convincing the Colonial Office in Berlin to grant permission for this particular show, which had been deemed illegal since 1901, to keep the "violent and devious" Tupua Tamasese "away from Samoa as long as possible" to prevent him from being a contender for Mata'afa's succession as ali'i sili. Despite his political intrigue, Solf had to acknowledge that "Tamasese did not see himself as a member of the Marquardts' Samoa troupe, but rather as an envoy of the Samoan chiefs, to pay his respect to His Majesty," the German emperor.[78] Tamasese succeeded, but let us return to Gauck's speech. Without mentioning the partially official nature of this prior visit, Gauck acknowledges the

Völkerschauen and the relative unawareness of this chapter in the German collective consciousness.[79] He refers to Die Brücke, an artist group in Dresden at the forefront of German expressionism in the early twentieth century, whose art works present some of the few media through which the mostly romanticized Sāmoan picture has been drawn in Germany.

The literature on Die Brücke is substantial.[80] It shows, among other things, how the involved artists found inspiration in the South Seas (or rather German colonies in the South Seas) by traveling there physically, like the artist-ethnographer Emil Nolde, or by visiting staged spectacles such as Völkerschauen and "exotic objects" in ethnographic museums, as the armchair traveler Ernst Ludwig Kirchner.[81] These orchestrated settings enabled the artists to travel imaginatively and appropriate the "primitive other" mainly as foil for the unfulfilled longings of the "civilized self."[82] "Although much has been written about the role of primitivism in modern art," Arnd Schneider concludes, "the encounter between artists from other cultures and Western art has received relatively less consideration." Such "reverse appropriation," moreover, aims not only at Western art genres but also, as we shall see, at colonial histories and their ethnographic condition.[83] This is not to claim a simple role reversal because a degree of impossibility remains in that the power dynamics associated with the original appropriation—for example, primitivism—are largely not reversed.[84]

Michel Tuffery is a prominent example and one of the first Sāmoan artists to address the Sāmoan-German legacy.[85] Tuffery is of Rarotongan, Sāmoan, and Tahitian descent and was born in Aotearoa New Zealand, thus embodying—at the level of personal life—the widespread "Pacific diaspora" and often associated "ambivalent kinship."[86] In his words, "If you're born here [Aotearoa/New Zealand], you've got no identity." Although he most strongly identifies as Sāmoan, he also feels that he has acquired rather than inherited his Sāmoan identity.[87] At the level of art practice, then, Tuffery exemplifies the resulting "art of in-betweenness" negotiating and expressing the inescapable diasporic "space between" multiple affiliations.[88] In his series *Siamani Samoa* (German Samoa), which was largely motivated by the still present yet deteriorating traces of imperial Germany in Sāmoa (as in architectural designs and industrial infrastructures), he produced, among other pieces, a painting inspired by a well-known photograph of Solf and Tamasese riding in a carriage on their way to see Kaiser Wilhelm.[89] The painting's title,

Mulinu'u to Berlin, Tamasese and Dr Wilhelm Solf off to visit the Kaiser, indicates that the relationship between Mulinu'u—the locality where the German colonial flag was raised—and Berlin is a significant aspect of Tuffery's work.[90]

Besides these obvious connections, which are reenacted through the reinscription and recirculation of a German colonial photograph through a Sāmoan artist's intervention, are a few more hidden aspects of relevance for this discussion. First is a genealogical connection that links Tuffery personally to the wider (post)colonial history. Second, his work is informed by detailed historical research to establish a link across archival records, photographs, and artistic responses. Third, he uses ethnographic museum collections as resource for inspiration, just as the expressionists did before him from the other side.[91] Tuffery seems to approach the joint legacy, however—despite clearly expressing a Sāmoan perspective from a Sāmoan position—in response to a German vantage point, as the order of the title *Siamani Samoa* indicates. The three artists I introduce, however, turn the vantage point from German-Sāmoan to Sāmoan-German. They do so by not only reversely appropriating ethnographic tools and thus perpetuating the ethnographic condition, but also by questioning, critiquing, and subverting the forms and ways in and through which the latter comes into existence.

Yuki Kihara: Rewriting Anthropological Perspectives

As an artist and independent curator, Yuki Kihara works across a range of media that includes photography, performance, and video. She has built a comprehensive and multifaceted body of art work and curatorial practice that addresses and examines—among other aspects—gender roles, consumerism, (mis)representations, and societal issues spanning past, present, and future from colonial and postcolonial perspectives.[92] Kihara was born in Sāmoa to a Japanese father and Sāmoan mother, and lived in Sāmoa, Japan, and Indonesia before moving to Aotearoa New Zealand. Her life has thus also been characterized by diasporic movements across the Pacific, and her art has given expression to a particular kind of "in-betweenness." In a series of photographs, *Fa'afafine: In a Manner of a Woman,* Kihara instrumentalizes her status as a *fa'afafine* (person occupying the space between male and female)—in this case as a "Pacific island woman of transgender experience"—to create an artistic statement that "exposes . . . the western binary opposition of gender and sexuality" and "shatters these colonial constructions imposed upon many Indigenous cultures in the Pacific."[93] Through photographic self-portraits, she is "counter-appropriating the media, technologies and concepts of ethnographic photography," thus collapsing the distinction between photographer and subject and reversing its othering gaze.[94] In a show called *Diva Siva—Fa'afafine Cabaret* at the Haus der Kulturen der Welt (House of World Cultures) in Berlin, Kihara moved from photography to aesthetic performance, participating under the pseudonym of Dusky-Geisha and presenting a "live ethnography" that looked at the Western idea of royalty and its various notions brought to the Pacific Islands in the Victorian era.[95]

Significant to this discussion, Kihara has deployed these techniques of ethnographic counterappropriation through artistic interventions to address, critique, and subvert the German-Sāmoan legacy. In another photographic series, *Where Do We Come From? What Are We? Where Are We Going?*, she shifts the emphasis from her body to the landscapes materializing Sāmoa's cultural and political history.[96] Taking inspiration from a late nineteenth-century photograph, *Samoan Half Caste,* by New Zealand photographer Thomas Andrew (who also captured the raising of the German flag), which features a nameless Sāmoan woman posed in black Victorian dress, Kihara assumes her alter ego Salome to redress history and return agency to the unnamed and depicted, just as Oscar Wilde used this biblical character in a controversial play to subvert political power.[97] Kihara dons a Victorian mourning dress, which she also wears in a performance called *Taualuga: The Last Dance* "as a signifier of colonialism" to "unlock the photograph to free the soul," and revisits sites of historical significance to speak to their reverberations in the present.[98] One of the locations is a monument devoted to the raising of the German flag on Mulinu'u.[99] The flag was hauled down but its (post)colonial repercussions continue.

This performative response to colonial histories and their contemporary legacies gains a more ethnographic quality in *Them and Us,* a mixture of hybrid choreography and film aimed at rewriting the German anthropological viewpoint of the former colony of German Sāmoa (see plate 8).[100] This *Folkoloniales Spektakel* switches between recorded sequences of a choreographed dance performance and scenes showing the performers strolling through the streets of Berlin. Here we see Sāmoan members of the Tatau Dance Group walking silently yet confidentially through German city streets named after the heroic figures Albert von Chamisso, Arthur Schopenhauer, and Immanuel Kant, thereby responding to quoted passages of the intellectual trinity's abstract (and dehumanizing) racial thinking through concrete (and rehumanizing) bodily presences.[101] This reclaiming of Sāmoan traces continues by the group's walking through and thus reoccupying Sāmoan places, such as the Samoa-Weg (Sāmoa alley) in a *Gartenkolonie* (garden colony) and Tropical Islands (a water park with a *fale* or Sāmoan house), and culminates when the Sāmoan protagonists impersonate Solf and other members of the Reichstag debating the *Mischehenverbot* (prohibition of mixed marriage) in front of a 'ie toga or fine mat.[102] Here, the ethnographically grounded colonial governance, which always had to reckon with 'ie toga, becomes rewritten by the formerly ethnographically studied and colonially governed; the use of parody as a performative utterance of resistance and subversion perforates the veil of colonialism and renders its totalizing ambition incomplete.

This becomes even more explicit in Kihara's latest projects. *Der Papālagi* (The White Man) series is a response to a book written by Erich Scheurmann, a German national who lived in Sāmoa during the German colonial administration. Published in 1920, the book contains descriptions of European life seen through the eyes of Tuiavi'i, a Sāmoan chief. However, it has been accused of being a fictional rather than a factual account, and been branded "Ethnokitsch."[103] Kihara's series features a public performance presented as a social, or rather ethnographic, experiment in which Christian and Barbara Durst—German migrants who have lived in Sāmoa for more than twenty-four years—"go native." Dressed in Sāmoan regalia, they make public appearances in different locations in and around the capital city of Apia. In this work, it is the Papālagi who are the disguised Other subjected to the Sāmoan gaze.[104]

In another photo series, *A Study of a Samoan Savage,* a man embodying the Pacific demigod Maui is being examined with instruments and through techniques used for anthropometrical studies in physical anthropology up until the mid-twentieth century.[105] The series is "both an indictment of the stereotyping of anthropometry and a re-presentation of its methodologies," and "conveys a provocative message by reusing a historical method of cultural categorisation to critique and rebut racial bias."[106] Its re-presentation is a response to still widespread perceptions of so-called Polynesian men as physically powerful yet intellectually primitive, as in rugby culture; the associated gaze is readdressed through Maui, the trickster and shapeshifter, who defiantly looks back at the viewer.[107] This anthropological inversion depends, somewhat paradoxically, on Kihara's detailed historical and ethnographic research into anthropological concepts and typologies as well as their photographic manifestations. Actively using and fiercely critiquing museum collections and archival records thus perpetuates the underlying ambivalent ethnographic condition and carries it from colonial governance into contemporary art.

Rosanna Raymond: Reactivāting Museum Spaces

I met with Rosanna Raymond several times in Europe and Aotearoa New Zealand to discuss German-Sāmoan colonial history and other issues of mutual interest. Raymond is an artist, curator, and performer as well as a published poet, scholar, and writer. She identifies as a New Zealand-born Pacific Islander of Sāmoan descent, and comments on contemporary Pacific Island realities around the globe by fusing customary practices with innovative techniques and by crossing boundaries between artistic media and genre. Her work has been greatly influenced by her association with the Pacific Sisters, a collective of artists with Pacific descent who created a wide range of works including visual art, film, music, and fashion. Raymond's work has continuously straddled the boundaries between art and academia, and often been conducted in partnership with museums and universities—across the Pacific as well across Europe, including Germany.[108]

A prominent example is the acclaimed *Pasifika Styles: Artists inside the Museum* exhibition co-curated by Raymond and Amiria Salmond, which set out to literally enliven the Museum of Anthropology and Archaeology at the University of Cambridge by opening up and drawing "artists inside the museum" to demonstrate the contemporary relevance of its historical collections and to shape a "new openness between Pacific art and anthropology" (see chapter 2). To achieve this goal, the curators did not, as Raymond stressed, "follow a conventional approach of selecting particular works and dictating how they should be exhibited, as we [the curators] wanted them [the artists] to react to the space on their own terms." Throughout the conceptual design of *Pasifika Styles,* Raymond and Salmond engaged with the anthropological literature that in many cases has explained Pacific Indigeneities away, such as through the "invention of tradition" debate (see chapter 2). These perspectives failed to see, according to Raymond, that "among and within Polynesian communities we were having our own debates on issues such as authenticity, hybridity and contemporaneity . . . using the arts to convey our own theories."[109]

Such a theoretically driven (and ethnographically informed) artistic expression becomes apparent in Raymond's *SaVAge K'lub*, which engages critically with notions of the savage Other and subverts the nineteenth-century gentlemen's Savage Club and its references to Indigenous people in ceremonies, regalia, and branding. Since 2010, she has set up a network of artists contributing to *SaVAge K'lub* events as part of multiart installation and performance events in museum and gallery spaces throughout the world. The Oceanic concept of the *vā*—the relational space that carries conceptual purchase particularly in Sāmoa (see chapter 2)—is, as the intervention's title indicates, central for its purpose. It allows for an embodied engagement with past, present, and future—from Savage Club to SaVAge K'lub and beyond—and across globally dispersed localities, thus turning museums into sites for the revision of old and the creation of new conversations and relationships.[110]

The ambivalent ethnographic condition materialized in the institution of the museum as a site of both colonial typification and artistic inspiration emerged also during Raymond's residency at the Humboldt Lab at Berlin's Ethnological Museum as part of the project *Indigeneity in the Contemporary World: Performance, Politics, and Belonging.*[111] There she discovered extensive holdings of textiles, images, and handcrafted items from Sāmoa, many of which were associated with its colonization by imperial Germany (figure 6.6). Drawing on her encounter with the collection and detailed research on its provenance, Raymond staged at the conclusion of her residency an *Acti.VA.tion* of the expansive *Südsee* (South Seas) exhibition, which featured outrigger canoes and ornate meeting houses among a myriad of other intricately fashioned things. Her performative intervention *Soli I Tai—Soli I Uta* (Tread on the Sea—Tread on the Land) proceeded through the galleries and activated the principle of the vā—"the space that holds things together in relation, the glue that binds us together across differences," as she explains—through her body, spoken words, chanted songs, and choreographed dances, to enliven so-called and so-staged artifacts (see chapter 2) and reconnect them with human biographies and histories.[112]

Interestingly, the event was promoted as a performance, a genre against which Raymond protests elsewhere: "I did an activation . . . a 'performance' is different, and I do perform. But when I'm working in the museum space I am creating a shared space through my body with

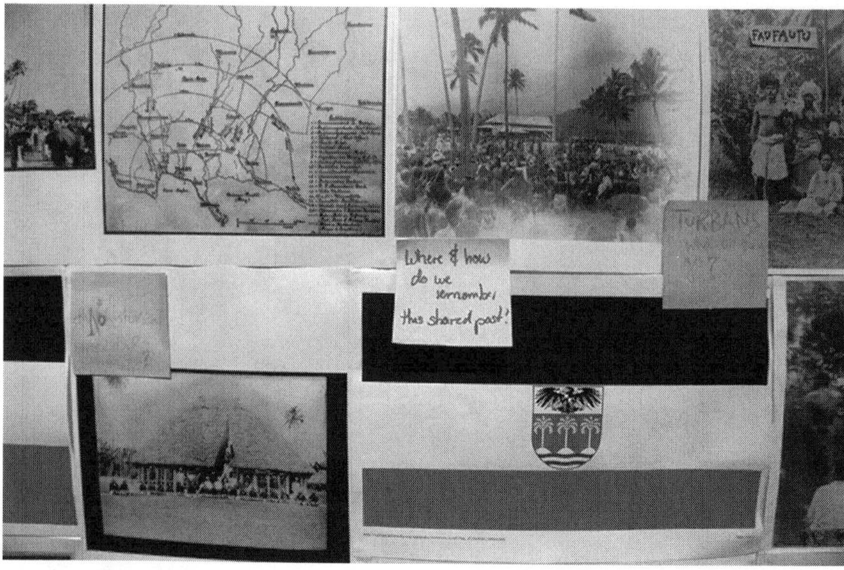

Figure 6.6 *Eyeland Part 6-Glass Walls and Dark Seas.* Interactive research notes, Ethnologisches Museum Berlin, 2014. Photograph courtesy of Rosanna Raymond.

the past." She goes on to explain that "activating the vā," the relational space spanning the temporal continuum between past, present, and future (see chapter 2), occurs through "the Pacific body, which is the vessel of the genealogical matter."[113] Significantly, her Pacific body is inherently and partially both Sāmoan and German because, as she put it in conversation to me,

> I think genealogically we are linked forever. German blood runs through my veins because of the physical presence they had in the island. . . . The fact the museums had so much of our *measina* [treasures], well it brought me there. I was able to connect in a much deeper way, through the collections. They are there for a reason, and they bring us together in the 21st century.[114]

Ethnographic museums thus emerge as prime sites through which genealogic links can be addressed by reactivating static ethnographic records or "artifacts" as through the vā, "a very lively space that needs to be maintained and reciprocated and kept alive, because it can go dormant."[115] As we have seen, artistic interventions aimed at doing so inevitably become profoundly embodied and personal affairs.

Leafa Wilson aka Olga Hedwig Krause: Recolonizing a Sāmoan-German Name and Body

Leafa Wilson is an artist and curator based at Waikato Museum Te Whare Taonga o Waikato. She curated, for example, *Letters to the Ancestors: Contemporary Indigenous Art from Aotearoa and the Pacific* (2005), which brought together artists from across the Pacific, many were seen for the first time in Aotearoa, to address notions of diaspora, genealogies, and relationship with the land.[116] Her artistic oeuvre includes interaction performances, multimedia installations, and photography.[117] When I met Leafa aka Olga in Waikato, it quickly became clear that we shared a strong interest in Sāmoa's German chapter. She appreciated my visit because, as she stressed, this conversation can hardly be had in Sāmoa or Aotearoa. I, in parallel, struggled to have the conversation on the German side. Her profoundly personal rather than purely intellectual involvement emerged clearly, so I feel it is most appropriate to leave most of the talking here to Leafa aka Olga. I do this out of personal and anthropological respect to further unsettle Said's conclusion (quoted earlier) that "the direct, even importunate solicitations of debate and intellectual engagement from the formerly colonized are left largely unattended."[118] "Anthropology's interlocutors" are indeed speaking back, in this context addressing a common legacy through similar conceptual lenses but different means and on their own terms.

Leafa aka Olga describes her curatorial position:

> I am possibly the first Polynesian woman to have the role of art curator in a museum institution. Not Pacific art, or Māori art . . . but the fine arts. I see this as a small triumph for the marginalized, and so I try never to see this as being about myself but about representing the suppressed voices within the dominion of Western art. Sounds very idealistic but it's a deeply held belief of mine. I am black (Samoan), I am a woman: My Samoan worldview can't help but be a tacit voice in my curatorial practice.[119]

Her role as an artist, on the other hand, is equally framed through a female Sāmoan worldview, but its inherent German dimension complicates matters, as is clear in the ongoing project *Ich heisse Olga Hedwig Krause—Deutsche Kuenstlerin* (My name is Olga Hedwig Krause: German Artist) (see chapter 5). Here, Leafa's German names given on her birth certificate become the site of installation art. Moving images advance and retreat her body and multiple selves with superimposed images of her birth certificate, her great-grandfather Paul Heinrich Krause, and images of women who look supposedly more German than she does.[120] She explains:

> Always, we are the *body corporate* and that's how in my head I approach these two names that signify me. Leafa Wilson. I am married to Craig Wilson, so that's a working/married name . . . but I was born *Olga Hedwig Janice Krause*—it's still me . . . no changes there. So I will often use Leafa Wilson's name as the curator for work because that's how I am known. . . . If I am curating or writing outside of work or exhibiting, I often use my birth name because it does honour my late father Charles *aka Sale* Krause who died in 1993. It's a sentimental connection to him as well as part of my practice to undermine the hegemonic reading of the body that doesn't equate my black body with my German names.[121]

She elaborates in conversation with me, explaining how the project continues her

> life's work of colonizing Germany through my black body and my name. They seem to me and feel to me incongruous with what one might expect an Olga Krause to be. She is someone who is white, German speaking, and living in Frankfurt or something. I am a Sāmoan woman, born in Aotearoa and raised in a small town called Tokoroa. Worlds apart. OLGA is VĀ or space [through which] I occupy Germany, and it is a place of utopic race relations.[122]

Leafa aka Olga explicates the biographical evolution of this process:

> I am philosophical about the Sāmoan-German relationship because it has happened, I exist and therefore it is very much just part of my psyche or what I understand to be my "make up" is, not just me but that of every Sāmoan German hybrid since Germany colonized Sāmoa. There was a time when I used to attribute my artistic and musical leanings to the German "part" of mind, but the older I grew

> and by the time I reached my late 20s, I deduced that I in fact had a colonized mind around my own identity. From whenever that point was, I started to filter out my own racist thought and decolonize my mind and retaining the stuff about Germany that was actually authentic, which turned out to be just my name. That is all. The one certainty and reminder of Germany.[123]

In her concluding comments, it emerges quite clearly how Leafa aka Olga has turned the German-Sāmoan past, by recolonizing her name and body, into a Sāmoan-German present and future, however utopian it might be or remain. At the personal level, this is not utopian at all but viscerally real because Leafa's body embodies the genealogical connection through which Sāmoans were colonized and turned into *Neue Landsleute* (new compatriots) of Germany, a process that led—despite attempts to maintain racial purity, as through the *Mischehenverbot* (prohibition of mixed marriages)—to the birth and growing up of "brown Germans."[124] The resulting question of "who or what is German" has been fought over to this day.[125] The wider (post)colonial "race relations" might indeed, as Leafea put it, remain "utopic." Yet it is impossible to deny her the following bodily concrete stance:

> I wrestled with this notion of being called a German-Sāmoan and I resented that the hierarchy was German first, Sāmoan second. I always call myself a Sāmoan (or Sāmoan-German) in that order because it is true, from a percentage ratio aspect as well as from my lived experience. I NEVER once lived as a German, so to place German first felt like an affectation or just bullshit, really.[126]

In his book *Pacific Performances: Theatricality and Cross-Cultural Encounter in the South Seas* (2007), Christopher Balme convincingly argues that the performative mimicry observed at the Polynesian Cultural Centre in Hawai'i corresponds—in contrast to Frantz Fanon and Homi Bhabha's definitions—to a "reverse colonial mimicry." Balme explains:

> instead of imitating the colonizer and developing forms of subversion by holding up a distorted image of the European, the Samoans and Tongans appear to be mimicking European projections of themselves. . . . This ironic use of parody depends on the performers'

> awareness of European and Euro-American projections and is evident in various subtle and not so subtle allusions.[127]

What is given expression in, and enacted through, the artwork of Yuki Kihara, Rosanna Raymond, and Leafa Wilson aka Olga Krause, I argue, is a reverse anthropological mimicry.[128] This entails the parody of anthropological imaginations through the counterappropriation of ethnographic tools as artistic strategy and intervention aimed not so much at ironical play, as seen in the acts of resistance toward the tourist gaze at the Polynesian Cultural Center (although this can certainly be discerned in the entertaining *Them and Us*), as at articulating fierce critique, turning the vantage point—from a colonial German-Sāmoan to a (post)colonial and utopian Sāmoan-German, and engaging with the politics of representation that embraces multiple perspectives on a common history. These artists actively add to and reshape this history by circulating images and allowing photographs and sites to resurface and be reinscribed into collective memory. Mimicry is used not as a way of adapting and surviving, as it has been historically promoted, but as a strategy of resistance in artistic practice geared toward rewriting anthropological perspectives (Kihara), reactivāting museum spaces (Raymond), and recolonizing a Sāmoan-German name and body (Wilson aka Krause).

In doing so, the three artists mobilize genealogical claims from different positions and to varying degrees: from the broader histories of colonialism and anthropology (Kihara), to their materialization in museum collections and exhibitions (Raymond), and the personal embodiment of Sāmoan-German descent and heritage (Wilson aka Krause). Consequently, they are each differently invested at the level of personal identity and differ in their Sāmoan or Sāmoan-German perspectives. They also vary in their motivation in pursuing this issue—from personal interest to its appropriation for its currency as topic of interest and marketability, just as I, as a German academic, am part of a changing national commemorative culture that has brought Germany's difficult colonial past back to the surface while subjecting it to international attention, critique, and protest (as through the artists under scrutiny).[129] In any case, perspectives and motivations are heterogeneous and cannot be reduced to a singular view and motive.

Yet all three artists have been subjected to the same dynamics of the Pacific diaspora and the associated "ambivalent kinship," which have also been provoked by the German colonial legacy and, as we have seen, have spurred different manifestations of self-inspection or self-ethnography—pursued and expressed through the "art of in-betweenness"—to address, negotiate, and revise the diasporic "space between" various locations and positions, including Sāmoa and Germany. Moreover, all three artists use ethnographic museums as resources and sites for interventions and expressions. Their historical research and fieldwork leave traces of "the ethnographic in artwork," thus further blurring the boundaries between art and anthropology.[130] Their staunch cultural and political positioning makes it "almost unthinkable," as Jonathan Mane-Wheoki notes in reference to Māori artists, to "seek mere aesthetic or intellectual gratification from their work."[131] Their methodological twist of a reverse anthropological mimicry unsettles the "artificial division between Western and non-Western artists," and transcends the "clear binary structures of colonizer and colonized."[132] Most important, this reverse anthropological mimicry perpetuates the ambivalent ethnographic condition and carries it from colonial governance into contemporary art. We shall see in due course where it travels from here.

CONCLUSION

An Ethnographic Kaleidoscope

This book began with the specific intention of refocusing ethnographic museums through Oceanic lenses and ended on the broad notion of "anthropology's interlocutors" navigating an all-encompassing and all-permeating ethnographic condition. As James Clifford observed some thirty years ago,

> It has become necessary to imagine a world of generalized ethnography. With expanded communication and intercultural influence, people interpret others, and themselves, in a bewildering diversity of idioms—a global condition of what Mikhail Bakhtin called "heteroglossia".[1]

It appears an irony of history that the same interpretive terrain through which often harmful anthropological categories, typologies, and hierarchies were created has not been left behind, as the frequently used prefix "post" (as in "post-ethnographic") seems to announce, but is rather critically renavigated and creatively reproduced. As we have seen in the preceding chapters, the ethnographic condition is inevitably and inescapably ambivalent; its anthropological steering might offer tools for racial profiling and colonial suppression as well as for liberating objects, humanizing types, revaluing informants, and articulating or performing artistic critique.

Apart from this analytical focus, and the historical and contemporary realities thus revealed, *Refocusing Ethnographic Museums through Oceanic Lenses* responds to the "heteroglossia" of the ethnographic condition through "polyphony," another concept introduced by Bakhtin.[2] That is, the book refocuses the ethnographic, and thus the ethnographic museum, through the conceptualization and execution of the inquiry itself: by decentering and multiplying the interpretive authority and by giving expression to plural voices engaged in the co-construction of knowledge. In doing so analytically and methodologically, the authors shape something that might be called an ethnographic kaleidoscope. *Merriam-Webster* defines a kaleidoscope as "an instrument containing loose bits of colored material (such as glass or plastic) between two flat plates and two plane mirrors so placed that changes of position of the bits of material are reflected in an endless variety of patterns."[3] The book has been written by and with several authors inspecting a common point of reference or "bits of material." The associated negotiation of this polyphonic texture necessarily implies constant "changes of position." It follows that the resulting text can only be seen as a momentarily tamed and tied down instant and state of an "endless variety of patterns." The same yet differently manifested kaleidoscopic effect will hold true for each individual reader because the ethnographic story told here lingers on in you, the reader, and in the process of reading becomes subjected to further examinations and dissections, and thus to further changes of position and an infinite variety of patterns. This book is, in fact—like any ethnographic study—unfinishable and, to a certain extent, a purely subjective phenomenon for both writer and reader. Consequently, it feels more like concluding a story about the book than the book as such. Paul Ricoeur's insights into the circular relationship of life and narrative reflect the condition of writing and reading.[4] On the one hand, I, or rather we, have been drawing on academic conventions and linguistic tools provided by cultural life to write this book. On the other hand, this specific form of narrative lives on in the interpretive world of you, the reader.

An ethnographic kaleidoscope responds to these ever-shifting interpretive positions and interpreted patterns, and is not only of metaphorical value for our purposes here. Instead, a kaleidoscope as an instrument materializes a way of ethnographically thinking and knowing about what can and should be ethnographically thought and known.[5] In other words, the kaleidoscope offers a lens through which the ethnographic museum can be refocused by moving intellectually from the impulse to freeze and close differences—perceived as cultural, ontological, or otherwise—into categories, types, and taxonomies, toward more dynamic and opening intellectual performances such as tracing and mapping ethnographic positions and patterns and doing and enacting ethnography itself. In this vein, this book has not been content with articulating an argument or formulating critique—however important both aspects of intellectual labor are—but has striven to present profound thinking deriving from, and feeding back into, concrete practices, while mobilizing this doing-thinking-doing to reimagine or refocus ethnographic museums. A concluding event and story illustrates this point.

On October 23, 2017, the Free State of Saxony in Germany returned, for the first time in its history, ancestral remains—in this case *iwi kūpuna*—to their descendants and place of origin, in this case Hawaiʻi. These iwi kūpuna were evidently stolen by German ship captains from burial caves in Hilo, Honolulu, and Waiʻalae in the Hawaiian Islands between 1896 and 1902 and sold directly to the Königliches Zoologisches und Anthropologisch-Ethnographisches Museum in Dresden.[6] There they *became* scientific specimens incorporated into the anthropological collection that later, in 1957, formed part of the Museum für Völkerkunde Dresden. This museum belongs, since 2004, to the Staatliche Ethnographische Sammlungen Sachsen, or SES (State Ethnographic Collections Saxony)—together with the Grassi Museum für Völkerkunde zu Leipzig and the Völkerkundemuseum Herrnhut—and, since 2010, to the Staatliche Kunstsammlungen Dresden, or SKD (Dresden State Art Collections).

When I began the fieldwork informing this book in Hawaiʻi in late 2014, I became aware of this particular and seemingly unsolvable claim, which was first lodged in 1991. I did so by engaging with Noelle Kahanu (coauthor of chapter 1) and Edward Halealoha Ayau, then executive director of Hui Mālama I Nā Kūpuna O Hawaiʻi Nei, a Hawaiian group devoted to the return of globally dispersed iwi kūpuna.[7] In October 2017, twenty-six years later, just a month after I started in my new role as head of research at the SES, this ordeal finally found its positive conclusion. My involvement on the Saxonian side in making this happen was minimal because my colleagues Nanette Snoep, Birgit Scheps-Bretschneider, and Vera Marusic had paved the way through the bureaucratic machinery for months before I joined the institution. It seemed as if I were drawn to this historical juncture beyond my control, but I am convinced that this remarkable constellation itself was no accident but the response to some higher calling. After reading this book, the reader should not be surprised that I unconditionally supported the cause and took charge of much of the external correspondence with the Hawaiian side, with whom I was also more familiar. I made any effort conceivable that this historic event would run culturally safe, diplomatically appropriate, and intellectually stimulating, and insisted that we should arrange a public roundtable discussion (after the political act sealing the return of the iwi kūpuna) so that museum staff and visitors could come along, meet, experience, listen, ask, and understand. Both sides, SES and Hawaiʻi, agreed to stage such an event.

As we have seen throughout this book, ethnographic museums are increasingly discussed and contested institutions in Germany, Europe, and beyond. The debate around issues such as the provenance of so-called ethnographic objects collected in colonial contexts and the restitution of illegitimately removed human remains to the descendants of the deceased is particularly intense.[8] This discussion, however, often remains at the level of political opinion and lacks critical and productive interrogation. Restitution is often seen as an individual and final act, as an end in itself, which could even threaten the survival of museum collections and research. But what happens if we reconsider restitution itself as anthropological work, which allows us to delve deeper into the meanings of material entities and the life of things? What can be gained, rather than lost, if we approach restitution as an integral dimension of the museum as process through which "ethnographic objects" and human remains can be reconnected with the cultural environments of their source societies and customary sources of knowledge? In short, what new can we study, learn, and understand through processes of restitution—due to their epistemological and ontological potentialities—while writing the next chapter of the ongoing relationships between here and there, us and them?[9]

The panel was conceived as part of the *Prolog #1–10 Stories of People, Things and Places,* a workshop exhibition that explores the museum in an ongoing process and invites the visitor to look behind the scenes. It tells local and global stories about people, things, and places.[10] The speakers were Dr. Kamanaʻopono Crabbe, Ka Pouhana/CEO of the Office of Hawaiian Affairs (OHA); Edward Halealoha Ayau, liaison to OHA on International Repatriation and former executive director of Hui Mālama I Nā Kūpuna O Hawaiʻi Nei; Kaleikoa Kaʻeo, leader and Hawaiian language and culture educator with the University of Hawaiʻi from the island of Maui; Kauila Kealiʻikanakaʻoleohaililani, grandson of Pualani and Edward L.H. Kanahele, founders of Hui Mālama I Nā Kūpuna O Hawaiʻi Nei; Noelle (coauthor of chapter 1) as well as Birgit, who is in charge of provenance research at SES; and myself. The panel discussion, including one film about Hui Mālama I Nā Kūpuna O Hawaiʻi Nei and another about the return of chief Kalaniʻōpuʻu's mahiole and ʻahu ʻula from Aotearoa to Hawaiʻi (see introduction),[11] provided insights into the underpinning (anthropological) work, which reconnects past, present, and future, to critically and productively address the key question: "Restitution: What Now?"[12]

It goes beyond the scope of this conclusion to analyze the event, and its bits of material, changes of position, and endless variety of patterns in detail. I—or rather we—shall do so in due course, however. What I end with are two anecdotes, one before and one after the roundtable discussion. On Sunday evening, the day before the political and public gatherings, a small group of museum staff, including myself, welcomed the Hawaiian delegation and opened the museum so that the iwi kūpuna could be ceremonially received and prepared for their journey home. As the ceremony was conducted in one staff room, my colleagues and I were sitting in another, waiting quietly so that the process could unfold without any disturbance. Suddenly, ear-piercing Hawaiian chants echoed through the hallway and filled the adjacent rooms. One of my colleagues asked me—assuming my Hawaiian expertise—what the lyrics were. I instinctively responded, "I do not know; I do not care—it is enough for me to feel it." Weeks later at Leipzig University, one of my students, Despoina, while presenting on the roundtable discussion, asked the other students who attended about their impressions. One of them, Julius, responded by describing how he entered the Prolog exhibition space without noting many of the things on display. After engaging with the faces and stories of the speakers, and watching the films about their work, he explained, he left through the same exhibition space "looking anew" and "with different eyes" at the same "things." These two anecdotes illustrate what ethnographic museums, and anthropology more broadly, can and should do: rather than explaining differences of others away, they make us refocus our own lenses so that any bits of material are enlightened through changes of position and emerge in an endless variety of patterns. Imagine how rich life can be, or become, if we dare to take a curious look through such an ethnographic kaleidoscope . . .

AFTERWORD

Regenerating Maka

Ty P. Kāwika Tengan

I write this piece in October during the Hawaiian lunar month of ʻIkuwā,[1] which in 2017 is characterized by the southerly storms that give this month's name its meaning of "noisy, clamorous, . . . din, . . . voices of the gods in the elements."[2] The last month of the Hawaiian year, ʻIkuwā, heralds the rising of the Makaliʻi (Little Eyes, or the Pleiades) constellation at sunset and the start of the four-month Makahiki (Arrival of the Eyes) New Year ceremonies that mark the return of Lono, deity of abundance and fertility. As explained by Dr. Pualani Kanakaʻole Kanahele, founder of the Papakū Makawalu methodology (whose name references "eight eyes"),[3] the Makahiki period calls on "man to be conscious of the rejuvenation of life forms, man being part of the regeneration process."[4] This period of transition and renewal enacts a return to the initial moment of creation described in the cosmogonic genealogy of the Kumulipo, which places the beginning of the world "at the time of the night of Makaliʻi [winter]."[5] Moved by the din of the thunder and pounding rain outside my window, and cognizant of the fact that the broader pan-Austronesian term mata reverberates across the Pacific and offers shared vantage points for the Hawaiian, Rapanui, Māori, Sāmoan, and Tongan actors in this book, I suggest we consider the regenerative potential of maka/mata as a way of "refocusing ethnographic museums through Oceanic lenses."[6]

Following the lead of the Kanaka ʻŌiwi (Indigenous Hawaiian) artist Carl Pao,[7] I explore the *kaona* (referred to in chapter 2 as "layers of teaching and meaning" that is also a cognate of *taonga*, the Māori concept for treasure explained in chapter 5)[8] of the concept "*maka*" by offering the following list of entries given in the *Hawaiian Dictionary:*

1. n. Eye, eye of a needle, face, countenance; presence, sight, view; lens of a camera.
2. n. Beloved one, favorite; person.
3. n. Point, bud, protuberance; center of a flower, including usually both the stamens and pistils; nipple, teat; sharp edge or blade of an instrument; point of a fishhook; beginning, commencement; source; any new plant shoot coming up. Fig., descendant. **ho'o. maka** To begin, start, initiate; commence; to appear, of a child's first tooth; to put forth buds; to come to a head, as a boil. *Mea ho'omaka,* beginner. (PPN mata.)
4. n. Mesh of a net, mesh in plaiting; stitch, in sewing.
5. vs. Raw, as fish; uncooked; green, unripe, as fruit; fresh as distinct from salted provisions; wet, as sand.
6. Probably same as manu, canoe bow and stern pieces.
7. n. A seaweed.
8. n. Varieties of sweet potato.
9. n. Recognition token.[9]

Recognizing that not all of these definitions pertain to the different cases that Philipp, Noelle, Sean, Mara, Cristián, and Nina discuss, I nevertheless suggest that maka points to a source of what Vicente Diaz calls "Indigenous discursive flourish"—a "penchant for meaning making and multiplication"[10]—characteristic of Native Pacific ontologies that genealogically connect people, place, potency, and portability. Eyes, faces, beloved persons, descendants, flower buds, seaweed, and sweet potatoes are—like Bishop Museum's *He Nae Akea* exhibition described in the introduction—bound together in a net strung between the end points of a canoe whose mobile interpretation initiates new presences.

To refocus this book and the ethnographic museums and things in it, let us look to maka's encompassing the "lens of a camera"—the device that brought the images of Pacific Islanders' engagements with empire into a particular kind of focus. This expansion of meaning from eye to camera lens points to Hawaiian propensities to adopt Western technologies in efforts to adapt to worlds increasingly difficult to recognize without the aid of multiple optics.[11] These are always fraught and unequal processes, as shown in chapter 5's multiple views on a double German-Sāmoan/Sāmoan-German lens. Like the institutions and histories the authors detail, I suggest this text be viewed as and through maka—a new shoot whose emergence begins a fresh—if still raw—process of regenerating and remaking the face of the ethnographic museum.[12]

By foregrounding (or, à la Kanahale, being part of) processes of regeneration, I respond to the work of Native or Indigenous studies scholars who argue for a return to spiritual, cultural, and land-based practices as the basis of Indigenous political and intellectual resurgence.[13] In the Hawaiian context, a primary biological and cultural concept for regeneration is the *kīpuka,* "a clear place or oasis within a lava bed where there may be vegetation."[14] As Davianna McGregor explains,

> The beauty of these natural kīpuka is not only their ability to resist and withstand destructive forces of change, but their ability to regenerate life on the barren lava that surrounds them. For from these kīpuka come the seeds and spores carried by birds and blown by the wind to sprout upon and regenerate the forest on the new lava, sparking a new dynamic cycle of coming into and passing out of life.[15]

McGregor goes on to show how rural communities can be viewed as "cultural kīpuka . . . from which Native Hawaiian culture can be regenerated and revitalized in the setting of contemporary Hawai'i."[16] Noelani Goodyear-Ka'ōpua applies McGregor's analytic to the efforts of Native Hawaiian educators to establish kīpuka, or zones of Indigenous cultural growth, through Hawaiian charter schools.[17] Similarly, we can also view the museums discussed in this book as potential kīpuka for the regeneration of Oceanic materialities, connectivities, and mana—to name just of few of the important sources of becoming that are discussed.

In pointing to the "generative potency"[18] of museum objects—or as they are reframed here as ships, vessels, things, and treasures (*mea makamae* in Hawaiian)—living in these kīpuka, I suggest the use of a related land-based metaphor, *makana'ā.* Mary Kawena Pukui and Samuel Elbert define the term as "plants growing on lava beds (probably a contraction of maka i nā 'a'ā, budding in the lava)."[19] Seen as makana'ā, the materials thrive in curatorial environments that nurture and are expanded by its growth. Intentional care of watchful maka—those individuals and groups who claim descent as well as those who nurture friendship—promotes the regeneration not only of a single shoot, but an entire ecosystem. This book offers numerous examples of just this phenomenon in the making, notably doing so in conversations coming from and between maka: the Hawaiian makaloa mat of Kala'i whose petition produces a material response 140 years later (chapter 2); the Ho'omaka Hou Research Initiative linking present-day Rapanui descendants to images of ancestors from 1934 and 1935 while producing new pictures of places photographed at that same time (chapter 3); and the defiant eyes and countenance of a modern "savage" rewriting old anthropological perspectives through the work of a contemporary Sāmoan artist (chapter 6).

My thinking on the regenerative capacity of Oceanic maka owes a great debt to my makamaka (friend) Carl Pao, a Native Hawaiian artist whose pieces were featured in the 2003 *E Kū Mau Mau* exhibit discussed in chapter 1. In his later artwork, he uses the motif of the maka (and all of its layered meanings, though particularly as the sexualized aspect of the stamens at the center of the flower) to restore mana (generative potency, spiritual power, and authority) to the carved images of Hawaiian male gods whose penises were chopped off sometime before they ended up in the various museums where they now are.[20] Pao's painting *Ki'i Kupuna: Maka* (2013) (figure 8.1) represents the maka of a flower (both stamens and pistil) at the center of the gaping mouth of a *ki'i* (carved image). Describing the work, Marata Tamaira writes, "The mouth of the ki'i functions as a sacred, protective space, safeguarding the maka—a metaphor for the Hawaiian people—as it regenerates itself in a perpetual cycle of growth and renewal."[21] Through this lens, we may revision all ki'i (as well as the museums they are found in) as kīpuka (sites of Indigenous regeneration) for makana'ā, new buddings of life and mana flowing from the "curatorial conversations" that have produced Pao's pieces as well as those embodied in this text—and thus the book itself.

To speak of regenerating maka is to necessarily foreground the centrality of Oceanic genealogical practices in the refocusing of ethnographic museums and anthropology more generally.[22] Genealogy as practice interweaves and activates multiple relational lines in order to draw from the generative past new and old pathways forward.[23] For Hawaiians, maka traces a lineage to Hāloa, which names both the chiefly progenitor of our people as well as his elder sibling the kalo (taro) plant.[24] We see this connection in a chant that makes reference to "nā maka o Hā-loa i luna," which Pukui and Elbert translate as

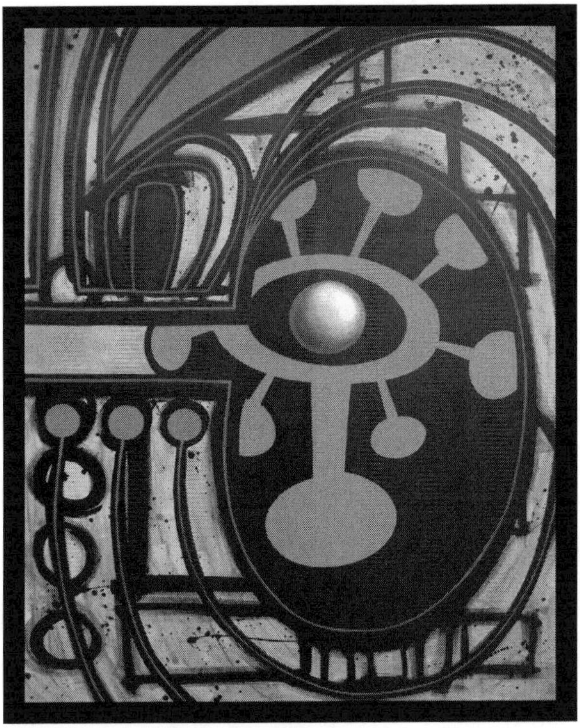

Figure 8.1 Art work, *Ki'i Kupuna: Maka,* by Carl F. K. Pao. Photograph courtesy of artist.

"descendants of Hā-loa above."[25] Jonathan Goldberg-Hiller and Noenoe Silva argue that the ability of Hāloa (as both kalo and genealogical links between land and people) to regenerate "by budding, moving underground, and arising again in new foliage, along themselves" expresses a "Kanaka [Hawaiian] ontology" of emergence that "recognizes cultural continuity and creation even in the context of thin political and material resources."[26] We might also view maka and makanaʻā as reflecting a "practical ontology"[27] through which contemporary objects and offspring become the living face of the ancestors, refuting colonial assertions of Indigenous death or containment (as Philipp shows of Rapa Nui in chapter 4). In the Māori context, the establishment and enactment of *whakapapa* (genealogical and kinship) connections transforms individuals and artifacts into "the living face" of both their ancestors as well as a new layer of ancestral relationship that generates "the continued flourishing of . . . well-being and mana."[28]

It is here that I need to briefly mark my own genealogical engagements with some of the maka in this book. My maternal grandmother Margaret's maiden name was Kamaka ("The maka"), and she first saw me in Wiesbaden, Germany, shortly after my birth—an event referred to metaphorically as *puka nā maka i ke ao* (the eyes appear in the light).[29] I was in Germany only for a few months before my father, who was in the U.S. Army, finished his tour of duty. I spent most of my life in Hawai'i, where a nagging sense of outsiderness as a Hawaiian evidently led me to anthropology. I later worked with mentors who were leaders in the Hawaiian repatriation and burial protection movement, and it was through that I first met Noelle Kahanu. In her various roles, Noelle has been a major part of almost every project I have been involved with at the Bishop Museum, and in large part I have her to thank (or blame!) for being a part of this book. It was through her hosting that Philipp came to be at the University of Hawai'i for three months and that he and I established a connection.

Although Philipp and I have a similar approach to thinking about museums, I was nonetheless wary when he and Noelle invited me to contribute to this text. What would it mean—for all of the coauthors—to be slotted into the "with" category below Philipp as the main author attributed with the reaching out to "collaborate"? How much would others actually be able to speak, and how would they be heard? As much of my subsequent conversation with him occurred over email, it was difficult for me to get a true sense of how he conducted himself as a scholar outside Hawai'i as I had not yet had the opportunity to 'ike maka (see for myself).

Then, in the summer of 2017, I attended the meeting of the European Society for Oceanists (ESfO) in Munich that Philipp helped host. This was my first time in Germany since 1975, and it was an important return not only to a land but also to the discipline that was a home for me. On numerous occasions, I observed Philipp pushing the dialogues to be truly regenerative of new ideas and practices. We sat and discussed my initial concerns at length, and he encouraged me to include them here while also raising new ones. I was encouraged.

When I finally received and read the draft of the book, I was heartened by what I saw as an emergence of multiple maka—both as perspectives and as presences. Nowhere is this more evident than in chapter 5, coauthored with Sean Mallon (a friend whose voice I was happy to imagine hearing) and Nina Tonga (whom I look forward to meeting one day). The critiques that Sean and Nina levy on Philipp's curatorial choices make space not only for their own Sāmoan and Tongan voices to be heard, but also for a recognition of the potentials and problems of mana taonga when multiple genealogies do or do not articulate in the co-collecting process. So too do the voices of Mara Mulrooney (a former Bishop Museum colleague whom I respect tremendously) and Cristián Moreno Pakarati (whom I would love to work with) shift the tenor of chapter 3, particularly because Cristián (a descendant of an early Rapanui "informant") brings a distinct form of genealogical bearing to the chapter's writing. Last is Noelle, whose writing with Philipp has produced a muliwai of words that, like the physical estuary at the meeting of river and sea, is a space for regeneration.

I trace and honor these relations because they are central to any form of genealogical practice. Indeed, the sprouting and nurturing of the makana'ā (budding shoots in the lava) requires an environment of care whose hallmark is a collaborative ethos that invites multiple others—scholars, museum staff, administrators, donors, community members, ancestors, lands, oceans, gods—to coauthor and co-configure the space of the ethnographic museum as a kīpuka (zone of Indigenous growth). The collaborative mode that Philipp, Noelle, Mara, Cristián, Sean, and Nina enact here is not perfect, but it is a powerful example of what can happen when anthropologists and curators rethink both the starting and end points of their interventions.

I conclude this essay where I began it, in the month of 'Ikuwā. It is the start of the Makahiki, a time of returns and renewals as the elemental form of the god Lono brings winter storms and drenched landscapes. Community groups are harvesting kalo for offerings and training their bodies for competition. In the spirit of Makahiki, Noelle and a contingent of Native Hawaiian leaders have just come back from Dresden where, working with Philipp, they were able to complete the first repatriation of iwi kupuna (ancestral human remains) from the German state of Saxony.[30] Accompanying this group was Kamana'opono Crabbe, the CEO/Pouhana of the Office of Hawaiian Affairs (and a good friend). When I asked him what he thought of Philipp, the first word out of his mouth was "makaihe" (spear tip). The reference here is to Lonomakaihe, a form of Lono prayed to by warriors who trained in lonomakaihe (the art of spear throwing), one of the games played during Makahiki.

Recalling Philipp's convening of an academic panel, Kamanaʻopono wrote, "When he launches a spear through his questions, and it has the ripple effect to alter a new direction in a field such as anthropology and archaeology, it was exciting."[31] Crabbe's statement reminds us that refocusing museums through maka also requires koa (courage) to both hurl and dodge the spears that will fly in the battles to decolonize ethnographic museums. This koa comes from the recitation of I-kū-wā, which was and is also the line shouted out by the people in response to the leaders of the *I Kū Mau Mau* chant (chapter 1). As our ancestors have done before us, so will our descendants—we bud, emerge, and regenerate.

Notes

Introduction

1. Friedrich von Bose, *Das Humboldt-Forum: Eine Ethnografie seiner Planung* (Berlin: Kulturverlag Kadmos, 2016); Horst Bredekamp and Peter-Klaus Schuster, eds., *Das Humboldt Forum: Die Widergewinnung der Idee* (Berlin: Wagenbach, 2016); and Stiftung Preußischer Kulturbesitz, *The Laboratory Concept: Museum Experiments in the Humboldt Lab Dahlem* (Berlin: Nicolai, 2015).
2. Thomas Thiemeyer, "Deutschland postkolonial: Ethnologische und genealogische Erinnerungskultur," *Merkur: Deutsche Zeitschrift für europäisches Denken* 70 (July 2016): 33–45. See "No Humboldt 21!," http://www.no-humboldt21.de, accessed June 27, 2019; Africanevir, *No Humboldt 21! Dekoloniale Einwände gegen das Humboldt-Forum* (Berlin: Africanevir, 2017); see also the exhibition in Berlin (Deutsches Historisches Museum, "German Colonialism," https://www.dhm.de/en/ausstellungen/archive/2016/german-colonialism.html, accessed June 27, 2019).
3. Michael M. Ames, *Cannibal Tours and Glass Boxes: The Anthropology of Museums* (Vancouver: UBC Press, 1992); James Clifford, *The Predicament of Culture* (Cambridge, MA: Harvard University Press, 1988); James Clifford, *Routes: Travel and Translation in the late Twentieth Century* (Cambridge, MA: Harvard University Press, 1997); Ivan Karp, Christine Mullen Kreamer, and Steven D. Lavine, eds., *Museums and Communities: The Politics of Public Culture* (Washington, DC: Smithsonian Institution Press, 1992); and Ivan Karp and Steven D. Lavine, *Exhibiting Cultures: The Poetics and Politics of Museum Display* (Washington, DC: Smithsonian Institution Press, 1991).
4. Tony Bennet, Ben Dibley, and Rodney Harrison, "Introduction: Anthropology, Collecting and Colonial Governmentalities," *History and Anthropology* 25, no. 2 (2014): 137–149; Rodney Harrison, Sarah Byrne, and Anne Clarke, eds., *Reassembling the Collection: Ethnographic Museums and Indigenous Agency* (Santa Fe, NM: SAR Press, 2013); and Chris Gosden and Frances Larson, *Knowing Things: Exploring the Collections at the Pitt Rivers Museum 1884–1945* (Oxford: Oxford University Press, 2007).

5. Bryony Onciul, *Museums, Heritage and Indigenous Voice: Decolonising Engagement* (London: Routledge, 2015); Philipp Schorch, Conal McCarthy, and Arapata Hakiwai, “Globalizing Māori Museology: Reconceptualizing Engagement, Knowledge and Virtuality through Mana Taonga,” *Museum Anthropology* 39, no. 1 (2016): 48–69; Conal McCarthy, “Indigenisation: Reconceptualising Museology,” in *The Contemporary Museum: Shaping Museums for the Global Now,* ed. Simon J. Knell (London: Routledge, 2018), 37–54; and Amy Lonetree, *Decolonizing Museums: Representing Native America in National and Tribal Museums* (Chapel Hill: University of North Carolina Press, 2012).
6. Christina Kreps, “The Theoretical Future of Indigenous Museums: Concept and Practice,” in *The Future of Indigenous Museums: Perspectives from the Southwest Pacific*, ed. Nick Stanley (Oxford: Berghahn Books, 2007), 223–234; and Stanley, *The Future of Indigenous Museums.*
7. Conal McCarthy, *Museums and Māori: Heritage Professionals, Indigenous Collections, Current Practice* (Wellington: Te Papa Press, 2011); and Philipp Schorch, “Assembling Communities: Curatorial Practices, Material Cultures, and Meanings,” in *Engaging Heritage, Engaging Communities*, eds. Bryony Onciul, Michelle L. Stefano, and Stephanie Hawke (Suffolk, UK: Boydell and Brewer, 2017), 31–46.
8. Philipp Schorch, Conal McCarthy, and Eveline Dürr, “Introduction: Conceptualising Curatopia,” in Schorch and McCarthy, *Curatopia,* 1–16.
9. Harrison, Byrne, and Clarke, *Reassembling the Collection*; Conal McCarthy, *Indigenous Museology: Insights from Australia and Aotearoa New Zealand* (London: Routledge, forthcoming 2020); Christina F. Kreps, *Liberating Culture: Cross-Cultural Perspectives on Museums, Curation, and Heritage Preservation* (London: Routledge, 2003); and Ruth B. Phillips, *Museum Pieces: Toward the Indigenization of Canadian Museums* (Montreal: McGill-Queen’s University Press, 2013).
10. Rainer F. Buschmann, “Oceanic Collections in German Museums Collections, Contexts, and Exhibits,” in *Pacific Presences: Oceanic Art and European Museums,* vol. 1, eds. Lucie Carreau, Alison Clark, Alana Jelinek, Erna Lilje, and Nicholas Thomas (Leiden: Sidestone Press, 2018), 197–227.
11. A variety of European conferences, which I attended throughout the course of this project, offered insights into productive initiatives while, above all, pointing to the ways in which the institution of the ethnographic (or ethnological) museum is being hotly debated and contested today. Examples include the following: “Difficult Heritage: Colonial Objects—Postcolonial Knowledge” at the Linden-Museum

Stuttgart in 2017 (see conference flyer, https://www.lindenmuseum.de/fileadmin/user_upload/images/fotogalerie/Schwieriges_Erbe/Faltblatt_Einladung_SchwierigesErbe.pdf, accessed May 28, 2017; conference report by Myriam Gröpl and Sara Capdeville, "Tagungsbericht: 'Schwieriges Erbe. Koloniale Objekte—Postkoloniales Wissen,'" Universität Hamburg, May 19, 2017, https://www.kolonialismus.uni-hamburg.de/tagungsbericht-schwieriges-erbe-koloniale-objekte-postkoloniales-wissen-24-04-2017-linden-museum-stuttgart, accessed June 7, 2017); "The Future of Ethnographic Museums" at the Pitt Rivers Museum in Oxford in 2013 (see Clare Harris and Michael O'Hanlon, "The Future of the Ethnographic Museum," *Anthropology Today* 29 [2013]: 8–12); "Positioning Ethnological Museums in the 21st Century" in Hanover, Germany, in 2015 (see Eckart Köhne, ed., "Positioning Ethnological Museums in the 21st Century," *Museumskunde* 81, no. 1 [2016]: 10–13).

12. Friedrich von Bose, "Strategische Reflexivität: Das Berliner Humboldt Forum und die postkoloniale Kritik," *Historische Anthropologie* 25, no. 3 (2017): 409–417; for a critical commentary, see Philipp Schorch, "Why has the ethnographic museum run out of steam?," *Wie weiter mit Humboldts Erbe?* (blog), 2018, https://blog.uni-koeln.de/gssc-humboldt/why-has-the-ethnographic-museum-run-out-of-steam, accessed November 27, 2018.
13. For the German context, see Larissa Förster, "Öffentliche Kulturinstitution, internationale Forschungsstätte und postkoloniale Kontaktzone: Was ist ethno am ethnologischen Museum?," in *Ethnologie im 21. Jahrhundert*, eds. Thomas Bierschenk, Matthias Krings, and Carola Lentz (Berlin: Dietrich Reimer Verlag, 2013), 189–210; Michael Kraus and Karoline Noack, eds., *Quo vadis, Völkerkundemuseum? Aktuelle Debatten zu ethnologischen Sammlungen in Museen und Universitäten* (Bielefeld: transcript, 2015); and Hans-Peter Hahn, ed., *Ethnologie und Weltkulturenmuseum*: Positionen für eine offene Weltsicht (Berlin: Vergangenheitsverlag, 2017).
14. James Clifford, "The Times of the Curator," in Schorch and McCarthy, *Curatopia*, 109.
15. Eileen Hooper-Greenhill, *Museums and the Interpretation of Visual Culture* (London: Routledge, 2000), 153.
16. Ciraj Rassool, "Towards the Postcolonial Museum" (paper presented at the "Difficult Heritage" conference, Linden-Museum Stuttgart, Germany, April 24, 2017).
17. Christopher B. Balme, *Pacific Performances: Theatricality and Cross-Cultural Encounter in the South Seas* (New York: Palgrave Macmillan, 2007), 9.

18. Arif Dirlik, ed., *What Is in a Rim? Critical Perspectives on the Pacific Region Idea,* 2nd ed. (Lanham, MD: Rowman & Littlefield, 1998).
19. Margaret Jolly, "Imagining Oceania: Indigenous and Foreign Representations of a Sea of Islands," *The Contemporary Pacific* 19, no. 2 (2007): 508–545; Epeli Hau'ofa, *We Are the Ocean: Selected Works* (Honolulu: University of Hawai'i Press, 2008); Vilsoni Hereniko and Rob Wilson, eds., *Inside Out: Literature, Cultural Politics and Identity in the New Pacific* (Lanham, MA: Rowman & Littlefield, 1999); Teresia K. Teaiwa, "Native Thoughts: A Pacific Studies Take on Cultural Studies and Diaspora," in *Indigenous Diasporas and Dislocations*, eds. Graham Harvey and Charles D. Thompson Jr. (Aldershot, UK: Ashgate, 2005), 15–35; Ty P. Kāwika Tengan, Tēvita O. Ka'ili, and Rochelle Tuitagava'a Fonoti, "Genealogies: Articulating Indigenous Anthropology in/of Oceania," Special issue, *Pacific Studies* 33, no. 2/3 (2010): 139–167; and Albert Wendt, "Towards a New Oceania," *Mana Review: A South Pacific Journal of Language and Literature* 1, no. 1 (1976): 49–60.
20. Philipp Schorch and Arno Pascht, eds., "Reimagining Oceania through Critical Junctures," special issue, *Oceania* 87, no. 2 (2017): 114–187.
21. Serge Tcherkézoff, "Inventing Polynesia," in Hermann, *Changing Contexts, Shifting Meanings,* 123.
22. Quoted in ibid., 124.
23. Serge Tcherkézoff, "A Long and Unfortunate Voyage Towards the 'Invention' of the Melanesia/Polynesia Dinstinction (1595–1832)," *Journal of Pacific History* 38, no. 2 (2003): 175–196; and Bronwen Douglas, "Encountering Agency: Islanders, European Voyagers, and the Production of Race in Oceania," in Herman, *Changing Contexts, Shifting Meanings,* 74–92; Bronwen Douglas and Christopher Ballard, "Race, Place and Civilisation: Colonial Encounters and Governance in Greater Oceania," *Journal of Pacific History* 47, no. 3 (2012): 1–18.
24. Nicholas Thomas et al., "The Force of Ethnology: Origins and Significance of the Melanesia/Polynesia Division [and Comments and Replies]," *Current Anthropology* 30, no. 1 (1989): 27–41; Nicholas Thomas, *In Oceania: Visions, Artifacts, Histories* (Durham, NC: Duke University Press, 1997); Margaret Jolly, "On the Edge? Deserts, Oceans, Islands," *The Contemporary Pacific* 13, no. 2 (2001): 417–466; Jolly, "Imagining Oceania"; Hau'ofa, "Our Sea of Islands"; Hau'ofa, *We Are the Ocean.*
25. Vilsoni Hereniko, "Dancing Oceania: The Oceania Dance Theatre in Context," in *The Fifth Asia-Pacific Triennial of Contemporary Art*, eds. Lynne Seear and Suhanya Raffel (Brisbane: Queensland Art Gallery, 2006); Albert Wendt, "Afterword: Tatauing the Post-Colonial Body," in *Inside Out: Literature, Cultural Politics, and Identity in the New Pacific,*

eds. Vilsoni Hereniko and Rob Wilson (New York: Rowman & Littlefield, 1999), 399–412.

26. Patrick V. Kirch, *On the Road of the Winds: An Archaeological History of the Pacific Islands before European Contact* (Oakland: University of California Press, 2017), 4.
27. Patrick V. Kirch and Roger C. Green. *Hawaiki, Ancestral Polynesia: An Essay in Historical Anthropology* (Cambridge: Cambridge University Press, 2001); Peter H. Buck (Te Rangi Hiroa), *Vikings of the Sunrise* (Philadelphia, PA: Lippincott, 1938).
28. Lilikalā Kame'eleihiwa, "Hawai'i-nui-akea Cousins: Ancestral Gods and Bodies of Knowledge Are Treasures for the Descendants," *Te Kaharoa* 2 (2009): 42–43.
29. Jolly, "Imagining Oceania."
30. Kame'eleihiwa, "Hawai'i-nui-akea Cousins," 50. The term receives a special emphasis at the Hawai'inuiākea School of Hawaiian Knowledge at the University of Hawai'i (where Kame'eleihiwa teaches) that may not reflect its usage in other parts of Oceania.
31. Lilikalā Kame'eleihiwa, *Native Land and Foreign Desires: Pehea La E Pono Ai? How Shall We Live in Harmony?* (Honolulu: Bishop Museum Press, 1992).
32. Eveline Dürr and Philipp Schorch, eds., *Transpacific Americas: Encounters and Engagements Between the Americas and the South Pacific* (London: Routledge, 2016).
33. J. C. Beaglehole, ed., *The Journals of Captain James Cook: The Voyage of the Resolution and Discovery, 1776–1780: Part I* (Cambridge: The Hakluyt Society, 1967), 512, quoted in Sean Mallon et al., "The 'ahu 'ula and mahiole of Kalani'ōpu'u: a journey of chiefly adornments [Introduction]," *Tuhinga* 28 (2017): 5.
34. Mallon et al., "The 'ahu 'ula and mahiole," 7–11.
35. Ibid., 11.
36. Te Waari Carkeek, "Reforged Connections—a Tangata Whenua Perspective," *Tuhinga* 28 (2017): 16–17, 16.
37. Mallon et al., "The 'ahu 'ula and mahiole," 4.
38. Arapata Hakiwai, "Te hokinga atu (the return): ōku whakaaro (reflections)," *Tuhinga* 28 (2017): 17–19; Conal McCarthy, Arapata Hakiwai, and Philipp Schorch, "The Figure of the Kaitiaki," in Schorch and McCarthy, *Curatopia,* 211–226.
39. Noelle M.K.Y. Kahanu, "Fated Feathers, Unfurling Futures," *Tuhinga* 28 (2017): 24–30; Noelle Kahanu, Moana Nepia, and Philipp Schorch, "He alo ā he alo/kanohi ki te kanohi/Face to Face: Curatorial Bodies, Encounters and Relations," in Schorch and McCarthy, *Curatopia,* 296–316.

40. Epeli Hau'ofa, "Our Sea of Islands," *The Contemporary Pacific* 6, no. 1 (1994): 147–161; and Chris Ballard, "Oceanic Historicities," *The Contemporary Pacific* 26, no. 1 (2014): 96–124.
41. Hau'ofa, "Our Sea of Islands;" see also Philipp Schorch and Eveline Dürr, "Transpacific Americas as Relational Space," in Dürr and Schorch, *Transpacific Americas,* xi–xxv.
42. Waltraud Kokot, "Diaspora and transnationale Verflechtungen," in *Ethnologie der Globalisierung: Perspektiven kulturelle Verflechtungen*, eds. Brigitta Hauser-Schäublin and Ulrich Braukämpfer (Berlin: Dietrich Reimer Verlag, 2002), 95–110); George E. Marcus, "Ethnography in/of the World System: The Emergence of Multi-Sited Ethnography," *Annual Review of Anthropology* 24 (1995): 95–117; Karen Fog Olwig and Kirsten Hatrup, *Siting Culture: The Shifting Anthropological Object* (London: Routledge, 1997); and Gisela Welz, "Moving Targets: Feldforschung unter Mobilitätsdruck," *Zeitschrift fur Völkerkunde* 94, no. 2 (1998): 177–194.
43. Paul Gilroy, *The Black Atlantic: Modernity and Double Consciousness* (Cambridge: Harvard University Press, 1993).
44. Schorch, McCarthy, and Dürr, "Introduction: Conceptualising Curatopia."
45. Deutsche Gesellschaft für Völkerkunde e. V., "Umbenennung in Deutsche Gesellschaft für Sozial- und Kulturanthropologie," https://www.dgv-net.de/wir-heissen-anders/, accessed December 2, 2017.
46. For a detailed discussion of this pervasive shift, see Clifford, "The Times of the Curator."
47. Marcus Banks, *Visual Methods in Social Research* (London: Sage, 2001); Gemma Orobitg Canal, "Photography in the Field: Word and Image in Ethnographic Research," in *Working Images: Visual Research and Representation in Ethnography*, eds. Sarah Pink, László Kürti, and Ana Isabel Afonso (London: Routledge, 2004), 31–46; Christine Hine, *Virtual Ethnography* (London: Sage, 2000); Sarah Pink, *Doing Visual Ethnography* (London: Sage, 2009); Donald A. Ritchie, *Doing Oral History* (Oxford: Oxford University Press, 2003); Gerd Spittler, "Teilnehmende Beobachtung als Dichte Teilnahme," *Zeitschrift für Ethnologie* 126 (2001): 1–25; and Tom Wengraf, *Qualitative Research Interviewing: Biographical Narrative and Semi-Structured Methods* (London: Sage, 2001).
48. James Clifford, *The Predicament of Culture* (Cambridge, MA: Harvard University Press, 1988); George E. Marcus, *Ethnography through Thick and Thin* (Princeton, NJ: Princeton University Press, 1998); and Luke Eric Lassiter, *The Chicago Guide to Collaborative Ethnography* (Chicago: Chicago University Press, 2005).

49. James Clifford, George E. Marcus, and School of American Research, *Writing Culture: The Poetics and Politics of Ethnography: A School of American Research Advanced Seminar* (Berkeley: University of California Press, 1986); and Clifford, *The Predicament of Culture.*
50. Martin Holbraad and Morten Pedersen, *The Ontological Turn* (Cambridge: Cambridge University Press, 2017).
51. Gildas Salmond quoted in Eduardo Viveiros de Castro, "Who Is Afraid of the Ontological Wolf? Some Comments on an Ongoing Anthropological Debate," CUSAS Annual Marilyn Strathern Lecture, May 30, 2014, *Cambridge Journal of Anthropology* 33, no. 1 (2015): 2–17.
52. Viveiros de Castro, "Who Is Afraid?," 14 (emphasis in the original).
53. Amiria Salmond, "Transforming Translations (Part 2): Addressing Ontological Alterity," *HAU: Journal of Ethnographic Theory* 4, no. 1 (2014): 155–187, 179 [emphasis in the original].
54. Zoe Todd, "An Indigenous Feminist's Take on the Ontological Turn: 'Ontology' Is Just Another Word for Colonialism," *Journal of Historical Sociology* 29, no. 1 (2016): 4–22.
55. Schorch, McCarthy, and Dürr, "Introduction: Conceptualising Curatopia."
56. Philipp Schorch and Noelle M.K.Y. Kahanu, "Anthropology's Interlocutors: Hawai'i Speaking Back to Ethnographic Museums in Europe," *Zeitschrift für Kulturwissenschaften* 1 (2015): 114–117.
57. Nicolas Peterson, Lindy Allen, and Louise Hamby, eds., *The Makers and Making of Indigenous Australian Museum Collections* (Melbourne: Melbourne University Press, 2008); Sarah Byrne et al., eds., *Unpacking the Collection: Networks of Material and Social Agency in the Museum* (New York: Springer, 2011); Aaron Glass, Judith Berman, and Rainer Hatoum, "Reassembling *The Social Organization*: Collaboration and Digital Media in (Re)making Boas's 1897 Book," *Museum Worlds: Advances in Research* 5, no. 1 (2017): 108–132; and Michelle Horwood, *Sharing Authority in the Museum: Distributed Objects, Reassembled Relationships* (London: Routledge, 2018).
58. Bernadette Lynch, "The Gate in the Wall: Beyond Happiness-Making in Museums Meanings," in Onciul, Stefano, and Hawke, *Engaging Heritage,* 11–29; and "Whose Cake Is It Anyway? A Collaborative Investigation into Engagement and Participation in 12 Museums and Galleries in the UK" (London: Paul Hamlyn Foundation, 2011).
59. Philipp Schorch and Noelle M.K.Y. Kahanu, "Forum as Laboratory: The Cross-Cultural Infrastructure of Ethnographic Knowledge and Material Potentialities," in *Prinzip Labor: Museumsexperimente im Humboldt Lab Dahlem,* eds. Martin Heller, Andrea Scholz, and Agnes Wagner (Berlin: Nicolai Publishing, 2015), 241–248.

60. Tengan, Ka'ili, and Fonoti, "Genealogies," 140.
61. Manulani Aluli Meyer, *Ho'oulu: Our Time of Becoming. Hawaiian Epistemology and Early Writings* (Honolulu: 'Ai Pohaku Press, 2003).
62. On the common sphere, Wilhelm Dilthey, *Selected Writings* (Cambridge: Cambridge University Press, 1976); on untranslatable, Homi K. Bhabha, *The Location of Culture* (London: Routledge, 1994).
63. Schorch and Kahanu, "Forum as Laboratory."
64. Lassiter, *The Chicago Guide.* Examples that point into this direction include Paul Sillitoe, *Indigenous Studies and Engaged Anthropology: The Collaborative Moment* (London: Routledge, 2015); Joy Hendry and Laara Fitznor, eds., *Anthropologists, Indigenous Scholars and the Research Endeavour: Seeking Bridges Towards Mutual Respect* (London: Routledge, 2012).
65. James Clifford, "On Ethnographic Authority," *Representations* 2 (1983): 140.
66. Aaron Glass, "Indigenous Ontologies, Digital Futures: Plural Provenances and the Kwakwaka'wakw Collection in Berlin and Beyond," in *Museum as Process: Translating Local and Global Knowledges*, ed. Raymond A. Silverman, 19–44 (London: Routledge, 2015).

Chapter 1: I Kū Mau Mau

1. Mary Kawena Pukui, "The Canoe Making Profession of Ancient Times," in *Occasional Papers of Bernice Pauahi Bishop Museum of Polynesian Ethnology and Natural History* 15, no. 13 (November 1939): 149–159.
2. David Malo, *Hawaiian Antiquities (Moolelo Hawaii),* trans. Nathaniel Bright Emerson, 1898 (Honolulu: Hawaiian Gazette, 1903), 247.
3. Noenoe K. Silva, "I Kū Mau Mau: How Kānaka Maoli Tried to Sustain National Identity within the United States Political System," *American Studies* 45, no. 3 (Fall 2004): 9–31; see also Kaiulani Kanoa-Martin, ed., "I Ku Mau Mau," *Huapala: Hawaiian Music and Hula Archives,* http://www.huapala.org/Chants/I_Ku_Mau_Mau.html, accessed August 4, 2016.
4. John Wise, "Ka Ninau Ike Hana o Ke Kanaka Hawaii," *Kuokoa,* December 30, 1921.
5. Noelani Goodyear-Ka'ōpua, introduction to *A Nation Rising: Hawaiian Movements for Life, Land, and Sovereignty,* eds. Noelani Goodyear-Ka'ōpua, Ikaika Hussey, and Erin Kahunawaika'ala Wright (Durham, NC: Duke University Press, 2014), 1–33.
6. Philipp Schorch and Noelle M.K.Y. Kahanu, "Anthropology's Interlocutors: Hawai'i Speaking Back to Ethnographic Museums in Europe," *Zeitschrift für Kulturwissenschaften* 1 (2015): 114–117.

7. Peter Buck used this spelling of his Māori name—Te Rangi Hiroa—when he was at medical school at Otago University because it was easier for Pākehā (settlers of European descent) to pronounce. Today this appears archaic and names like this—Te Rangihīroa—usually follow Māori conventions established in the *Ngā Tāngata Taumata Tau Rau Dictionary of New Zealand Biography*. Consequently, we use Te Rangihīroa throughout this chapter and the book.
8. On genealogies, Arjun A. Appadurai, *Modernity at Large: Cultural Dimensions of Globalization* (Minneapolis: University of Minnesota Press, 1996).
9. Manulani Aluli Meyer, *Hoʻoulu: Our Time of Becoming: Hawaiian Epistemology and Early Writings* (Honolulu: ʻAi Pohaku Press, 2003); and Philipp Schorch and Noelle M.K.Y. Kahanu, "Forum as Laboratory: The Cross-Cultural Infrastructure of Ethnographic Knowledge and Material Potentialities," in *Prinzip Labor: Museumsexperimente im Humboldt Lab Dahlem,* eds. Martin Heller, Andrea Scholz, and Agnes Wagner (Berlin: Nicolai Publishing, 2015), 241–248; see also the introduction.
10. Kamanamaikalani Beamer, *No Mākou Ka Mana: Liberating the Nation* (Honolulu: Kamehameha Publishing, 2014); Lorenz Gonschor, "'A Power in the World': The Hawaiian Kingdom as a Model of Hybrid Statecraft in Oceania and a Progenitor of Pan-Oceanism" (PhD diss., University of Hawaiʻi, 2016); and Lorenz Gonschor, "Ka Hoku o Osiania: Promoting the Hawaiian Kingdom as a Model for Political Transformation in Nineteenth-Century Oceania," in *Agents of Transculturation: Border-Crossers, Mediators, Go-Betweens,* eds. Sebastian Jobs and Gesa Mackenthun (Münster: Waxmann, 2013), 157–188.
11. Roger Rose, "Hawaiian Hall—A Brief Historical Sketch" (unpublished paper, Bernice Pauahi Bishop Museum, 2003).
12. Roger Rose, *A Museum to Instruct and Delight: William T. Brigham and the Founding of Bernice Pauahi Bishop Museum* (Honolulu: Bishop Museum Press, 1980).
13. Haunani-Kay Trask, *From a Native Daughter: Colonialism and Sovereignty in Hawaiʻi* (Honolulu: University of Hawaiʻi Press, 1999).
14. Beamer, *No Mākou Ka Mana,* 12.
15. Tony Bennett, *The Birth of the Museum: History, Theory, Politics* (London: Routledge, 1995).
16. DeSoto Brown, personal communication with Philipp Schorch, October 15, 2014.
17. Beamer, *No Mākou Ka Mana,* 13.
18. Stacy L. Kamehiro, *The Arts of Kingship: Hawaiian Art and National Culture of the Kalakaua Era* (Honolulu: University of Hawaiʻi Press, 2009), 97.

19. Rose, *A Museum,* 17.
20. Ibid., 10–13. Queen Emmalani's 1884 codicil was initially questioned; it was not implemented until 1886, more than a year after her death.
21. "Ka Hale Hoikeike o Bihopa" (The Bishop Museum), *Ka Leo o ka Lahui,* September 21, 1894, 2; translated and reproduced in *nupepa,* April 28, 2016, accessed April 20, 2017, https://nupepa-hawaii.com/2016/04/28/e-ola-mau-ka-hale-hoikeike-o-bihopa-1894/.
22. Bernice Pauahi Bishop Museum [Bishop Museum], "Director's Report for 1903," in *Occasional Papers of Bernice Pauahi Bishop Museum of Polynesian Ethnology and Natural History* [*Occasional Papers*] 2, no. 2 (1904): 5.
23. William T. Brigham, *A Handbook for Visitors to the Bernice Pauahi Bishop Museum of Polynesian Ethnology and Natural History* (Honolulu: Bishop Museum Press, 1903), 7.
24. On primitive people and savage races, William T. Brigham, *Mat and Basket Weaving of the Ancient Hawaiians* (Honolulu: Bishop Museum Press, 1906), 1; on kapa-making, *Ka Hana Kapa: The Making of Bark-Cloth in Hawaii* (Honolulu: Bishop Museum Press, 1911), 1.
25. Emma Metcalf Beckley Nākuina, "Not Courteous Treatment of Ladies at Bishop Museum: An Open Protest to the Trustees of the Kamehameha Schools," *Pacific Commercial Advertiser,* May 19, 1897, 6.
26. Rose, *A Museum,* 67.
27. Bishop Museum, "Director's Report for 1899," *in Occasional Papers* 1, no. 2 (1900), 9.
28. Ibid., "Director's Report for 1903."
29. Herbert E. Gregory, "Report of the Director for 1924," *Bernice P. Bishop Museum Bulletin* 21 (1925), 51.
30. Ibid.
31. Bishop Museum, "Report of the Director for 1920," *Occasional Papers* 8, no. 1 (1921), 25.
32. Bishop Museum, *Annual Report* (Honolulu: Bishop Museum Press, 1919), 3.
33. Bishop Museum, "Report of the Director for 1921" (1922), 10.
34. Herbert E. Gregory, "Report of the Director for 1922," *Bernice P. Bishop Museum Bulletin* 4, (1923), 12; and "Report of the Director for 1924," *Bernice P. Bishop Museum Bulletin* 21 (1925), 3.
35. Herbert E. Gregory, "Report of the Director for 1926," *Bernice P. Bishop Museum Bulletin* 41 (1927), 34; and "Report of the Director for 1927," *Bernice P. Bishop Museum Bulletin* 57 (1928), 29.
36. Rose, "Hawaiian Hall," 138.
37. See Bishop Museum, "Reports of the Director," 1944–1949, in which staff listings note Lahilahi Webb as a consultant.

38. Peter H. Buck, "Report of the Director for 1949," *Bernice P. Bishop Museum Bulletin* 199 (1950), 25.
39. Herbert E. Gregory, "Report of the Director for 1924," 3.
40. From 1899 to 1921, annual reports note several Hawaiians who served as janitors: Moses Kauahi, James Kalei, William Aipu, and Thomas Keolanui.
41. Pukui to Webb, note, May 19, 1938, Webb Signature Book, translated by Todd Tukushima, Bishop Museum Archives.
42. Conal McCarthy, "'Empirical Anthropologists Advocating Cultural Adjustments': The Anthropological Governance of Āpirana Ngata and the Native Affairs Department," *History and Anthropology* 25, no. 2 (2014): 280–295; see also chapter 3.
43. Philipp Schorch, Conal McCarthy, and Arapata Hakiwai, "Globalizing Māori Museology: Reconceptualizing Engagement, Knowledge and Virtuality through Mana Taonga," *Museum Anthropology* 39, no. 1 (2016): 48–69.
44. Sebastian Conrad, "Enlightenment in Global History: A Historiographical Critique," *American Historical Review* 117, no. 4 (October 2012): 999–1027.
45. Philipp Schorch, Conal McCarthy, and Evelyn Dürr, "Introduction: Conceptualising Curatopia," in Schorch and McCarthy, *Curatopia,* 1–16; see also introduction.
46. Naomi Losch,"Mary Kawena Pukui," *Ōiwi: A Native Hawaiian Journal* 3 (2005); Katherine Luomala, "Necrology: Peter Henry Buck (Te Rangi Hiroa)," in "Report of the Director for 1951," ed. C. H. Edmondson, *Bernice P. Bishop Museum Bulletin* 208 (1952), 36–41; and John Bell Condliffe, *Te Rangi Hiroa: The Life of Sir Peter Buck* (Christchurch: Whitcombe and Tombs, 1971).
47. Bishop Museum, *Annual Report* (Honolulu: Bishop Museum Press, 1945), 38.
48. Rose, "Hawaiian Hall," 50.
49. See Eleanor Lilihana-a-I Williamson, introduction to Mary Kawena Pukui, *'Ōlelo No'eau: Hawaiian Proverbs and Poetical Sayings* (Honolulu: Bishop Museum Press, 1983).
50. Schorch, McCarthy, and Hakiwai, "Globalizing Māori Museology."
51. Homi K. Bhabha, *The Location of Culture* (London: Routledge, 1994).
52. Jan Nederveen Pieterse, "Globalization as Hybridization," in *Global Modernities,* eds. Mike Featherstone, Scott Lash, and Roland Robertson (London: Sage, 1995), 66.
53. See *Connecting Materialities/Material Connectivities [mat ~ con],* accessed September 15, 2017, http://www.highlandasia.net/projects/matcon.html. The project has been developed into an edited volume titled *Exploring*

Materiality and Connectivity in Anthropology and Beyond (UCL Press, 2020). See also chapters 4 and 5 of this book.

54. Paul Gilroy, *The Black Atlantic: Modernity and Double Consciousness* (Cambridge, MA: Harvard University Press, 1993).
55. Philipp Schorch, "Assembling Communities: Curatorial Practices, Material Cultures, and Meanings," *in Engaging Heritage, Engaging Communities*, eds. Bryony Onciul, Michelle L. Stefano, and Stephanie Hawke (Martlesham, Suffolk, UK: Boydell and Brewer, 2017), 31–46; and Schorch, McCarthy, and Dürr, "Introduction: Conceptualising Curatopia."
56. Marshall Sahlins, "Goodbye to Triste Tropes: Ethnography in the Context of Modern World History," *Journal of Modern History* 65, no. 1 (1993): 1–25.
57. Kenneth P. Emory, "Memorial for Peter Buck," February 13, 1952, Staff file, Bishop Museum Archives, 2.
58. Hirini Moko Mead, *Tikanga Māori: Living by Māori Values* (Wellington: Huia Publishers, 2003), 264.
59. On performing Indigeneity, Laura R. Graham and H. Glenn Penny, *Performing Indigeneity: Global Histories and Contemporary Experiences* (Lincoln: University of Nebraska Press, 2014); on Indigenous cosmopolitans, Maximilian C. Forte, ed., *Indigenous Cosmopolitans: Transnational and Transcultural Indigeneity in the Twenty-First Century* (New York: Peter Lang, 2010); on Indigenous scholars, Joy Hendry and Laara Fitznoor, *Anthropologists, Indigenous Scholars and the Research Endeavour: Seeking Bridges Towards Mutual Respect* (London: Routledge, 2012).
60. For example, Peter H. Buck (Te Rangi Hiroa), *Vikings of the Sunrise* (New York: J. B. Lippincott, 1938); Te Rangi Hiroa (Peter H. Buck), "An Introduction to Polynesian Anthropology," *Bernice P. Bishop Museum Bulletin* 187 (1945); Te Rangi Hiroa (Peter H. Buck), *Arts and Crafts of Hawaii* (Honolulu: Bishop Museum Press, 1957).
61. Geoffrey M. White and Ty P. Kawika Tengan, "Disappearing Worlds: Anthropology and Cultural Studies in Hawai'i and the Pacific," *Contemporary Pacific* 13, no. 2 (Fall 2001): 390.
62. For example, Mary Kawena Pukui, *Echo of Our Song: Chants and Poems of the Hawaiians* (Honolulu: University of Hawai'i Press, 1973); *'Ōlelo No'eau: Hawaiian Proverbs and Poetical Sayings* (Honolulu: Bishop Museum Press, 1983); with Samuel H. Elbert, *Hawaiian Dictionary: Hawaiian-English, English-Hawaiian* (Honolulu: University of Hawai'i Press, 1986).
63. US Government, Federal Register Notice, April 22, 1998, vol. 63, no. 77, 19939–19940.

64. The committee consisted of a dozen Native Hawaiian community leaders, scholars, activists, artists, and cultural practitioners. After about six committee meetings, the final theme arrived at for the overall draft concept was *"E Ola Mau"—Life Everlasting.*
65. Inspired by Malo's chant, the exhibition title "E Kū Mau Mau" replaced the "I" with the more imperative command "E" while simultaneously emphasizing the god Kū and his enduring nature.
66. Ty P. Kāwika Tengan, "The Return of Kū? Remembering Hawaiian Masculinity, Warriorhood, and Nation, " in Graham and Penny, *Performing Indigeneity,* 206–246; Ty P. Kāwika Tengan, "The Return of Kū, " in *E Kū Ana Ka Paia: Unification, Responsibility and the Kū Images* (Honolulu: Bishop Museum Press, 2010).
67. Throughout my time at the Bishop Museum, I was a cultural inventory specialist (identifying funerary objects), an education project manager, and director of community affairs.
68. On the community conduit, Noelle M.K.Y. Kahanu, Moana Nepia, and Philipp Schorch, "He alo ā he alo/kanohi ki te kanohi/face to face: Curatorial bodies, encounters and relations," in Schorch and McCarthy, *Curatopia,* 296–316.
69. I received a BA in political science and a JD from the University of Hawai'i at Manoa, and worked for the U.S. Senate Committee on Indian Affairs for five years before working at the Bishop Museum.
70. For more information on the renovation process, see Noelle M.K.Y. Kahanu, "E Kū Ana Ka Paia: Finding Contemorary Relevance in an Ancient Prophecy," in *Restoring Bishop Museum's Hawaiian Hall: Ho'i hou ka wena i Kaiwi'ula,* Samuel M. Gon et al. (Honolulu: Bishop Museum Press, 2009).
71. Bishop Museum, "Director's Report for 1903," 145.
72. For a detailed discussion on mana, see chapters 2 and 5.
73. Bishop Museum, "Hawaiian Hall's Grand Reopening Ceremony," *Ka 'Elele, the Journal of Bishop* (Fall 2009).
74. This evaluation is also referenced in Nicholas Thomas with Noelle M.K.Y. Kahanu, introduction to *Pacific Presences,* vol. 1, and Noelle M.K.Y. Kahanu, "Ka Hale Hō'ike'ike Pihopa: A Bishop Museum Love Story" in *Detours: A Decolonial Guide to Hawai'i,* eds. Hokulani K. Aikau and Vernadette Vicuna Gonzalez (Durham, NC: Duke University Press, 2019).
75. Bishop Museum, "New Acquisitions—A New Dawn," *Ka 'Elele, the Journal of Bishop* (Fall 2009), 10.
76. Western Museums Association, *Museums and Race,* https://museumsandrace.org, accessed October 10, 2016.
77. Ibid.

78. For example, *Seeding Authority: A Symposium on Decolonizing the Museum*, Honolulu, Hawaiʻi, November 10, 2018, and panel presentations *Museums and Race 2016: Transformation and Justice*, Western Museums Association, Phoenix, AZ, September 2016; and *Race, Diversity and Institutional Change*, Honolulu, Hawaiʻi, November 2016.
79. Sahlins, "Goodbye to Triste Tropes"; Ruth B. Phillips and Elizabeth Harney, "Multiple Modernities: Twentieth-Century Artistic Modernisms in Global Perspective" (Carleton University, 2017), https://carleton.ca/culturalmediations/mappingmodernisms/multiple-modernisms-project, accessed October 9, 2017. The project led to the volume *Mapping Modernisms: Art, Indigeneity, Colonialism*, edited by Elizabeth Harney and Ruth B. Phillips (Durham, NC: Duke University Press, 2018).

Chapter 2: Rethinking Temporalities

1. Nélia Dias, "Looking at Objects: Memory, Knowledge in Nineteenth-Century Ethnographic Displays," in *Travellers' Tales: Narratives of Home and Displacement*, ed. George Robertson et al. (London: Routledge, 1994), 166; and Nicholas Thomas, *Possessions: Indigenous Art/Colonial Culture* (London: Thames and Hudson, 1999), 259–260.
2. Johannes Fabian, *Time and the Other: How Anthropology Makes Its Object* (New York: Columbia University Press, 2002); Marc Augé, *A Sense for the Other: The Timeliness and Relevance of Anthropology*, trans. Amy Jacobs (Stanford, CA: Stanford University Press, 1998); and Kate Sturge, *Representing Others: Translation, Ethnography and the Museum* (London: Routledge, 2007).
3. Research Center for Material Culture, *Museum Temporalities: Time, History and the Ethnographic Museum* (conference website), http://www.materialculture.nl/en/events/museum-temporalities-time-history-and-the-ethnographic-museum, accessed February 15, 2017.
4. Research Center for Material Culture, *Museum Temporalities* (conference program), http://www.materialculture.nl/sites/default/files/files/201511/abstracts_and_biographies_museum_temporalities_0.pdf, accessed February 15, 2017.
5. Philipp Schorch and Noelle M.K.Y. Kahanu, "Anthropology's Interlocutors: Hawaiʻi Speaking Back to Ethnographic Museums in Europe," *Zeitschrift für Kulturwissenschaften* 1 (2015): 114–117.
6. *Positioning Ethnological Museums in the 21st Century* (conference website), https://www.volkswagenstiftung.de/veranstaltungen/veranstaltungsarchiv/detailansicht-veranstaltung/news/detail/artikel/positioning-ethnological-museums-in-the-21st-century/marginal/4670.html, accessed August 25, 2016.

7. Mark Elliott, "Some Anxious Moments: The Mechanics and Pragmatics of a Collaborative Exhibition," in *Pasifika Styles: Artists Inside the Museum,* ed. Rosanna Raymond and Amiria Salmond (Dunedin: Otago University Press, 2008), 93. See also James Clifford, "On Collecting Art and Culture," chap. 10 in *The Predicament of Culture: Twentieth-Century Ethnography, Literature, and Art* (Cambridge, MA: Harvard University Press, 1988); Carine Ayélé Durand, "Indexing (in) Authenticity: Art and Artefact in Ethnography Museums," *AlterNative: An International Journal of Indigenous Peoples* 6, no. 3 (2010), 248–260; and Haidy Geismar, "The Art of Anthropology: Questioning Contemporary Art in Ethnographic Display," in *Museum Theory,* vol. ed. Andrea Whitcomb and Kylie Message, *The International Handbooks of Museum Studies,* ed. Sharon Macdonald and Helen Rees Leahy (Malden, MA: Wiley-Blackwell, 2015), 183–210.
8. Ty P. Kāwika Tengan, "The Return of Kū? Remembering Hawaiian Masculinity, Warriorhood, and Nation," in *Performing Indigeneity: Global Histories and Contemporary Experiences*, ed. Laura R. Graham and H. Glenn Penny (Lincoln: University of Nebraska Press, 2014), 206–246; and Ty P. Kāwika Tengan, "The Return of Kū," in *E Kū Ana Ka Paia: Unification, Responsibility and the Kū Images* (Honolulu: Bishop Museum Press, 2010).
9. James Clifford, "The Times of the Curator," in Schorch and McCarthy, *Curatopia,* 109–123.
10. Rosanna Raymond and Amiria Salmond, eds., *Pasifika Styles: Artists Inside the Museum* (Dunedin: Otago University Press, 2008), 19.
11. On "undisciplining" museums and their debates, see also Larissa Förster and Friedrich von Bose, "Concerning Curatorial Practice in Ethnological Museums: An Epistemology of Postcolonial Debate," in Schorch and McCarthy, *Curatopia,* 44–55.
12. Philipp Schorch and Noelle M.K.Y. Kahanu, "Forum as Laboratory: The Cross-Cultural Infrastructure of Ethnographic Knowledge and Material Potentialities," in Heller, Scholz, and Wagner, *Prinzip Labor,* 241–248.
13. The Bishop Museum, in many ways a profoundly U.S. institution, is not immune to the often conflicting relationship between so-called contemporary art work and ethnographic artifact, as could be witnessed during the restoration of Hawaiian Hall in 2009 (Noelle Kahanu, personal communication, November 20, 2014) and can be detected throughout its institutional history (see chapter 1).
14. Philipp Schorch, Conal McCarthy, and Arapata Hakiwai, "Globalizing Māori Museology: Reconceptualizing Engagement, Knowledge and Virtuality through Mana Taonga," *Museum Anthropology* 39, no. 1

(2016): 48–69; Schorch and Kahanu, "Anthropology's Interlocutors"; and Schorch and Kahanu, "Forum as Laboratory."

15. Amiria Henare [Salmond], Martin Holbraad, and Sari Wastell, eds., *Thinking Through Things: Theorising Artefacts Ethnographically* (London: Routledge, 2007), 5.
16. Philipp Schorch, "Assembling Communities: Curatorial Practices, Material Cultures, and Meanings," in Onciul, Stefano, and Hawke, *Engaging Heritage, Engaging Communities,* 31–46. James Clifford alludes to the practice of translation at the heart of the cultural concept of the museum and the cultural practice of curatorship ("The Times of the Curator"). For the closely related discussion on the processes of translation at the core of Indigeneity, see James Clifford, *Returns: Becoming Indigenous in the Twenty-First Century* (Cambridge, MA: Harvard University Press, 2013). For that on the practice of ethnographic translation and its implications for ethnographic theory and methodology, see Amiria Salmond, "Transforming Translations (Part I): 'The Owner of These Bones,'" *HAU: Journal of Ethnographic Theory* 3, no. 3 (2013): 1–32. See also Paul Ricoeur, *On Translation,* trans. Eileen Brennan (London: Routledge, 2006); and Kate Sturge, *Representing Others: Translation, Ethnography and Museum* (London: Routledge, 2007).
17. Philipp Schorch, Conal McCarthy, and Eveline Dürr, "Introduction: Conceptualising Curatopia," in Schorch and McCarthy, *Curatopia*, 1–16; Philipp Schorch, "Assembling Communities"; Schorch, McCarthy, and Hakiwai, "Globalizing Māori Museology"; Schorch and Kahanu, "Forum as Laboratory"; Schorch and Kahanu, "Anthropology's Interlocutors"; and Philipp Schorch and Arapata Hakiwai, "Mana Taonga and the Public Sphere: A Dialogue Between Indigenous Practice and Western Theory," *International Journal of Cultural Studies* 17, no. 2 (2014): 191–205. See also the introduction and conclusion of this book.
18. Michelle Kamalu Dupreez [du Preez], "Eia Hawai'inuiākea: Reflections on the Protocol for the Opening of the *Pacific Encounters* [illegible]," *Journal of Museum Ethnography* 21 (2009): 104–105. In a related Oceanic context and for Māori people, *taonga* (or material treasures) *are* ancestors and therefore *are* people and instantiate relations. See Henare [Salmond], "Taonga Māori: Encompassing Rights and Property in New Zealand," in Henare [Salmond], Holbraad, and Wastell, *Thinking Through Things,* 47–67.
19. Intriguingly, this vocabulary derived from Pacific worlds resonates cross-culturally with the old German word *Ding* (thing) and its early meanings as meeting, assembly, or gathering (Bruno Latour and Peter Weibel, *Making Things Public: Atmospheres of Democracy* [Cambridge,

MA: MIT Press, 2005]). Tim Ingold points to its inherent narrative quality by arguing "things *are* their relations"; "the things of this world *are* their stories" (*Being Alive: Essays on Movement, Knowledge and Description* [London: Routledge, 2011], 70, 160).

20. Quoted in Marsha MacDowell, C. Kurt Dewhurst, and Marques Hanalai Marzan, "'Ike Pāpale: Lau Hala in Hawaiian Cultural Heritage," in *'Ike Ulana Lau Hala: The Vitality and Vibrancy of Lau Hala Weaving Traditions in Hawai'i,* ed. Lia O'Neill et al. (Honolulu: University of Hawai'i Press, 2014), 12–40, 33.
21. For contemporary manifestations of mana, see Matt Tomlinson and Ty P. Kāwika Tengan, *New Mana: Transformations of a Classic Concept in Pacific Languages and Cultures* (Canberra: Australian National University Press, 2016).
22. See Schorch, McCarthy, and Dürr, "Introduction: Conceptualizing Curatopia"; and Clifford, "The Times of the Curator."
23. Martin Hollbraad, "The Power of Powder: Multiplicity and Motion in the Divinatory Cosmology of Cuban Ifa or Mana, Again," in Henare [Salmond], Holbraad, and Wastell, *Thinking through Things,* 189–226; and Schorch, McCarthy, and Hakiwai, "Globalizing Māori Museology."
24. On the "space between," Sean Mallon, "Afterword: Pacific Voices in the Bicultural Museum," in *Museums and Māori: Heritage Professionals, Indigenous Collections, Current Practice,* ed. Conal McCarthy (Wellington: Te Papa Press, 2011); Albert Wendt, "Afterword: Tatauing the Post-Colonial Body," in *Inside Out: Literature, Cultural Politics, and Identity in the New Pacific,* ed. Vilsoni Hereniko and Rob Wilson (New York: Rowman & Littlefield, 1999), 399–412; and Vilsoni Hereniko, "Taualuga: Decolonising and Globalising the Pacific," in *Transpacific Americas: Encounters and Engagements Between the Americas and the South Pacific*, ed. Eveline Dürr and Philipp Schorch (London: Routledge, 2016), 167–174.
25. Hereniko, "Taualuga," 167.
26. I use the Sāmoan spelling (vā) because this is the most common form used in the literature across Oceania, including Hawai'i. For a Tongan philosophical perspective, see Hūfanga 'Okusitino Māhina, "Tā, Vā, and Moana: Temporality, Spatiality, and Indigeneity," in "Genealogies: Articulating Indigenous Anthropology in/of Oceania," special issue, *Pacific Studies* 33, no. 2/3 (2010): 168–202; for a Sāmoan philosophical view materialized in architecture, see Albert L. Refiti, "Mavae and Tofiga: Spatial Exposition of the Samoan Cosmogony and Architecture," chap. 1 (PhD diss., Auckland University of Technology, 2015).

27. Wendt, "Afterword," 402.
28. Hereniko, "Taualuga," 168.
29. See also chapter 6.
30. I thank Noelle Kahanu for those subtle points in conversation.
31. Rodney Harrison, "Reassembling Ethnographic Museum Collections," in Harrison, Byrne, and Clarke, *Reassembling the Collection*, 3–35.
32. Schorch, "Assembling Communities."
33. Dipesh Chakrabarty, *Provincializing Europe: Postcolonial Thought and Historical Difference* (Princeton, NJ: Princeton University Press, 2008), 175.
34. Henare [Salmond], Holbraad, and Wastell, *Thinking Through Things*, 4.
35. On narrative interviews, Philipp Schorch, "Museum Encounters and Narrative Engagements," in *Museum Theory*, ed. Andrea Witcomb and Kylie Message (Malden, MA: Blackwell Publishing, 2015), 437–457; and Tom Wengraf, *Qualitative Research Interviewing: Biographical Narrative and Semi-Structured Methods* (London: Sage, 2001).
36. On photography, Marcus Banks and David Zeitlyn, *Visual Methods in Social Research* (London: Sage, 2001); Gemma Orobitg Canal, "Photography in the Field: Word and Image in Ethnographic Research," in *Working Images: Visual Research and Representation in Ethnography*, ed. Ana Isabel Alfonso, Laszlo Kurti, and Sarah Pink (London: Routledge, 2004), 31–46; Sarah Pink, *Doing Visual Ethnography* (London: Sage, 2009); on feelings, Philipp Schorch, Emma Waterton, and Steve Watson, "Museum Canopies and Affective Cosmopolitanism: Cultivating Cross-Cultural Landscapes for Ethical Embodied Responses," in *Heritage, Affect and Emotion: Politics, Practices and Infrastructures*, ed. Divya P. Tolia-Kelly, Emma Waterton, and Steve Watson (London: Routledge, 2017), 93–113; and Philipp Schorch, "Cultural Feelings and the Making of Meaning," *International Journal of Heritage Studies* 20, no. 1 (2014): 22–35.
37. Jonathan K.K. Osorio, *Dismembering the Lāhui: A History of the Hawaiian Nation to 1887* (Honolulu: University of Hawai'i Press, 2002).
38. Quoted in Lorenz Gonschor, "Ka Hoku o Osiania: Promoting the Hawaiian Kingdom as a Model for Political Transformation in Nineteenth-Century Oceania," *in Agents of Transculturation: Border-Crossers, Mediators, Go-Betweens*, ed. Sebastian Jobs and Gesa Mackenthun (New York: Waxmann, 2013), 74.
39. Osorio, *Dismembering the Lāhui*; and Gonschor, "Ka Hoku o Osiania."
40. I thank Marques Marzan and Noelle Kahanu for information pertaining to Kala'i and her woven protest.
41. Quoted in Roger Rose, "Patterns of Protest: A Hawaiian Mat-Weaver's Response to 19th-Century Taxation and Change," *Bishop Museum Occasional Papers* 30 (1990): 97–98.

42. Ibid., 88.
43. Bernice Pauahi Bishop Museum, *A Preliminary Catalogue of the Bernice Pauahi Bishop Museum of Polynesian Ethnology and Natural History* (Honolulu: Bishop Museum Press, 1892), 67.
44. William T. Brigham, *Mat and Basket Weaving of the Ancient Hawaiians* (Honolulu: Bishop Museum Press, 1906), 83.
45. Te Rangi Hiroa, *Arts and Crafts of Hawaii* (Honolulu: Bishop Museum Press, 1957), 132.
46. Rose, "Patterns of Protest," 95; on the dialectics between adaptation and adaptation in the case of Rapa Nui, see chapter 3.
47. Marques Marzan, interviews, October 15 and November 19, 2014, Bishop Museum.
48. The program taught by Maile Andrade at the Kamakakūokalani Center for Hawaiian Studies at the University of Hawai'i at Mānoa is called Native Hawaiian Creative Expression (rather than art): http://manoa.hawaii.edu/hshk/people/ivy-h-andrade/, accessed December 10, 2016.
49. *Marques Hanalei Marzan* (website), http://www.marquesmarzan.com, accessed July 11, 2019.
50. Lilikala Kame'eleihiwa, *Native Land and Foreign Desires: Pehea La E Pono Ai? How Shall We Live in Harmony?* (Honolulu: Bishop Museum Press, 1992), 22–23.
51. Kamanamaikalani Beamer, *No Mākou Ka Mana: Liberating the Nation* (Honolulu: Kamehameha Publishing, 2014); Noelani Goodyear-Ka'ōpua, Ikaika Hussey, and Erin Kahunawaika'ala Wright, eds., *A Nation Rising: Hawaiian Movements for Life, Land, and Sovereignty* (Durham, NC: Duke University Press, 2014).
52. Deidre Brown, "Islands of Opportunity: Pasifika Styles and Museums," in *Pasifika Styles: Artists Inside the Museum*, ed. Rosanna Raymond and Amiria Salmond (Dunedin: Otago University Press, 2008), 28.
53. Conal McCarthy, *Museums and Māori: Heritage Professionals, Indigenous Collections, Current Practice* (Wellington: Te Papa Press, 2011); and Ruth B. Phillips, *Museum Pieces: Toward the Indigenization of Canadian Museums* (Montreal: McGill-Queen's University Press, 2013).
54. Richard Sennett, *The Craftsman* (London: Penguin Books, 2008), 20, 125. Emphasis in original.
55. Kamalu du Preez, interviews, October 14 and November 25, 2014, Bishop Museum.
56. Vilsoni Hereniko, "The Pā Boys dir. by Himiona Grace" (review), *The Contemporary Pacific* 27, no. 2 (2015): 573–576.
57. I thank Noelle Kahanu for these clarifications on the nā'au.

58. Quoted in Sam Low, "Na'au: The Heart of Wayfinding," *Hana Hou Magazine,* http://www.samlow.com/sail-nav/wayfinding.html, accessed September 29, 2016.
59. For a discussion of the nā'au in relation to the context of the fierce controversy around Mauna Kea, see Vilsoni Hereniko and Philipp Schorch, "The Canoe, the Wind, and the Mountain: Shunting the 'Rashomon effect' of Mauna Kea," *Pacific Studies* 41, no. 3 (2018): 119–130.
60. Hereniko, "The Pā Boys."
61. Bernice Pauahi Bishop Museum, *Ili Iho: The Surface Within* (Honolulu: Bishop Museum Press, 2009).
62. See similar point made in regard to Māori people, who have always represented themselves in the here and now rather than the then and there—as seen, for example, in carvings of ancestors in meeting houses who are viewed as living and facilitating communion with their descendants (Schorch, McCarthy, and Hakiwai, "Globalizing Māori Museology," 52).
63. Chakrabarty, *Provincializing Europe,* 251.
64. Clifford, "The Times of the Curator," 121.
65. See Schorch, McCarthy, and Hakiwai, "Globalizing Māori Museology"; Schorch, McCarthy. and Dürr, "Introduction: Conceptualizing Curatopia."
66. See also Schorch and Kahanu, "Forum as Laboratory."
67. See also Conal McCarthy, Arapata Hakiwai, and Philipp Schorch, "The Figure of the Kaitiaki: Learning from Māori Curatorship Past and Present," in Schorch and McCarthy, *Curatopia,* 211–226.
68. Martin Holbraad, "Can the Thing Speak?" *OAC Press Working Papers Series* no. 7 (2011): 1–26, 11.
69. Karl Benediktsson and Katrín Anna Lund, "Introduction: Starting a Conversation with Landscape," in *Conversations with Landscape* (Farnham, Surrey, UK: Ashgate, 2010), 1–12.
70. On art as interpretation, Nicholas Thomas and Diane Losche, introduction to *Double Vision: Art Histories and Colonial Histories in the Pacific* (Cambridge: Cambridge University Press, 1999); on art as ethnography, Carine Ayélé Durand, *Anthropology in a Glass Case: Indigeneity, Collaboration, and Artistic Practice in Museums* (Saarbrücken: VDM Verlag Dr. Müller, 2010).
71. Tim Ingold, *Making: Anthropology, Archaeology, Art and Architecture* (London: Routledge, 2013), xi, 31, 45.
72. For a related discussion on artistic practice, see Garry L. Hagberg, *Art as Language: Wittgenstein, Meaning, and Aesthetic Theory* (Ithaca, NY: Cornell University Press, 1995), 113.

73. I thank Noelle Kahanu for comments in developing this point.
74. Amiria Salmond and Rosanna Raymond, "Show and Tell: Weaving a Basket of Knowledge," in *Between Art and Anthropology: Contemporary Ethnographic Practice*, ed. Arnd Schneider and Christopher Wright (Oxford: Berg, 2010), 101.
75. Salmond, "Transforming Translations (Part 1)," 17.
76. Lilikala Kameʻeleihiwa, "Hawaiʻi-nui-akea Cousins: Ancestral Gods and Bodies of Knowledge Are Treasures for the Descendants," *Te Kahora* 2 (2009): 52.
77. I appreciate the comments made by Chris Ballard and refer the reader to one of his attempts: Chris Ballard, "The Return of the Past: On Drawing and Dialogic History," *The Asia Pacific Journal of Anthropology* 14, no. 2 (2013): 136–148.
78. University of Hawaiʻi at Mānoa, Department of Art & Art History, "Schedule of Events," http://www.hawaii.edu/art/exhibitions+events/exhibitions, accessed August 14, 2019.
79. Dürr and Schorch, *Transpacific Americas*.
80. Chapter 4.
81. Hagberg, *Art as Language*, 4.
82. John Dewey, *Art as Experience* (London: George Allen & Unwin, 1934), 106.
83. Walter Benjamin, "On Language as Such and on the Language of Man," in *One-Way Street and Other Writings*, trans. Edmund Jephcott and Kingsley Shorter (London: Verso, 1979), 107–123.
84. Schorch, Waterton, and Watson, "Museum Canopies."
85. Arjun A. Appadurai, *Modernity at Large: Cultural Dimensions of Globalization* (Minneapolis: University of Minnesota Press, 1996); Clifford Geertz, "Deep Play: Notes on the Balinese Cockfight," in *The Interpretation of Cultures: Selected Essays* (London: Hutchinson, 1975), 412–53; and Paul Ricoeur, *From Text to Action: Essays in Hermeneutics*, II (Evanston, IL: Northwestern University Press. 1991).
86. Ingold, *Making*, 109, 111.
87. Tim Ingold, *The Perception of the Environment: Essays on Livelihood, Dwelling and Skill* (London: Routledge, 2000).
88. Durand, *Anthropology in a Glass Case*; Ingold, *Making*; Ingold, *Perception of the Environment*; and Sennett, *The Craftsman*.
89. On operating as ships, Paul Gilroy, *The Black Atlantic Modernity and Double-Consciousness* (Cambridge, MA: Harvard University Press, 1993).
90. On double vision, Thomas and Losche, *Double Vision*.
91. Chris Ballard, "Oceanic Historicities," *The Contemporary Pacific* 26, no. 1 (2014): 103.

92. Epeli Hau'ofa, *We Are the Ocean: Selected Works* (Honolulu: University of Hawai'i Press, 2008), 69. See also Robert Sullivan, "The English Moko: Exploring a Spiral," in *Figuring the Pacific: Aotearoa & Pacific Cultural Studies*, ed. Howard Douglas McNaughton and John Newton (Christchurch: Canterbury University Press, 2005), 12–28. See also chapter 4 of this book.
93. Brigham, *Mat and Basket Weaving*, 1; *Ka Hana Kapa: The Making of Bark-Cloth in Hawaii* (Honolulu: Bishop Museum Press, 1911), 1.
94. Vicente M. Diaz and J. Kehaulani Kauanui, "Native Pacific Cultural Studies on the Edge," *The Contemporary Pacific* 13, no. 2 (2001): 315–341.
95. Marshall Sahlins, *Culture in Practice: Selected Essays* (Brooklyn, NY: Zone Books, 2005), 479.
96. Clifford, *Returns*; and Sahlins, *Culture in Practice*. For a critique of the renaissance discourse, see Aaron Glass, "History and Critique of the Renaissance Discourse," in *Native Art of the Northwest Coast: A History of Changing Ideas*, ed. Charlotte Townsend-Gault, Jennifer Kramer, and Ki-Ke-In (Toronto: UBC Press, 2013).
97. Philipp Schorch and Arno Pascht, introduction to "Reimagining Oceania through Critical Junctures," Special issue, *Oceania*, 87, no. 2 (2017): 114–123; and Philipp Schorch, "The Hermeneutics of Transpacific Assemblages," *Alfred Deakin Research Institute Working Paper Series* 2, no. 41 (2013): 1–15.
98. James West Turner, "Continuity and Constraint: Reconstructing the Concept of Tradition from a Pacific Perspective," *The Contemporary Pacific* 9, no. 2 (1997): 345–381.
99. Clifford, *Returns*; David W. Gegeo, "Cultural Rupture and Indigeneity: The Challenge of (Re)visioning "Place" in the Pacific," *The Contemporary Pacific* 13, no. 2 (2001): 491–506; Graham Harvey and Charles D. Thompson, eds., *Indigenous Diasporas and Dislocations* (Aldershot, Hampshire, UK: Ashgate, 2005); Hau'ofa, *We Are the Ocean*; and Margaret Jolly, "On the Edge? Deserts, Oceans, Islands," *The Contemporary Pacific* 13, no. 2 (2001): 417–466.
100. See also dialectics of Indigeneity in chapter 4.
101. Hereniko and Schorch, "The Canoe, the Wind, and the Mountain."

Chapter 3: Cross-Cultural Journeys

1. In so-called Polynesian languages and ontologies, a separation does not exist between people and land, or subject and object (see chapter 4). Writing any such language, however, is merely a convention derived from a consensus. Moreover, claiming that there is a right way to write Polynesian using Latin script seems spurious. Thus, though we insist on the unison of people and land as a key thread running through this book,

we still stick to the convention of writing Rapa Nui for the island and Rapanui for the people. This seems simple and appropriate, and avoids confusion for the reader.

2. Other Rapa Nui photo collections are those of Percy Edmunds (1911–1929), Robert Gerstmann (1946), and an unknown photographer (perhaps William Allanson Bryan, who was hired by the Compañía Explotadora de Isla de Pascua) whose photos were taken between 1910 and 1925 and accessioned by the museum in 1935. On Gerstmann photographs, see Tania Basterrica Brockman and Betty Haoa Rapahango, "The 1946 Trip to Rapa Nui through the Photographs of Gerstmann, Helfritz, and Felbermayer," *Rapa Nui Journal* 29, no. 2 (October 2015): 23–38.
3. Mara A. Mulrooney, Charmaine Wong, Kelley Esh, Scott Belluomini, and Mark D. McCoy, "Integrating Research and Collections Management: The Hoʻomaka Hou Research Initiative at the Bishop Museum," *Museum Worlds: Advances in Research* 4 (2016): 51–62.
4. See Philipp Schorch, "Assembling Communities: Curatorial Practices, Material Cultures and Meanings," in Onciul, Stefano, and Hawke, *Engaging Heritage, Engaging Communities,* 31–46.
5. Alfred Métraux, *Ethnology of Easter Island* (Honolulu: Bishop Museum Press, 1940); and *Easter Island: A Stone-Age Civilization of the Pacific,* trans. Michael Bullock (London: André Deutsch, 1957).
6. Elizabeth Edwards, "Talking Visual Histories: Introduction," in *Museums and Source Communities: A Routledge Reader,* ed. Laura Lynn Peers and Alison Kay Brown (London: Routledge, 2003), 83–99; and Laura Peers and Alison K. Brown, "'Just by Bringing these Photographs . . .': On the Other Meanings of Anthropological Images," in Morton and Edwards, *Photography, Anthropology and History,* 265–280.
7. For clarification and use of the terms anthropological and ethnological, see the introduction.
8. See Tony Bennett et al., *Collecting, Ordering, Governing: Anthropology, Museums, and Liberal Government* (Durham, NC: Duke University Press, 2017); and Elizabeth Edwards and Christopher Morton, introduction to *Photography, Anthropology and History,* 1–26.
9. See Peter Mesenhöller and Jutta-Beate Engelhard, eds., *Bilder aus dem Paradies: Koloniale Fotografie aus Samoa 1875–1925*, exhibition catalog (Marburg, DE: Jonas Verlag, 1995); Wulf Köpke and Bernd Schmelz, eds., *A Glimpse into Paradise: Historical Photographs of Polynesia*, exhibition catalog (Hamburg: Museum für Völkerkunde Hamburg, 2014); and Max Quanchi, "History of Photography in the Pacific Islands," in Köpke and Schmelz, *A Glimpse into Paradise,* 67–85.

10. In regard to Māori people and photography, see Christopher Pinney, "The Phenomenology of Colonial Photography," in *Bilder des Fremden: Mediale Inszenierung von Alterität im 19. Jahrhundert,* ed. Hans-Peter Bayerdörfer, Bettina Barbara Dietz, Frank Heidemann, and Paul Hempel (Berlin: Lit Verlag, 2007), 19–39; and Arapata Hakiwai, "The Meaning of Ancestral Photographs in Māori Culture," in Köpke and Schmelz, *A Glimpse into Paradise,* 145–154.
11. Nicholas Thomas and Diane Losche, eds., *Double Vision: Art Histories and Colonial Histories in the Pacific* (Cambridge: Cambridge University Press, 1999).
12. Aaron Glass, "Indigenous Ontologies, Digital Futures: Plural Provenances and the Kwakwaka'wakw Collection in Berlin and Beyond," in *Museum as Process: Translating Local and Global Knowledges,* ed. Raymond A. Silverman (London: Routledge, 2015), 19–44; and Philipp Schorch, Conal McCarthy, and Arapata Hakiwai, "Globalizing Māori Museology: Reconceptualizing Engagement, Knowledge and Virtuality through Mana Taonga," *Museum Anthropology* 39, no. 1 (2016): 48–69. See also the introduction to this book.
13. Sarah Byrne et al., eds., *Unpacking the Collection: Networks of Material and Social Agency in the Museum* (New York: Springer, 2011); and Rodney Harrison, Sarah Byrne, and Anne Clarke, eds., *Reassembling the Collection: Ethnographic Museums and Indigenous Agency* (Santa Fe, NM: SAR Press, 2013).
14. Te Rangi Hiroa (Peter H. Buck), "An Introduction to Polynesian Anthropology," *Bernice Pauahi Bishop Museum Bulletin 187* (1945), 47.
15. See chapters 1 and 2.
16. See Peter H. Buck (Te Rangi Hiroa), "Bishop Museum—Yale's partner in the Pacific," *Yale Alumni Magazine* 14, no. 7 (April 1951): 5–7.
17. See Conal McCarthy, "'Empirical Anthropologists Advocating Cultural Adjustments': The Anthropological Governance of Āpirana Ngata and the Native Affairs Department," *History and Anthropology* 25, no. 2 (2014): 280–295; Conal McCarthy, "Historicising the 'Indigenous International': Museums, Anthropology, and Transpacific Networks," in *Transpacific Americas: Encounters and Engagements Between the Americas and the South Pacific,* eds. Eveline Dürr and Philipp Schorch (New York: Routledge, 2016), 3–26; Schorch, McCarthy, and Hakiwai, "Globalizing Māori Museology"; and chapter 1 of this volume.
18. Letter on June 24, 1935, in M.P.K. Sorrenson, ed., *Na To Hoa Aroha: From Your Dear Friend: The Correspondence between Sir Apirana Ngata and Sir Peter Buck 1925–1950, vol. 3, 1932–1950* (Auckland: Auckland University Press, 1986).

19. Métraux, *Easter Island,* 12.
20. See McCarthy, "Historicising the 'Indigenous International'"; and Schorch, McCarthy, and Hakiwai, "Globalizing Māori Museology."
21. Mara A. Mulrooney et al., "New Dates from Old Samples: A Revised Radiocarbon Chronology for the Wai'ahukini Rockshelter Site (H8), Ka'u District, Hawai'i Island," *Society for Hawaiian Archaeology, Special Publication* 4 (2014): 17–26.
22. Deidre Brown, "Te Ahua Hiko: Digital Cultural Heritage and Indigenous Objects, People, and Environments," in *Theorizing Digital Cultural Heritage: A Critical Discourse,* eds. Fiona Cameron and Sarah Kenderdine (Cambridge, MA: MIT Press, 2007), 77–91; Fiona R. Cameron and Helena Robinson, "Digital Knowledgescapes: Cultural, Theoretical, Practical, and Usage Issues Facing Museum Collection Databases in a Digital Epoch," in Cameron and Kenderdine, *Theorizing Digital Cultural Heritage,* 165–191; Jenny Newell, "Old Objects, New Media: Historical Collections, Digitization and Affect," *Journal of Material Culture* 17, no. 3 (2012): 287–306; Amiria Salmond, "Digital Subjects, Cultural Objects: Special Issue Introduction," *Journal of Material Culture* 17, no. 3 (2012): 211–228; Supriya Singh and Meredith Blake, "The Digitization of Pacific Cultural Collections: Consulting with Pacific Diasporic Communities and Museum Experts," *Curator: The Museum Journal* 55, no. 1 (2012): 95–105; and Supriya Singh, Meredith Blake, and Jonathan O'Donnell, "Digitizing Pacific Cultural Collections: The Australian Experience," *International Journal of Cultural Property* 20 (2013): 77–107.
23. Alfred Métraux, "Arribo a la isla de Pascua" in *Sur,* no. 10 (1941): 39–52, 50 [original written in Spanish by Métraux]. A similar version, translated from the French, is available in Alfred Métraux, *La Isla de Pascua* (México: Fondo de Cultura Económica, 1950), 23. This is our translation into English and our emphasis.
24. Steven Roger Fischer, *Rongorongo: The Easter Island Script. History, Traditions, Texts* (Oxford: Clarendon Press, 1997), 47–57.
25. Thomas S. Barthel, *The Eighth Land: The Polynesian Discovery and Settlement of Easter Island* (Honolulu: University Press of Hawai'i, 1978).
26. On the Mohican Expedition of 1886, see William J. Thomson, *Te Pito te Henua, or Easter Island* (Washington, DC: Smithsonian Institution, 1891). Many sources about the German-Chilean Walter Knoche expedition exist. The most comprehensive is Walter Knoche, *Die Osterinsel: Eine Zusammenfassung der chilenischen Osterinselexpedition des Jahres 1911* (Chile: Concepción, Soc. Imp. y Lit., 1925).

27. See Cristián Moreno Pakarati, "The Land Commission of 1917: Analysis and Participation of the Rapanui," *Rapa Nui Journal* 26, no. 2 (2012): 29–41. Several books and articles cover the de Estella research. See especially Bienvenido de Estella, *La Isla de Pascua* (Santiago de Chile: Imprenta Cervantes, 1920).
28. The most distinguished first-branch "informants" were Veriamo a Huki (~1830–1936); Joseph Maherenga, "Ioteva" (~1835–1918); María Ana Veri Topa Tahi (~1837–1917); Mihaera Keremuti, "Timikore" (~1838–1916); Gabriel Revahiva, "Kapiera" (~1840–1918); Ioane "Nuku" Vavara, also called "Juan Cruz" (~1842–1926); Buenaventura Tehatirenga, "Fati" (~1859–1932); Tomenika a Vakatukuonge (1843–1915); Eutimio Rangitopa, "Haro Mamoe" (~1845–1922); Porotu a Ure 'Ao Viri, "Hongi A Tu'a Kava" (~1845–1924); Ramón Tehaha a Ure 'Iti (~1845–1918); Román Hei a Pa'enga, "Oromana" (~1851–1927); and Nicolás Pakarati Urepotahi (~1855–1927).
29. The leper colony was a transforming place, north of Haŋa Roa. It went from a ravaged hut to a full-fledged leprosarium where the ill were looked after by Chilean nuns. See Rolf Foerster and Sonia Montecino, "Rapa Nui: la lepra y sus derivados (estado de excepción, cárcel, . . .)" in *Escrituras Americanas,* no. 1 (2012): 270–353. The second branch's most distinguished sources were Timoteo Ureatoro, "Te Kohou a Tematangi" (~1833–1917); Pakomio Ma'ori, "Urekino" (~1836–1908); Akutino Veriheka (~1836–1913); Arakilio Pua'arahoa (~1837–1912); Bernabé Tori a Papaveri, "Harakura" (~1840–1918); Felipe Ikahiva, "Arariko" (~1847–1910); and Atamu Tuputahi a Hare Kai Hiva (~1847–1912).
30. See Thor Heyerdahl, "The Concept of Rongo-Rongo Among the Historic Population of Easter Island," in *Reports of the Norwegian Archaeological Expedition to Easter Island and the East Pacific,* vol. 2 *Miscellaneous Papers,* eds. Thor Heyerdahl and Edwin Ferdon Jr. (Stockholm: Forum Publishing House, 1965), 359–385; see also Thomas S. Barthel, "Native Documents from Easter Island," 387–389.
31. Englert, despite being (and remaining) a controversial figure, does not speak of informants but of *colaboradores* (collaborators) in *Idioma Rapanui: Gramática y diccionario del antiguo idioma de la Isla de Pascua* (Santiago de Chile: Universidad de Chile, 1978) and *Diccionario Rapa Nui-Español* (Santiago de Chile: Prensas de la Universidad de Chile, 1938). Moreover, he speaks of "la primera and principal fuente de información" (the primary and principal source of information) and calls Teao "la voz de la antigüedad" (the voice of antiquity). See *La Tierra de Hotu Mat'ua* (Santiago de Chile: Rapanui Press, 2006), 10. In a sense, then, Englert was forerunner of our own collaborative work.

32. For a detailed study of these informants, see Barthel, *The Eighth Land,* 287–299.
33. The pioneers in this were Simeón Riroroko, Juan Araki, Gabriel and Mateo Veriveri, and Pio Haoa, among others.
34. At around the same time, the Rapanui appropriated another Western idea to support their own views: maps. "Ethnic" maps were prepared to claim the whole surface of the island that was being disputed between a foreign company and the Chilean state. See Moreno Pakarati, "The Land Commission of 1917"; Rolf Foerster, Jimena Ramirez, and Cristián Moreno Pakarati, *Cartografía y conflicto en Rapa Nui* (Santiago de Chile: Rapanui Press, 2014).
35. Métraux mentions this behavior several times throughout his monograph and the popular account of his trip (see *La Isla de Pascua*). Tepano's birth year has been estimated by different sources from the early 1860s to the early 1880s. He appears as younger than fifteen (and obviously not yet married) in the 1886 census, and considering his mother's age, his siblings, and his age estimated by various censuses, we have chosen to use his most commonly used date of birth: 1872.
36. About this trip, see Rolf Foerster, "Voluntary Trip of Deportation? The Case of King Riroroko and Policies of Deporation on Easter Island (1897–1916)," *Rapa Nui Journal* 24, no. 2 (2010); and Cristián Moreno Pakarati, "Rebelión Sumisión y Mediación en Rapa Nui (1897–1915)," in *La Compañía Explotadora de Isla de Pascua: Patrimonio, Memoria e Identidad en Rapa Nui,* ed. Claudio Cristino and Miguel Fuentes (Concepción: Ediciones Escaparate, 2010).
37. Compañía Explotadora de Isla de Pascua (CEDIP) was a transnational, Scottish-owned Chilean company that managed a sheep ranch on Rapa Nui and exported wool to different markets. It controlled the territory of most of the island, and almost monopolized access to goods, contact to the mainland through ships, and job opportunities. The manager of the company was de facto ruler of the Island until 1914. See Miguel Fuentes, ed., *Rapa Nui y la Compañía Explotadora* (Hanga Roa: Rapanui Press, 2013).
38. Consejo de Jefes de Rapanui and Alberto Hotus, *Te mau hatu'o Rapa Nui: Los soberanos de Rapa Nui; Pasado, presente y futuro* (Santiago de Chile: Editorial Emisión, 1988), 357.
39. Steven Roger Fischer, *Island at the End of the World: The Turbulent History of Easter Island* (London: Reaktion Books, 2005), 155.
40. Zósimo Valenzuela, "La Isla de Pascua," *Revista Católica* 13, nos. 259–261 (1912).

41. Knoche, *Die Osterinsel;* see also Knoche, *Die Osterinsel: Die chilenische Osterinsel-Expedition von 1911,* ed. Hermann Mückler (Wiesbaden: Harrassowitz Verlag, 2015).
42. See Jo Anne Van Tilburg, *Among Stone Giants: The Life of Katherine Routledge and her Remarkable Expedition to Easter Island* (New York: Scribner, 2003).
43. Van Tilburg has argued that the relationship between Tepano and Routledge went far beyond the professional level. The speculation is interesting despite the lack of related contemporary sources and nothing explicit from Routledge. See Jo Anne Van Tilburg, "Easter Island's Ethnographic Triangle: Katherine Routledge (1866–1935), Alfred Métraux (1906–1963) and Juan Tepano (c. 1867–1947)," on the Easter Island Statue Project website (http://www.eisp.org/1853/, accessed April 12, 2017).
44. Katherine Routledge, *The Mystery of Easter Island* (London: Sifton Praed & Co., 1919).
45. Estella, *La Isla de Pascua.*
46. John MacMillan Brown, *The Riddle of the Pacific* (Kempton, IL: Adventures Unlimited Press, 2015).
47. Rolf Foerster, "Rapa Nui y Chile: Cuatro seducciones y sus lecturas," *Mapocho* 67 (2010): 51–73.
48. Métraux, *Easter Island,* 24.
49. Métraux, *La Isla de Pascua,* 22–25.
50. Métraux, *Ethnology of Easter Island,* 3.
51. The full story appears in Patricia Stambuk, *Rongo: La Historia Oculta de Isla de Pascua.* (Santiago de Chile: Pehuén, 2010) and in Thomas Lavachery and Denis Roussel, *L'homme de Pâques* (Y.C. Aligator film, 2002).
52. Métraux, *Ethnology of Easter Island,* 4.
53. Van Tilburg, "Easter Island's Ethnographic Triangle."
54. Magdalena Haoa Araki (1904–1983), called "Matarena" or "Mata" by the islanders. See Steven Roger Fischer, "The Métraux-Barthel Correspondence (1956–1961) and the Métraux Field-Notes of Easter Island [Part Two]," *Rapa Nui Journal* 23, no. 1 (2009): 55–64, 56.
55. See Patricia Vargas, Claudio Cristino, and Roberto Izaurieta, *1000 años en Rapa Nui. Arqueología del asentamiento* (Santiago de Chile: Editorial Universitaria, 2006).
56. By far the most successful and prolific is Grant McCall, whose work about the island is essential for understanding Rapa Nui in the nineteenth and twentieth centuries. See, for example, *Rapanui. Tradition and Survival on Easter Island,* 2nd ed. (Sydney: George Allen and Unwin, and Honolulu: University of Hawai'i Press, 1994).

57. Durba Ghosh, "Decoding the Nameless: Gender, Subjectivity, and Historical Methodologies in Reading the Archives of Colonial India," in *A New Imperial History: Culture, Identity and Modernity in Britain and the Empire, 1660–1840,* ed. Kathleen Wilson (Cambridge: Cambridge University Press, 2004), 301.
58. Oxenham quoted in the Elizabeth Edwards and Christopher Morton, introduction to *Photography, Anthropology and History,* 13.
59. For example, see Van Tilburg on Tepano: "he single-handedly identified, collected, recorded, influenced, shaped and reconstructed the quintessential data all researchers today regard as the ethnography of Rapa Nui," quoted in Felix Driver, "Intermediaries and the Archive of Exploration," in *Indigenous Intermediaries: New Perspectives on Exploration Archives,* ed. Shino Konishi, Maria Nugent, and Tiffany Shellam (Canberra: ANU Press, 2015), 24.
60. See Onciul, Stefano, and Hawke, eds., *Engaging Heritage, Engaging Communities*; Schorch, "Assembling Communities"; and Philipp Schorch, Conal McCarthy, and Eveline Dürr, "Introduction: Conceptualizing Curatopia," in Schorch and McCarthy, *Curatopia*, 1–16.
61. On the Council of Elders, toward the end of 2016, Alberto Hotus named Carlos Edmunds Paoa, "Karito," as his successor. On Indigenous representations, see Fischer, *Island at the End of the World.*
62. On the cession of the island, see also Fischer, *Island at the End of the World*; Grant McCall, "Riro, Rapu and Rapanui: Refoundations in Easter Island Colonial History," *Rapa Nui Journal* 11, no. 3 (1997): 112–122; and Carlos López, "How Did Chile Acquire Easter Island?," *Rapa Nui Journal* 12, no. 4 (1998): 118–122. On the book, Consejo de Jefes de Rapanui and Alberto Hotus, *Te mau hatu'o Rapa Nui.*
63. See Lorenz Gonschor, "Facing Land Challenges in Rapa Nui (Easter Island)," *Pacific Studies* 34, no. 2–3 (2011).
64. Consejo de Jefes de Rapanui and Alberto Hotus, *Te mau hatu'o Rapa Nui,* 374.
65. Musées royaux d'Art e d'Histoire, *Île de Pâques 1934–1935: Expédition Métraux-Lavachery* (Brussels: Buch, 1995); see review by Paul G. Bahn, "Pictures from an Expedition: Île de Pâques 1934–1935. Expedition Metraux-Lavachery, 1995," *Rapa Nui Journal* 12, no. 2 (June 1998): 58.
66. Christine Laurière, *L'Odyssée pascuane Mission Métraux-Lavachery, Île de Pâques 1934–1935* (Lahic/DPRPS, 2014), 139.
67. H. Porter Abbott, *The Cambridge Introduction to Narrative* (Cambridge: Cambridge University Press, 2002), 129.
68. Roslyn Poignant and Axel Poignant, *Encounter at Nagalarramba* (Canberra: National Library of Australia, 1996), 9.
69. Peers and Brown, "Just by Bringing These Photographs," 273.

70. For related arguments on humanizing abstract totalities such as culture through stories and faces, see Philipp Schorch, "The Cosmohermeneutics of Migration Encounters at the Immigration Museum Melbourne," *Museum Worlds: Advances in Research* 2, no. 1 (2014): 81–98; "Cultural Feelings and the Making of Meaning," *International Journal of Heritage Studies* 20, no. 1 (2014): 22–35; and "Contact Zones, Third Spaces, and the Act of Interpretation," *Museum and Society* 11, no. 1 (2013): 68–81.
71. Ministerio de Educación Publica, Dirección de Bibliotecas, Archivos y Museos, "Decreto 1373," Santiago, October 10, 1973.
72. See grant proposal by Lilian López on "Reposicionamiento del Museo Antropológico P. Sebastián Englert dentro de la comunidad de Isla de Pascua" (2011), Biblioteca William Mulloy Archives.
73. See multivolume report Paula Valenzuela Contreras, "Diagnóstico de la situación actual y plan de desarrollo del Museo Padre Sebastián Englert de Isla de Pascua," Multivolume report 2007, Biblioteca William Mulloy.
74. See exhibition catalog, Cristián Moreno Pakarati, *Englert Expo* (Museo Antropológico Padre Sebastián Englert, 2012).
75. Another recent exhibition, in 2015, *More Manava,* was devoted to the two political revolutions of the twentieth century and communicated largely through photographs. See also the subsequent book: Rolf Foerster and Cristián Moreno Pakarati, *More Manava* (Santiago de Chile: Rapanui Press, 2016).
76. Francisco Torres Hochstetter, "Editorial," *Apuntes del Museo Padre Sebastián Englert* 3 (2014).
77. Francisco Torres Hochstetter, interview by Philipp Schorch, February 16, 2016.
78. Fischer, *Island at the End of the World.*
79. Divya P. Tolia-Kelly, Emma Waterton, and Steve Watson, "Heritage, Affect and Emotion," in *Heritage, Affect and Emotion: Politics, Practices and Infrastructures,* ed. Tolia-Kelly, Waterton, and Watson (London: Routledge, 2017), 3–5.
80. Herle Anita, "John Layard long Malakula 1914–1915: The Potency of Field Photography," in Morton and Edwards, *Photography, Anthropology and History,* 256–257.
81. Foerster, Ramirez, and Moreno Pakarati, "Cartografía y conflicto en Rapa Nui," 64.
82. Britton L. Shepardson et al., "Terevaka Archaeological Outreach (TAO) 2015 Field Report: Archaeology, Conservation, and Toponymy," *Rapa Nui Journal* 29, no. 2 (2015): 47–51. See online database, http://www.terevaka.net/toponymy/index.html, accessed August 3, 2017.
83. Edwards, "Talking Visual Histories," 84.

84. László Munteán, "Touching Time: Photography, Affect and the Digital Archive," in Tolia-Kelly, Waterton, and Watson, *Heritage, Affect and Emotion,* 201–218.

Chapter 4: Curating an Island, Curing Rapa Nui

1. Steven Roger Fischer, *Island at the End of the World: The Turbulent History of Easter Island,* chap. 5 (Chicago: University of Chicago Press, 2005).
2. David C. Harvey, "Heritage Pasts and Heritage Presents: Temporality, Meaning and the Scope of Heritage Studies," *International Journal of Heritage Studies* 7, no. 4 (2001): 319–338.
3. Grant McCall, "Japan, Rapanui and Chile's Uncertain Sovereignty," *Rapa Nui Journal* 9, no. 1 (1995): 1–7.
4. Camila Zurob Dreckmann, "Familia, propiedad y herencia en Rapa Nui," *Revista Anales* 7, no. 2 (November 2011): 165–185.
5. I follow Steven Roger Fischer's conventions here in capitalizing "Museum Island" and lowercasing "company island."
6. Miguel Fuentes, ed., *Rapa Nui y la Compañia Explotadora* (Santiago de Chile: Rapanui Press, 2013); see also chapter 3.
7. Fischer, *Island at the End of the World*, 200. The correct name is Ahu Ature Huki, which was, moreover, not practically reerected by Heyerdahl and his team, but by Rapanui people led by Pedro Atán and Lázaro Hotu. The reerection of Ahu Tongariki, on the other hand, did not amount to a full restoration because several *pukao* (topknots) are still laying in front of the ahu (Cristián Moreno Pakarati, email correspondence, May 15, 2017).
8. See Consejo de Monumentos Nacionales de Chile, "Isla de Pascua," http://www.monumentos.cl/catalogo/625/w3-article-26080.html, accessed December 7, 2016.
9. This moai named Pou Hakanononga is now housed at the Musées Royaux d'Art et d'Histoire situated in the Parc du Cinquantenaire in Brussels. See Peter Mason, "Moai on the Move," *Journal of the History of Collections* 24, no. 1 (2012): 117–130. This text uses "moai," the more common usage, rather than "mo'ai."
10. Fischer, *Island at the End of the World,* 190–191.
11. On the first inventory and restoration, Francisco Torres Hochstetter, "La Tierra de Hotu Matu'a, un viaje espiritual y científico al pasado de Rapanui," in Englert, *La Tierra de Hotu Mat'ua*. The archaeological jewel reference appears in Englert, *La Tierra de Hotu Mat'ua* (Apendice arqueologico, 99); the most significant reference stems from Carlos Paoa Huke, "Vida y Obra del Padre Sebastian Englert, O.F.M. Cap. en la Isla de Pascua desde 1935 hasta 1968," unpublished document held at the

Biblioteca William Mulloy of the Museo Antropológico Padre Sebastián Englert.

12. William Mulloy and Gonzalo Figueroa, *The Archaeological Heritage of Easter Island* (Paris: UNESCO, 1966).
13. Some of the institutions constituting and governing the Rapanui heritage complex are, among others: Gobernación Provincia de Isla de Pascua, Ministerio del Interior y Seguridad Pública, Corporación Cultural de Rapa Nui, Municipalidad de Rapa Nui, Comisión de Desarrollo de Isla de Pascua, Corporación Nacional de Desarrollo Indígena, Servicio Nacional de Turismo, Secretaría Técnica de Patrimonio Rapa Nui del Consejo de Monumentos Nacionales, Museo Antropológico Padre Sebastián Englert, Subdirección de Bibliotecas, Archivos y Museos de Chile, Parque Nacional Rapa Nui, and Corporación Nacional Forestal.
14. McCall, "Japan, Rapanui and Chile."
15. Dreckmann, "Familia, propiedad y herencia."
16. See UNESCO, World Heritage List, "Rapa Nui National Park," http://whc.unesco.org/en/list/715, accessed December 10, 2016.
17. Fischer, *Island at the End of the World*, 244.
18. The distinction between curational and curatorial is a product of the conversations with Martin Saxer with whom I co-convened the project Connecting Materialities/Material Connectivities [mat~con], which has been developed into the volume *Exploring Materiality and Connectivity in Anthropology and Beyond* (London: UCL Press, 2020). See http://www.highlandasia.net/projects/matcon.html, accessed February 14, 2017.
19. This is not a direct translation. The Spanish, Rapanui, and English texts are individual tributes given by Figueroa, Juan Edmunds Rapahango, and Mulloy's widow, Emily Ross. The direct translation from Rapanui into English would be "With his studies/teachings and the reerection of the Aringa Ora he showed us his great love for Rapa Nui" (Cristián Moreno Pakarati, email correspondence, May 15, 2017).
20. Fischer, *Island at the End of the World*, 206–207.
21. See the institutional history on the Museo Antropológico Padre Sebastián Englert website (http://www.museorapanui.cl/679/w3-propertyvalue-96753.html, accessed December 18, 2016); see also Claudio Gómez Papic, "El Padre Sebastián, el patrimonio rapanui y el museo de Isla de Pascua," in Englert, *La Tierra de Hotu Mat'ua*. Copies of the proposition (1967), resolution (1969), and decree (1973) to establish the museum are held at the library. On the 1984 appointment, Fischer, *Island at the End of the World*, 231.
22. Sergio Rapu, interview in English by Philipp Schorch, February 20, 2017, Rapa Nui.

23. On the reerection of the moai, see Fischer, *Island at the End of the World*, 229.
24. See Conal McCarthy, "'Empirical Anthropologists Advocating Cultural Adjustments': The Anthropological Governance of Āpirana Ngata and the Native Affairs Department," *History and Anthropology* 25, no. 2 (2014): 280–295; Conal McCarthy, "Historicising the 'Indigenous International': Museums, Anthropology, and Transpacific Networks," in Dürr and Schorch, *Transpacific Americas,* 3–26; Philipp Schorch, Conal McCarthy, and Arapata Hakiwai, "Globalizing Māori Museology: Reconceptualizing Engagement, Knowledge and Virtuality through Mana Taonga," *Museum Anthropology* 39, no. 1 (2016): 48–69; chapters 1 and 3.
25. See Comunidad Indígena Ma'u Henua, Facebook, https://es-la.facebook.com/Mau-Henua-179457969167170, accessed August 14, 2019; Cooperativa, "Comunidad Ma'u Henua entregó cuenta pública de administración en Rapa Nui," April 13, 2017, http://www.cooperativa.cl/noticias/pais/pueblos-originarios/comunidad-ma-u-henua-entrego-cuenta-publica-de-administracion-en-rapa/2017-04-13/185535.html, accessed August 14, 2019; MoeVarua, "Comunidad Indígena Ma'u Henua Coadministra el Parque Nacional Rapa Nui," November 16, 2016, http://www.moevarua.com/mau-henua, accessed May 6, 2017.
26. Fischer, *Island at the End of the World*, 200.
27. Tony Bennett, Ben Dibley, and Rodney Harrison, "Introduction: Anthropology, Collecting and Colonial Governmentalities," *History and Anthropology* 25, no. 2 (2014): 145.
28. See CMN, "Secretaría Técnica CMN destaca representatividad de Comisión Asesora de Monumentos Nacionales en visita Rapa Nui," June 17, 2016, http://www.monumentos.cl/consejo/606/w3-article-63117.html, accessed August 14, 2019; Museo Antropológico Padre Sebastián Englert, "Programa de Educación Patrimonial Manu Iri," http://www.museorapanui.cl/679/w3-article-63864.html, accessed July 8, 2019. Both initiatives still largely proceed through a Republic of Chile institution, which consults but ultimately decides based on its principles, unlike the Indigenous community institution Ma'u Henua, which sets out to govern the national park based on Rapanui principles.
29. Consejo de Jefes de Rapanui and Alberto Hotus, *Te mau hatu'o Rapa Nui: Los soberanos de Rapa Nui; Pasado, presente y futuro* (Santiago de Chile: Editorial Emisión, 1988), 21 (author's translation).
30. This text opts for "kaiŋa" instead of "kainga" to comply with contemporary conventions in the Rapanui language.
31. Sebastian Englert, *Diccionario Rapa Nui-Español* (Santiago de Chile: Prensas de la Universidad de Chile, 1938), 6.

32. Ibid., 89.
33. Hau'ofa Epeli, *We Are the Ocean: Selected Works* (Honolulu: University of Hawai'i Press, 2008), 69.
34. Englert, *La Tierra de Hotu Mat'ua*, 96.
35. Fischer, *Island at the End of the World*, 233.
36. Katherine Routledge, *The Mystery of Easter Island* (London: Sifton Praed & Co., 1919), 165.
37. Alfred Métraux, *Easter Island: A Stone-Age Civilization of the Pacific*, trans. Michael Bullock (London: André Deutsch, 1957), 24.
38. Fischer, *Island at the End of the World*, 242.
39. Mason, "Moai on the Move."
40. Peter Mason, "Siete maneras de ser moai: Seven Ways of Being Moai," *Boletín del Museo Chileno de Arte Precolombino* 10, no. 2 (2005): 9.
41. Jacinta Arthur, "Reclaiming Mana Repatriation in Rapa Nui" (PhD diss., University of California, 2015), 60.
42. Ibid.
43. In the Māori language, the word "iwi" refers to both kinship group or tribe and bone. A related Hawaiian proverb is "Ola nā iwi—The bones live."
44. "Jacinta Arthur y su lucha por la repatriacion junto a Ka Haka Hoki Mai Te Mana Tupuna," November 24, 2016, http://www.uchileindigena.cl/jacinta-arthur-y-su-lucha-por-la-repatriacion-junto-a-ka-haka-hoki-mai-te-mana-tupuna-2, accessed February 20, 2017.
45. Jacinta Arthur, "Ka Haka Hoki Mai Te Mana Tupuna," *Apuntes del Museo Padre Sebastián Englert,* no. 3 (2014): 73–94.
46. Pelayo Tuki, interview by Philipp Schorch, March 6, 2016, Museo Antropológico Padre Sebastián Englert (author's translation).
47. Arthur, "Reclaiming Mana Repatriation"; see Museum of New Zealand Te Papa Tongarewa, "Repatriation: Karanga Aotearoa," https://www.tepapa.govt.nz/about/repatriation, accessed February 20, 2017. For the Hawaiian context, see Edward Halealoha Ayau and Ty Kāwika Tengan, "Ka Huaka'i o Nā 'Ōiwi: The Journey Home," in *The Dead and their Possessions: Repatriation in Principle, Policy and Practice,* ed. Cressida Fforde, Jane Hubert, and Paul Turnbull (London: Routledge, 2002), 171–189.
48. Paulina Torres, "Te Kuhane o te Kainga: El paisaje y la persona en Rapa Nui" (master's thesis, Universidad Academica de Humanismo Christiano, 2010).
49. See Wikcionario, "toki," https://es.wiktionary.org/wiki/toki#Rapa_nui (accessed August 14, 2019); Facebook, "Toki Rapa Nui," https://www.facebook.com/EscuelaDeMusicaDeRapaNui (accessed August 14, 2019).

50. See Mason, "Moai on the Move"; Fischer, *Island at the End of the World*; National Geographic, *Moái: Vivir para el futuro. Las relaciones entre Japón y Chile través de los moái* (Comité de Ejecución del Proyecto Moái, 2013).
51. See Mahatua Producciones. "Sinopsis: Un viaje en busca del espíritu de los ancestros." *Te Kuhane o Te Tupuna: El Espíritu de los Ancestros,* http://www.mahatua.cl/sinopsis.html, accessed March 12, 2017 (author's translation).
52. A Rapanui delegation, backed up by the Chilean government, visited the British Museum in November 2018 to begin discussion on a potential return of this emblematic moai to the island (John Bartlett, "'Moai are family': Easter Island people to head to London to request statue back," *The Guardian,* November 16, 2018, https://www.theguardian.com/world/2018/nov/16/maoi-easter-island-statue-british-museum-talks-return, accessed August 14, 2019).
53. Coauthors Mara Mulrooney, Noelle Kahanu, and Ty Tengan helped facilitating the film's screening at the University of Hawai'i; I assisted in making contacts with Arapata Hakiwai, Kaihautū (Māori leader) of Te Papa, and arranged the screening at the European Society for Oceanists conference in Munich, June 29–July 2, 2017.
54. I thank Mara Mulrooney for this crucial information.
55. Ty P. Kāwika Tengan, "The Mana of Kū: Indigenous Nationhood, Masculinity and Authority in Hawai'i," in Tomlinson and Tengan, *New Mana,* 55–76.
56. Tomlinson and Tengan, *New Mana.*
57. Fischer, *Island at the End of the World*, 151.
58. Rolf Foerster and Sonia Montecino, "Rapa Nui: la lepra y sus derivados (Estado de excepción, cárcel)," *Escrituras Americanas* 1 (2012): 270–353, 270.
59. No written rule or law was in place, but the captains of the ships generally refused to take Rapanui people, who had no means to leave the island, to Chile (I thank Cristián Moreno Pakarati for this information).
60. Foerster and Montesino, "Rapa Nui," 273; Patricia Stambuk, *Rongo: La Historia Oculta de Isla de Pascua* (Santiago de Chile: Pehuen, 2010), 222.
61. Fischer, *Island at the End of the World*, 214–215; for a detailed account on the revolution, see Rolf Foerster and Cristián Moreno Pakarati, *More Manava* (Santiago de Chile: Rapanui Press, 2016).
62. Quoted in Stambuk, *Rongo,* 308 (author's translation).
63. Tania Basterrica Brockman, "Museo de Sitio Leprosario de Isla de Pascua" (unpublished master's thesis, Instituto Iberoamericano de Museología, 2014).
64. Aldea Educativa Rapa Nui, "Hoŋa'a o te Mana—Aldea Educativa Rapa Nui," http://www.aerp.cl, accessed January 19, 2017 (author's translation).

65. This is taken by an unpublished document titled "Aldea Educativa Rapa Nui—Casa del Arte Isla de Pascua" provided by Tania Basterrica Brockman (author's translation).
66. Ibid.
67. Both quotes, including the one from Walter Benjamin, are from Þióra Pétursdóttir and Bjørnar Olsen, introduction to *Ruin Memories: Materiality, Aesthetics and the Archaeology of the Recent Past,* ed. Bjørnar Olsen and Þióra Pétursdóttir (London: Routledge, 2014), 9, 22.
68. Walter Benjamin, *The Origin of German Tragic Drama* (New York: Verso, 1977), 177–178.
69. See Educarchile, "Liceo de Rapa Nui: un espacio multicultural," June 10, 2006, http://ww2.educarchile.cl/PORTAL.HERRAMIENTAS/autoaprendizaje/article-104210.html, accessed January 10, 2017.
70. Fischer, *Island at the End of the World*, 222.
71. I thank Cristián Moreno Pakarati for this information. This text uses "Tapati," the more common usage, rather than "Tāpati."
72. On contemporary Indigeneity see, for example, James Clifford, *Returns: Becoming Indigenous in the Twenty-First Century* (Cambridge, MA: Harvard University Press, 2013); Maximilian C. Forte, ed., *Indigenous Cosmopolitans: Transnational and Transcultural Indigeneity in the Twenty-First Century* (New York: Peter Lang, 2010); Laura R. Graham and H. Glenn Penny, eds., *Performing Indigeneity: Global Histories and Contemporary Experiences* (Lincoln: University of Nebraska Press, 2014); Charles D. Thompson Jr. and Graham Harvey, eds., *Indigenous Diasporas and Dislocations* (London: Routledge, 2005).
73. James Clifford, "Indigenous Articulations," *The Contemporary Pacific* 13, no. 2 (2001): 467–490.
74. Dan Bendrups, "Pacific Festivals as Dynamic Contact Zones," *Shima: The International Journal of Research into Island Cultures* 2, no. 1 (2008): 14–28, 14.
75. Riet Delsing, "Cultural Politics and Globalization on Rapa Nui," *Rapa Nui Journal* 12, no. 4 (1998): 99–108; see also Riet Deslsing, *Articulating Rapa Nui: Polynesian Cultural Politics in a Latin American Nation-State* (Honolulu: University of Hawaiʻi Press, 2015).
76. Grant McCall, "Culture Bursting Out All Over on Rapanui 2001–2002," *Rapa Nui Journal* 15, no. 2 (2001): 78–82.
77. Maxi Haase, "Popular Perceptions and Local Negotiations of Easter Island Culture," in *Rapa Nui—Easter Island: Cultural and Historical Perspectives,* ed. Ian Conrich and Herman Mückler (Berlin: Frank & Timme, 2016), 35–50, 43.
78. See chapter 2.

79. See, for example, Fischer, *Island at the End of the World.*
80. See chapter 2.
81. On these distinctions, see Jacinta Arthur, "Hakari o te Rapa Nui: Myth Representation in Rapa Nui: From Ancestral Ritual to Postmodern Performance," *Cátedra de Artes* 7 (2009): 65–92.
82. Fischer, *Island at the End of the World*, 258.
83. I build here on ideas and vocabulary collectively developed in the Connecting Materialities/Material Connectivities [mat~con] project.
84. See chapter 2.
85. Philipp Schorch, "Two Germanies: Ethnographic Museums, (Post) Colonial Exhibitions, and the 'Cold Odyssey' of Pacific Objects between East and West," in Carreau et al., *Pacific Presences,* vol. 2, 171–185.
86. See Miguel Fuentes, ed., *Rapa Nui y la La Compañia Explotadora, 1895–1953* (Santiago de Chile: Rapanui Press, 2013), especially the chapter by Georgianna Pineda, "Protección patrimonial para sitios históricos: una aproximación de puesta en valor para el complejo industrial de Vaitea (Rapa Nui)," 194–311.
87. For more information, see Portal del Plan Nacional de Conservación del *Sophora toromiro*, "Visión general del toromiro," http://plantoromiro.org/educacion/vision-general-del-toromiro, accessed August 4, 2017.

Chapter 5: Materializing German-Samoan Colonial Legacies

1. The online narrative brings together related and diverse information about a particular object, collection of objects or subject, linking a collection in significant ways. This information appears on the museum's collection database-catalogue known commercially as the EMu Collections Management System. This is available only to staff. Selected information from this catalogue is also made publicly accessible on the museum's website.
2. On the interplay of cross-cultural resonance and dissonance, see Philipp Schorch and Noelle M.K.Y. Kahanu, "Forum as Laboratory: The Cross-Cultural Infrastructure of Ethnographic Knowledge and Material Potentialities," in Heller, Scholz, and Wagner, *Prinzip Labor,* 241–248.
3. On mana, Marshall Sahlins, *Islands of History* (Chicago: University of Chicago Press, 1985); on taonga, Patrick Vinton Kirch and Roger C. Green, *Hawaiki, Ancestral Polynesia: An Essay in Historical Anthropology* (Cambridge: Cambridge University Press, 2001).
4. On Indigenous articulation, James Clifford, "Indigenous Articulations," *The Contemporary Pacific* 13, no. 2 (2001): 468–490; on inauthenticity, Alan Hanson, "The Making of the Maori: Cultural Invention and Its Logic," *American Anthropologist* 91, no. 4 (1989): 890–902;

and Eric Hobsbawm and Terences Ranger, eds., *The Invention of Tradition* (Cambridge: Cambridge University Press, 1983); see also chapter 2.

5. Apirana T. Mahuika, "Maori Culture and the New Museum," *Museum Anthropology* 15, no. 4 (1991): 9–10.
6. Museum of New Zealand Te Papa Tongarewa, *2005–2006 Annual Report of the Museum of New Zealand Te Papa Tongarewa* (Wellington: Museum of New Zealand Te Papa Tongarewa, 2006), 12–13.
7. Philipp Schorch, Conal McCarthy, and Arapata Hakiwai, "Globalizing Māori Museology: Reconceptualizing Engagement, Knowledge and Virtuality through Mana Taonga," *Museum Anthropology* 39, no.1 (2016), 48–69; Conal McCarthy et al., "Mana Taonga: Connecting Communities with New Zealand Museums through Ancestral Māori Culture," *Museum International* 65 (2015): 5–15; Philipp Schorch and Arapata Hakiwai, "Mana Taonga and the Public Sphere: A Dialogue Between Indigenous Practice and Western Theory," *International Journal of Cultural Studies* 17, no. 2 (2014): 191–205; Arapata Hakiwai, "The Search for Legitimacy: Museums in Aotearoa, New Zealand—A Māori Viewpoint," in *Heritage, Museums and Galleries: An Introductory Reader,* ed. Gerard Corsane (London: Routledge, 2005), 154–162; Arapata Hakiwai, "Māori Taonga—Māori Identity,“ in *Art and Cultural Heritage: Law, Policy and Practice,* ed. Barbara T. Hoffman (New York: Cambridge University Press, 2006), 409–412; Arapata Hakiwai, "The Protection of Taonga and Māori Heritage in Aotearoa (New Zealand)," in *Decolonizing Conservation: Caring for Māori Meeting Houses Outside New Zealand,* ed. Dean Sally (Walnut Creek, CA: Left Coast Press, 2008), 45–58; Conal McCarthy, *Museums and Māori: Heritage Professionals, Indigenous Collections, Current Practice* (Wellington: Te Papa Press, 2011); Conal McCarthy, *Te Papa: Reinventing New Zealand's National Museum 1998–2018* (Wellington: Te Papa Press, 2018); Huhana Smith, "The Museum of New Zealand Te Papa Tongarewa," in Healy and Witcomb, *South Pacific Museums,* 10.11–10.13; and Huhana Smith, "Mana Taonga and the Micro World of Intricate Research and Findings around Taonga Māori at the Museum of New Zealand Te Papa Tongarewa," Special Issue, *Matter in Place, SITES: Journal of Social Anthropology and Cultural Studies* 6, no. 2 (2009): 7–31.
8. Paul Tapsell, "Taonga, Marae, Whenua—Negotiating Custodianship: A Maori Tribal Response to Te Papa: The Museum of New Zealand," in *Rethinking Settler Colonialism: History and Memory in Australia, Canada, Aotearoa, New Zealand, and South Africa,* ed. Annie Coombes (Manchester, UK: Manchester University Press, 2006), 86–99. For an overview of iwi associated with the Wellington region, see Greater

Wellington Regional Council, "Māori of the Wellington Region," February 18, 2016, http://www.gw.govt.nz/maori-of-the-wellington-region/, accessed June 6, 2017.

9. Merata Kawharu, "Gilbert Mair and the Taumata-a-Iwi," in *Ko Tawa: Maori Treasures from New Zealand,* ed. Paul Tapsell (Auckland: David Bateman, 2006), 154–181.
10. Arapata Hakiwai, "He Mana Taonga, He Mana Tangata: Maori Taonga and the Politics of Maori Tribal Identity and Development" (PhD diss., Victoria University of Wellington, Museum and Heritage Studies, 2014); Michelle Horwood, "Worlds Apart: Indigenous Re-engagement with Museum-Held Heritage: A New Zealand–United Kingdom Case Study" (PhD diss., Victoria University of Wellington, 2015); and McCarthy, *Museums and Māori.*
11. On Pacific Cultures, Sean Mallon, "Afterword—Pacific Voices in the Bicultural Museum," in McCarthy, *Museums and Māori,* 248–253; on New Zealand History, Stephanie Gibson, "Te Papa and New Zealand's Indian Communities: A Case Study about Exhibition Development," *Tuhinga: Records of the Museum of New Zealand Te Papa Tongarewa* 14 (2003): 61–75; Pushpa Wood, "Community Consultation: Te Papa and New Zealand Indian Communities: The Other Side of the Coin." *Tuhinga: Records of the Museum of New Zealand Te Papa Tongarewa* 16 (2005): 127–135; and Stephanie Gibson and Sean Mallon. "Representing Community Exhibitions at the Museum of New Zealand Te Papa Tongarewa." *Tuhinga: Records of the Museum of New Zealand Te Papa Tongarewa* 21 (2010): 43–58.
12. On other museums, McCarthy et al., "Mana Taonga"; globally, Schorch, McCarthy, and Hakiwai, "Globalizing Māori Museology."
13. Sean Mallon, "Agency and Authority: The Politics of Co-Collecting," in Schorch and McCarthy, *Curatopia,* 279–295; and Schorch and Hakiwai, "Mana Taonga and the Public Sphere."
14. Mallon, "Agency and Authority."
15. Stephanie Gibson, "Case Study: Museum of New Zealand Te Papa Tongarewa," in *Collecting the Contemporary: A Handbook for Social History Museums,* ed. Owain Rhys and Zelda Baveystock (Edinburgh: MuseumsEtc, 2014), 440–446; and Lynette Townsend, "Collecting Childhood—in more than one way," *Uni News, The University of Auckland News for Staff* 44, no. 8 (2015), 5.
16. Lissant Bolton, ed., "Fieldwork, Fieldworkers, Developments in Vanuatu Research," Special issue, *Oceania* 70, no. 1 (1999); Lissant Bolton, *Unfolding the Moon: Enacting Women's Kastom in Vanuatu* (Honolulu: University of Hawai'i Press, 2003), 44–50.

17. Gerd Spittler, “Teilnehmende Beobachtung als Dichte Teilnahme,” *Zeitschrift für Ethnologie* 126, no. 1 (2001), 1–25.
18. Schorch and Hakiwai, “Mana Taonga and the Public Sphere”; Schorch, McCarthy and Hakiwai, “Globalizing Māori Museology”; Schorch and Kahanu, “Forum as Laboratory”; Philipp Schorch and Noelle M.K.Y Kahanu, “Anthropology’s Interlocutors: Hawai‘i Speaking Back to Ethnographic Museums in Europe,” *Zeitschrift für Kulturwissenschaften* 1 (2015): 114–117; Philipp Schorch, “Assembling Communities: Curatorial Practices, Material Cultures, and Meanings,” in Onciul, Stefano, and Hawke, *Engaging Heritage, Engaging Communities,* 31–46; see also introduction.
19. Luke E. Lassiter, *The Chicago Guide to Collaborative Ethnography* (Chicago: Chicago University Press, 2005).
20. The project Connecting Materialities/Material Connectivities [mat~con] has been developed into the volume *Exploring Materiality and Connectivity in Anthropology and Beyond* (London: UCL Press, 2020). See http://www.highlandasia.net/projects/matcon.html, accessed February 14, 2017.
21. This characterization was offered by Gabriel Koureas in response to a paper Philipp delivered on our behalf at the conference Museums and Their Publics at Sites of Conflicted History in Warsaw on March 13, 2017.
22. On virtual ethnography, Christine Hine, *Virtual Ethnography* (London: Sage, 2000); on global connections, Anna Lowenhaupt Tsing, *Friction: An Ethnography of Global Connection* (Princeton, NJ: Princeton University Press, 2005).
23. Museum Fünf Kontinente, “Sammlung Ozeanien,” http://www.museum-fuenf-kontinente.de/forschung/sammlung-ozeanien/, accessed March 9, 2017.
24. Tsing, *Friction.*
25. Kathrin DiPaola, “Samoa, ‘Perle’ der deutschen Kolonien?: ‘Bilder’ des Exotischen Anderen in Geschichte(n) des 20. Jahrhunderts” (PhD diss., University of Maryland, 2004), 324.
26. Glyn Williams, “Railways in Samoa,” http://www.sinfin.net/railways/world/samoa.html, accessed March 30, 2017.
27. Ilia L. Likou, “Vailima beer bound for United States market,” *Samoa Observer,* March 7, 2018, http://www.samoaobserver.ws/en/07_03_2018/local/30852/Vailima-beer-bound-for-United-States-market.htm, accessed December 3, 2018.
28. Facebook, Hamburg Samoanischer Club e.V., https://www.facebook.com/Hamburg-Samoanischer-Club-eV-1797646333805558, accessed August 14, 2019; and website, http://www.hamburg-samoanischer-club.de, accessed August 14, 2019.

29. Christopher B. Balme, *Pacific Performances: Theatricality and Cross-Cultural Encounter in the South Seas* (New York: Palgrave Macmillan, 2007), chap. 5, 122–145.
30. Leafa Wilson aka Olga Krause, "Ich heisse Olga Hedwig Krause—Deutsche Kuenstlerin," http://www.gettheswitch.com/ongoing.html, accessed November 28, 2017.
31. Jochen Roller, "Them and Us: Ein folkoloniales Spektakel," http://www.jochenroller.de/them-and-us, accessed April 20, 2017.
32. Nicholas Thomas and Diane Losche, eds., *Double Vision: Art Histories and Colonial Histories in the Pacific* (Cambridge: Cambridge University Press, 1999), 4, emphasis in the original.
33. Christine Winter, "Changing Frames: Identity and Citizenship of New Guineans of German Heritage during the Inter-war Years," *Journal of Pacific History* 47, no. 3 (2012): 347–367.
34. Simon Knell, "Altered Values: Searching for a New Collecting" in *Museums and the Future of Collecting* (Farnham, Surrey, UK: Ashgate Publishing, 2004), 17.
35. See Misa Telefoni Retzlaff, "An Enduring Legacy: The German Influence in Samoan Culture and History," Scribd, https://www.scribd.com/document/89983188/Misa-Telefoni-Retzlaff-Samoa-Enduring-legacy-german-influence, accessed August 14, 2019.
36. Sean Mallon, *Samoan Art & Artists: O Measina a Samoa* (Honolulu: University of Hawai'i Press, 2002), 208; see also the *Siamani Samoa* series by Michel Tuffery (chapter 6).
37. Philipp Schorch, Conal McCarthy, and Eveline Dürr, "Introduction: Conceptualising Curatopia," in Schorch and McCarthy, *Curatopia*, 1–16.
38. See Karen Stevenson, *The Frangipani Is Dead: Contemporary Pacific Art in New Zealand* (Wellington: Huia Publishers, 2008).
39. See Linda Herrick, "Pictures Tell Story of Pacific Colony," *New Zealand Herald*, April 28, 2002, http://www.nzherald.co.nz/lifestyle/news/article.cfm?c_id=6&objectid=1842345, accessed June 6, 2017.
40. Louis Owens, "Afterword: Their Shadows before Them: Photographing Indians," in *Trading Gazes: Euro-American Women Photographers and Native North Americans, 1880–1940*, ed. Susan Bernardin et al. (New Brunswick, NJ: Rutgers University Press, 2003), 192; see also chapter 3.
41. Olga Janice Hedwig Krause (Leafa Wilson), "Ich heiße Olga Hedwig Krause; Deutsche Künstlerin—My Name is Olga Hedwig Krause: German Artist," in *National Socialism in Oceania: A Critical Evaluation of its Effect and Aftermath*, ed. Emily Turner-Graham and Christine Winter (New York: Peter Lang, 2010), 234–238.

42. Malama Meleisea, *The Making of Modern Samoa: Traditional Authority and Colonial Administration in the History of Western Samoa* (Suva: University of the South Pacific, 1987), 170.
43. Ibid.
44. Tony Brunt, *'To Walk Under Palm Trees': The Germans in Samoa: Snapshots from Albums—Part One* (Auckland: Tony Brunt, 2016), http://germansinsamoa.net/wp-content/uploads/2013/09/Palm_Trees_Ebook.pdf, accessed October 10, 2017.
45. James Clifford, "The Times of the Curator," in Schorch and McCarthy, *Curatopia*, 109–123.
46. Chris Healy and Andrea Witcomb, eds., *South Pacific Museums: Experiments in Culture* (Melbourne: Monash University ePress, 2006); Viv Golding and Wayne Modest, eds., *Museums and Communities: Curators, Collections and Collaboration* (London: Bloomsbury, 2013).
47. Conal McCarthy, Arapata Haikwai, and Philipp Schorch, "The Figure of the Kaitiaki: Learning from Māori Curatorship Past and Present," in Schorch and McCarthy, *Curatopia*, 211–226.
48. Ciraj Rassool, "Towards the Postcolonial Museum" (paper presented at the "Schwieriges Erbe: Koloniale Objekte—Postkoloniales Wissen" [Difficult Heritage: Colonial Objects—Postcolonial Knowledge] at the Linden-Museum Stuttgart, April 24, 2017.
49. Rebekka Habermas in response to the papers delivered by Rassool and Schorch on our behalf.
50. See Linden Museum, "Schwieriges Erbe," https://www.lindenmuseum.de/erleben/veranstaltungen/veranstaltung/schwieriges-erbe, accessed June 18, 2017.
51. Ty P. Kāwika Tengan, Tēvita O. Ka'ili, and Rochelle Tuitagava'a Fonoti, eds., *Genealogies: Articulating Indigenous Anthropology in/of Oceania*, Special issue of *Pacific Studies* 33, no. 2/3 (2010): 140; see also afterword.
52. Epeli Hau'ofa, *We Are the Ocean: Selected Works* (Honolulu: University of Hawai'i Press, 2008); Geoffrey M. White and Ty P. Kāwika Tengan, "Disappearing Worlds: Anthropology and Cultural Studies in Hawai'i and the Pacific," *The Contemporary Pacific* 13, no. 2 (Fall 2001): 390.
53. Vilsoni Hereniko and Rob Wilson, *Inside Out: Literature, Cultural Politics, and Identity in the New Pacific* (New York: Rowman & Littlefield, 1999).

Chapter 6: "Anthropology's Interlocutors" and the Ethnographic Condition

1. Edward W. Said, *Orientalism* (New York: Pantheon, 1978); "Representing the Colonized: Anthropology's Interlocutors," *Critical Inquiry* 15, no. 2 (Winter 1989): 205–225.

2. Georg Steinmetz, *The Devil's Handwriting: Precoloniality and the German State in Qingdao, Samoa and Southwest Africa* (Chicago: University of Chicago Press, 2007); Talal Assad, ed., *Anthropology and the Colonial Encounter* (London: Ithaca Press, 1973).
3. Steinmetz, *The Devil's Handwriting,* 27.
4. Matthew Jefferies, *Contesting the German Empire, 1871–1918* (Oxford: Blackwell, 2008), 201.
5. Bronwyn Labrum, "Collecting, Curating and Exhibiting Cross-Cultural Material Histories in a Post-Settler Society," in Schorch and McCarthy, *Curatopia,* 244–261.
6. Said, "Representing the Colonized," 219.
7. Rainer F. Buschmann, *Anthropology's Global Histories: The Ethnographic Frontier in German New Guinea, 1870–1935* (Honolulu: University of Hawai'i Press, 2008).
8. Conal McCarthy, "'Empirical Anthropologists Advocating Cultural Adjustments': The Anthropological Governance of Āpirana Ngata and the Native Affairs Department," *History and Anthropology* 25, no. 2 (2014): 280–295.
9. Amiria Henare [Salmond], "Nga Rakau a te Pakeha: Reconsidering Māori Anthropology," in *Anthropologies and Science: Epistomologies in Practice*, eds. Jeanette Edwards, Penny Harvey, and Peter Wade (Oxford: Berg, 2007), 93–113.
10. Geoffrey M. White and Ty P. Kāwika Tengan, "Disappearing Worlds: Anthropology and Cultural Studies in Hawai'i and the Pacific," *The Contemporary Pacific* 13, no. 2 (Fall 2001): 381–416, 390.
11. See introduction and chapter 3.
12. Ruth B. Phillips, "Swings and Roundabouts: Pluralism and the Politics of Change in Canada's National Museums," in Schorch and McCarthy, *Curatopia*, 143–158.
13. *Samoa Weekly Herald,* Saturday, March 3, 1900.
14. Peter J. Hempenstall, *Pacific Islanders under German Rule: A Study in the Meaning of Colonial Resistance* (Canberra: Australian National University Press, 1978); Paul M. Kennedy, *The Samoan Tangle: A Study in Anglo-German-American Relations 1878–1900* (Dublin: Irish University Press, 1974); Malama Meleisea, *The Making of Modern Samoa: Traditional Authority and Colonial Administration in the History of Western Samoa* (Suva: Institute of Pacific Studies of the University of the South Pacific, 1987); and Steinmetz, *The Devil's Handwriting.*
15. Nicholas Thomas and Julie Adams, introduction to *Artefacts of Encounter: Cook's Voyages, Colonial Collecting and Museum Histories,* ed. Nicholas Thomas et al. (Dunedin: Otago University Press, 2016), 19.

16. Jan Lederbogen, "Frühe Fotografie auf Samoa zwischen Wissenschaftsanspruch und kolonialem Denken," in Engelhard and Mesenhöller, *Bilder aus dem Paradies,* 28–30.
17. Kennedy, *The Samoan Tangle*, 77.
18. Steinmetz, *The Devil's Handwriting*, 342, 340; see also *Samoanische Zeitung*, August 2, 1901, in which the author writing under the pseudonym of "Spectator" reports about the "difficulties" and "dangers" posed to the colonial government by the installment of the ali'i sili and the "necessary distribution of fine mats."
19. *Auckland Star*, March 15, April 5, 1900.
20. Christopher B. Balme, *Pacific Performances: Theatricality and Cross-Cultural Encounter in the South Seas* (New York: Palgrave Macmillan, 2007), 138.
21. *Samoa Weekly Herald*, March 3, 1900.
22. Bundesarchiv, "Eine deutsche 'Musterkolonie'—Samoa unter dem Kosmopoliten Wilhelm Solf," Web gallery, https://www.bundesarchiv.de/oeffentlichkeitsarbeit/bilder_dokumente/01081/index.html.de, accessed June 10, 2017.
23. Peter J. Hempenstall and Paula T. Mochida, *The Lost Man: Wilhelm Solf in German History* (Wiesbaden: Harrassowitz Verlag, 2005), 59–60.
24. Sean Mallon, "German Samoa Captured by New Zealand Troops—29 August 1914," *Te Papa Blog,* August 29, 2014, http://blog.tepapa.govt.nz/2014/08/29/german-samoa-captured-by-new-zealand-troops-august-1914/, accessed January 5, 2017.
25. *Evening Post*, Saturday, August 2, 1930.
26. *Auckland Star*, Wednesday, October 8, 1930.
27. Te Papa also houses a total of nine flags (see Mallon, "German Samoa Captured").
28. *New Zealand Herald*, January 14, 1938; see also *Auckland Star*, January 13, 1938.
29. *New Zealand Herald*, January 29, 1938.
30. Ibid., February 13, 1934.
31. Museum of New Zealand Te Papa Tongarewa, Poster: "German Colonial Possessions" (United Kingdom: Johnson Riddle & Co. Ltd., 1915), http://collections.tepapa.govt.nz/object/1081465, accessed August 14, 2019.
32. Kirstie Ross, "August 1914: This Month Last Century," *Te Papa Blog,* August 29, 2012, http://blog.tepapa.govt.nz/2012/08/29/august-1914-this-month-last-century, accessed August 14, 2019.
33. James Belich, *Paradise Reforged: A History of the New Zealanders from the 1880s to the Year 2000* (Rosedale, NZ: Penguin Books, 2001).

34. Kennedy, *The Samoan Tangle*, 305.
35. Damon Salesa, "A Pacific Destiny: New Zealand's Overseas Empire 1840–1945," in *Tangata O Le Moana: New Zealand and the People of the Pacific*, ed. Sean Mallon, Kolokesa Māhina-Tuai, and Damon Salesa (Wellington: Te Papa Press, 2012), 97–122.
36. *The Dominion,* September 11, 1914; *The Press*, September 11, 1914.
37. *The Wairarapa Age*, September 18, 1914. The folder "Copies of letters to and from Dr. Schultz and others" held at Archives New Zealand, Te Rua Mahara o te Kāwanatanga contains a chain of letters in which Schultz, while in internment on Motuihe Island, protests to the New Zealand government against such governmental, military, and media misrepresentations of the takeover (Archives Reference No. G47 1).
38. Alexander Turnbull Library, Ref: Eph-B-POSTCARD-Vol-1–125-top (W. Blomfield, "Samoa yielded without a struggle," *Observer Print,* 1914), http://mp.natlib.govt.nz/detail/?id=10325&l=en, accessed March 11, 2017.
39. *New Zealand Herald*, June 26, 1935.
40. Ibid., September 9, 1914; *The Dominion*, November 24, 1915.
41. *Samoanische Zeitung*, September 5, 1914.
42. Steinmetz, *The Devil's Handwriting*, 324.
43. Hempenstall and Mochida, *The Lost Man,* 63.
44. Feelix M. Keesing, *Modern Samoa: Its Government and Changing Life* (London: George Allen & Unwin, 1934), 327.
45. *Samoanische Zeitung*, August 2, 1901.
46. Steinmetz, *The Devil's Handwriting*, 339–341.
47. Ibid.
48. *Samoanische Zeitung*, April 13, 1912.
49. Julius Riese, "Die *Samoanische Zeitung* (1901–1914): Images of the Samoan People and Culture in a German Newspaper," in *Sprachwissenschaft und kolonialzeitlicher Sprachkontakt: Sprachliche Begegnungen und Auseinandersetzungen,* ed. Stefan Engelberg and Doris Stolberg (Berlin: Akademie Verlag, 2012), 182.
50. *Samoanische Zeitung*, October 28, 1912.
51. Steinmetz, *The Devil's Handwriting.*
52. Tony Brunt, "Werner von Bulow: The Mystery Man of Matapo'o," chap. 7 in *"To Walk Under Palm Trees": The Germans in Samoa: Snapshots from Albums—Part One* (Auckland; Tony Brunt, 2016), 143, http://germansinsamoa.net/wp-content/uploads/2013/09/Palm_Trees_Ebook.pdf, accessed April 8, 2017.
53. Steinmetz, *The Devil's Handwriting*, 341, 313. On Krämer, see Sven Mönter, "Dr. Augustin Krämer: a German Ethnologist in the Pacific"

(PhD diss., The University of Auckland, 2010); for more on Solf, see Peter Hempenstall and Paula Mochida, *The Lost Man: Wilhelm Solf in German History* (Wiesbaden: Harrassowitz Verlag, 2005); on Schultz, see Dorothee Piesbergen, "Erich Schultz-Ewerth," in *Rechtsvergleicher: Verkannt, Vergessen, Verdrängt*, ed. Bernhard Großfeld (Münster: LIT, 2000), 75–85.

54. Hempenstall and Mochida, *The Lost Man*, 61.
55. Thomas Schwarz, "Hybridität: Ein begriffsgeschichtlicher Aufriss," *Zeitschrift für interkulturelle Germanistik* 6, no. 1 (2015): 163–180, 171 (author's translation); see also Thomas Schwarz, *Ozeanische Affekte: Die literarische Modellierung Samoas im kolonialen Diskurs* (Kelheim: EIA AG—Internet Akademie und Lehrbuch Verlag, 2013). The intermarrage of Sāmoans with Chinese was also discouraged by both German and New Zealand colonial administrations (Sean Mallon, email correspondence, March 17, 2017).
56. For the celebratory strand of the literature, see Hermann Joseph Hiery, *Das Deutsche Reich in der Südsee (1900–1921): Eine Annäherung an die Erfahrungen verschiedener Kulturen* (Göttingen: Vandenhoeck & Ruprecht, 1995); for the condemning strand, see Meleisea, *The Making of Modern Samoa*.
57. Steinmetz, *The Devil's Handwriting*, 331.
58. M.P.K. Sorrenson, *Manifest Duty: The Polynesian Society over 100 Years* (Auckland: The Polynesian Society, 1992), 7.
59. Erich Schultz, *Proverbial Expressions of the Samoans* (Auckland: The Polynesian Society, 1948).
60. See Archives New Zealand file on Julius Henniger (reference no. AAAB W291 482, Box 3); see also "Statement of a case of a German who is prevented by the New Zealand Administration of Samoa to carry on scientific research on the Islands," written by Henniger and held at the Turnbull Library (call no. P Q920 HEN 1920); *Grey River Argus*, "The Case of Julius Henniger," June 17, 1920: "His treatment by us [New Zealand] is not merely an act of gross injustice to the individual; it is and unforgivable crime against Science itself."
61. Conal McCarthy, "'Two Branches of the Brown Polynesians': Ethnological Fieldwork, Colonial Governmentality and the 'Dance of Agency'," in *New Zealand's Empire*, ed. Katie Pickles and Catharine Coleborne (London: Manchester University Press, 2016), 51–67.
62. Memorandum on Solf for C. W. Butterfield, Government House, Apia, May 16, 1928, Archives New Zealand.
63. On anthropological governance, McCarthy, "Empirical Anthropologists Advocating Cultural Adjustments"; see also chapters 1–3; on "Maori

methods" and ethnological research, McCarthy, "'Two Branches of the Brown Polynesians,'" 61; for the letter exchange between Ngata and Buck, see M.P.K. Sorrenson, *Na to Hoa Aroha, from Your Dear Friend: The Correspondence of Sir Apirana Ngata and Sir Peter Buck, Volume One (1925–29)* (Auckland: Auckland University Press, 1986), 61.

64. Letter by H.R.H. Balneavis, Secretary of Maori Ethnological Research Board to Dora H. de Beer, May 10, 1928. See letter exchange at Alexander Turnbull Library between Maori Ethnological Research Board and Dora H. de Beer, who was hired to translate Augustin Krämer's *Die Samoa-Inseln*. It took until 1938, however, to translate part of the book on behalf of the New Zealand government as guiding document for colonial administrative staff. In 1994, the full version was translated by Theodore Verhaaren and published as *The Samoa Islands: An Outline of a Monograph with Particular Consideration of German Samoa* (Honolulu: University of Hawai'i Press). For more information on Krämer, see Mönter, "Dr. Augustin Krämer"; and Dietrich Schleip, "Ozeanische Ethnographie und Koloniale Praxis, Das Beispiel Augustin Krämer" (master's thesis, Eberhard-Karls-Universität Tübingen, 1989).
65. Te Rangi Hiroa (Peter H. Buck), *Samoan Material Culture* (Honolulu: Bishop Museum Press. 1930), 283; see also chapter 2.
66. Hilke Thode-Arora mentioned in conversation that the stamp was also used to prevent the trading of mats beyond German Sāmoa so that they could circulate only within the German colonial setting and economic sphere (April 5, 2017, Munich).
67. See Safua Akeli, "Remembering Malifa School in Samoa," *Te Papa blog*, May 28, 2012, http://blog.tepapa.govt.nz/2012/05/28/remembering-malifa-school-in-samoa, accessed August 14, 2019.
68. *Evening Post*, December 3, 1936.
69. Universität Bayreuth, "Die deutsche Schule und die Regierungsschule für Eingeborene in Apia," http://www.neueste.uni-bayreuth.de/Suedsee SchuleAusbIX.htm, accessed May 9, 2017.
70. Peggy Fairbairn-Dunlop, *Tamatai Samoa: Their Stories* (Suva: University of the South Pacific, 1998), 143.
71. Steinmetz, *The Devil's Handwriting*, 321–322.
72. Universität Bayreuth, "Die deutsche Schule."
73. Steinmetz, *The Devil's Handwriting*, 317.
74. Albert Wendt, "Afterword: Tatauing the Post-Colonial Body," in *Inside Out: Literature, Cultural Politics, and Identity in the New Pacific*, ed. Vilsoni Hereniko and Rob Wilson (New York: Rowman & Littlefield, 1999), 410–411.

75. Thomas and Adams, introduction, 19.
76. Bundespräsidialamt, "Bundespräsident Joachim Gauck beim Mittagessen zu Ehren des Staatsoberhaupts des Unabhängigen Staates Samoa," January 28, 2014, http://www.bundespraesident.de/SharedDocs/Downloads/DE/Reden/2014/01/140128-Staatsoberhaupt-Samoa.pdf, accessed August 14, 2019.
77. In the context of this chapter and argument, I prefer "ethnic shows" over "human zoos," as suggested by Hilke Thode-Arora ("Walking the Fine Line: *From Samoa with Love?* at the Museum Fünf Kontinente, Munich," in Schorch and McCarthy, *Curatopia*, 56–71). Yet I also acknowledge the equally valid use of "human zoos" (see, for example, Meleisea, *The Making of Modern Samoa,* and Yuki Kihara, the contemporary artist who features in detail in this chapter).
78. Hilke Thode-Arora, *From Samoa with Love? Samoa-Völkerschauen im Deutschen Kaiserreich: Eine Spurensuche* (Munich: Hirmer, 2014), 140, 172.
79. "After Mata'afa's death, the German regime abolished ali'i sili and created the position of *fautua*, jointly held by my grandfather Tupua Tamasese Lealofi and Malietoa Tanumafili" (His Highness Tui Atua Tupua Tamasese Efi in Thode-Arora, *From Samoa with Love?*, 8).
80. For publications, see Jill Loyd, *German Expressionism, Primitivism and Modernity* (New Haven, CT: Yale University Press, 1991); Birgit Dalbajewa and Ulrich Bischoff, eds., *Die BRÜCKE in Dresden 1905–1911* (Cologne: Verlag der Buchhandlung König, 2001); Andrea Rüth, "Auf der Suche nach der ursprünglichen Einheit von Mensch und Natur." Eine Untersuchung zum antizivilisatorischen Aspekt im deutschen Expressionismus am Beispiel der Künstlergruppe "Brücke" (PhD diss., Ludwig-Maximilians-Universität München, 2008); and Mathias Krüger, "Künstlerkolonien: Gründungsorte im Abseits der Moderne," in *Gründungsorte der Moderne: Von St. Petersburg bis Occupy Wall Street*, ed. Maha El Hissy and Sascha Pöhlmann (Paderborn, DE: Wilhelm Fink, 2014), 161–176; for exhibitions, see *Die Brücke in der Südsee: Exotik der Farbe* (Saarlandmuseum, Saarbrücken, October 22, 2005–January 8, 2006), http://www.hatjecantz.de/die-bruecke-in-der-suedsee-1631-0.html; *BRÜCKE und die Lebensreform* (Buchheim Museum, July 2–October 9, 2016), https://www.buchheimmuseum.de/aktuell/2016/lebensreform.php; and Brücke Museum http://www.bruecke-museum.de/, accessed , accessed July 10, 2019.
81. Emil Nolde, *Welt und Heimat: Die Südseereise 1913–1918,* 4th ed. (Cologne: Dumont, 2002).
82. These broad characterizations were confirmed and enriched in an excellent seminar on "German Expressionism, Anthropology, and

Colonialism" hosted by the Statens Museum for Kunst—National Gallery of Denmark and the Stedelijk Museum Amsterdam in Copenhagen, December 8–9, 2017, in which I participated.

83. Arnd Schneider, "Appropriations," in *Contemporary Art and Anthropology*, ed. Arnd Schneider and Christopher Wright (Oxford: Berg, 2006), 34.
84. I thank Nina Tonga for this point.
85. Nicholas Netzler's exhibition Unsere Neuen Landsleute (Our New Countrymen) at Lopdell House Gallery (now Te Uru Waitakere Contemporary Gallery) in Titirangi, West Auckland, in 2002 precedes Michel Tuffery's *Siamani Samoa* (see chapter 5).
86. For a discussion of Pacific diasporas underpinning Pacific life in general and artistic performance in particular, see Balme, *Pacific Performances*; on ambivalent kinship, Teresia Teaiwa and Sean Mallon, "Ambivalent Kinships? Pacific People in New Zealand," in *New Zealand Identities: Departures and Destinations*, ed. James H. Liu et al. (Wellington: Victoria University Press, 2005), 207–229.
87. Graeme Whimp, "Working in the Space Between: Pacific Artists in Aotearoa/New Zealand," in *The Space Between: Negotiating Culture, Place, and Identity in the Pacific*, Occasional Paper Series 44, ed. A. Marata Tamaira (Honolulu: Center for Pacific Islands Studies, University of Hawai'i, 2009), 13.
88. Sean Mallon, "The Art of In-Betweenness: Reflecting on Pacific Art Practice in New Zealand," *SPAN Journal of the South Pacific Association for Commonwealth Literature and Language Studies* 53 (2004): 44–56; Whimp, "Working in the Space Between."
89. Michel Tuffery, *Siamani Samoa* (Bowen Hills, AU: Andrew Baker Art Dealer, 2012).
90. Tuffery, *Siamani Samoa*.
91. See Thode-Arora, *From Samoa with Love?*; see also Thode-Arora, "Walking the Fine Line."
92. Milford Galleries Dunedin, "Yuji Kihara," https://www.milfordgalleries.co.nz/dunedin/artists/232-Yuki-Kihara, accessed July 10, 2019.
93. Quoted in Erika Wolf, "Shigeyuki Kihara's 'Fa'a fafine; In a Manner of a Woman': The Photographic Theater of Cross-Cultural Encounter," *Pacific Arts* 10, no. 2 (2010): 24; see also "Fa'afafine: In the Manner of a Woman, Triptych 1," TheMet, 2004–2005, http://www.metmuseum.org/art/collection/search/538528, accessed July 10, 2019.
94. Deidre Brown, "Islands of Opportunity: Pasifika Styles and Museums," in Raymond and Salmond, *Pasifika Styles*, 27.

95. Balme, *Pacific Performances*, 209; see discussion of fa'afafine in Balme, *Pacific Performances*, 200–212.
96. Yuki Kihara, *Where Do We Come From? What Are We? Where Are We Going?*, exhibition at Milford Galleries, Dunedin, March 16–April 10, 2013, https://www.milfordgalleries.co.nz/dunedin/exhibitions/328-Yuki-Kihara-Where-do-we-come-from-What-are-we-Where-are-we-going, accessed February 10, 2017; Mandy Treagus and Madeleine Seys, "Looking Back at Samoa: History, Memory, and the Figure of Mourning in *Yuki Kihara's Where Do We Come From? What Are We? Where Are We Going?*," *Asian Diasporic Visual Cultures and the Americas* 3, no. 1–2 (2017): 86–109; and Maia Nuku, "Standing on the Edge of the Abyss: Shigeyuki Kihara, Catalyst for Change," *Broadsheet/Contemporary Art Centre of Australia, S.A.* 44, no. 3 (2015): 10–11, 14.
97. Singapore Art Museum, "Shigeyuki Kihara: Artist Statement and Biography," 2014, https://www.singaporeartmuseum.sg/downloads/apbf/new_zealand/Shigeyuki_Kihara.pdf, accessed February 10, 2017.
98. Shigeyuki Kihara, "Taualuga: The Last Dance," https://www.youtube.com/watch?v=ev-vIeSDb4I, accessed July 10, 2019.
99. Yuki Kihara, *Where Do We Come From?*.
100. Jochen Roller, "Them and Us: Ein folkoloniales Spektakel," 2015, http://www.jochenroller.de/them-and-us, accessed February 10, 2017.
101. "Tatau Dance Group," Facebook, https://www.facebook.com/TatauDanceGroup, accessed July 10, 2019.
102. Jochen Roller and Yuki Kihara, *Them and Us: Ein folkoloniales Spektakel*, 2015, https://vimeo.com/154989326, accessed March 12, 2017.
103. See Sabine teHeesen's critique "Freude am fremden Volk: Erich Scheurmann in der Maske des Papalagi," updated 2016, http://literaturkritik.de/id/3043, accessed March 12, 2017.
104. Yuki Kihara, *Der Papālagi (The White Man): Exhibition Preview*, Milford Galleries, Dunedin, https://www.milfordgalleries.co.nz/dunedin/submissions/10321-9b5290a9, accessed February 5, 2017.
105. Andrew Clifford, ed., *Yuki Kihara: A Study of a Samoan Savage* (Waitakere: Te Uru Waitakere Contemporary Gallery, 2016).
106. Yuki Kihara, *A Study of a Samoan Savage: Head with Pelvimeter*, 2015, Auckland Art Gallery Toi o Tāmaki, http://www.aucklandartgallery.com/explore-art-and-ideas/artwork/22715/a-study-of-a-samoan-savage-head-with-pelvimeter, accessed March 11, 2017.
107. Kihara, *Study of a Samoan Savage*.
108. Divya P. Tolia-Kelly, "Dark Seas and Glass Walls—Feeling Injustice at the Museum. Practitioner Perspectives: Rosanna Raymond," in

Tolia-Kelly, Waterton, and Watson, *Heritage, Affect and Emotion*, 276–292; see also "Rosanna Raymond," Facebook, https://de-de.facebook.com/rosanna.raymond, accessed March 16, 2017.

109. Rosanna Raymond and Amiria Salmond, introduction to *Pasifika Styles: Artists Inside the Museum* (Dunedin: Otago University Press, 2008), 19, 9.
110. Billie Lythberg, "21st Century South Sea Savagery: Rosanna Raymond's SaVAge K'lub at APT8," *Broadsheet Journal* 45, no. 1 (2016): 14–17; see also interview with Raymond in Divya P. Tolia-Kelly, "Dark Seas and Glass Walls."
111. Heller, Martin, Andrea Scholz, and Agnes Wagner, eds., *Prinzip Labor: Museumsexperimente im Humboldt Lab Dahlem* (Berlin: Nicolai, 2015). The project publication, *Hands On: Indigenous Artists and European Cultural Institutions: The Story of Two Art Residencies* gives a behind-the-scenes glimpse of the processes involved in negotiating the residency for an Indigenous artist, which is common in Canada, the United States, Australia, and Oceania, but still uncommon in Europe given, among other aspects, the tyranny of distance between museums and so-called source communities, and the privileging of certain knowledge systems as one of the (post)colonial legacies (see http://www.indigeneity.net).
112. Indigeneity in the Contemporary World: Performance, Politics, and Belonging, "Residencies," http://indigeneity.net/residencies; see intervention, "Rosanna Raymond—Acti.VA.tion," https://vimeo.com/110965423, accessed August 14, 2019.
113. Tolia-Kelly, "Dark Seas and Glass Walls," 283, 290.
114. Rosanna Raymond, email to the author, August 28, 2016.
115. Tolia-Kelly, "Dark Seas and Glass Walls," 290.
116. Rober Jahnke, ed., and Leafa Wilson, exhibition curator, *Letters to the Ancestors: Contemporary Indigenous Art from Aotearoa and the Pacific*, exhibition catalog (Hamilton, NZ: Waikato Museum, 2005).
117. "Art: Olga/Hedwig/Janice Krause," http://www.gettheswitch.com, accessed March 22, 2017.
118. Said, *Representing the Colonized*, 219.
119. #500words, "WWLD? In Conversation with Leafa Wilson aka Olga Krause," December 3, 2014, https://hashtag500words.com/2014/12/03/wwld-in-conversation-with-leafa-wilson-aka-olga-krause/, accessed July 10, 2019.
120. Sofa Gallery, *Ich heisse Olga Hedwig Krause: Deutsche Künstlerin. My name is Olga Hedwig Krause: German Artists,* exhibition brochure (Christchurch, 2005).
121. #500words, "WWLD?"
122. Leafa Wilson, email to the author, July 22, 2016.

123. Ibid.
124. On *Neue Landsleute,* Balme, *Pacific Performances,* chap. 5, 122–145; on "brown Germans," Christine Winter, "National Socialism and the German (Mixed-Race) Diasporas in Oceania," in *Europa Jenseits der Genzen,* eds. Michael Mann and Jürgen G. Nagel (Heidelberg: Draupadi-Verlag, 2015), 228–248.
125. Christine Winter, "Changing Frames Identity and Citizenship of New Guineans of German Heritage during the Interwar Years," *Journal of Pacific History* 47, no. 3 (2012): 347–367.
126. Leafa Wilson, email to the author, July 22, 2016.
127. Balme, *Pacific Performances,* 182.
128. On reverse anthropology, see Stuart Kirsch, *Reverse Anthropology: Indigenous Analysis of Social and Environmental Relations in New Guinea* (Redwood City, CA: Stanford University Press, 2006).
129. Philipp Schorch, "Two Germanies: Ethnographic Museums, (Post) Colonial Exhibitions, and the 'Cold Odyssey' of Pacific Objects Between East and West," in Carreau et al., *Pacific Presences,* vol. 2, 171–185.
130. On the traces, George E. Marcus, "Affinities: Fieldwork in Anthropology Today and the Ethnographic in Artwork," in Schneider and Wright, *Between Art and Anthropology,* 83–94; on the boundaries, George E. Marcus and Fred R. Myers, eds., *The Traffic in Culture: Refiguring Art and Anthropology* (Oakland: University of California Press, 1995); Arnd Schneider and Christopher Wright, *Between Art and Anthropology: Contemporary Ethnographic Practice* (London: Bloomsbury, 2010); and Arnd Schneider and Christopher Wright, eds., *Contemporary Art and Anthropology* (Oxford: Berg, 2006).
131. Jonathan Mane-Wheoki, "The Resurgence of Maori Art: Conflicts and Continuities in the Eighties," *The Contemporary Pacific* 7 (1995): 1–19, 5.
132. On the division, Schneider, "Appropriations," 30; on the structures, Balme, *Pacific Performances,* 217.

Conclusion

1. James Clifford, *The Predicament of Culture* (Cambridge, MA: Harvard University Press, 1988), 22–23.
2. Michael Holquist, *Dialogism: Bakhtin and His World* (London: Routledge, 2002).
3. *Merriam-Webster Dictionary,* s.v. "kaleidoscope," https://www.merriam-webster.com/dictionary/kaleidoscope, accessed July 11, 2019.
4. Paul Ricoeur, "Life in Quest of Narrative," in *On Paul Ricoeur: Narrative and Interpretation,* edited by David Wood (London: Routledge, 1991), 20–33.

5. In regard to new directions of anthropology within and beyond museums see “Engaging Anthropological Legacies,” *Museum Worlds* 5 (2017), http://journals.berghahnbooks.com/museum-worlds; and, in particular, Andrea Scholz, “Sharing Knowledge as a Step toward an Epistemological Pluralization of the Museum,” 133–148. For new directions of the ethnographic, see the ongoing research area “Transforming the Ethnographic” at the Centre for Anthropological Research on Museums and Heritage (CARMAH), http://www.carmah.berlin/making-differences-in-berlin/, accessed November 10, 2017.
6. See Staatliche Kunstsammlungen Dresden, “Freistaat Sachsen gibt menschliche Gebeine aus Museum für Völkerkunde Dresden an Hawaiʻi zurück,” Press Release, October 23, 2017, https://www.skd.museum/presse/2017/freistaat-sachsen-gibt-menschliche-gebeine-aus-museum-fuer-voelkerkunde-dresden-an-hawaii-zurueck, accessed November 12, 2017; see also the unpublished provenance research report on Hawaiʻi compiled by Birgit Scheps-Bretschneider in 2017 held at the Grassi Museum für Völkerkunde.
7. Edward Halealoha Ayau and Ty Kāwika Tengan, “Ka Huakaʻi o Nā ʻŌiwi: The Journey Home,” in *The Dead and Their Possessions: Repatriation in Principle, Policy and Practice,* eds. Cressida Fforde, Jane Hubert, and Paul Turnbull (London: Routledge, 2002), 171–189; Edward Halealoha Ayau and Honor Keeler, “Injustice, Human Rights, and Intellectual Savagery. A Review,” April 14, 2017, http://www.hsozkult.de/debate/id/diskussionen-3987, accessed November 21, 2018.
8. The literature on restitution or repatriation is broad. See, for example, Tiffany Jenkins, *Contesting Human Remains in Museum Collections: The Crisis of Cultural Authority* (New York: Routledge, 2011); “Ritual Repatriation” in *Museum Worlds* 5 (2017), https://www.berghahnjournals.com/view/journals/museum-worlds/5/1/museum-worlds.5.issue-1.xml, accessed December 18, 2018; for the German context, see “Human Remains in Museums and Collections. A Critical Engagement with the Recommendations of the German Museums Association (2013),” February 3, 2017, https://www.hsozkult.de/debate/id/diskussionen-3909, accessed November 21, 2018; for the French context, the groundbreaking report Felwine Sarr and Bénédicte Savoy, “The Restitution of African Cultural Heritage: Toward a New Relational Ethics,” November 2018, http://restitutionreport2018.com/, accessed November 24, 2018.
9. These questions also informed our subsequent international conference, “Sensitive Heritage: Ethnographic Museums and Material/Immaterial Restitutions,” https://grassi-voelkerkunde.skd.museum/ausstellungen

/sensitive-heritage-ethnographic-museums-and-materialimmaterial-restitutions, accessed November 21, 2018.

10. Staatliche Kunstsammlungen Dresden, *Prolog #1–10,* http://prolog-ausstellung.info/about/, accessed November 21, 2017.
11. See Kamakako'i, "Ka Ho'ina: Going Home," uploaded December 16, 2014, https://vimeo.com/114712444; and Office of Hawaiian Affairs, "Nā Hulu Lehua: The Royal Cloak and Helmet of Kalani'ōpu'u," uploaded October 27, 2016, https://vimeo.com/189245734, accessed November 23, 2017.
12. Staatliche Kunstsammlungen Dresden, "Restitution: Was Jetzt?" *Prolog #1–10,* http://prolog-ausstellung.info/calender/2017/10/23/podiumsdiskussion-restitution-was-jetzt, accessed November 29, 2017.

Afterword

1. I typically do not italicize Hawaiian because it is not a foreign language for me, or in Hawai'i, where the publisher of this book is located. The first instance of a common word in Hawaiian in this essay is italicized, however, in keeping with Philipp's "Note on the Text."
2. Kalei Nu'uhiwa, *Kaulana Mahina 2016–2017,* (2016); Mary Kawena Pukui and Samuel H. Elbert, eds., *Hawaiian Dictionary: Hawaiian-English, English-Hawaiian* (Honolulu: University of Hawai'i Press, 1986), 97.
3. See Dr. Pualani Kanaka'ole Kanahele, "Papakū Makawalu Part 1," Presentation in Keauhou, Hawai'i, April 24, 2009, https://vimeo.com/4621142, accessed October 23, 2017.
4. Dr. Pualani Kanaka'ole Kanahele, "Ke Au Makahiki," handout at the *Papakū Makawalu: Makahiki* workshop, University of Hawai'i, Hilo, January 16–18, 2016.
5. Liliuokalani, trans., *The Kumulipo: An Hawaiian Creation Myth* (Kentfield, CA: Pueo Press, 1978). Rpt. of *An Account of the Creation of the World According to Hawaiian Tradition,* 1897.
6. Mata is the cognate term used in other Austronesian languages, including Rapanui, Māori, Sāmoan, and Tongan.
7. Carl F.K. Pao, artist statement posted at *Pewa II: Remasculation and Human Seed Ships* show at SPF Projects, Honolulu, May 8–June 8, 2014; Marata Tamaira, "About the Cover Art," in *New Mana: Transformations of a Classic Concept in Pacific Languages and Cultures,* eds. Matt Tomlinson and Ty P. Kāwika Tengan (Canberra: ANU Press, 2016), xiii-xiv; Ty P. Kāwika Tengan, "The Mana of Kū: Indigenous Nationhood, Masculinity and Authority in Hawai'i," in Tomlinson and Tengan, *New Mana,* 55–75.

8. For a discussion of kaona as a decolonial interpretive methodology, see Brandy Nālani McDougall, *Finding Meaning: Kaona and Contemporary Hawaiian Literature* (Tucson: University of Arizona Press, 2016).
9. Pukui and Elbert, *Hawaiian Dictionary,* 224.
10. Vicente M. Diaz, "Native Pacific Studies and the Illinois Debacle: Indigeneity at the Edge of Nationalist Belongings and the Limits of Signification," *American Quarterly* 67, no. 3 (2015): 597–608.
11. Compare with Kamanamaikalani Beamer, *Na Mākou ka Mana: Liberating the Nation* (Honolulu: Kamehameha Schools Press, 2014).
12. Jonathan Goldberg-Hiller and Noenoe K. Silva, "The Botany of Emergence: Kanaka Ontology and Biocolonialism in Hawai'i," *Native American and Indigenous Studies* 2, no. 2 (2015): 1–26.
13. See, for example, Hokulani K. Aikau, "Following the Alaloa Kīpapa of Our Ancestors: A Trans-Indigenous Futurity without the State (United States or Otherwise)," *American Quarterly* 67, no. 3 (2015): 653–661; Alfred Taiaiake, *Wasáse: Indigenous Pathways of Action and Freedom* (Toronto: University of Toronto Press, 2015); Jeff Corntassel, "Re-Envisioning Resurgence: Indigenous Pathways to Decolonization and Self-determination," *Decolonization: Indigeneity, Education & Society* 1, no. 1 (2012): 86–101; Noelani Goodyear-Ka'ōpua, *The Seeds We Planted: Portaits of a Native Hawaiian Charter School* (Minneapolis: University of Minnesota Press, 2013); Noenoe K. Silva, *The Power of the Steel-tipped Pen: Reconstructing Native Hawaiian Intellectual History* (Durham, NC: Duke University Press, 2017); Leanne Betasamosake Simpson, *As We Have Always Done: Indigenous Freedom Through Radical Resistance* (Minneapolis: University of Minnesota Press, 2017).
14. Pukui and Elbert, *Hawaiian Dictionary,*155.
15. Davianna Pōmaika'i McGregor, *Nā Kua'āina: Living Hawaiian Culture* (Honolulu: University of Hawai'i Press, 2007), 7–8.
16. Ibid., 8.
17. Goodyear-Ka'ōpua, *The Seeds We Planted,* 7.
18. As Bradd Shore explains, "either directly or indirectly *mana* is linked to generative potency, to the sources of organic creation" (140). Bradd Shore, "*Mana* and *Tapu,*" in *Developments in Polynesian Ethnology,* ed. Alan Howard and Robert Borofsky (Honolulu: University of Hawai'i Press, 1989), 137–173.
19. Pukui and Elbert, *Hawaiian Dictionary,* 27. For an example of how the ecological concept of makana'ā has been mobilized in efforts to regenerate dryland forests in Ka'ūpūlehu on Hawai'i Island, see the work of Ho'ōla ka Makana'ā at Ka'ūpūlehu, http://www.dryland forest.org/hoola-ka-makanaa-at-kaupulehu-dryland-forest, and

https://www.hawaiiforestinstitute.org/our-projects/dryland-forest-projects/kaupulehu-dryland-forest, accessed September 30, 2017.

20. See Pao, *Pewa II*; Tamaira, "About the Cover Art" and Tengan "The Mana of Kū." In the 2003 *E Kū Mau Mau* exhibit, he featured a four-foot-tall carved wooden ule (penis) with shark's teeth embedded in it.
21. Tamaira, "About the Cover Art."
22. Ty P. Kāwika Tengan, "Shifting the 'We' in Oceania: Anthropology and Pacific Islanders Regenerated," in *Who Are We? Reimagining Alterity and Affinity in Anthropology,* eds. Liana Chua and Nayanika Mathur (Berghan Books, 2018), 151–176; Ty P. Kāwika Tengan, Tēvita O. Ka'ili, and Rochelle Tuitagava'a Fonoti, "Genealogies: Articulating Indigenous Anthropology in/of Oceania," *Pacific Studies* 33, no. 2 (2010): 139–167.
23. See especially James Clifford, *Returns: Becoming Indigenous in the Twenty-First Century* (Cambridge, MA: Harvard University Press, 2013); and Epeli Hau'ofa, *We Are the Ocean: Selected Works* (Honolulu: University of Hawai'i Press, 2008).
24. Goldberg-Hiller and Silva, "Botany of Emergence," 11–13.
25. Pukui and Elbert, *Hawaiian Dictionary,* 224.
26. Goldberg-Hiller and Silva, "Botany of Emergence," 4.
27. The abstract for the 2017 ESfO panel "Genealogical Methods: Kinship as Practical Ontology" organized by Anne Salmond, Amiria Salmond, Billy Jane Lythberg, Dan Hikuroa, Conal McCarthy, and Albert Refiti argued for "approaching kinship as philosophy, empirical analysis, and political action—practical ontology" (Conference Programme for the 11th Conference of the European Society for Oceanists, "Experiencing Pacific Environments" [Munich: Ludwig-Maximilians-Universität, 2017], 125). See also Amiria Salmond ("Uncommon Things," *Anthropologica* 59, no. 2 [2017], 264), who cites Christopher Gad, Casper Bruun Jensen, and Brit Ross Winthereik, "Practical Ontology: Worlds in STS and Anthropology," *NatureCulture* 3 (2015): 67–86.
28. Wayne Ngata, Hera Ngata-Gibson, and Amiria Salmond, "Te Ataakura: Digital Taonga and Cultural Innovation," *Journal of Material Culture* 17, no. 3 (2012): 242, 243; Amiria Salmond, "Transforming Translations (Part I): 'The Owner of These Bones'," *Hau: Journal of Ethnographic Theory* 3, no. 3 (2013), 18; Salmond, "Uncommon Things," 256. I owe a great debt to Amiria Salmond for pushing my thinking on genealogical practice. On arguments I have made elsewhere on the capacity of genealogical practices to shift the boundaries of Indigeneity and anthropology through tactical forms of pronominal inclusion and exclusion (Tengan, "Shifting the 'We' in Oceania"), she has noted a resonance with whakapapa where "appearing in one instant as the living

face of one line, and in the next as the living face of quite another relational constellation, is common practice and does not necessarily imply the sacrifice of one identity for another" (email to author, October 1, 2015).

29. Pukui and Elbert, *Hawaiian Dictionary,* 224.
30. Timothy Hurley, "Native Hawaiian Remains Arrive Home after 100 Years," *Honolulu Star-Advertiser,* October 29, 2017, B1. I prefer to spell kupuna without the kahakō as it refers to the adjectival case here rather than the countable plural noun.
31. Kamanaʻopono, email to author, November 1, 2017.

Bibliography

Primary Sources

Correspondence, Files, and Other Archival Material

Alexander Turnbull Library. "MS Papers 1005: Dora de Beer: Correspondence, 1924–1938."

———. "Samoa Yielded without a Struggle." Postcard drawn by W. Blomfield. Observer Print., 1914. Reference no. Eph-B-POSTCARD-Vol-1–125-top. http://mp.natlib.govt.nz/detail/?id=10325&l=en. Accessed March 11, 2017.

———. "Statement of a Case of a German Who Is Prevented by the New Zealand Administration of Samoa to Carry on Scientific Research on the Islands," written by Julius Henniger, 1920. Reference no. P Q920 HEN 1920.

Archives New Zealand, Te Rua Mahara o te Kāwanatanga. File on Julius Henniger. Reference no. AAAB W291 482 Box 3.

———. Folder "Copies of letters to and from Dr. Schultz and others." Reference no. G47 1.

———. Memorandum by Dr. Solf for C. W. Butterfield. Government House, Apia, May 16, 1928.

Emory, Kenneth P. "Memorial for Peter Buck," February 13, 1952. Staff file. Bishop Museum Archives.

López, Lilian. "Reposicionamiento del Museo Antropológico P. Sebastián Englert dentro de la comunidad de Isla de Pascua." Grant proposal 2011. Biblioteca William Mulloy Archives.

Ministerio de Educación Publica, Dirección de Bibliotecas, Archivos y Museos. "Decreto 1373." Santiago, October 10, 1973.

Mulloy, William, and Gonzalo Figueroa. *The Archaeological Heritage of Easter Island.* Microfiche no. 69fr0242. Catalog no. 7875. UNESCO Archives. Paris: UNESCO, 1966.

Municipalidad de Isla de Pascua. "Aldea Educativa Rapa Nui—Casa del Arte Isla de Pascua." Unpublished document. Tania Basterrica Brockman.

Paoa Huke, Carlos. "Vida y Obra del Padre Sebastian Englert, O.F.M. Cap. en la Isla de Pascua desde 1935 hasta 1968." Unpublished document. Biblioteca William Mulloy.

Pukui, Mary Kawena. Note to Lahilahi Webb, May 19, 1938, translated by Todd Fukushima. Webb Signature Book. Bishop Museum Archives.

Rose, Roger. "Hawaiian Hall—A Brief Historical Sketch." Unpublished file, 2003. Bernice Pauahi Bishop Museum.

Scheps-Bretschneider, Birgit. Unpublished provenance research report on Hawai'i, compiled 2017. GRASSI Museum für Völkerkunde zu Leipzig.

Thomson, William J. *Te Pito te Henua, or Easter Island.* Smithsonian Institution, 1891. From the Report of the National Museum, 1888–1889. Washington, DC.

US Government. Federal Register Notice, April 22, 1998, vol. 63, no. 77, 19939–19940.

Valenzuela Contreras, Paula. "Diagnóstico de la situación actual y plan de desarrollo del Museo Padre Sebastián Englert de Isla de Pascua." Multivolume report 2007. Biblioteca William Mulloy.

Historic Newspapers

Auckland Star. March 15, 1900.

———. April 5, 1900.

———. October 8, 1930.

———. January 13, 1938.

The Dominion, September 11, 1914.

———. November 24, 1915.

Evening Post. August 2, 1930.

———. December 3, 1936.

Gray River Argus. June 17, 1920.

New Zealand Herald. September 9, 1914.

———. February 13, 1934.

———. Wednesday, June 26, 1935.

———. January 14, 1938.

———. January 29, 1938.

The Press. September 11, 1914.

Samoa Weekly Herald. March 3, 1900.

Samoanische Zeitung. August 2, 1901.

———. April 13, 1912.

———. October 28, 1912.

———. September 5, 1914.

The Wairarapa Age. September 18, 1914.

Secondary Sources: Books, Articles, Catalogs

Abbott, H. Porter. *The Cambridge Introduction to Narrative.* Cambridge: Cambridge University Press, 2002.

Africanevir. *No Humboldt 21! Dekoloniale Einwände gegen das Humboldt-Forum.* Africanevir: Berlin, 2017.

Aikau, Hokulani K. "Following the Alaloa Kīpapa of Our Ancestors: A Trans-Indigenous Futurity without the State (United States or otherwise)." *American Quarterly* 67, no. 3 (2015): 653–661.

Ames, Michael M. *Cannibal Tours and Glass Boxes: The Anthropology of Museums.* Vancouver: UBC Press, 1992.

Anita, Herle. "John Layard Long Malakula 1914–1915: The Potency of Field Photography." In Morton and Edwards, *Photography, Anthropology and History,* 241–263.

Appadurai, Arjun A. *Modernity at Large: Cultural Dimensions of Globalization.* Minneapolis: University of Minnesota Press, 1996.

Arthur, Jacinta. "Hakari o te Rapa Nui: Myth Representation in Rapa Nui: From Ancestral Ritual to Postmodern Performance." *Cátedra de Artes* 7 (2009): 65–92.

———. "Ka Haka Hoki Mai Te Mana Tupuna." *Apuntes del Museo Padre Sebastián Englert* no. 3 (2014): 73–94.

———. "Reclaiming Mana Repatriation in Rapa Nui." PhD diss., University of California, 2015.

Assad, Talal, ed. *Anthropology and the Colonial Encounter.* London: Ithaca Press, 1973.

Augé, Marc. *A Sense for the Other: The Timeliness and Relevance of Anthropology.* Translated by Amy Jacobs. Stanford, CA: Stanford University Press, 1998.

Ayau, Edward Halealoha, and Ty Kāwika Tengan. "Ka Huaka'i o Nā 'Ōiwi: The Journey Home." In *The Dead and their Possessions: Repatriation in Principle, Policy and Practice,* edited by Cressida Fforde, Jane Hubert, and Paul Turnbull, 171–189. London: Routledge, 2002.

Bahn, Paul G. "Pictures from an Expedition: Île de Pâques 1934–1935. Expedition Metraux-Lavachery, 1995." *Rapa Nui Journal* 12, no. 2 (June 1998).

Ballard, Chris. "Oceanic Historicities." *The Contemporary Pacific* 26, no. 1 (2014): 96–124.

———. "The Return of the Past: On Drawing and Dialogic History." *The Asia Pacific Journal of Anthropology* 14, no. 2 (2013): 136–148.

Balme, Christopher B. *Pacific Performances: Theatricality and Cross-Cultural Encounter in the South Seas.* New York: Palgrave Macmillan, 2007.

Banks, Marcus. *Visual Methods in Social Research.* London: Sage, 2001.

Banks, Marcus, and David Zeitlyn. *Visual Methods in Social Research.* London: Sage, 2001.

Barthel, Thomas S. *The Eighth Land: The Polynesian Discovery and Settlement of Easter Island.* Honolulu: University Press of Hawai'i, 1978.

———. "Native Documents from Easter Island." In *Reports of the Norwegian Archaeological Expedition to Easter Island and the East Pacific.* Vol. 2: *Miscellaneous Papers,* ed. Thor Heyerdahl and Edwin Ferdon Jr., 387–389. Stockholm: Forum Publishing House, 1965.

Basterrica Brockman, Tania. "Museo de Sitio Leprosario de Isla de Pascua." Master's thesis, Instituto Iberoamericano de Museología, 2014.

Basterrica Brockman, Tania, and Betty Haoa Rapahango. "The 1946 Trip to Rapa Nui Through the Photographs of Gerstmann, Helfritz, and Felbermayer." *Rapa Nui Journal* 29, no. 2 (October 2015): 23–38.

Basu, Paul. "Object Diasporas, Resourcing Communities: Sierra Leonean Collections in the Global Museumscape." *Museum Anthropology* 34, no. 1 (2011): 28–42.

Beaglehole, J. C. ed. *The Journals of Captain James Cook: The Voyage of the* Resolution *and* Discovery, *1776–1780: Part I.* Cambridge: The Hakluyt Society, 1967.

Beamer, Kamanamaikalani. *No Mākou Ka Mana: Liberating the Nation.* Honolulu: Kamehameha Publishing, 2014.

Belich, James. *Paradise Reforged: A History of the New Zealanders from the 1880s to the Year 2000.* Rosedale, NZ: Penguin Books, 2001.

Bendrups, Dan. "Pacific Festivals as Dynamic Contact Zones." *Shima: The International Journal of Research into Island Cultures* 2, no. 1 (2008): 14–28.

Benediktsson, Karl, and Katrín Anna Lund. Introduction to *Conversations with Landscape,* 1–12. Farnham, Surrey, UK: Ashgate, 2010.

Benjamin, Walter. "On Language as Such and on the Language of Man." In *One-Way Street and Other Writings.* Translated by Edmund Jephcott and Kingsley Shorter, 107–123. London: Verso, 1979.

———. *The Origin of German Tragic Drama.* New York: Verso, 1977.

Bennett, Tony. *The Birth of the Museum: History, Theory, Politics.* London: Routledge, 1995.

Bennett, Tony, Fiona Cameron, Nélia Dias, Ben Dibley, Rodney Harrison, Ira Jacknis, and Conal McCarthy. *Collecting, Ordering, Governing: Anthropology, Museums, and Liberal Government.* Durham, NC: Duke University Press, 2017.

Bennett, Tony, Ben Dibley, and Rodney Harrison. "Introduction: Anthropology, Collecting and Colonial Governmentalities." *History and Anthropology* 25, no. 2 (2014): 137–149.

Bernice Pauahi Bishop Museum. *Annual Report.* Honolulu: Bishop Museum Press, 1919.

———. *Annual Report.* Honolulu: Bishop Museum Press, 1945.

———. "Director's Report for 1899." In *Occasional Papers of Bernice Pauahi Bishop Museum of Polynesian Ethnology and Natural History* 1, no. 2 (1900).

———. "Director's Report for 1903." In *Occasional Papers of Bernice Pauahi Bishop Museum of Polynesian Ethnology and Natural History* 2, no. 2 (1904).

———. "Hawaiian Hall's Grand Reopening Ceremony." *Ka 'Elele, the Journal of Bishop* (Fall 2009).

———. *Ili Iho: The Surface Within*. Honolulu: Bishop Museum Press, 2009.

———. "New Acquisitions—A New Dawn." *Ka 'Elele, the Journal of Bishop* (Fall 2009).

———. *A Preliminary Catalogue of the Bernice Pauahi Bishop Museum of Polynesian Ethnology and Natural History*. Honolulu: Bishop Museum Press, 1892.

———. "Report of the Director for 1920." In *Occasional Papers of Bernice Pauahi Bishop Museum of Polynesian Ethnology and Natural History* 8, no. 1 (1921).

———. "Report of the Director for 1921." In *Occasional Papers of Bernice Pauahi Bishop Museum of Polynesian Ethnology and Natural History* 8, no. 5 (1922).

Bhabha, Homi K. *The Location of Culture*. London: Routledge, 1994.

Bolton, Lissant, ed. "Fieldwork, Fieldworkers, Developments in Vanuatu Research." Special issue, *Oceania* 70, no. 1 (1999).

———. *Unfolding the Moon: Enacting Women's Kastom in Vanuatu*. Honolulu: University of Hawai'i Press, 2003.

Bose, Friedrich von. *Das Humboldt-Forum: Eine Ethnografie seiner Planung*. Berlin: Kulturverlag Kadmos, 2016.

Bredekamp, Horst, and Schuster, Peter-Klaus, eds. *Das Humboldt Forum: Die Widergewinnung der Idee*. Berlin: Wagenbach, 2016.

Brigham, William T. *A Handbook for Visitors to the Bernice Pauahi Bishop Museum of Polynesian Ethnology and Natural History*. Honolulu: Bishop Museum Press, 1903.

———. *Ka Hana Kapa: The Making of Bark-Cloth in Hawaii*. Honolulu: Bishop Museum Press, 1911.

———. *Mat and Basket Weaving of the Ancient Hawaiians*. Honolulu: Bishop Museum Press, 1906.

Brown, Deidre. "Islands of Opportunity: Pasifika Styles and Museums." In Raymond and Salmond, *Pasifika Styles*, 23–29.

———. "Te Ahua Hiko: Digital Cultural Heritage and Indigenous Objects, People, and Environments." In *Theorizing Digital Cultural Heritage: A Critical Discourse*, edited by Fiona Cameron and Sarah Kenderdine, 77–91. Cambridge, MA: MIT Press, 2007.

Brown, John Macmillan. *The Riddle of the Pacific.* London: George Allen & Unwin, 1924. Reprint, Kempton, IL: Adventures Unlimited Press, 2015.

Buck, Peter H. (Te Rangi Hiroa). "Bishop Museum—Yale's partner in the Pacific." *Yale Alumni Magazine* 14, no. 7 (April 1951): 5–7.

———. "Report of the Director for 1949." *Bernice P. Bishop Museum Bulletin* 199 (1950).

———. *Vikings of the Sunrise.* Philadelphia, PA: Lippincott, 1938.

Buschmann, Rainer F. *Anthropology's Global Histories: The Ethnographic Frontier in German New Guinea, 1870–1935.* Honolulu: University of Hawai'i Press, 2008.

———. "Oceanic Collections in German Museums: Collections, Contexts, and Exhibits." In Carreau et al., *Pacific Presences,* vol. 1, 197–227.

Byrne, Sarah, Anne Clarke, Rodney Harrison, and Robin Torrence, eds. *Unpacking the Collection: Networks of Material and Social Agency in the Museum.* New York: Springer, 2011.

Cameron, Fiona R., and Sarah Kenderdine, eds. *Theorizing Digital Cultural Heritage: A Critical Discourse.* Cambridge, MA: MIT Press, 2007.

Cameron, Fiona R., and Helena Robinson. "Digital Knowledgescapes: Cultural, Theoretical, Practical, and Usage Issues Facing Museum Collection Databases in a Digital Epoch." In Cameron and Kenderdine, *Theorizing Digital Cultural Heritage,* 165–191.

Canal, Gemma Orobitg. "Photography in the Field: Word and Image in Ethnographic Research." In *Working Images: Visual Research and Representation in Ethnography,* edited by Ana Isabel Alfonso, Laszlo Kurti, and Sarah Pink, 31–46. London: Routledge, 2004.

Carreau, Lucie, Alison Clark, Alana Jelinek, Erna Lilje, and Nicholas Thomas, eds. *Pacific Presences: Oceanic Art and European Museums.* Vol. 1. Leiden: Sidestone Press, 2018.

———. *Pacific Presences: Oceanic Art and European Museums.* Vol. 2. Leiden: Sidestone Press, 2018.

Carkeek, Te Waari. "Reforged Connections—a Tangata Whenua Perspective." *Tuhinga* 28 (2017): 16–17.

Chakrabarty, Dipesh. *Provincializing Europe: Postcolonial Thought and Historical Difference.* Princeton, NJ: Princeton University Press, 2008.

Clifford, Andrew, ed. *Yuki Kihara: A Study of a Samoan Savage.* Exhibition brochure. Waitakere: Te Uru Waitakere Contemporary Gallery, 2016.

Clifford, James. "Indigenous Articulations." *The Contemporary Pacific* 13, no. 2 (2001): 467–490.

———. "On Collecting Art and Culture." Chap. 10 in *The Predicament of Culture: Twentieth-Century Ethnography, Literature, and Art.* Cambridge, MA: Harvard University Press, 1988.

———. "On Ethnographic Authority." *Representations* 2 (1983): 118–146.
———. *The Predicament of Culture.* Cambridge, MA: Harvard University Press, 1988.
———. *Returns: Becoming Indigenous in the Twenty-First Century.* Cambridge, MA: Harvard University Press, 2013.
———. *Routes: Travel and Translation in the Late Twentieth Century.* Cambridge, MA: Harvard University Press, 1997.
———. "The Times of the Curator." In Schorch and McCarthy, *Curatopia,* 109–123.
Clifford, James, George E. Marcus, and School of American Research. *Writing Culture: The Poetics and Politics of Ethnography: A School of American Research Advanced Seminar.* Berkeley: University of California Press, 1986.
Condliffe, John Bell. *Te Rangi Hiroa: The Life of Sir Peter Buck.* Christchurch: Whitcombe and Tombs, 1971.
Conrad, Sebastian. "Enlightenment in Global History: A Historiographical Critique." *American Historical Review* 117, no. 4 (October 2012): 999–1027.
Consejo de Jefes de Rapanui and Alberto Hotus. *Te mau hatu'o Rapa Nui: Los soberanos de Rapa Nui; Pasado, presente y future.* Santiago de Chile: Editorial Emisión, 1988.
Corntassel, Jeff. "Re-Envisioning Resurgence: Indigenous Pathways to Decolonization and Self-Determination." *Decolonization: Indigeneity, Education & Society* 1, no. 1 (2012): 86–101.
Dalbajewa, Birgit, and Ulrich Bischoff, eds. *Die BRÜCKE in Dresden 1905–1911.* Cologne: Verlag der Buchhandlung König, 2001.
Delsing, Riet. "Cultural Politics and Globalization on Rapa Nui." *Rapa Nui Journal* 12, no. 4 (1998): 99–108.
Delsing, Riet. *Articulating Rapa Nui: Polynesian Cultural Politics in a Latin American Nation-State.* Honolulu: University of Hawai'i Press, 2015.
Dewey, John. *Art as Experience.* London: George Allen & Unwin, 1934.
Dias, Nélia. "Looking at Objects: Memory, Knowledge in Nineteenth-Century Ethnographic Displays." In *Travellers' Tales: Narratives of Home and Displacement,* edited by George Robertson, Melinda Mash, Lisa Tickner, Jon Bird, Barry Curtis, and Tim Putnam, 164–176. London: Routledge, 1994.
Diaz, Vicente M. "Native Pacific Studies and the Illinois Debacle: Indigeneity at the Edge of Nationalist Belongings and the Limits of Signification." *American Quarterly* 67, no. 3 (2015): 597–608.
Diaz, Vicente M., and J. Kehaulani Kauanui. "Native Pacific Cultural Studies on the Edge." *The Contemporary Pacific* 13, no. 2 (2001): 315–341.

Dilthey, Wilhelm. *Selected Writings.* Cambridge: Cambridge University Press, 1976.

DiPaola, Kathrin. "Samoa, 'Perle' der deutschen Kolonien?: 'Bilder' des Exotischen Anderen in Geschichte(n) des 20. Jahrhunderts." PhD diss., University of Maryland, 2004.

Dirlik, Arif, ed. *What Is in a Rim? Critical Perspectives on the Pacific Region Idea.* 2nd ed. Lanham, MD: Rowman & Littlefield, 1998.

Douglas, Bronwen. "Encountering Agency: Islanders, European Voyagers, and the Production of Race in Oceania." In Hermann, *Changing Contexts, Shifting Meanings*, 74–92.

Douglas, Bronwen, and Christopher Ballard. "Race, Place and Civilisation: Colonial Encounters and Governance in Greater Oceania." *Journal of Pacific History* 47, no. 3 (2012): 1–18.

Driver, Felix. "Intermediaries and the Archive of Exploration." In *Indigenous Intermediaries: New Perspectives on Exploration Archives,* edited by Shino Konishi, Maria Nugent, and Tiffany Shellam, 11–29. Canberra: ANU Press, 2015.

Dupreez [du Preez], Michelle Kamalu. "Eia Hawai'inuiākea: Reflections on the Protocol for the Opening of the *Pacific Encounters* Exhibition." *Journal of Museum Ethnography* 21 (2009): 103–109.

Durand, Carine Ayélé. *Anthropology in a Glass Case: Indigeneity, Collaboration, and Artistic Practice in Museums.* Saarbrücken: VDM Verlag Dr. Müller, 2010.

———. "Indexing (in) Authenticity: Art and Artefact in Ethnography Museums." *AlterNative: An International Journal of Indigenous Peoples* 6, no. 3 (2010): 248–260.

Dürr, Eveline, and Philipp Schorch, eds. *Transpacific Americas: Encounters and Engagements Between the Americas and the South Pacific.* London: Routledge, 2016.

Edwards, Elizabeth. "Talking Visual Histories: Introduction." In *Museums and Source Communities: A Routledge Reader,* edited by Laura Lynn Peers and Alison Kay Brown, 83–99. London: Routledge, 2003.

Edwards, Elizabeth, and Christopher Morton. Introduction to *Photography, Anthropology and History,* 1–26.

Elliott, Mark. "Some Anxious Moments: The Mechanics and Pragmatics of a Collaborative Exhibition." In Raymond and Salmond, *Pasifika Styles,* 89–95.

Englert, Sebastián. *Diccionario Rapa Nui-Español.* Santiago de Chile: Prensas de la Universidad de Chile, 1938.

———. *Idioma Rapanui: Gramática y diccionario del antiguo idioma de la Isla de Pascua.* Santiago de Chile: Universidad de Chile, 1978.

———. *La Tierra de Hotu Mat'ua.* 1948. Facsimile of the first edition. Santiago de Chile: Rapanui Press, 2006.

Estella, Bienvenido de. *La Isla de Pascua.* Santiago de Chile: Imprenta Cervantes, 1920.

Fabian, Johannes. *Time and the Other: How Anthropology Makes Its Object.* New York: Columbia University Press, 2002.

Fairbairn-Dunlop, Peggy. *Tamatai Samoa: Their Stories.* Suva: University of the South Pacific, 1998.

Fischer, Steven Roger. *Island at the End of the World: The Turbulent History of Easter Island.* London: Reaktion Books, 2005.

———. "The Métraux-Barthel Correspondence (1956–1961) and the Métraux Field-Notes of Easter Island [Part Two]." *Rapa Nui Journal* 23, no. 1 (2009): 55–64.

———. *Rongorongo: The Easter Island Script. History, Traditions, Texts.* Oxford: Clarendon Press, 1997.

Foerster, Rolf. "Rapa Nui y Chile: Cuatro seducciones y sus lecturas." *Mapocho* 67 (2010): 51–73.

———. "Voluntary Trip of Deportation? The Case of King Riroroko and Policies of Deporation on Easter Island (1897–1916)." *Rapa Nui Journal* 24, no. 2 (2010).

Foerster, Rolf, and Sonia Montecino. "Rapa Nui: la lepra y sus derivados (Estado de excepción, cárcel . . .)." *Escrituras Americanas* 1 (2012): 270–353.

Foerster, Rolf, and Cristián Moreno Pakarati. *More Manava.* Santiago de Chile: Rapanui Press, 2016.

Foerster, Rolf, Jimena Ramirez, and Cristián Moreno Pakarati. *Cartografía y conflicto en Rapa Nui.* Santiago de Chile: Rapanui Press, 2014.

Förster, Larissa. "Öffentliche Kulturinstitution, internationale Forschungsstätte und postkoloniale Kontaktzone: Was ist ethno am ethnologischen Museum?" *Ethnologie im 21. Jahrhundert,* edited by Thomas Bierschenk, Matthias Krings, and Carola Lentz, 189–210. Berlin: Dietrich Reimer Verlag, 2013.

Förster, Larissa, and Friedrich von Bose. "Concerning Curatorial Practice in Ethnological Museums: An Epistemology of Postcolonial Debate." In Schorch and McCarthy, *Curatopia,* 44–55.

Forte, Maximilian C., ed. *Indigenous Cosmopolitans: Transnational and Transcultural Indigeneity in the Twenty-First Century.* New York: Peter Lang, 2010.

Fuentes, Miguel, ed. *Rapa Nui y la Compañia Explotadora, 1895–1953.* Hanga Roa: Rapanui Press, 2013.

Gad, Christopher, Casper Bruun Jensen, and Brit Ross Winthereik. "Practical Ontology: Worlds in STS and Anthropology." *NatureCulture* 3 (2015): 67–86.

Geertz, Clifford. "Deep Play: Notes on the Balinese Cockfight." In *The Interpretation of Cultures: Selected Essays,* 412–453. London: Hutchinson, 1975.

Gegeo, David W. "Cultural Rupture and Indigeneity: The Challenge of (Re) visioning "Place" in the Pacific." *The Contemporary Pacific* 13, no. 2 (2001): 491–506.

Geismar, Haidy. "The Art of Anthropology: Questioning Contemporary Art in Ethnographic Display." Chap. 10 in *Museum Theory: An Expanded Field,* edited by Andrea Whitcomb and Kylie Message, 183–210. Part 2 of *The International Handbooks of Museum Studies,* edited by Sharon Macdonald and Helen Rees Leahy. Malden, MA: Wiley-Blackwell, 2015.

Ghosh, Durba. "Decoding the Nameless: Gender, Subjectivity, and Historical Methodologies in Reading the Archives of Colonial India." In *A New Imperial History: Culture, Identity and Modernity in Britain and the Empire, 1660–1840,* edited by Kathleen Wilson, 297–316. Cambridge: Cambridge University Press, 2004.

Gibson, Stephanie. "Case Study: Museum of New Zealand Te Papa Tongarewa." In *Collecting the Contemporary: A Handbook for Social History Museums,* edited by Owain Rhys and Zelda Baveystock, 440–446. Edinburgh: MuseumsEtc, 2014.

———. "Te Papa and New Zealand's Indian Communities: A Case Study about Exhibition Development." *Tuhinga: Records of the Museum of New Zealand Te Papa Tongarewa* 14 (2003): 61–75.

Gibson, Stephanie, and Sean Mallon. "Representing Community Exhibitions at the Museum of New Zealand Te Papa Tongarewa." *Tuhinga: Records of the Museum of New Zealand Te Papa Tongarewa* 21 (2010): 43–58.

Gilbert, Helen, and J. Phillipson. *Hands On: Indigenous Artists and European Cultural Institutions: The Story of Two Artist Residencies.* London: Streamline Press, 2014.

Gilroy, Paul. *The Black Atlantic: Modernity and Double Consciousness.* Cambridge, MA: Harvard University Press, 1993.

Glass, Aaron. "History and Critique of the Renaissance Discourse." In *Native Art of the Northwest Coast: A History of Changing Ideas,* edited by Charlotte Townsend-Gault, Jennifer Kramer, and Ki-Ke-In. Toronto: UBC Press, 2013.

———. "Indigenous Ontologies, Digital Futures: Plural Provenances and the Kwakwaka'wakw Collection in Berlin and Beyond." In *Museum as Process: Translating Local and Global Knowledges,* edited by Raymond A. Silverman, 19–44. London: Routledge, 2015.

Glass, Aaron, Judith Berman, and Rainer Hatoum. "Reassembling *The Social Organization:* Collaboration and Digital Media in (Re)making Boas's 1897 Book." *Museum Worlds: Advances in Research* 5, no. 1 (2017): 108–132.

Goldberg-Hiller, Jonathan, and Noenoe K. Silva. "The Botany of Emergence: Kanaka Ontology and Biocolonialism in Hawai'i." *Native American and Indigenous Studies* 2, no. 2 (2015): 1–26.

Golding, Viv, and Wayne Modest, eds. *Museums and Communities: Curators, Collections, and Collobarations.* London: Bloomsbury, 2013.

Gómez Papic, Claudio. "El Padre Sebastián, el patrimonio rapanui y el museo de Isla de Pascua." In Englert, *La Tierra de Hotu Mat'ua.*

Gon, Samuel M., Linny Morris, Bernice Pauahi Bishop Museum, and Melanie Ide, eds. *Restoring Bishop Museum's Hawaiian Hall: Ho'i hou ka wena i Kaiwi'ula.* Honolulu: Bishop Museum Press, 2009.

Gonschor, Lorenz. "Facing Land Challenges in Rapa Nui (Easter Island)." *Pacific Studies* 34, no. 2–3 (2011).

———. "Ka Hoku o Osiania: Promoting the Hawaiian Kingdom as a Model for Political Transformation in Nineteenth-Century Oceania." In *Agents of Transculturation: Border-Crossers, Mediators, Go-Betweens,* edited by Sebastian Jobs and Gesa Mackenthun, 157–188. Münster: Waxmann, 2013.

———. "'A Power in the World': The Hawaiian Kingdom as a Model of Hybrid Statecraft in Oceania and a Progenitor of Pan-Oceanism." Phd diss., University of Hawai'i, 2016.

Goodyear-Ka'ōpua, Noelani. Introduction to *A Nation Rising: Hawaiian Movements for Life, Land, and Sovereignty,* edited by Noelani Goodyear-Ka'ōpua, Ikaika Hussey, and Erin Kahunawaika'ala Wright, 1–33. Durham, NC: Duke University Press, 2014.

———. *The Seeds We Planted: Portaits of a Native Hawaiian Charter School.* Minneapolis: University of Minnesota Press, 2013.

Goodyear-Ka'ōpua, Noelani, Ikaika Hussey, and Erin Kahunawaika'ala Wright, eds. *A Nation Rising: Hawaiian Movements for Life, Land, and Sovereignty.* Durham, NC: Duke University Press, 2014.

Gosden, Chris, and Frances Larson. *Knowing Things: Exploring the Collections at the Pitt Rivers Museum 1884–1945.* Oxford: Oxford University Press, 2007.

Graham, Laura R., and H. Glenn Penny. *Performing Indigeneity: Global Histories and Contemporary Experiences.* Lincoln: University of Nebraska Press, 2014.

Gregory, Derek. *Geographical Imaginations.* Oxford: Blackwell, 1994.

Gregory, Herbert E. "Report of the Director for 1922." In *Bernice P. Bishop Museum Bulletin* 4 (1923).

———. "Report of the Director for 1924." In *Bernice P. Bishop Museum Bulletin* 21 (1925).

———. "Report of the Director for 1926." In *Bernice P. Bishop Museum Bulletin* 41 (1927).

———. "Report of the Director for 1927." In *Bernice P. Bishop Museum Bulletin* 57 (1928).

Haase, Maxi. "Popular Perceptions and Local Negotiations of Easter Island Culture." In *Rapa Nui—Easter Island: Cultural and Historical Perspectives,* edited by Ian Conrich and Herman Mückler, 35–50. Berlin: Frank & Timme, 2016.

Hagberg. Garry L. *Art as Language: Wittgenstein, Meaning, and Aesthetic Theory.* Ithaca, NY: Cornell University Press, 1995.

Hahn, Hans-Peter, ed. *Ethnologie und Weltkulturenmuseum: Positionen für eine offene Weltsicht.* Berlin: Vergangenheitsverlag, 2017.

Hakiwai, Arapata. "He Mana Taonga, He Mana Tangata: Maori Taonga and the Politics of Maori Tribal Identity and Development." PhD diss., Victoria University of Wellington, 2014.

———. "Māori Taonga—Māori Identity." In *Art and Cultural Heritage: Law, Policy and Practice,* edited by Barbara T. Hoffman, 409–412. New York: Cambridge University Press, 2006.

———. "Te hokinga atu (the return): ōku whakaaro (reflections)." *Tuhinga* 28 (2017): 17–19.

———. "The Meaning of Ancestral Photographs in Māori Culture." In Köpke and Schmelz, *A Glimpse into Paradise,* 145–154.

———. "The Protection of Taonga and Māori Heritage in Aotearoa (New Zealand)." In *Decolonizing Conservation: Caring for Māori Meeting Houses Outside New Zealand,* edited by Dean Sally, 45–58. Walnut Creek, CA: Left Coast Press, 2008.

———. "The Search for Legitimacy: Museums in Aotearoa, New Zealand—A Māori Viewpoint." In *Heritage, Museums and Galleries: An Introductory Reader,* edited by Gerard Corsane, 154–162. London: Routledge, 2005.

Hanson, Alan. "The Making of the Maori: Cultural Invention and Its Logic." *American Anthropologist* 91, no. 4 (1989): 890–902.

Harley, J. Brian. "Maps, Knowledge and Power." In *The Iconography of Landscape,* edited by Denis Cosgrove and Stephen Daniels, 277–312. Cambridge: University of Cambridge Press, 1988.

Harris, Clare, and Michael O'Hanlon. "The Future of the Ethnographic Museum." *Anthropology Today* 29 (2013): 8–12.

Harrison, Rodney. "Reassembling Ethnographic Museum Collections." In Harrison, Byrne, and Clarke, *Reassembling the Collection,* 3–35.

Harrison, Rodney, Sarah Byrne, and Anne Clarke, eds. *Reassembling the Collection: Ethnographic Museums and Indigenous Agency.* Santa Fe, NM: SAR Press, 2013.

Harvey, David C. "Heritage Pasts and Heritage Presents: Temporality, Meaning and the Scope of Heritage Studies." *International Journal of Heritage Studies* 7, no. 4 (2001): 319–338.

Harvey, Graham, and Charles D. Thompson, eds. *Indigenous Diasporas and Dislocations.* Aldershot, Hampshire, UK: Ashgate, 2005.

Hau'ofa, Epeli. "Our Sea of Islands." *The Contemporary Pacific* 6, no. 1 (1994): 147–161.

———. *We Are the Ocean: Selected Works.* Honolulu: University of Hawai'i Press, 2008.

Hauser-Schäublin, Brigitta. "Exchanged Value: The Winding Paths of the Objects." In *James Cook: Gifts and Treasures from the South Seas (The Cook/Forster Collection, Göttingen),* edited by Brigitta Hauser-Schäublin, Gundolf Kruger, and Christian F. Feest, 11–29. Munich: Prestel, 1998.

Healy, Chris, and Andrea Witcomb, eds. *South Pacific Museums: Experiments in Culture.* Melbourne: Monash University ePress, 2006.

Hempenstall, Peter J. *Pacific Islanders under German Rule: A Study in the Meaning of Colonial Resistance.* Canberra: Australian National University Press, 1978.

Hempenstall, Peter J., and Paula T. Mochida. *The Lost Man: Wilhelm Solf in German History.* Wiesbaden: Harrassowitz Verlag, 2005.

Henare [Salmond], Amiria. "Nga Rakau a te Pakeha: Reconsidering Māori Anthropology." In *Anthropologies and Science: Epistomologies in Practice,* edited by Jeanette Edwards, Penny Harvey, and Peter Wade, 93–113. Oxford: Berg, 2007.

———. "Taonga Māori: Encompassing Rights and Property in New Zealand." In Henare [Salmond], Holbraad, and Wastell, *Thinking Through Things,* 47–67.

Henare [Salmond], Amiria, Martin Holbraad, and Sari Wastell, eds. *Thinking Through Things: Theorising Artefacts Ethnographically.* London: Routledge, 2007.

Hendry, Joy, and Laara Fitznoor, eds. *Anthropologists, Indigenous Scholars and the Research Endeavour: Seeking Bridges Towards Mutual Respect.* London: Routledge, 2012.

Hereniko, Vilsoni. "Dancing Oceania: The Oceania Dance Theatre in Context." In *The Fifth Asia-Pacific Triennial of Contemporary Art,* edited by Lynne Seear and Suhanya Raffel. Brisbane: Queensland Art Gallery Publishing, 2006.

———. "Taualuga: Decolonising and Globalising the Pacific." In Dürr and Schorch, *Transpacific Americas,* 167–174.

———. "The Pā Boys dir. by Himiona Grace" (Review). *The Contemporary Pacific* 27, no. 2 (2015): 573–576.

Hereniko, Vilsoni, and Philipp Schorch. "The Canoe, the Wind, and the Mountain: Shunting the 'Rashomon Effect' of Mauna Kea," *Pacific Studies* 41, no. 3 (2018): 119–130.

Hereniko, Vilsoni, and Rob Wilson, eds. *Inside Out: Literature, Cultural Politics and Identity in the New Pacific*. New York: Rowman & Littlefield, 1999.

Hermann, Elfriede, ed. *Changing Contexts, Shifting Meanings: Transformations of Cultural Traditions in Oceania*. Honolulu: University of Hawai'i Press, 2011.

Heyerdahl, Thor. "The Concept of Rongo-Rongo Among the Historic Population of Easter Island." In *Reports of the Norwegian Archaeological Expedition to Easter Island and the East Pacific*. Vol. 2: *Miscellaneous Papers*, edited by Thor Heyerdahl and Edwin Ferdon Jr., 359–385. Stockholm: Forum Publishing House, 1965.

Hiery, Hermann Joseph. *Das Deutsche Reich in der Südsee (1900–1921): Eine Annäherung an die Erfahrungen verschiedener Kulturen*. Göttingen: Vandenhoeck & Ruprecht, 1995.

Hine, Christine. *Virtual Ethnography*. London: Sage, 2000.

Hiroa, Te Rangi (Peter H. Buck). *Arts and Crafts of Hawaii*. Honolulu: Bishop Museum Press, 1957.

———. "An Introduction to Polynesian Anthropology." *Bernice P. Bishop Museum Bulletin* 187 (1945).

———. "Samoan Material Culture." *Bernice P. Bishop Museum Bulletin* 75 (1930).

Hobsbawm, Eric, and Terences Ranger, eds. *The Invention of Tradition*. Cambridge: Cambridge University Press, 1983.

Hogsden, Carl, and Emma K. Poulter. "The Real Other? Museum Objects in Digital Contact Networks." *Journal of Material Culture* 17, no. 3 (2012): 265–286.

Holbraad, Martin. "Can the Thing Speak?" *OAC Press Working Papers Series* 7 (2011): 1–26.

Holbraad, Martin. "The Power of Powder: Multiplicity and Motion in the Divinatory Cosmology of Cuban Ifa or Mana, Again." In Henare [Salmond], Holbraad, and Wastell, *Thinking through Things*, 189–226.

Holbraad, Martin, and Morten Axel Pedersen. *The Ontological Turn*. Cambridge: Cambridge University Press, 2017.

Holquist, Michael. *Dialogism: Bakhtin and His World*. London: Routledge, 2002.

Hooper-Greenhill, Eileen. *Museums and the Interpretation of Visual Culture*. London: Routledge, 2000.

Horwood, Michelle. *Sharing Authority in the Museum: Distributed Objects, Reassembled Relationships*. London: Routledge, 2018.

———. "Worlds Apart: Indigenous Re-engagement with Museum-held Heritage: A New Zealand–United Kingdom Case Study." PhD diss., Victoria University of Wellington, 2015.

Harney, Elizabeth, and Ruth B. Phillips, eds. *Mapping Modernisms: Art, Indigeneity, Colonialism.* Durham, NC: Duke University Press, 2018.

Heller, Martin, Andrea Scholz, and Agnes Wagner, eds. *Prinzip Labor: Museumsexperimente im Humboldt Lab Dahlem.* Berlin: Nicolai Publishing, 2015.

Hurley, Timothy. "Native Hawaiian Remains Arrive Home After 100 Years," *Honolulu Star-Advertiser,* October 29, 2017, B1.

Ingold, Tim. *Being Alive: Essays on Movement, Knowledge and Description.* London: Routledge, 2011.

———. *Making: Anthropology, Archaeology, Art and Architecture.* London: Routledge, 2013.

———. *The Perception of the Environment: Essays on Livelihood, Dwelling and Skill.* London: Routledge, 2000.

Jahnke, Robert, ed., and Leafa Wilson, exhibition curator. *Letters to the Ancestors: Contemporary Indigenous Art from Aotearoa and the Pacific.* Exhibition catalog. Hamilton, NZ: Waikato Museum, 2005.

Jefferies, Matthew. *Contesting the German Empire, 1871–1918.* Oxford: Blackwell, 2008.

Jenkins, Tiffany. *Contesting Human Remains in Museum Collections: The Crisis of Cultural Authority.* New York: Routledge, 2011.

Jolly, Margaret. "Imagining Oceania: Indigenous and Foreign Representations of a Sea of Islands." *The Contemporary Pacific* 19, no. 2 (2007): 508–545.

———. "On the Edge? Deserts, Oceans, Islands." *The Contemporary Pacific* 13, no. 2 (2001): 417–466.

Kahanu, Noelle M.K.Y. "Ka Hale Hōʻikeʻike Pihopa: A Bishop Museum Love Story." In *Detours: A Decolonial Guide to Hawaiʻi,* edited by Hokulani K. Aikau and Vernadette Vicuna Gonzalez, 164–172. Durham, NC: Duke University Press, 2019.

———. "E Kū Ana Ka Paia: Finding Contemorary Relevance in an Ancient Prophecy." In Gon et al., *Restoring Bishop Museum's Hawaiian Hall,* 1–5.

———. "Fated Feathers, Unfurling Futures." *Tuhinga* 28 (2017): 24–30.

Kahanu, Noelle M.K.Y., Moana Nepia, and Philipp Schorch. "He alo ā he alo/kanohi ki te kanohi/Face to Face: Curatorial Bodies, Encounters and Relations." In Schorch and McCarthy, *Curatopia,* 296–316.

Kameʻeleihiwa, Lilikalā. "Hawaiʻi-nui-akea Cousins: Ancestral Gods and Bodies of Knowledge Are Treasures for the Descendants." *Te Kaharoa* 2 (2009): 42–63.

———. *Native Land and Foreign Desires: Pehea La E Pono Ai? How Shall We Live in Harmony?* Honolulu: Bishop Museum Press, 1992.

Kamehiro, Stacy L. *The Arts of Kingship: Hawaiian Art and National Culture of the Kalakaua Era.* Honolulu: University of Hawaiʻi Press, 2009.

Kanakaʻole Kanahele, Pualani. "Ke Au Makahiki." Handout. *Papakū Makawalu: Makahiki* workshop, University of Hawaiʻi, Hilo, January 16–18, 2016.

Karp, Ivan, Christine Mullen Kreamer, and Steven D. Lavine, eds. *Museums and Communities: The Politics of Public Culture.* Washington, DC: Smithsonian Institution Press, 1992.

Karp, Ivan, and Steven D. Lavine, *Exhibiting Cultures: The Poetics and Politics of Museum Display.* Washington, DC: Smithsonian Institution Press, 1991.

Kawharu, Merata. "Gilbert Mair and the Taumata-a-Iwi." In *Ko Tawa: Maori Treasures from New Zealand,* edited by Paul Tapsell, 154–181. Auckland: David Bateman, 2006.

Keesing, Feelix M. *Modern Samoa: Its Government and Changing Life.* London: George Allen & Unwin, 1934.

Kennedy, Paul M. *The Samoan Tangle: A Study in Anglo-German-American Relations 1878–1900.* Dublin: Irish University Press, 1974.

Kirch, Patrick V. *On the Road of the Winds: An Archaeological History of the Pacific Islands before European Contact.* Oakland: University of California Press, 2017.

Kirch, Patrick V., and Roger C. Green. *Hawaiki, Ancestral Polynesia: An Essay in Historical Anthropology.* Cambridge: Cambridge University Press, 2001.

Kirsch, Stuart. *Reverse Anthropology: Indigenous Analysis of Social and Environmental Relations in New Guinea.* Redwood City, CA: Stanford University Press, 2006.

Kirshenblatt-Gimblett, Barbara. "Objects of Ethnography." In *Exhibiting Cultures: The Poetics and Politics of Museum Display,* edited by Ivan Karp and Steven D. Lavine, 386–443. Washington, DC: Smithsonian Institution Press, 1991.

Knell, Simon. "Altered Values: Searching for a New Collecting." In *Museums and the Future of Collecting.* 2nd ed., edited by Simon Knell. Farnham, Surrey, UK: Ashgate Publishing, 2004.

Knoche, Walter. *Die Osterinsel: Die chilenische Osterinsel-Expedition von 1911,* edited by Hermann Mückler. Wiesbaden: Harrassowitz Verlag, 2015.

———. *Die Osterinsel: Eine Zusammenfassung der chilenischen Osterinselexpedition des Jahres 1911.* Chile: Concepción, Soc. Imp. y Lit., 1925.

Köhne, Eckart, ed. "Positioning Ethnological Museums in the 21st Century." *Museumskunde* 81, no. 1 (2016): 10–13.

Kokot, Waltraud. "Diaspora and transnationale Verflechtungen." In *Ethnologie der Globalisierung: Perspektiven kulturelle Verflechtungen,* edited by Brigitta Hauser-Schäublin and Ulrich Braukämpfer, 95–110. Berlin: Dietrich Reimer Verlag, 2002.

Köpke, Wulf, and Bernd Schmelz, eds. *A Glimpse into Paradise: Historical Photographs of Polynesia.* Exhibition catalogue. Hamburg: Museum für Völkerkunde Hamburg, 2014.

Krämer, Augustin. *The Samoa Islands: An Outline of a Monograph with Particular Consideration of German Samoa,* translated by Theodore Verhaaren. Honolulu: University of Hawai'i Press, 1994.

Kraus, Michael, and Karoline Noack, eds. *Quo vadis, Völkerkundemuseum? Aktuelle Debatten zu ethnologischen Sammlungen in Museen und Universitäten.* Bielefeld: transcript, 2015.

Krause, Olga Janice Hedwig (Leafa Wilson). "Ich heiße Olga Hedwig Krause; Deutsche Künstlerin—My Name is Olga Hedwig Krause: German Artist." In *National Socialism in Oceania: A Critical Evaluation of its Effect and Aftermath* (Germanica Pacifica Series), edited by Emily Turner-Graham and Christine Winter, 234–238. New York: Peter Lang, 2010.

Kreps, Christina F. *Liberating Culture: Cross-Cultural Perspectives on Museums, Curation, and Heritage Preservation.* London: Routledge, 2003.

———. "The Theoretical Future of Indigenous Museums: Concept and Practice." In *The Future of Indigenous Museums: Perspectives from the Southwest Pacific,* edited by Nick Stanley, 223–234. Oxford: Berghahn Books, 2007.

Krüger, Mathias. "Künstlerkolonien: Gründungsorte im Abseits der Moderne." In *Gründungsorte der Moderne: Von St. Petersburg bis Occupy Wall Street,* edited by Maha El Hissy and Sascha Pöhlmann, 161–176. Paderborn, DE: Wilhelm Fink, 2014.

Labrum, Bronwyn. "Collecting, Curating and Exhibiting Cross-Cultural Material Histories in a Post-Settler Society." In Schorch and McCarthy, *Curatopia,* 244–261.

Lassiter, Luke Eric. *The Chicago Guide to Collaborative Ethnography.* Chicago: Chicago University Press, 2005.

Latour, Bruno, and Peter Weibel, eds. *Making Things Public: Atmospheres of Democracy.* Cambridge, MA: MIT Press, 2005.

Laurière, Christine. *L'Odyssée pascuane Mission Métraux-Lavachery, Île de Pâques 1934-1935.* Paris: Lahic/DPRPS, 2014.

Lavachery, Thomas, and Denis Roussel. *L'homme de Pâques.* Y.C. Aligator Film, 2002.

Lederbogen, Jan. "Frühe Fotografie auf Samoa zwischen Wissenschaftsanspruch und kolonialem Denken." In Engelhard and Mesenhöller, *Bilder aus dem Paradies,* 28–30.

Liliuokalani, Queen of Hawai'i, trans. *The Kumulipo: An Hawaiian Creation Myth.* Kentfield, CA: Pueo Press, 1978.

Lonetree, Amy. *Decolonizing Museums: Representing Native America in National and Tribal Museums.* Chapel Hill: University of North Carolina Press, 2012.

López, Carlos. "How Did Chile Acquire Easter Island?" *Rapa Nui Journal* 12, no. 4 (1998): 118–122.

Losch, Naomi. "Mary Kawena Pukui." *Ōiwi: A Native Hawaiian Journal* 3 (2005).

Loyd, Jill. *German Expressionism, Primitivism and Modernity.* New Haven, CT: Yale University Press, 1991.

Luomala, Katherine. "Necrology: Peter Henry Buck (Te Rangi Hiroa)." In "Report of the Director for 1951," edited by C. H. Edmondson. *Bishop Museum Bulletin* 208 (1952).

Lynch, Bernadette. "The Gate in the Wall: Beyond Happiness-making in Museums Meanings." in Onciul, Stefano, and Hawke, *Engaging Heritage, Engaging Communities,* 11–29.

———. "Whose Cake Is It Anyway? A Collaborative Investigation into Engagement and Participation in 12 Museums and Galleries in the UK." London: Paul Hamlyn Foundation, 2011.

Lythberg, Billie. "21st Century South Sea Savagery: Rosanna Raymond's SaVAge K'lub at APT8." *Broadsheet Journal* 45, no. 1 (2016): 14–17.

MacDowell, Marsha, C. Kurt Dewhurst, and Marques Hanalai Marzan. "'Ike Pāpale: Lau Hala in Hawaiian Cultural Heritage." In *'Ike Ulana Lau Hala: The Vitality and Vibrancy of Lau Hala Weaving Traditions in Hawai'i,* edited by Lia O'Neill, M. A. Keawe, Marsha MacDowell, and C. Kurt Dewhurst, 12–40. Honolulu: University of Hawai'i Press, 2014.

Māhina, Hūfanga 'Okusitino. "Tā, Vā, and Moana: Temporality, Spatiality, and Indigeneity." In "Genealogies: Articulating Indigenous Anthropology in/of Oceania," edited by Ty P. Kāwika Tengan, Tēvita O. Ka'ili, and Rochelle Tuitagava'a Fonoti. Special issue, *Pacific Studies* 33, no. 2/3 (2010): 168–202.

Mahuika, Apirana T. "Maori Culture and the New Museum." *Museum Anthropology* 15, no. 4 (1991): 9–10.

Mallon, Sean. "Afterword: Pacific Voices in the Bicultural Museum." In McCarthy, *Museums and Māori*, 248–253.

———. "Agency and Authority: The Politics of Co-Collecting." In Schorch and McCarthy, *Curatopia,* 279–295.

———. “The Art of In-Betweenness: Reflecting on Pacific Art Practice in New Zealand.” *SPAN Journal of the South Pacific Association For Commonwealth Literature and Language Studies* 53 (2004): 44–56.

———. “German Samoa Captured by New Zealand Troops—29 August 1914.” *Te Papa Blog* (Museum of New Zealand Te Papa Tongarewa), August 29, 2014. http://blog.tepapa.govt.nz/2014/08/29/german-samoa-captured-by-new-zealand-troops-august-1914. Accessed January 5, 2017.

———. *Samoan Art & Artists: O Measina a Samoa.* Honolulu: University of Hawaiʻi Press, 2002.

Mallon, Sean, Rangi Te Kanawa, Rachael Collinge, Nirmala Balram, Grace Hutton, Te Waari Carkeek, Arapata Hakiwai, Emalani Case, Kawikakaʻiulani Aipa, and Kamalani Kapeliela. “The ʻahu ʻula and mahiole of Kalaniʻōpuʻu: a journey of chiefly adornments.” *Tuhinga* 28 (2017): 4–23.

Malo, David. *Hawaiian Antiquities (Moolelo Hawaii).* Translated by Nathaniel Bright Emerson, 1898. Honolulu: Hawaiian Gazette, 1903.

Mane-Wheoki, Jonathan. “The Resurgence of Maori Art: Conflicts and Continuities in the Eighties.” *The Contemporary Pacific* 7 (1995): 1–19.

Marata, Tamaira. “About the Cover Art.” In Tomlinson and Tengan, *New Mana,* xiii–xiv.

Marcus, George E. “Affinities: Fieldwork in Anthropology Today and the Ethnographic in Artwork,” in Schneider and Wright, *Between Art and Anthropology,* 83–94.

———. “Ethnography in/of the World System: The Emergence of Multi-Sited Ethnography.” *Annual Review of Anthropology* 24 (1995): 95–117.

———. *Ethnography through Thick and Thin.* Princeton, NJ: Princeton University Press, 1998.

Marcus, George E., and Fred R. Myers, eds. *The Traffic in Culture: Refiguring Art and Anthropology.* Oakland: University of California Press, 1995.

Mason, Peter. “Moai on the Move.” *Journal of the History of Collections* 24, no. 1 (2012): 117–130.

———. “Siete maneras de ser moai: Seven Ways of Being Moai.” *Boletín del Museo Chileno de Arte Precolombino* 10, no. 2 (2005): 9–27.

McCall, Grant. “Culture Bursting Out All Over on Rapanui 2001–2002.” *Rapa Nui Journal* 15, no. 2 (2001): 78–82.

———. “Japan, Rapanui and Chile’s Uncertain Sovereignty.” *Rapa Nui Journal* 9, no. 1 (March 1995): 1–7.

———. *Rapanui. Tradition and Survival on Easter Island.* 2nd rev. ed. Sydney: George Allen & Unwin, and Honolulu: The University of Hawaiʻi Press, 1994.

———. "Riro, Rapu and Rapanui: Refoundations in Easter Island Colonial History." *Rapa Nui Journal* 11, no. 3 (1997): 112–122.

McCarthy, Conal. "'Empirical Anthropologists Advocating Cultural Adjustments': The Anthropological Governance of Āpirana Ngata and the Native Affairs Department." *History and Anthropology* 25, no. 2 (2014): 280–95.

———. *Exhibiting Māori: A History of the Colonial Cultures of Display.* Wellington: Te Papa Press, 2007.

———. "Historicising the 'Indigenous International': Museums, Anthropology, and Transpacific Networks." In Dürr and Schorch, *Transpacific Americas,* 3–26.

———. "Indigenisation: Reconceptualising museology." In *The Contemporary Museum: Shaping Museums for the Global Now,* edited by Simon J. Knell, 37–54. London: Routledge, 2018.

———. *Indigenous Museology: Insights from Australia and Aotearoa New Zealand.* Museums in Focus series. London: Routledge, forthcoming 2020.

———. *Museums and Māori: Heritage Professionals, Indigenous Collections, Current Practice.* Wellington: Te Papa Press, 2011.

———. *Te Papa: Reinventing New Zealand's national museum 1998–2018.* Wellington: Te Papa Press, 2018.

———. "'Two Branches of the Brown Polynesians': Ethnological Fieldwork, Colonial Governmentality and the 'Dance of Agency.'" In *New Zealand's Empire,* edited by Katie Pickles and Catharine Coleborne, 51–67. London: Manchester University Press, 2016.

McCarthy, Conal, Arapata Hakiwai, and Philipp Schorch. "The Figure of the Kaitiaki: Learning from Māori Curatorship Past and Present." In Schorch and McCarthy, *Curatopia,* 211–226.

McCarthy, Conal, Eric Dorfman, Arapata Hakiwai, and Āwhina Twomey. "Mana Taonga: Connecting Communities with New Zealand Museums through Ancestral Māori Culture." *Museum International* 65 (2015): 5–15.

McDougall, Brandy Nālani. *Finding Meaning: Kaona and Contemporary Hawaiian Literature.* Tucson: University of Arizona Press, 2016.

McGregor, Davianna. *Nā Kua'āina: Living Hawaiian Culture.* Honolulu: University of Hawai'i Press, 2007.

Mead, Hirini Moko. *Tikanga Māori: Living by Māori Values.* Wellington: Huia Publishers, 2003.

Meleisea, Malama. *The Making of Modern Samoa: Traditional Authority and Colonial Administration in the History of Western Samoa.* Suva: University of the South Pacific, 1987.

Mesenhöller, Peter, and Jutta-Beate Engelhard, eds. *Bilder aus dem Paradies: Koloniale Fotografie aus Samoa 1875–1925*. Exhibition catalog. Marburg, DE: Jonas Verlag, 1995.

Métraux, Alfred. "Arribo a la isla de Pascua." *Sur*, no. 10 (1941): 39–52.

———. *Easter Island: A Stone-Age Civilization of the Pacific*, translated by Michael Bullock. London: André Deutsch, 1957.

———. *Ethnology of Easter Island*. Honolulu: Bishop Museum Press, 1940.

———. *La Isla de Pascua*. México: Fondo de Cultura Económica, 1950.

Meyer, Manulani Aluli. *Hoʻoulu: Our Time of Becoming: Hawaiian Epistemology and Early Writings*. Honolulu: ʻAi Pohaku Press, 2003.

Mönter, Sven. "Dr. Augustin Krämer: a German Ethnologist in the Pacific." PhD diss., University of Auckland, 2010.

Moreno Pakarati, Cristián. *Englert Expo*. Exhibition catalog. Hanga Roa: Museo Antropológico Padre Sebastián Englert, 2012.

———. "Rebelión Sumisión y Mediación en Rapa Nui (1897–1915)." In *La Compañía Explotadora de Isla de Pascua: Patrimonio, Memoria e Identidad en Rapa Nui*, edited by Claudio Cristino and Miguel Fuentes. Concepcion: Ediciones Escaparate, 2010.

———. "The Land Commission of 1917: Analysis and Participation of the Rapanui." *Rapa Nui Journal* 26, no. 2 (2012): 29–41.

Morton, Christopher, and Elizabeth Edwards, eds. *Photography, Anthropology and History: Expanding the Frame*. Farnham, Surrey, UK: Ashgate, 2009.

Mulrooney, Mara A., Kelly S. Esh, Mark D. McCoy, Simon H. Bickler, and Yosihiko H. Sinoto. "New Dates from Old Samples: A Revised Radiocarbon Chronology for the Waiʻahukini Rockshelter Site (H8), Kaʻu District, Hawaiʻi Island." *Society for Hawaiian Archaeology, Special Publication* 4 (2014): 17–26.

Mulrooney, Mara A., Charmaine Wong, Kelley Esh, Scott Belluomini, and Mark D. McCoy. "Integrating Research and Collections Management: The Hoʻomaka Hou Research Initiative at the Bishop Museum." *Museum Worlds: Advances in Research* 4 (2016): 51–62.

Munteán, László. "Touching Time: Photography, Affect and the Digital Archive." In Tolia-Kelly, Waterton, and Watson, *Heritage, Affect and Emotion*, 201–218.

Musées Royaux d'Art e d'Histoire. *Île de Pâques 1934–1935: Expédition Métraux-Lavachery*. Brussels: Buch, 1995.

Museum of New Zealand Te Papa Tongarewa. *2005–2006 Annual Report of the Museum of New Zealand Te Papa Tongarewa*. Wellington, 2006.

Nākuina, Emma Metcalf Beckley. "Not Courteous Treatment of Ladies at Bishop Museum: An Open Protest to the Trustees of the Kamehameha Schools." *Pacific Commercial Advertiser*, May 19, 1897.

National Geographic. *Moái: Vivir para el future: Las relaciones entre Japón y Chile través de los moái.* Comité de Ejecución del Proyecto Moái, 2013.

Newell, Jenny. "Old Objects, New Media: Historical Collections, Digitization and Affect." *Journal of Material Culture* 17, no. 3 (2012): 287–306.

Ngata, Wayne, Hera Ngata-Gibson, and Amiria Salmond. "Te Ataakura: Digital *Taonga* and Cultural Innovation." *Journal of Material Culture* 17, no. 3 (2012): 229–244.

Nolde, Emil. *Welt und Heimat: Die Südseereise 1913–1918,* 4th ed. Cologne: Dumont, 2002.

Nuku, Maia. "Standing on the Edge of the Abyss: Shigeyuki Kihara, Catalyst for Change." *Broadsheet/Contemporary Art Centre of Australia, S.A.* 44, no. 3 (2015): 10–11.

Office of Hawaiian Affairs. "Nā Hulu Lehua: The Royal Cloak and Helmet of Kalaniʻōpuʻu." Video uploaded October 27, 2016. https://vimeo.com/189245734. Accessed November 23, 2017.

Olwig, Karen Fog, and Kirsten Hatrup. *Siting Culture: The Shifting Anthropological Object.* London: Routledge, 1997.

Onciul, Bryony. *Museums, Heritage and Indigenous Voice: Decolonising Engagement.* London: Routledge, 2015.

Onciul, Bryony, Michelle L. Stefano, and Stephanie Hawke, eds. *Engaging Heritage, Engaging Communities.* Martlesham, Suffolk, UK: Boydell and Brewer, 2017.

Osorio, Jonathan K.K. *Dismembering the Lāhui: A History of the Hawaiian Nation to 1887.* Honolulu: University of Hawaiʻi Press, 2002.

Owens, Louis. "Afterword: Their Shadows before Them: Photographing Indians." In *Trading Gazes: Euro-American Women Photographers and Native North Americans, 1880–1940,* edited by Susan Bernardin, Melody Graulich, Lisa MacFarlane, and Nicole Tonkovich. New Brunswick, NJ: Rutgers University Press, 2003.

Pao, Carl F.K. Artist statement posted at *Pewa II: Remasculation and Human Seed Ships* show at SPF Projects, Honolulu, May 8–June 8, 2014.

Peers, Laura, and Alison K. Brown. "'Just by Bringing these Photographs . . .': On the Other Meanings of Anthropological Images." In Morton and Edwards, *Photography, Anthropology and History,* 265–280.

———. "Museums and Source Communities." In *Museums and Their Communities,* edited by Sheila Watson, 519–537. London: Routledge, 2007.

Peterson, Nicolas, Lindy Allen, and Louise Hamby, eds. *The Makers and Making of Indigenous Australian Museum Collections.* Melbourne: Melbourne University Press, 2008.

Pétursdóttir, Þióra, and Bjørnar Olsen. Introduction to *Ruin Memories: Materiality, Aesthetics and the Archaeology of the Recent Past,* edited by Bjørnar Olsen and Þióra Pétursdóttir, 3–30. London: Routledge, 2014.

Phillips, Ruth B. *Museum Pieces: Toward the Indigenization of Canadian Museums.* Montreal: McGill-Queen's University Press, 2013.

———. "Swings and Roundabouts: Pluralism and the Politics of Change in Canada's National Museums." In Schorch and McCarthy, *Curatopia,* 143–158.

Piesbergen, Dorothee. "Erich Schultz-Ewerth." In *Rechtsvergleicher: Verkannt, Vergessen, Verdrängt,* edited by Bernhard Großfeld, 75–85. Münster: LIT, 2000.

Pieterse, Jan Nederveen. "Globalization as Hybridization." In *Global Modernities,* edited by Mike Featherstone, Scott Lash, and Roland Robertson, 45–68. London: Sage, 1995.

Pineda, Georgianna. "Protección patrimonial para sitios históricos: una aproximación de puesta en valor para el complejo industrial de Vaitea (Rapa Nui)." In Fuentes, *Rapa Nui,* 194–311.

Pink, Sarah. *Doing Visual Ethnography.* London: Sage, 2009.

Pinney, Christopher. "The Phenomenology of Colonial Photography." In *Bilder des Fremden: Mediale Inszenierung von Alterität im 19. Jahrhundert,* edited by Hans-Peter Bayerdörfer, Bettina Barbara Dietz, Frank Heidemann, and Paul Hempel, 19–39. Berlin: Lit Verlag, 2007.

Poignant, Roslyn, and Axel Poignant. *Encounter at Nagalarramba.* Canberra: National Library of Australia, 1996.

Pukui, Mary Kawena. *Echo of Our Song: Chants and Poems of the Hawaiians.* Honolulu: University of Hawai'i Press, 1973.

———. *'Ōlelo No'eau: Hawaiian Proverbs and Poetical Sayings.* Honolulu: Bishop Museum Press, 1983.

———. "The Canoe Making Profession of Ancient Times." In *Occasional Papers of Bernice Pauahi Bishop Museum of Polynesian Ethnology and Natural History* 15, no. 13 (November 1939): 149–159.

Pukui, Mary Kawena, and Samuel H. Elbert, eds. *Hawaiian Dictionary: Hawaiian-English, English-Hawaiian.* Honolulu: University of Hawai'i Press, 1986.

Quanchi, Max. "History of Photography in the Pacific Islands." In Köpke and Schmelz, *A Glimpse into Paradise,* 67–85.

Rassool, Ciraj. "Towards the Postcolonial Museum." Paper presented at the "Schwieriges Erbe: Koloniale Objekte—Postkoloniales Wissen" (Difficult Heritage: Colonial Objects—Postcolonial Knowledge) conference at the Linden-Museum Stuttgart, April 24, 2017.

Raymond, Rosanna, and Amiria Salmond. Introduction to *Pasifika Styles: Artists Inside the Museum.* Dunedin: Otago University Press, 2008.

Raymond, Rosanna, and Amiria Salmond, ed. *Pasifika Styles: Artists Inside the Museum.* Dunedin: Otago University Press, 2008.

Refiti, Albert L. "Lau tofiga lea: Vā and the contemporary understanding of space as identity." Chap. 1 in "Mavae and Tofiga: Spatial Exposition of the Samoan Cosmogony and Architecture." PhD diss., Auckland University of Technology, 2015.

Ricoeur, Paul. *From Text to Action: Essays in Hermeneutics,* II. Evanston, IL: Northwestern University Press, 1989.

———. "Life in Quest of Narrative." In *On Paul Ricoeur: Narrative and Interpretation,* edited by David Wood, 20–33. London: Routledge, 1991.

———. *On Translation.* Translated by Eileen Brennan. London: Routledge, 2006.

Riese, Julius. "Die *Samoanische Zeitung* (1901–1914): Images of the Samoan People and Culture in a German Newspaper." In *Sprachwissenschaft und kolonialzeitlicher Sprachkontakt: Sprachliche Begegnungen und Auseinandersetzungen,* edited by Stefan Engelberg and Doris Stolberg, 163–189. Berlin: Akademie Verlag, 2012.

Ritchie, Donald A. *Doing Oral History.* Oxford: Oxford University Press, 2003.

Rose, Roger. *A Museum to Instruct and Delight: William T. Brigham and the Founding of Bernice Pauahi Bishop Museum.* Honolulu: Bishop Museum Press, 1980.

———. "Patterns of Protest: A Hawaiian Mat-Weaver's Response to 19th-Century Taxation and Change." *Bernice P. Bishop Museum Occasional Papers* 30 (1990): 88–117.

Routledge, Katherine. *The Mystery of Easter Island.* London: Sifton Praed & Co., 1919.

Rüth, Andrea. "Auf der Suche nach der ursprünglichen Einheit von Mensch und Natur.' Eine Untersuchung zum antizivilisatorischen Aspekt im deutschen Expressionismus am Beispiel der Künstlergruppe 'Brücke.'" PhD diss., Ludwig-Maximilians-Universität München, 2008.

Sahlins, Marshall. *Culture in Practice: Selected Essays.* Brooklyn, NY: Zone Books, 2005.

———. "Goodbye to Triste Tropes: Ethnography in the Context of Modern World History." *Journal of Modern History* 65, no. 1 (1993): 1–25.

———. *Islands of History.* Chicago: University of Chicago Press, 1985.

Said, Edward W. *Orientalism.* New York: Pantheon, 1978.

———. "Representing the Colonized: Anthropology's Interlocutors." *Critical Inquiry* 15, no. 2 (Winter 1989): 205–225.

Salesa, Damon. "A Pacific Destiny: New Zealand's Overseas Empire 1840–1945." In *Tangata O Le Moana: New Zealand and the People of the Pacific,* edited by Sean Mallon, Kolokesa Māhina-Tuai, and Damon Salesa, 97–122. Wellington: Te Papa Press, 2012.

Salmond, Amiria. "Digital Subjects, Cultural Objects: Special Issue Introduction," *Journal of Material Culture* 17, no. 3 (2012): 211–228.

———. "Transforming Translations (Part 1): 'The Owner of These Bones.'" *HAU: Journal of Ethnographic Theory* 3, no. 3 (2013): 1–32.

———. "Transforming Translations (Part 2): Addressing Ontological Alterity." *HAU: Journal of Ethnographic Theory* 4, no. 1 (2014): 155–187.

———. "Uncommon Things." *Anthropologica* 59, no. 2 (2017).

Salmond, Amiria, and Rosanna Raymond. "Show and Tell: Weaving a Basket of Knowledge." In Schneider and Wright, *Between Art and Anthropology,* 95–102.

Saxer, Martin. "A Spectacle of Maps: Cartographic Hopes and Anxieties in the Pamirs." *Cross-Currents: East Asian History and Culture Review* 12 (2016): 11–136.

Schleip, Dietrich. "Ozeanische Ethnographie und Koloniale Praxis, Das Beispiel Augustin Krämer." Master's thesis, Eberhard-Karls-Universität Tübingen, 1989.

Schneider, Arnd. "Appropriations." In *Contemporary Art and Anthropology,* edited by Arnd Schneider and Christopher Wright. Oxford: Berg, 2006.

Schneider, Arnd, and Christopher Wright. *Between Art and Anthropology: Contemporary Ethnographic Practice.* London: Bloomsbury, 2010.

———, eds. *Contemporary Art and Anthropology.* Oxford: Berg, 2006.

Scholz, Andrea. "Sharing Knowledge as a Step toward an Epistemological Pluralization of the Museum." In "Engaging Anthropological Legacies," special section of *Museum Worlds* 5 (2017), edited by Sharon Macdonald, Henrietta Lidchi, and Margareta von Oswald, 133–148.

Schorch, Philipp. "Assembling Communities: Curatorial Practices, Material Cultures, and Meanings." In Onciul, Stefano, and Hawke, *Engaging Heritage, Engaging Communities,* 31–46.

———. "Contact Zones, Third Spaces, and the Act of Interpretation." *Museum and Society* 11, no. 1 (2013): 68–81.

———. "The Cosmohermeneutics of Migration Encounters at the Immigration Museum Melbourne." *Museum Worlds: Advances in Research* 2, no. 1 (2014): 81–98.

———. "Cultural Feelings and the Making of Meaning." *International Journal of Heritage Studies* 20, no. 1 (2014): 22–35.

———. "The Hermeneutics of Transpacific Assemblages." *Alfred Deakin Research Institute Working Paper Series* 2, no. 41 (2013): 1–15.

———. “Museum Encounters and Narrative Engagements.” In Witcomb and Message, *Museum Theory,* 437–457.

———. “Two Germanies: Ethnographic Museums, (Post)Colonial Exhibitions, and the ‘Cold Odyssey’ of Pacific Objects between East and West.” In Carreau et al., *Pacific Presences,* vol. 2, 171–185.

———. “Why Has the Ethnographic Museum Run Out of Steam?” *Wie weiter mit Humboldts Erbe? Ethnographische Sammlungen neu denken* (blog), 2018. https://blog.uni-koeln.de/gssc-humboldt/why-has-the-ethnographic-museum-run-out-of-steam. Accessed November 27, 2018.

Schorch, Philipp, and Eveline Dürr. “Transpacific Americas as Relational Space.” In Dürr and Schorch, *Transpacific Americas*, xi–xxv.

Schorch, Philipp, and Arapata Hakiwai. “Mana Taonga and the Public Sphere: A Dialogue Between Indigenous Practice and Western Theory.” *International Journal of Cultural Studies* 17, no. 2 (2014): 191–205.

Schorch, Philipp, and Noelle M.K.Y. Kahanu. “Anthropology’s Interlocutors: Hawai‘i Speaking Back to Ethnographic Museums in Europe.” *Zeitschrift für Kulturwissenschaften* 1 (2015): 114–117.

———. “Forum as Laboratory: The Cross-Cultural Infrastructure of Ethnographic Knowledge and Material Potentialities.” In Heller, Scholz, and Wagner, *Prinzip Labor,* 241–248.

Schorch, Philipp, and Conal McCarthy, eds. *Curatopia: Museums and the Future of Curatorship.* Manchester, UK: Manchester University Press, 2019.

Schorch, Philipp, Conal McCarthy, and Eveline Dürr. “Introduction: Conceptualising Curatopia.” In Schorch and McCarthy, *Curatopia,* 1–16.

Schorch, Philipp, Conal McCarthy, and Arapata Hakiwai. “Globalizing Māori Museology: Reconceptualizing Engagement, Knowledge, and Virtuality through Mana Taonga.” *Museum Anthropology* 39, no. 1 (2016): 48–69.

Schorch, Philipp, and Arno Pascht. Introduction to “Reimagining Oceania,” 114–123.

———, eds. “Reimagining Oceania through Critical Junctures.” Special issue, *Oceania* 87, no. 2 (2017): 114–187.

Schorch, Philipp, Martin Saxer, and Marlen Elders, eds. *Exploring Materiality and Connectivity in Anthropology and Beyond.* London: UCL Press, 2020.

Schorch, Philipp, Emma Waterton, and Steve Watson. “Museum Canopies and Affective Cosmopolitanism: Cultivating Cross-Cultural Landscapes for Ethical Embodied Responses.” In Tolia-Kelly, Waterton, and Watson, *Heritage, Affect and Emotion,* 93–113.

Schultz, Erich. *Proverbial Expressions of the Samoans.* Auckland: The Polynesian Society, 1948.

Schwarz, Thomas. "Hybridität: Ein begriffsgeschichtlicher Aufriss." *Zeitschrift für interkulturelle Germanistik* 6, no. 1 (2015): 163–180.

———. *Ozeanische Affekte: Die literarische Modellierung Samoas im kolonialen Diskurs.* Kelheim: EIA AG—Internet Akademie und Lehrbuch Verlag, 2013.

Sennett, Richard. *The Craftsman.* London: Penguin Books, 2008.

Shepardson, Britton L., Beno Atán, Toria Calderón, Gonzalo Droppelmann, Julia Godinez, Catalina González, Victoria Guerrero, Yumi Ika, Madison Ledesma, Omar Monares, Erin Mullin, Ariki Nahoe, Tiare Pakarati, Franco Pérez, Ietu Quezada, Sara Sanford, Dylan Shepardson, and Ma'eha Te Ra'a. "Terevaka Archaeological Outreach (TAO) 2015 Field Report: Archaeology, Conservation, and Toponymy." *Rapa Nui Journal* 29, no. 2 (2015): 47–51.

Shore, Bradd. "Mana and Tapu." In *Developments in Polynesian Ethnology,* edited by Alan Howard and Robert Borofsky, 137–173. Honolulu: University of Hawai'i Press.

Sillitoe, Paul. *Indigenous Studies and Engaged Anthropology: The Collaborative Moment.* London: Routledge, 2015.

Silva, Noenoe K. "I Kū Mau Mau: How Kānaka Maoli Tried to Sustain National Identity within the United States Political System," *American Studies* 45, no. 3 (Fall 2004): 9–31.

———. *The Power of the Steel-Tipped Pen: Reconstructing Native Hawaiian Intellectual History.* Durham, NC: Duke University Press, 2017.

Silverman, Ray, ed. *Museum as Process: Translating Local and Global Knowledges.* London: Routledge, 2015.

Simpson, Leanne Betasamosake. *As We Have Always Done: Indigenous Freedom Through Radical Resistance.* Minneapolis: University of Minnesota Press, 2017.

Singh, Supriya, and Meredith Blake. "The Digitization of Pacific Cultural Collections: Consulting with Pacific Diasporic Communities and Museum Experts." *Curator: The Museum Journal* 55, no. 1 (2012): 95–105.

Singh, Supriya, Meredith Blake, and Jonathan O'Donnell, "Digitizing Pacific Cultural Collections: The Australian Experience." *International Journal of Cultural Property* 20 (2013): 77–107.

Smith, Huhana. "Mana Taonga and the Micro World of Intricate Research and Findings around Taonga Māori at the Museum of New Zealand Te Papa Tongarewa." Special issue, *Matter in Place. SITES: Journal of Social Anthropology and Cultural Studies* 6, no. 2 (2009): 7–31.

———. "The Museum of New Zealand Te Papa Tongarewa." In Healy and Witcomb, *South Pacific Museums,* 10.11–10.13.

Sofa Gallery. *Ich heisse Olga Hedwig Krause: Deutsche Künstlerin. My name is Olga Hedwig Krause: German Artists.* Exhibition brochure. Christchurch, 2005.

Sorrenson, M.P.K. [Maurice Peter Keith]. *Manifest Duty: The Polynesian Society over 100 Years.* Auckland: The Polynesian Society, 1992.

———, ed. *Na To Hoa Aroha: From Your Dear Friend: The Correspondence between Sir Apirana Ngata and Sir Peter Buck 1925–1950, vol. 3, 1932–1950.* Auckland: Auckland University Press, 1986.

Spittler, Gerd. "Teilnehmende Beobachtung als Dichte Teilnahme." *Zeitschrift für Ethnologie* 126, no. 1 (2001): 1–25.

Stambuk, Patricia. *Rongo: La Historia Oculta de Isla de Pascua.* Santiago de Chile: Pehuén, 2010.

Stanley, Nick, ed. *The Future of Indigenous Museums: Perspectives from the Southwest Pacific.* Oxford: Berghahn Books, 2007.

Steinmetz, Georg. *The Devil's Handwriting: Precoloniality and the German State in Qingdao, Samoa and Southwest Africa.* Chicago: University of Chicago Press, 2007.

Stevenson, Karen. *The Frangipani Is Dead: Contemporary Pacific Art in New Zealand.* Wellington: Huia Publishers, 2008.

Stiftung Preußischer Kulturbesitz. *The Laboratory Concept: Museum Experiments in the Humboldt Lab Dahlem.* Berlin: Nicolai, 2015.

Sturge, Kate. *Representing Others: Translation, Ethnography and the Museum.* London: Routledge, 2007.

Sullivan, Robert. "The English Moko: Exploring a Spiral." In *Figuring the Pacific: Aotearoa & Pacific Cultural Studies,* edited by Howard Douglas McNaughton and John Newton, 12–28. Christchurch, NZ: Canterbury University Press, 2005.

Taiaiake, Alfred. *Wasáse: Indigenous Pathways of Action and Freedom.* Toronto: University of Toronto Press, 2015.

Tapsell, Paul. "Taonga, Marae, Whenua—Negotiating Custodianship: A Maori Tribal Response to Te Papa: The Museum of New Zealand." In *Rethinking Settler Colonialism: History and Memory in Australia, Canada, Aotearoa, New Zealand, and South Africa,* edited by Annie Coombes, 86–99. Manchester, UK: Manchester University Press, 2006.

Tcherkézoff, Serge. "Inventing Polynesia." In Hermann, *Changing Contexts, Shifting Meanings,* 123–138.

———. "A Long and Unfortunate Voyage Towards the 'Invention' of the Melanesia/Polynesia Distinction (1595–1832)." *Journal of Pacific History* 38, no. 2 (2003): 175–196.

Teaiwa, Teresia K. "Native Thoughts: A Pacific Studies Take on Cultural Studies and Diaspora." In *Indigenous Diasporas and Dislocations,* edited by Graham Harvey and Charles D. Thompson Jr., 15–35. Aldershot, UK: Ashgate, 2005.

Teaiwa, Teresia, and Sean Mallon. "Ambivalent Kinships? Pacific People in New Zealand." In *New Zealand Identities: Departures and Destinations,* edited by James H. Liu, Tim McCreanor, Tracey McIntosh, and Teresia Teaiwa, 207–229. Wellington: Victoria University Press, 2005.

Tengan, Ty P. Kāwika. "The Mana of Kū: Indigenous Nationhood, Masculinity and Authority in Hawai'i." In Tomlinson and Tengan, *New Mana,* 55–76.

———. "The Return of Kū." In *E Kū Ana Ka Paia: Unification, Responsibility and the Kū Images.* Honolulu: Bishop Museum Press, 2010.

———. "The Return of Kū? Remembering Hawaiian Masculinity, Warriorhood, and Nation. " In *Performing Indigeneity: Global Histories and Contemporary Experiences,* edited by Laura R. Graham and H. Glenn Penny, 206–246. Lincoln: University of Nebraska Press, 2014.

———. "Shifting the 'We' in Oceania: Anthropology and Pacific Islanders Regenerated." In *Who Are We? Reimagining Alterity and Affinity in Anthropology,* edited by Liana Chua and Nayanika Mathur. Oxford: Berghan Books, 2018.

Tengan, Ty P. Kāwika, Tēvita O. Ka'ili, and Rochelle Tuitagava'a Fonoti, eds. "Genealogies: Articulating Indigenous Anthropology in/of Oceania." Special issue, *Pacific Studies* 33, no. 2/3 (2010): 139–167.

Thiemeyer, Thomas. "Deutschland postkolonial: Ethnologische und genealogische Erinnerungskultur." *Merkur: Deutsche Zeitschrift für europäisches Denken* 70 (July 2016): 33–45.

Thode-Arora, Hilke. *From Samoa with Love? Samoa-Völkerschauen im Deutschen Kaiserreich: Eine Spurensuche.* Munich: Hirmer, 2014.

———. "Walking the Fine Line: *From Samoa with Love?* at the Museum Fünf Kontinente, Munich." In Schorch and McCarthy, *Curatopia,* 56–71.

Thomas, Nicholas. *In Oceania: Visions, Artifacts, Histories.* Durham, NC: Duke University Press, 1997.

———. *Possessions: Indigenous Art/Colonial Culture.* London: Thames and Hudson, 1999.

Thomas, Nicholas, and Julie Adams. Introduction to *Artefacts of Encounter: Cook's Voyages, Colonial Collecting and Museum Histories,* edited by Nicholas Thomas, Julie Adams, Billie Lythberg, Maia Nuku, and Amiria Salmond. Dunedin: Otago University Press, 2016.

Thomas, Nicholas, Allen Abramson, Ivan Brady, R. C. Green, Marshall Sahlins, Rebecca A. Stephenson, Friedrich Valjavec, and Ralph Gardner White. "The Force of Ethnology: Origins and Significance of the Melanesia/Polynesia Division [and Comments and Replies]," *Current Anthropology* 30, no. 1 (1989): 27–41.

Thomas, Nicholas, with Noelle M.K.Y. Kahanu. Introduction to Carreau et al., *Pacific Presences,* vol. 1, 13–35.

Thomas, Nicholas, and Diane Losche, eds. *Double Vision: Art Histories and Colonial Histories in the Pacific.* Cambridge: Cambridge University Press, 1999.

———. Introduction to *Double Vision: Art Histories and Colonial Histories in the Pacific,* 1–18. Cambridge: Cambridge University Press, 1999.

Todd, Zoe. "An Indigenous Feminist's Take on the Ontological Turn: 'Ontology' Is Just Another Word for Colonialism." *Journal of Historical Sociology* 29, no. 1 (2016): 4–22.

Tolia-Kelly, Divya P. "Dark Seas and Glass Walls—Feeling Injustice at the Museum. Practitioner Perspectives: Rosanna Raymond." In Tolia-Kelly, Waterton, and Watson, *Heritage, Affect and Emotion,* 276–292.

Tolia-Kelly, Divya P., Emma Waterton, and Steve Watson. "Heritage, Affect and Emotion." In *Heritage, Affect and Emotion,* 1–11.

Tolia-Kelly, Divya P., Emma Waterton, and Steve Watson, eds. *Heritage, Affect and Emotion: Politics, Practices and Infrastructures.* London: Routledge, 2017.

Tomlinson, Matt, and Ty P. Kāwika Tengan. *New Mana: Transformations of a Classic Concept in Pacific Languages and Cultures.* Canberra: Australian National University Press, 2016.

Torres Hochstetter, Francisco. "Editorial." *Apuntes del Museo Antropológico Padre Sebastián Englert* 3 (2014).

———. "La Tierra de Hotu Matu'a, un viaje espiritual y científico al pasado de Rapanui." In Englert, *La Tierra de Hotu Mat'ua.*

Torres, Paulina. "Te Kuhane o te Kainga: El paisaje y la persona en Rapa Nui." Master's thesis, Universidad Academica de Humanismo Christiano, 2010.

Townsend, Lynette. "Collecting Childhood—in more than one way." *Uni News, The University of Auckland News for Staff* 44, no. 8 (2015).

Trask, Haunani-Kay. *From a Native Daughter: Colonialism and Sovereignty in Hawai'i.* Honolulu: University of Hawai'i Press, 1999.

Treagus, Mandy, and Madeleine Seys. "Looking Back at Samoa: History, Memory, and the Figure of Mourning in *Yuki Kihara's Where Do We Come From? What Are We? Where Are We Going?*" *Asian Diasporic Visual Cultures and the Americas* 3, no. 1–2 (2017): 86–109.

Tsing, Anna Lowenhaupt. *Friction: An Ethnography of Global Connection.* Princeton, NJ: Princeton University Press, 2005.

Tuffery, Michel. *Siamani Samoa.* Bowen Hills, Queensland, AU: Andrew Baker Art Dealer, 2012.

Turner, James West. "Continuity and Constraint: Reconstructing the Concept of Tradition from a Pacific Perspective." *The Contemporary Pacific* 9, no. 2 (1997): 345–381.

Valenzuela, Zósimo. "La Isla de Pascua." *Revista Católica* 13, nos. 259–261 (1912).

Van Tilburg, Jo Anne. *Among Stone Giants: The Life of Katherine Routledge and her Remarkable Expedition to Easter Island.* New York: Scribner, 2003.

Vargas, Patricia, Claudio Cristino, and Roberto Izaurieta. *1000 años en Rapa Nui. Arqueología del asentamiento.* Santiago: Editorial Universitaria, 2006.

Viveiros de Castro, Eduardo. "Who is Afraid of the Ontological Wolf? Some Comments on an Ongoing Anthropological Debate." CUSAS Annual Marilyn Strathern Lecture, May 30, 2014. *Cambridge Journal of Anthropology* 33, no. 1 (2015): 2–17.

Welz, Gisela. "Moving Targets: Feldforschung unter Mobilitätsdruck." *Zeitschrift fur Völkerkunde 94,* no. 2 (1998): 177–194.

Wendt, Albert. "Afterword: Tatauing the Post-Colonial Body." In *Inside Out: Literature, Cultural Politics, and Identity in the New Pacific,* edited by Vilsoni Hereniko and Rob Wilson, 399–412. New York: Rowman & Littlefield, 1999.

———. "Towards a New Oceania." *Mana Review: A South Pacific Journal of Language and Literature* 1, no. 1 (1976): 49–60.

Wengraf, Tom. *Qualitative Research Interviewing: Biographical Narrative and Semi-Structured Methods.* London: Sage, 2001.

Whimp, Graeme. "Working in the Space Between: Pacific Artists in Aotearoa/New Zealand." In *The Space Between: Negotiating Culture, Place, and Identity in the Pacific,* Occasional Paper Series 44, edited by A. Marata Tamaira, 9–23. Honolulu: Center for Pacific Islands Studies, University of Hawai'i, 2009.

White, Geoffrey M., and Ty P. Kāwika Tengan. "Disappearing Worlds: Anthropology and Cultural Studies in Hawai'i and the Pacific." *The Contemporary Pacific* 13, no. 2 (Fall 2001): 381–416.

Williamson, Eleanor Lilihana-a-I. Introduction to *'Ōlelo No'eau: Hawaiian Proverbs and Poetical Sayings,* edited by Mary Kawena Pukui. Honolulu: Bishop Museum Press, 1983.

Winter, Christine. "Changing Frames: Identity and Citizenship of New Guineans of German Heritage during the Inter-war Years." *Journal of Pacific History* 47, no. 3 (2012): 347–367.

———. "National Socialism and the German (Mixed-Race) Diasporas in Oceania." In *Europa Jenseits der Genzen,* edited by Michael Mann and Jürgen G. Nagel, 228–248. Heidelberg: Draupadi-Verlag, 2015.

Wise, John. "Ka Ninau Ike Hana o Ke Kanaka Hawaii." *Kuokoa.* December 30, 1921.

Wolf, Erika. "Shigeyuki Kihara's Fa'a Fafine; In a Manner of a Woman': The Photographic Theater of Cross-Cultural Encounter." *Pacific Arts* 10, no. 2 (2010): 23–33.

Wood, Pushpa. "Community Consultation: Te Papa and New Zealand Indian Communities: The Other Side of the Coin." *Tuhinga: Records of the Museum of New Zealand Te Papa Tongarewa* 16 (2005): 127–135.

Zurob Dreckmann, Camila. "Familia, propiedad y herencia en Rapa Nui." *Revista Anales* 7, no. 2 (November 2011): 165–185.

Online Sources

"No Humboldt 21!". http://www.no-humboldt21.de. Accessed November 16, 2017.

#500words. "WWLD? In Conversation with Leafa Wilson aka Olga Krause." December 3, 2014. https://hashtag500words.com/2014/12/03/wwld-in-conversation-with-leafa-wilson-aka-olga-krause. Accessed March 18, 2017.

Akeli, Safua. "Remembering Malifa School in Samoa." *Te Papa Blog* (Museum of New Zealand Te Papa Tongarewa), May 28, 2012. http://blog.tepapa.govt.nz/2012/05/28/remembering-malifa-school-in-samoa. Accessed August 14, 2019.

Aldea Educativa Rapa Nui. "Hoŋa'a o te Mana—Aldea Educativa Rapa Nui." http://www.aerp.cl. Accessed January 19, 2017.

Ayau, Edward Halealoha, and Honor Keeler. "Injustice, Human Rights, and Intellectual Savagery. A Review." *H/Soz/Kult,* April 14, 2017. http://www.hsozkult.de/debate/id/diskussionen-3987. Accessed August 14, 2019.

Bartlett, John. "'Moai are family': Easter Island people to head to London to request statue back," *The Guardian,* November 16, 2018. https://www.theguardian.com/world/2018/nov/16/maoi-easter-island-statue-british-museum-talks-return. Accessed August 14, 2019.

Brücke Museum. Website. http://www.bruecke-museum.de. Accessed February 10, 2017.

Brunt, Tony. '*To Walk under Palm Trees': The Germans in Samoa: Snapshots from Albums—Part One.* Auckland: Tony Brunt, 2016. E-book:

http://germansinsamoa.net/wp-content/uploads/2013/09/Palm_Trees_Ebook.pdf. Accessed October 10, 2017.

Brunt, Tony. "Werner von Bulow: The Mystery Man of Matapo'o." Chap. 7 in *'To Walk Under Palm Trees': The Germans in Samoa: Snapshots from Albums—Part One*. Auckland: Tony Brunt, 2016. http://germansinsamoa.net/wp-content/uploads/2013/09/Palm_Trees_Ebook.pdf. Accessed April 8, 2017.

Buchheim Museum. "BRÜCKE und die Lebensreform." Exhibition held at Buchheim Museum, July 2–October 9, 2016. Press release, July 2, 2016. https://www.buchheimmuseum.de/aktuell/2016/lebensreform.php. Accessed February 10, 2017.

Bundesarchiv [German Federal Archive]. "Eine deutsche 'Musterkolonie'—Samoa unter dem Kosmopoliten Wilhelm Solf." Web gallery. https://www.bundesarchiv.de/oeffentlichkeitsarbeit/bilder_dokumente/01081/index.html.de. Accessed June 10, 2017.

Bundespräsidialamt. "Bundespräsident Joachim Gauck beim Mittagessen zu Ehren des Staatsoberhaupts des Unabhängigen Staates Samoa, Seiner Hoheit Tui Atua Tupua Tamasese Efi." Speech by President Joachim Gauck at Schloss Bellevue, January 28, 2014. http://www.bundespraesident.de/SharedDocs/Downloads/DE/Reden/2014/01/140128-Staatsoberhaupt-Samoa.pdf;jsessionid=90F1CCECB987A06392B1D6748C3FF8C5.2_cid293?__blob=publicationFile. Accessed June 8, 2017.

Centre for Anthropological Research on Museums and Heritage (CARMAH). *Making Differences in Berlin: Transforming Museums and Heritage in the 21st Century*." Project website. http://www.carmah.berlin/making-differences-in-berlin. Accessed November 10, 2017.

CMN. "Secretaría Técnica CMN destaca representatividad de Comisión Asesora de Monumentos Nacionales en visita Rapa Nui." June 17, 2016. http://www.monumentos.cl/consejo/606/w3-article-63117.html. Accessed August 14, 2019.

"Comunidad Indígena Ma'u Henua." Facebook. https://es-la.facebook.com/Mau-Henua-179457969167170. Accessed August 14, 2019.

Consejo de Monumentos Nacionales de Chile. "Isla de Pascua." http://www.monumentos.cl/catalogo/625/w3-article-26080.html. Accessed August 14, 2019.

Cooperativa. "Comunidad Ma'u Henua entregó cuenta pública de administración en Rapa Nui," April 13, 2017. http://www.cooperativa.cl/noticias/pais/pueblos-originarios/comunidad-ma-u-henua-entrego-cuenta-publica-de-administracion-en-rapa/2017–04–13/185535.html. Accessed August 14, 2019.

Deutsche Gesellschaft für Völkerkunde e.V. "Umbenennung in Deutsche Gesellschaft für Sozial- und Kulturanthropologie." https://www.dgv-net.de/wir-heissen-anders. Accessed December 2, 2017.

Deutsches Historisches Museum. "German Colonialism: Fragments Past and Present." Exhibition website, 2016. https://www.dhm.de/en/ausstellungen/archive/2016/german-colonialism.html. Accessed August 14, 2019.

Educarchile. "Liceo de Rapa Nui: un espacio multicultural." June 10, 2006. http://ww2.educarchile.cl/PORTAL.HERRAMIENTAS/autoaprendizaje/article-104210.html. Accessed January 10, 2017.

European Society for Oceanists (ESfO). *Experiencing Pacific Environments.* 11th EsfO conference held at Ludwig-Maximilians-Universität München, June 29—July 2, 2017. Conference program. http://esfo-org.eu/wp-content/uploads/2017/06/ESfO_booklet.pdf. Accessed November 20, 2017.

GRASSI Museum für Völkerkunde zu Leipzig. "Sensitive Heritage: Ethnographic Museums and Material/Immaterial Restitutions." Conference website, 2018. https://grassi-voelkerkunde.skd.museum/ausstellungen/sensitive-heritage-ethnographic-museums-and-materialimmaterial-restitutions. Accessed November 21, 2018.

Greater Wellington Regional Council. "Māori of the Wellington Region." February 18, 2016, http://www.gw.govt.nz/maori-of-the-wellington-region. Accessed June 6, 2017.

Gröpl, Myriam, and Sara Capdeville. "Tagungsbericht: 'Schwieriges Erbe. Koloniale Objekte—Postkoloniales Wissen.' 24.04.2017, Linden-Museum Stuttgart." Conference report. Universität Hamburg, May 19, 2017. https://www.kolonialismus.uni-hamburg.de/tagungsbericht-schwieriges-erbe-koloniale-objekte-postkoloniales-wissen-24-04-2017-linden-museum-stuttgart. Accessed August 14, 2019.

H/Soz/Kult. "Diskussionen." http://www.hsozkult.de/debate/page. Accessed November 20, 2017.

"Hamburg Samoanischer Club e.V." Facebook. https://www.facebook.com/Hamburg-Samoanischer-Club-eV-1797646333805558/?ref=nf. Accessed March 30, 2017.

———. Website. http://www.hamburg-samoanischer-club.de. Accessed November 20, 2018.

Hatje Cantz Verlag. *Die Brücke in der Südsee: Exotik der Farbe* [exhibition held at Saarlandmuseum, Saarbrücken, October 22, 2005–January 8, 2006]. Exhibition catalog page. http://www.hatjecantz.de/die-bruecke-in-der-suedsee-1631–0.html. Accessed February 10, 2017.

Hawai'i Forest Institute. "Ho'ola Ka Makana'a at Ka'ūpūlehu." https://www.hawaiiforestinstitute.org/our-projects/dryland-forest-projects/kaupulehu-dryland-forest. Accessed September 30, 2017.

Hawai'inuiākea School of Hawaiian Knowledge. "Faculty & Staff: Ivy Andrade." http://manoa.hawaii.edu/hshk/people/ivy-h-andrade. Accessed December 10, 2016.

Herrick, Linda. "Pictures Tell Story of Pacific Colony." *New Zealand Herald,* April 28, 2002. http://www.nzherald.co.nz/lifestyle/news/article.cfm?c_id=6&objectid=1842345. Accessed June 6, 2017.

Human Remains in Museums and Collections. "A Critical Engagement with the Recommendations of the German Museums Association (2013)." Discussion forum, February 3, 2017. *H-Soz-Kult.* http://www.hsozkult.de/debate/id/diskussionen-3909. Accessed November 21, 2018.

Indigeneity in the Contemporary World: Performance, Politics, and Belonging. Project website. http://www.indigeneity.net. Accessed March 12, 2017.

———. "Residencies." http://indigeneity.net/residencies. Accessed March 12, 2017.

———. "Rosanna Raymond—Acti.VA.tion." Video uploaded November 4, 2014. Accessed March 12, 2017. https://vimeo.com/110965423. Accessed March 12, 2017.

"Ka Haka Hoki Mai Te Mana Tupuna." Facebook. https://www.facebook.com/rapanui.repatriation. Accessed January 17, 2017.

Ka'ahahui 'O Ka Nāhelehele. "Ho'ōla Ka Makana'ā At Ka'ūpūlehu Dryland Forest." http://drylandforest.org/ho'ola-ka-makana'ā-ka'ūpūlehu-dryland-forest. Accessed September 30, 2017.

Kamakako'i, "Ka Ho'ina: Going Home." Video uploaded December 16, 2014. https://vimeo.com/114712444. Accessed November 23, 2017.

Kamehameha Schools. "Ola nā iwi." https://apps.ksbe.edu/kaiwakiloumoku/ola-na-iwi. Accessed January 17, 2017.

Kanaka'ole Kanahele, Pualani. "Papakū Makawalu Part 1." Presentation in Keauhou, Hawai'i, April 24, 2009. https://vimeo.com/4621142. Accessed October 23, 2017.

Kanoa-Martin, Kaiulani, ed. "I Ku Mau Mau." *Huapala: Hawaiian Music and Hula Archives.* http://www.huapala.org/Chants/I_Ku_Mau_Mau.html. Accessed August 4, 2016.

Kihara, Shigeyuki. "Fa'a fafine: In the Manner of a Woman, Triptych 1." Print dated 2004–2005. Acquired by museum 2007. *Metropolitan Museum of Art.* http://www.metmuseum.org/art/collection/search/538528. Accessed February 10, 2017.

Kihara, Yuki. *Der Papālagi (The White Man): Exhibition Preview*. Milford Galleries, Dunedin. https://www.milfordgalleries.co.nz/dunedin/submissions/10321–9b5290a9. Accessed February 5, 2017.

———. *A Study of a Samoan Savage: Head with Pelvimeter*. Auckland Art Gallery Toi o Tāmaki, 2015. http://www.aucklandartgallery.com/explore-art-and-ideas/artwork/22715/a-study-of-a-samoan-savage-head-with-pelvimeter. Accessed March 11, 2017.

———. *Where Do We Come From? What Are We? Where Are We Going?* Exhibition at Milford Galleries, Dunedin, March 16–April 10, 2013. https://www.milfordgalleries.co.nz/dunedin/exhibitions/328-Yuki-Kihara-Where-do-we-come-from-What-are-we-Where-are-we-going. Accessed February 10, 2017.

Landesmuseum Hannover. "Heikles Erbe (bis 26. Februar 2017): Koloniale Spuren bis in die Gegenwart." Exhibition website. https://www.landesmuseum-hannover.niedersachsen.de/startseite/sonderausstellungen/heikles_erbe/heikles-erbe-30-september-2016-bis-26-february-2017–139276.html. Accessed November 16, 2017.

Linden-Museum Stuttgart. *Schwieriges Erbe*. Conference website. https://www.lindenmuseum.de/service-menue/presse/schwieriges-erbe/. Accessed August 19, 2019.

———. *Schwieriges Erbe: Koloniale Objekte—Postkoloniales Wissen*. Conference flyer, 2017. https://www.lindenmuseum.de/fileadmin/user_upload/images/fotogalerie/Schwieriges_Erbe/Faltblatt_Einladung_SchwierigesErbe.pdf. Accessed May 28, 2017.

Likou, Ilia L. "Vailima beer bound for United States market." *Samoa Observer*, March 7, 2018. http://www.samoaobserver.ws/en/07_03_2018/local/30852/Vailima-beer-bound-for-United-States-market.htm. Accessed December 3, 2018.

Low, Sam. "Na'au: The Heart of Wayfinding." *Hana Hou Magazine*. http://www.samlow.com/sail-nav/wayfinding.html. Accessed September 29, 2016.

Macdonald, Sharon, Henrietta Lidchi, and Margareta von Oswald. "Engaging Anthropological Legacies." Special section of *Museum Worlds* 5 (2017). http://journals.berghahnbooks.com/museum-worlds. Accessed November 10, 2017.

Mahatua Producciones. "Sinopsis: Un viaje en busca del espíritu de los ancestros." *Te Kuhane o Te Tupuna: El Espíritu de los Ancestros*. http://www.mahatua.cl/sinopsis.html. Accessed March 12, 2017.

Māori Dictionary, s.v. "iwi" http://maoridictionary.co.nz/search?idiom=&phrase=&proverb=&loan=&histLoanWords=&keywords=iwi. Accessed January 17, 2017.

Marzan, Marques Hanalei. Artist website. http://www.marquesmarzan.com. Accessed December 10, 2016.

Merriam-Webster Dictionary, s.v. "kaleidoscope." https://www.merriam-webster.com/dictionary/kaleidoscope. Accessed November 30, 2017.

Milford Galleries Dunedin. "Yuki Kihara." Artist website. https://www.milfordgalleries.co.nz/dunedin/artists/232-Yuki-Kihara?a=232. Accessed February 10, 2017.

MoeVarua. "Comunidad Indígena Ma'u Henua Coadministra el Parque Nacional Rapa Nui." November 16, 2016. http://www.moevarua.com/mau-henua. Accessed May 6, 2017.

Museo Antropológico Padre Sebastián Englert. "Historia." http://www.museorapanui.cl/679/w3-propertyvalue-96753.html. Accessed December 18, 2016.

———. "Programa de Educación Patrimonial Manu Iri." http://www.museorapanui.cl/679/w3-article-63864.html. Accessed September 17, 2016.

Museum Fünf Kontinente. "Sammlung Ozeanien." http://www.museum-fuenf-kontinente.de/forschung/sammlung-ozeanien. Accessed March 9, 2017.

Museum of New Zealand Te Papa Tongarewa. "German Colonial Possessions" (London: Johnson Riddle & Co. Ltd, 1915). Poster in History Collection. http://collections.tepapa.govt.nz/object/1081465. Accessed August 14, 2019.

———. "Repatriation: Karanga Aotearoa." https://www.tepapa.govt.nz/about/repatriation. Accessed February 20, 2017.

———. "Shigeyuki Kihara—Taualuga: The Last Dance." Video published December 28, 2015. https://www.youtube.com/watch?v=ev-vIeSDb4I. Accessed February 10, 2017.

National Museum of the American Indian. "E Mau Ke Ea: The Sovereign Hawaiian Nation." http://www.nmai.si.edu/explore/exhibitions/item/?id=952. Accessed May 03, 2017.

nupepa, trans. "E ola mau ka Hale Hoikeike o Bihopa! 1894: The Bishop Museum." April 28, 2016 (translation of newspaper article "Ka Hale Hoikeike o Bihopa." *Ka Leo o ka Lahui,* September 21, 1894). https://nupepa-hawaii.com/2016/04/28/e-ola-mau-ka-hale-hoikeike-o-bihopa-1894. Accessed April 20, 2017.

Peers, Laura, Lotten Gustafsson Reinius, and Jennifer Shannon. "Ritual Repatriation." Special section of *Museum Worlds* 5 (2017). http://journals.berghahnbooks.com/museum-worlds. Accessed November 10, 2017.

Phillips, Ruth B., and Elizabeth Harney. "Multiple Modernities: Twentieth-Century Artistic Modernisms in Global Perspective: Project Summary." Carleton University, 2017. https://carleton.ca/culturalmediations/mappingmodernisms/multiple-modernisms-project. Accessed October 9, 2017.

Portal del Plan Nacional de Conservación del *Sophora toromiro*. "Visión general del toromiro." http://plantoromiro.org/educacion/vision-general-del-toromiro. Accessed August 4, 2017.

Research Center for Material Culture. *Museum Temporalities: Time, History and the Ethnographic Museum*. Conference website. http://www.materialculture.nl/en/events/museum-temporalities-time-history-and-the-ethnographic-museum. Accessed February 15, 2017.

———. *Museum Temporalities: Time, History and the (Ethnographic) Museum*. Conference program. http://www.materialculture.nl/sites/default/files/files/201511/abstracts_and_biographies_museum_temporalities_0.pdf. Accessed February 15, 2017.

Retzlaff, Misa Telefoni. "An Enduring Legacy: The German Influence in Samoan Culture and History." Scribd. https://www.scribd.com/document/89983188/Misa-Telefoni-Retzlaff-Samoa-Enduring-legacy-german-influence. Accessed August 14, 2019.

Roller, Jochen. "Them and Us: Ein folkoloniales Spektakel." http://www.jochenroller.de/them-and-us. Accessed April 20, 2017.

Roller, Jochen, and Yuki Kihara. *Them and Us*. Video published February 11, 2016. https://vimeo.com/154989326. Accessed March 12, 2017.

Ross, Kirstie. "August 1914: This Month Last Century." *Te Papa Blog* (Museum of New Zealand Te Papa Tongarewa), August 29, 2012. http://blog.tepapa.govt.nz/2012/08/29/august-1914-this-month-last-century. Accessed January 15, 2017.

"Rossana Raymond." Facebook. https://de-de.facebook.com/rosanna.raymond. Accessed March 16, 2017.

Sarr, Felwine, and Bénédicte Savoy. "The Restitution of African Cultural Heritage: Toward a New Relational Ethics." Restitution report, November 2018. http://restitutionreport2018.com. Accessed November 24, 2018.

Schorch, Philipp, and Martin Saxer. *Connecting Materialities/Material Connectivities [mat ~ con]*. Project website. http://www.highlandasia.net/projects/matcon.html. Accessed September 15, 2017.

Terevaka Archaeological Outreach. Project website. http://www.terevaka.net/toponymy/index.html. Accessed August 3, 2017.

"Toki Rapa Nui." Facebook. https://www.facebook.com/EscuelaDeMusicaDeRapaNui. Accessed March 1, 2017.

———. Website. http://tokirapanui.com. Accessed March 1, 2017.

UNESCO. "Rapa Nui National Park." World Heritage List. http://whc.unesco.org/en/list/715. Accessed December 10, 2016.

Universidad de Chile y la Corporación Nacional de Desarrollo Indígena. "Jacinta Arthur y su lucha por la repatriacion junto a Ka Haka Hoki Mai

Te Mana Tupuna." November 24, 2016, http://www.uchileindigena.cl/jacinta-arthur-y-su-lucha-por-la-repatriacion-junto-a-ka-haka-hoki-mai-te-mana-tupuna-2. Accessed February 20, 2017.

Universität Bayreuth. "Die deutsche Schule und die Regierungsschule für Eingeborene in Apia." http://www.neueste.uni-bayreuth.de/SuedseeSchuleAusbIX.htm. Accessed May 9, 2017.

Van Tilburg, Jo Anne. "Easter Island's Ethnographic Triangle." Easter Island Statue Project. http://www.eisp.org/1853. Accessed April 12, 2017.

VolkswagenStiftung. *Positioning Ethnological Museums in the 21. Century.* Conference website. https://www.volkswagenstiftung.de/veranstaltungen/veranstaltungsarchiv/detailansicht-veranstaltung/news/detail/artikel/positioning-ethnological-museums-in-the-21st-century/marginal/4670.html. Accessed August 25, 2016.

Waite, Deborah. *Binding & Looping: Transfer of Presence in Contemporary Pacific Art.* Exhibition at the University of Hawai'i, October 5–December 5, 2014. http://www.hawaii.edu/art/exhibitions+events/exhibitions/?p=1. Accessed November 2, 2016.

Western Museums Association. *Museums and Race: Transformation and Justice.* Project website and gathering held in Phoenix, AZ, September 2016. https://museumsandrace.org. Accessed October 10, 2016.

Wikipedia, s.v. "toki." Last modified May 7, 2017. https://es.wiktionary.org/wiki/toki#Rapa_nui. Accessed March 1, 2017.

Williams, Glyn. "Railways in Samoa." http://www.sinfin.net/railways/world/samoa.html. Accessed March 30, 2017.

Wilson, Leafa, aka Olga Krause. "Art: Olga/Hedwig/Janice Krause," http://www.gettheswitch.com. Accessed March 22, 2017.

———. "Ich heisse Olga Hedwig Krause—Deutsche Kuenstlerin." http://www.gettheswitch.com/ongoing.html. Last accessed November 28, 2017.

Singapore Art Museum. "Shigeyuki Kihara: Artist Statement and Biography." 2014. https://www.singaporeartmuseum.sg/downloads/apbf/new_zealand/Shigeyuki_Kihara.pdf. Accessed February 10, 2017.

Staatliche Kunstsammlungen Dresden. "Freistaat Sachsen gibt menschliche Gebeine aus Museum für Völkerkunde Dresden an Hawai'i zurück." Press release, October 23, 2017. https://www.skd.museum/presse/2017/freistaat-sachsen-gibt-menschliche-gebeine-aus-museum-fuer-voelkerkunde-dresden-an-hawaii-zurueck. Accessed November 12, 2017.

———. *Prolog #1–10.* http://prolog-ausstellung.info/about. Accessed November 21, 2017.

———. "Restitution: Was Jetzt?" *Prolog #1–10.* http://prolog-ausstellung.info/calender/2017/10/23/podiumsdiskussion-restitution-was-jetzt. Accessed November 29, 2017.

"Tatau Dance Group." Facebook. https://www.facebook.com/TatauDanceGroup. Accessed February 10, 2017.

teHeesen, Sabine. "Freude am fremden Volk: Erich Scheurmann in der Maske des Papalagi." Last updated in 2016. http://literaturkritik.de/id/3043. Accessed March 12, 2017.

Contributors

Philipp Schorch is a professor of museum anthropology at Ludwig-Maximilians-Universität in Munich, Germany, where he leads the ERC-funded five-year research project Indigeneities in the 21st Century. He is also an honorary fellow at the Alfred Deakin Institute for Citizenship and Globalisation, Deakin University, Australia. Philipp is coeditor of *Exploring Materiality and Connectivity in Anthropology and Beyond* (UCL Press, 2020), *Curatopia: Museums and the Future of Curatorship* (Manchester University Press, 2019), and *Transpacific Americas: Encounters and Engagements between the Americas and the South Pacific* (Routledge, 2016).

Noelle M.K.Y. Kahanu is a Native Hawaiian writer, artist, curator, and filmmaker with extensive program and exhibition experience. For fifteen years, she worked at Bishop Museum in Hawai'i as a cultural inventory specialist, project manager, and director of community affairs. She developed more than twenty-five exhibitions featuring more than a hundred Native artists and was a member of the project team for the restorations of Bishop Museum's Hawaiian Hall (2009), Pacific Hall (2013), and the landmark exhibition *E Kū Ana Ka Paia* (2010). She is currently an assistant specialist of public humanities and Native Hawaiian programs at the Department of American Studies, University of Hawai'i.

Sean Mallon is of Sāmoan and Irish descent. He is senior curator of Pacific Cultures at the Museum of New Zealand Te Papa Tongarewa. The author or lead editor of several books, including *Tangata o le Moana: The Story of New Zealand and the People of the Pacific* (2012), he is coauthor with Sébastien Galliot of *Tatau: A History of Sāmoan Tattooing* (2018). His exhibitions include *Paperskin: The Art of Tapa Cloth* (2009), *Tangata o le Moana* (2007), and *Voyagers: Discovering the Pacific and Tatau/Tattoo* (2002).

Cristián Moreno Pakarati is a Rapanui historian who graduated from the Pontificia Universidad Católica de Chile. He has authored and coauthored some two dozen publications related to the postcontact history of Rapa Nui (Easter Island) and collaborates frequently with renowned scholars and specialists dedicated to the island. Cristián is a founding member of the research and educational organization Rapanui Pioneers Society (RPS) based in Haŋa Roa. As a great-great-grandson of the legendary Polynesian sage Juan Tepano Rano, and great-grandson of outstanding mid-twentieth-century cultural figures Santiago Pakarati and Amelia Tepano, he aims to continue their legacy through his academic work on Rapa Nui.

Mara Mulrooney is a senior project supervisor at Pacific Legacy, Inc. in its Kailua, Hawai'i, office. Previously, she worked at the Bishop Museum in Honolulu as director of cultural resources and as the museum's anthropologist. She founded the Ho'omaka Hou Research Initiative, a collections-based research program focused on the re-analysis of archaeological, ethnographic, and archival collections. Mara has served as editor of the *Rapa Nui Journal* since 2010 and has published extensively on archaeological research on Rapa Nui and the Hawaiian Islands.

Nina Tonga is curator of Contemporary Art at the Museum of New Zealand Te Papa Tongarewa. From the villages of Vaini and Kolofo'ou in Tonga, she was born and raised in Aotearoa New Zealand. Nina specializes in contemporary Pacific art and is a doctoral candidate in Art History at the University of Auckland. Her exhibitions include *Home AKL* (2012) at Auckland Art Gallery Toi o Tāmaki, *Tonga 'i Onopooni: Tonga Contemporary* (2014) at Pataka Art + Museum, *Pacific Sisters: Fashion Activists* (2018) at Te Papa, and the Honolulu Biennial 2019, *To Make Wrong/Right/Now*.

Ty P. Kāwika Tengan is an associate professor of ethnic studies and anthropology at the University of Hawai'i at Mānoa. Author of *Native Men Remade: Gender and Nation in Contemporary Hawai'i* (2008), he is coeditor of special issues on Indigenous anthropology and Native Pacific studies that appear in *Pacific Studies* (2010) and *American Quarterly* (2015), and coeditor of *New Mana: Transformations of a Classic Concept in Pacific Languages and Cultures* (2016). He is presently working on a manuscript on Native Hawaiian veterans.

Index